Julia Grieve Smith

THE MUSICIAN'S WORLD

THE MUSICIAN'S WORLD

Letters of the great composers

EDITED BY HANS GAL

THAMES AND HUDSON

Originally published in hardback in 1965 as
The Musician's World: Great Composers in their Letters

First paperback edition 1978

Printed in Great Britain at
The Camelot Press Ltd, Southampton

CONTENTS

ACKNOWLEDGEMENTS

The editor and the publishers would like to thank the following publishers for permission to reproduce letters contained in the books listed below: Harvill Press Ltd: *Béla Bartók*, Serge Moreux, transl. G. S. Fraser and E. de Mauny, London, 1953; Collins, Publishers: *The Correspondence between Richard Strauss and Hugo von Hofmannsthal*, transl. H. Hammelmann and E. Osers, London, 1961; Faber and Faber Ltd, Publishers: *Arnold Schoenberg, Letters*, ed. E. Stein, transl. E. Wilkins and E. Kaiser, London, 1964; W. W. Norton and Co. Inc: *The Mussorgsky Reader*, ed. and transl. J. Leyda and S. Bertensson, New York, 1947; Oxford University Press: *Heirs and Rebels*, ed. Ursula Vaughan Williams, London, 1959, and *Gustav Holst*, Imogen Holst, London, 1938; The Bodley Head Ltd.: *The Life and Letters of Peter Ilich Tchaikovsky*, Modest Tchaikovsky, ed. and transl. Rosa Newmarch, London, 1906.

They would also like to thank the publishers and private individuals who have given permission for the publication of the following letters: Debussy to P-J. Toulet: Librarie Édition Galerie le Divan, Paris; Debussy to A. Messager: Librarie Dorbon-Ainé, Paris; Debussy to R. Godet: Éditions de la Pensée Moderne, Paris; Debussy to J. Durand: Durand et Cie, Éditeurs-proprietaires, Paris; Elgar: Dr Percy M. Blake, Mrs Elgar Blake, The Trustees of the Elgar Estate, and Messrs Geoffrey Bles Ltd; Fauré to his wife: M. Emmanuel Fauré-Fremiet; Puccini to G. Adami: Renier Adami and D. Adami-Rota, Milan; Ravel: Editions Robert Laffont, Paris; Strauss and Zweig: S. Fischer Verlag, Frankfurt.

The letters were translated by Daphne Woodward, with the exception of those taken from the English editions mentioned above. The excerpts from Heine (pp. 189–190, 203), George Sand (pp. 190-191, 193) and Stendhal (pp. 229–232) were translated by the editor.

The editor wishes to express his kindest thanks to Mrs Carolyn Coxon for her valuable help in preparing this publication.

INTRODUCTION

There is more than idle curiosity in our interest in everything regarding the life of a great artist. The phenomenon called a great work is an expression of personality and those who love the work extend that love to its creator. Whatever reflects the circumstances of his life, his relations with the world, the problems of his creative process, the tendencies of his thought, is relevant in a general as well as in a personal respect. True, such manifestations are rare and only incidental, but they are invaluable. Considering the unreliability of personal recollections, letters are the most precious and revealing illustration of the writer's mind. A letter is a direct communication with the addressee. Recollection of a conversation is, as a rule, subject to memory and its natural fallibility. A letter, on the contrary, is a document. With rare exceptions, a letter is more or less an improvisation, and more revealing therefore than any utterance of an autobiographical kind, more revealing than a preface or a dedication. Of the latter, however, some specimens will be included, for their topical interest. Occasionally a contemporary witness will be able to add relevant points or to elucidate a situation.

The aim of this anthology is to present a significant selection from an immensely extensive literature, and every single item should, in one way or another, throw light on the writer as well as, occasionally, on the addressee and, most of all, on personal, aesthetic, social and economic conditions of the world in which great musicians lived, suffered, and created. We may also gain some insight into the psychology of the creative process. In an anthology of this kind, the choice is obviously conditioned by the wish to show items of general interest or of picturesque significance. Irrelevant passages have been omitted, and also formalities and polite circumlocutions, which abound especially in specimens from earlier periods. Such omissions, however, are always indicated by . . ., and the reader with a special interest, who wants to see the complete original, will find the source listed.

The habit of writing letters, a result of general literacy, is comparatively modern. Medieval man wrote little, and the raw material, paper, was not readily available before the fifteenth century. Furthermore, that material is extremely perishable, apart from the fact that letters only survive by chance at a time when nobody is aware of their value. This accounts for the rarity of musicians' letters even of the sixteenth and seventeenth centuries. Starting from the eighteenth, the material becomes more and more substantial and musicians' letters, in ever increasing abundance, afford a fascinating view of the artistic and practical problems that confronted the Great, along with the most picturesque sidelights on cultural history. In addition, one will see that the close-up provided by an artist's own spontaneous utterance is incomparably more alive and moving than any other possible approach.

The average musician in the eighteenth century had a scanty general education and, with an enormous pressure of daily toil and trouble, little time for intellectual pursuits. Employed by the Church or by princes or nobles, he was kept in his place as an obedient servant. Beethoven was the first great musician who, in a climate already changed by the French Revolution, could assert himself as a proud personality, conscious of his dignity, without fear or submission. Even Beethoven, with the poor upbringing of a musician of his time, shows in his letters the pathetic struggle of a lofty, comprehensive mind with the intricacies of grammar, spelling, and style. With improved social conditions and a decent education, his successors in the nineteenth century had an easier start and a more direct access to literacy in a higher sense.

It is obvious that the capacity to give a lively, readable account of thoughts and feelings has become more frequent with a rising standard of general education. But there have always been artists whose capacity for spontaneous utterance was totally concentrated on their specific medium of expression. Schubert, at the threshold of the nineteenth century, shows but little in his letters of the incomparably rich humanity and expressiveness of his music; he writes a correct schoolmaster's style – he was indeed a schoolmaster for some years of his later adolescence. Mendelssohn, Schumann, Chopin, Berlioz, on the other hand, are delightful letter-writers, each in his own way. Wagner, a born writer, is quite extraordinary in his urge for verbal expression, stunning his opponent by sheer eloquence, pleading passionately for his ideas and amazingly successful with this method.

Considering this, the reader will realize that the larger or smaller contribution of an individual artist to this anthology is no measure of his comparative artistic importance, but is due to his larger or smaller contribution to an art very different from the one that made him great – to his achievement as a letter-writer.

Musicians are curious people. The language of their art is a world of its own, on a plane apart from reality, which explains why not all great musicians have been articulate in a literary sense. As a rule, however, they are extremely outspoken. Impatient with everything pertaining to a realm outside their artistic activity, they are liable to be fragmentary in their utterance, but they know what they mean and can be as blunt, as outspoken, as rude, as epigrammatic as any person alive. One must admit, however, that musicians can be as dull as anyone else when writing on matters of business, or when they are formal or obsequious, and exasperating whenever their vanity or profit is involved. One may find that the trivial affairs of money, of loss or gain, play a surprisingly important part in these letters of great men. No wonder: very few of them had a life of tolerable material security. We have to grasp the unpleasant fact that up to the end of the nineteenth century the social and economic conditions of our highly civilized society left, strictly speaking, no place for the creative musician, as there was no proper market for his goods. The privilege of writing music had to be bought by hard additional work, including untold drudgery. Brahms, who was very modest in his style of life, was practically the first great composer of non-operatic music who from his forties could live without being dependent on anyone. Even composers who wrote for the stage and who had to satisfy a more direct demand had to make up for a scanty reward by an enormous output. Only towards the end of the nineteenth century was the duty of paying a royalty to the author or composer of a dramatic work universally accepted by the theatres.

Musicians can be just as human in their foibles as they are divine in their achievements. Their jokes are by no means always in the best of taste. Fun seems to be a necessary relaxation from the fervent concentration and passionate struggle for perfection inherent in the musician's creative work. His propensity for punning, moreover, seems to stem from a turn of mind acquired in the practice of an art whose material is very much based on a process of variation and combination. Some of Mozart's letters are almost unprintable; many of Beethoven's, which abound in puns, are hardly translatable.

From one point of view, reading a letter seems almost an act of indiscretion. It would be impossible to explain this more succinctly and more earnestly than Brahms did in a letter to Maria Lipsius (pseudonym as a writer: La Mara), editor of 'Musikerbriefe', who had asked for his permission to publish some of his letters in a collection. It may open this anthology, expressing, as it does, an artist's feeling about publishing letters, and the reason why such publication should be confined to the dead.

JOHANNES BRAHMS TO MARIA LIPSIUS

Vienna, 27 May 1885

Dear Madam,
To be sure, I have the courage to ask you not to print the letters in question. I know and admit that I invariably write reluctantly, hurriedly and carelessly; but when I see an example like yours, I feel ashamed.

It takes a kind of courage to write to an unknown, cultivated and sympathetic man in such a slipshod style as I did in this instance.

But to allow such letters to be printed, to give one's explicit agreement, would be something other than courage!

If you will allow me to say categorically, here and now, that no one could give me greater displeasure than by printing any letter of mine – I will gladly make an exception of this particular one.

You can include it in your book all the more readily, because it will show your readers that it is not you but I who bear the blame for the absence of others, and because I am careful not to draw any conclusion from your proposal to include my own letters, regarding the other contents and the value of your book.

I know, not merely from 'Schiller and Goethe' but from the most agreeable personal experience as well, that there are plenty of people who enjoy letter-writing and write good ones.

But there are others like myself, and their letters – if the writer deserves it in other respects – should be read and interpreted indulgently and warily.

For instance, I am delighted to have a letter of Beethoven's to treasure as a relic; but it makes me shudder to think how much such a letter is supposed to signify and explain!

The same applies to unpublished works a musician leaves behind him.

I have always followed up such things eagerly, studied them, copied and re-copied them. For instance, I have cherished the uncounted surplus evidences of their industry and genius left by Haydn and by Franz Schubert.

I have always wished that such valuable and instructive treasures might be copied for the large libraries, where they would be accessible to people seriously interested in them. I will not dwell on the very different feelings with which I see those beloved treasures in print – or arrange them for publication myself, to make sure it will at least be done as decently as possible!

The amount of misunderstanding and misinterpretation that occurs in such cases is quite unbelievable, and whether such publications are necessary, desirable or superfluous and even harmful – I do not know!

At the risk that you will regard the beginning of this letter as sheer hypocrisy,

I sign myself,

Yours respectfully and devotedly,

J. Brahms

PART ONE

Sixteenth to Nineteenth Century

RENAISSANCE AND BAROQUE

From Lasso to Bach

The first truly characteristic letters of musicians that have survived were written by one of the latest and greatest of the noble dynasty of Flemish composers, whose art had spread all over the civilized parts of Europe by the middle of the sixteenth century, Orlando Lasso (1532–94) *who, after an international career as a musician of European fame, became master of music to the Duke of Bavaria in Munich. He addresses his patron in a free and easy way, joking, fooling, punning, sometimes rather coarsely, in a manner natural to a period of tremendous vitality, straightforwardness and freedom from restraint. One of his standard jokes is mixing four languages – Italian, French, Latin, and German – in an inimitable jargon of his own, which makes his letters wellnigh untranslatable and only accessible to a reader with the necessary smattering of linguistic knowledge. But they have a real style of their own, reminiscent of the composer's precious French, Italian, and German madrigals. One cannot but admit that the Latin of this composer, who set Latin words to music all his life, is as barbarous and ungrammatical as his German, Italian, and French. A sample of this kind seems, however, worth quoting:*

LASSO TO PRINCE WILLIAM, DUKE OF BAVARIA

Al Illustrissimo et eccellentissimo Sign. Principe Guilhelmo, Duca de la Baviera alta e bassa, et mio Signore et patrone sempre ossero.^{mo}, dove si trova sua Ex.^{ia}

Mons. mon prince, mon duc, mon seigneur, mon maître, va del resto, salus et gaudio.

Moi pauvre gentilhomme charbonnier, delaissé de tous, si non de celui qui peut plus que tous. Abandonné, loin du né [?], de maison, de buisson, de jardin au matin, de tout fruit, non pas cuit, et de fleurs, et d'odeurs, et en somme moi, pauvre homme de tout bien n'a plus rien. Voilà la feste que me fait la male peste. Je veux dire, mon très excellent Prince et Seigneur, que après avoir demeuré par 6 Wochen en mon jardin, il gran Duca Alberto misit mihi litteram, ut irem at Starnbergem, ut visitarem suam Altitudinem, et sic fuit factum; mais le temps fuit tantum temperatus par trop; par ainsi interrogavi Ducum de ce que je devois faire. Respondit placido quod deberem exire

Dachau, come les aliis sodalibus erant, ad evitandum morbum pestiferum. Ego respondit, quod familia mea erat plus quam satis, ou assez de gens, et quod libentius exirem à faire pénitence in der Elend zu Landshut pour la mémoire de mon prince, qui trop me pince; sein Fürstl. Gnaden antwortet mihi: ich bin woll zufrieden, du möchtest auch ein' Zeit zu den andern zu uns spazieren und also hin und her ziehen; na na, disje moi, wenn Eure F. Gn. meiner bedarf, si scriberem videbo, subito ad te venio. Respondit sua Exc. darauf: nun wol, wol; et etiam mihi dare fecit pevelhem [Befehl] ad regierum in civitatem Landsfutum, ut me cum fustibus et lanternis deberant accipere. A cosi, ou per ainsi, ich bin aspettando il mio prudentissimo Signore, si come fanno Judaei il Messiah, sed illos non veniat, mais mon maître si, ma de si. Ma potta del gran turco, è possibil ch'el mio patron possa star senza il suo poltron? Parlo di mi et de moi, non lo credete sate voi; se ti può star senza mi, mi non vo star senza ti. Je parle comme un couillon, mais c'est la conclusion, jour et nuit pour vous prions en bonne dévotion: tourné maître à la maison, garde bien le clef du con[?], car sans elle rien de bon. Ici fais fin à ma leçon, baisant en toute humilité les mains de votre Excellence et de Mons. le prince Ferdinando. Notre Seigneur maintienne vos Excellences saines, gagliardes et désireux de retourner, car il est temps sans plus tarder. De Landshut, 7e d'ottobre 1572.

De notre Excellences très humble serviteur
Orlando de Lassus

Here is a free rendering, stripped of paraphernalia and all untranslatable fooling, punning, and rhyming. The facts touched upon in this letter, however, are no joke but grim reality. The plague, a frequent visitor to Europe during these centuries, had driven the Court out of town and seriously disrupted Lasso's activities.

. . . My Prince, my Duke, my Master, etc., etc., health and joy! Poor me, a menial forsaken by all except for the one who means more than all, living far from the places I cherish – poor me has nothing left to enjoy. That's the feast bestowed upon me by the evil plague! What I want to say, my most excellent prince and master, is that I had stayed for six weeks in my garden when a letter arrived from Grand Duke Albert, ordering me to visit him at Starnberg. This I did. When I asked the prince what I was to do, he kindly told me to move to Dachau, to join the other fellows there, to avoid the plague. I replied that, considering my rather large family, I would prefer to do penance in the solitude of Landshut. Said his Grace: 'Quite all right; but you will come to us, now and then, as occasion demands, moving from the one place to the other.' 'Now then,' said I, 'whenever your Grace desires me to come, send me a missive and I will instantly appear.' And His Excellency said: 'All right.' He also gave me an order to the municipality at Landshut, to receive me with bag and baggage. So here I am, waiting for my wisest Lord as eagerly as the Jews are waiting for the Messiah. May he never come to them! Whereas you, my Master, may you come indeed, indeed! But the deuce, is it really possible that my patron could do without his fool? I am speaking of myself, of course. Well, if you can do without me, I cannot do without you. I speak as a lout; and so I conclude, praying for you day and night in all devotion, etc., etc.

Another letter of Lasso follows, in uneven verse, which is definitely untranslatable, not only owing to four intermixed languages. Those, however, who can read it, will certainly enjoy the fun and appreciate a gloriously uninhibited style.

Al Illustrissimo et Excellentissimo Signor Principe Guilhelmo, duce de le due Baviere, et mio Signor et patrone sempre oss.^{mo}, in Landshut.

Signor patron, Orlando Lasso
ha di presente poco spasso
in ogni cosa poco bono
multi danzano a questo sono.

S'à moi me plait manger et boire,
cela n'est pas trop fort à croire.
Je serais bien un gran cochin
si ne laissais l'eau pour le vin;
quand mon cul sonne de trombette,
aucun soudain son nez y mette.

Scatula cum literas votre Eccellentiae
manu propria recepi hodie.
Wenn die Arbeit Ihrer fürstl. Gnaden wohlgefällt,
das bringt mir in mein Säckel kein Geld;
soll mir aber fort Furz fahren,
schickt uns ein Wagen oder Karren.
Liegt Euer Gnaden mit Euer Gemahl
so lieg ich doch auch nit im Stall;
Euer Fürstl. Gnaden will ich Diener sein
dieweil ich leb, für mein allerliebster Herr mein,

das und dat mein ich mit Treuen,
und hoff es wird mich nit gereuen.
De votre Excellence umilissimo e cordialissimo servo,
Orlando dolce e non protervo

Datum il di della nostra Madonna
de i peccator è la ferma colonna;
a 25, del mese di Marzo [157?]
dopo la cena scrissi per solazzo.

We may find the fact uncomfortable that one of the supreme artists of his century had to pay for the safety of an honourable appointment, and for the freedom of creating music to his heart's content, by accepting the function of a sort of court jester to his noble prince. One may also remember that Rigoletto's privilege to speak the truth was counterbalanced by much humiliation. But if he has not been aware of it before, the reader will learn in these pages that freedom, based on tolerance and economic independence, is a very modern phenomenon, even for the greatest of artists.

The following business letter shows not only the high esteem which Lasso enjoyed among the potentates of his time, but also his good judgement and kind generosity. Jacob Regnart, whom he recommends in his own place, was one of his most distinguished Flemish contemporaries.

LASSO TO AUGUST, ELECTOR OF SAXONY

Munich, 13 February 1580

Most illustrious and right noble Prince, most gracious Elector and Lord. I humbly beg to inform your gracious Highness that I have received your letter and have noted all the contents thereof, and I hasten before aught else to offer my most humble thanks for the peculiar honour vouchsafed me by your gracious Highness in desiring to engage my trifling services; and I call God to witness that were I able, I would obey with the greatest readiness, for I know your gracious Highness ever deigns to give gracious hearing to your servants' petitions. But since, after the death of my most gracious Prince and Master, Duke Albert of Bavaria, of most pious memory, I allowed myself to be re-engaged by the beloved son of that revered Prince, my gracious Prince and Master, Duke William, and since moreover I am now growing old, and further more have a house, garden and other property in Bavaria, together with a yearly provision of 400 florins graciously bestowed upon me by the revered and well-remembered Duke Albert, in addition to what the present ruling Prince gives me, I humbly beg your gracious Highness, in consideration of all these circumstances, most graciously to excuse my inability to consent to serve you. . . . There is one, it seems to me, could likely serve your gracious Highness; he is now at Prague in the Chapel of His Imperial Majesty, where he instructs the boys in singing and composition. Should your gracious Highness be disposed to make use of him, you could let him know it. I can truthfully say that he is an excellent fellow, modest and of good sense, and his name, I think, is Jacobus Regnart. He is a Dutchman, speaks good German and has a knowledge of other tongues as well. And in short he is a good Musicus, and well fitted for this service. . . .

One generation later Claudio Monteverdi (1567–1643) *found himself confronted with the artistic problems of a new, fascinating type of theatrical entertainment – opera – which, owing to its extraordinary costliness, could be afforded only by princes, and on particularly special occasions. Monteverdi, like Lasso, was in the service of a sovereign prince, the Duke of Mantua. When in 1613, on the death of his patron, he found an appointment as 'Maestro di cappella' (head of music) at San Marco in Venice, he still maintained his close relations with the Gonzaga Court at Mantua, especially with respect to operatic commissions, in which he was interested most of all.*

His letters to the Court, referring to such commissions, are tremendously revealing. They show how much the first great operatic composer of history was already conscious of the paramount problem in all opera – the character and structure of the libretto. And they give an impressive account of the writer's independence of mind and artistic integrity when, duly accepting his humble duty of complying with every wish or whim of his mighty patron, he does not hesitate to express his own opinion with devastating accuracy when he happens to disagree on the merits or suitability of an operatic subject or its treatment by the poet. Alessandro Striggio was Chancellor of the Duke of Mantua.

MONTEVERDI TO ALESSANDRO STRIGGIO

Venice, 9 December 1616

I have received with great delight of spirit, from Sig. Carlo de Torri, Your Excellency's letter and the little book containing the sea-fable of the *Marriage of Thetis*; Your Excellency writes that you send it to me that I may study it diligently and thereafter write to you my opinion whether it should be set to music for use at the marriage of His Serene Highness; I, most illustrious Lord, having no other desire than to be of service to His Highness in whatsoever manner, will say no more by way of first reply, than that I am ready promptly to fulfil such orders as His Serene Highness may deign to give me and that I shall ever, without demur, be honoured to receive all his commands: so that if his Most Serene Highness approves this fable, I should hold it most beautiful and much to my taste; but if you require me to speak, I obey Your Excellency's command with all respect and readiness, on the understanding that my words are naught, as coming from a person of little worth, in all matters, and a person who ever honours virtue, in particular the present poet whose name I do not know, and the more so since this profession of poetry is not my own, I will say, therefore, with all reverence to obey you since you so command, I will say first in general that music wishes to be mistress of the air [*aria*] and not only of the water – I mean to say in my own language that the actions described in the said fable are all low and close to the earth, a thing most unsuitable for fine harmonies . . . it may also be added that the winds have to sing: namely, the Zephyrs and Boreas with his train; how, dear Sir, can I imitate the speech of the winds? Since they do not speak and how can I by their means stir the emotions! Ariadne moved by being a woman, and Orpheus likewise moved by being a man and not a wind. . . . The whole fable, moreover, in my no small ignorance I do not find moves me, indeed I find it difficult to understand, nor do I feel that it carries me by a natural progress towards an end that moves me. Ariadne carries me to merited lamentation, Orpheus to merited prayer, but this to I know not what end. . . . Howbeit the whole shall ever be accepted by me with all reverence and honour if His Serene Highness so commands and wishes it, for he is my master beyond all demur. . . . I ask forgiveness, dear Sir, if I have said too much, not with the wish to belittle anything whatsoever, but in the desire to obey your commands and so that, should I be ordered to set this fable to music, Your Excellency may give consideration to what I think. . . .

MONTEVERDI TO ALESSANDRO STRIGGIO

Venice, 1 May 1627

. . . I would, however, beg and implore Your Excellency, that if His Serene Highness deigns to command that I set to music the comedy he indicates to me, he may deign to consider two points, one, that I may have convenient time to compose it, and the other, that it may be by an excellent hand, for I should none the less find no small fatigue and little to my taste and much agitation in setting to music verses of a very simple nature, were I required to do it in too short a time; for the shortness of the time was the reason why I brought myself near to death when writing *Ariadne*. I know it could be done quickly, but quickly and well do not go together. If therefore there were time enough, and were I to have the opera or part thereof from your own most noble invention, you may be most assured that I should feel infinitely delighted, for I know what ease and propriety Your Excellency would bring me. If the task should relate to interludes for a long comedy, it would not be so laborious or so long; but a comedy to be sung, which is as much as to say a dramatic poem, believe me Your Excellency, it cannot be done in a short time without falling into one of two errors – either to do the thing badly, or to make oneself ill. . . . I have also given much thought to a small work by Sig. Giulio Strozzi, very fine and curious, from which I could take some four hundred lines entitled *Licori finta pazza inamorata d'Aminta* – the which, after a thousand absurd fancies, concludes with a marriage accompanied by excellent effects of illusion, and these and other such things may be used as trifling episodes among other pieces of music which are not unsuccessful and I know would not displease Your Excellency. . . .

There are some more letters on the opera mentioned above, 'La finta pazza Licori'. Unfortunately neither the music nor the libretto of this opera, on which Monteverdi passes such interesting comments in the following letters, has survived. The great composer of madrigals and sacred music had a passionate interest in the new problems of opera and in the dramatic and expressive components of the music required for this pioneering venture.

MONTEVERDI TO ALESSANDRO STRIGGIO

Venice, 7 May 1627

. . . I send Your Excellency *La Finta Pazza Licori* by Sig. Strozzi, as you commanded in your most kind letter, not yet set to music, not printed nor ever performed on the stage, for no sooner had the author written it out than he gave me with his own hand the copy, which was this one; if the said Sig. Giulio learns that it has found favour with His Serene Highness I am most assured that with rapid devotion and effect he will put it into order, dividing it into three acts or as it may please His Serene Highness, he being greatly desirous to have it set to music by me, and happy to see my feeble notes clothing his most lovely compositions, which truly, both for beauty of the verses and for invention, I have found to be a most worthy subject; and if this work be to Your Excellency's taste, do not delay in making known your decision, for I am certain the author will complete it to satisfaction within a very short time; the invention I do not think bad, nor the development of the plot; it is true that the role of Licori, being greatly varied, must not fall into the hands of any woman who is unable to be now man, now woman, with lively gestures and clearly distinguished passions; for since this feigned madness must relate only to the present and not to the past or the future, the mimicry must be based upon the words and not upon the cadence of the music; so that when war is spoken of, war must be mimed, when peace, then peace, when death, then death and so forth, and in order that the changes shall take place within the briefest space, and the mimicry. . .

MONTEVERDI TO ALESSANDRO STRIGGIO

Venice, 22 May 1627

. . . I have received by the post not only Your Excellency's most welcome letter, but also *Narciso* and *La Finta Pazza*. I have likewise received Your Excellency's pleasure and orders concerning *La Finta Pazza* and indeed I hold the same opinion as Your Excellency, that on the stage this *Finta Pazza* will appear the more novel and more varied and more diverting. But now that I have understood your mind, I will not fail (when the said Sig. Giulio Strozzi comes here from Florence, which will be in three or four days' time), I will not fail, as I say, to talk with him, and as you shall see, that gentleman shall enrich the piece with other varied and novel and diverse scenes, as I shall tell him according to my pleasure, and we shall see whether it can be enriched with other novelties and with additional characters, so that the *Finta Pazza* shall not be constrained to appear so frequently; and we shall see that each time she appears on the stage she shall bring new pleasures and new changes of harmony and gesture, as to all of which I will most fully inform Your Excellency. To my mind it is most excellently expressed in two or three places, in two others I think it could be expressed better, not indeed as to the verses but in the manner of novelty, and one such, if you will permit me, is Aminta's discourse when she is sleeping, when I would wish her to speak so that her own voice would not awaken her, for the consideration of being obliged to speak *sotto voce* will give me occasion to put forth new harmonies different from those of the past, in such manner and form as I may determine and with particular cause and difference the dance which is to come in the middle, and as I have said, I will make a scrupulous report thereon to Your Excellency. . . .

MONTEVERDI TO ALESSANDRO STRIGGIO

10 July 1627

I send Your Excellency the first act of *La Finta Pazza Licori* by Sig. Giulio Strozzi as you commanded. I wished to send the original itself, so that Your Excellency might see not so much the verses as the argument of the fable in the author's own hand and the characters. Two interludes have been finished which the author will give me tomorrow or the day after, and he says the feigned madness will begin in the third act, so soon as I have these I will send them likewise. There will be a dance for every act, all different and fantastic. Your Excellency, I am making up for the slight sickness which God be praised has almost entirely left me, and Sig. Giulio tells me that every act will display new events, so that I continue to believe that the thing will certainly not turn out badly, provided only that Signora Margherita [the singer intended for the principal role] will be now a brave soldier, now timorous, now ardent, well controlling her movements, without fear or constraint. . . .

The following letter could be called a historic document. It opens the perennial war between artist and critic, which has continued through the ages to the present day. The problem is insoluble. The critic, lacking the artist's vision and technical background, and the naïve listener's impressionability and enthusiasm, will never fully see the point. And the artist who turns critic will be worse, as his own strong convictions and prejudices will act as insuperable limitations to his appreciation. In this, Robert Schumann was a rare, wonderful exception. So the feud goes on and the reader will find further illustration of it in this collection.

Monteverdi had been attacked by a learned theorist, Artusi, for some harmonic eccentricities. He had replied to it in the preface to his Fifth Book of Madrigals (1605), which was duly followed by another attack by Artusi. As Monteverdi explains in this letter, he intended to write a book on what he called 'seconda pratica', his new, expressive style, as opposed to 'prima pratica', the traditional, pure style represented by Palestrina. But it is unlikely that this plan was realized.

MONTEVERDI TO AN UNKNOWN ADDRESS

Venice, 22 October 1633

. . . You must know therefore that it is true that I am writing, but under compulsion; for the event which years ago drove me to do so was of such a nature that without being aware that I was doing so, I promised to the world what I later found was beyond my feeble powers. I promised, as I say, in print to make known to a certain Theorist of *prima pratica* that in harmony there was another to be considered, unknown to him, and which I named *seconda*; for the reason that he had been pleased to print in opposition to one of my Madrigals certain passages of his own harmony founded on the arguments of *prima pratica*, namely on the ordinary rules, which resembled sol-fa written by a boy just beginning to study note by note, and not in cognizance of the art of melody. . . .

The title of the book will be: *Melodia, ovvero seconda pratica musicale.* Second (I mean) considered in respect of the modern, first in respect of the ancient; I am dividing the book into three parts, corresponding to the three components of Melody. In the first I treat of speech, in the second of harmony, in the third of what is rhythmic. I am of the opinion that this will not be unacceptable to the world, for I discovered by experience that when about to write Ariadne's Lament, finding no book which showed me the natural path to imitation or even which revealed to me that I ought to be an imitator, save for Plato, and he in such veiled fashion that with my weak eyes I could scarcely see afar off what little he could show me; I experienced, as I say, the great effort that is needed to do what little I did by way of imitation; and therefore I hope that I may not displease, but come what may, in the last resort I shall be better pleased with a little praise for this new manner of writing, than with much for the ordinary; and I again ask pardon for venturing along this other course. . . .

A dark episode in Monteverdi's life is illustrated in this anguished letter to the Councillor at Mantua; it has nothing to do with music, and it throws a sidelight on irrational aspects of a time when oppressive forces could suddenly fall upon a helpless victim. Monteverdi's son Massimiliano, a young physician, had been arrested and was to be tried by the Inquisition, accused of owning or having read a book prohibited by the Church.

MONTEVERDI TO ALESSANDRO STRIGGIO

Venice, 8 July 1628

. . . I understand from your most gracious letter that you went in person to speak to the Most Reverend Father Inquisitor, a favour so extreme that it makes me blush, and that he replied to Your Excellency that Massimiliano will be set free after only two days in prison. I suspect, Your Excellency, and forgive me if I speak so frankly, in face of your so great confidence, I suspect, and my son also suspects, that it may come to the rack or that it may come to some more than ordinary fine, or to some prison sentence of far, far more than two days; if they wish to examine him in everything he has ever thought or done, and even should their suspicions prove completely groundless, nevertheless the dread that fills his mind appals him greatly, and believe me, Your Excellency, scarce a day goes by but he weeps and laments over this persistent thought. The Most Reverend Father has written to me; if therefore he has this good intention, and has enquired into my son's life during six months in prison why does he not vouchsafe to relieve him from this tribulation and me likewise, and leave him to practise medicine to his and my satisfaction, and if need be that he pay twenty or twenty-five ducats as a token of punishment, and vow that he will never more read things vain and impertinent, let that be done also, since I know for certain that in any case he will never do so again, and I would pay the money willingly. Dear my Lord, if it were possible to obtain the favour of which I speak, I beg you with all my heart and soul to do me that favour that I may receive it, and I assure you that it will give life both to the boy and to me, for truly I feel my affection tormented by this thought; console me, I beseech you, if it be at all possible, for I can never receive a greater boon, the goods of this world are most dear to me, but much dearer are peace of mind and my own honour; forgive me, I beseech you, for thus troubling you while with heartfelt affection I make my most humble reverence and kiss your hand. . . .

Fortunately young Massimiliano was acquitted in the end, perhaps owing to some powerful intervention, but he would not have been the first innocent, nor the last, to die on the rack.

Monteverdi's most outstanding contemporary, the great German composer Heinrich Schütz *(1585–1672), must have crossed his path in Venice, where he stayed from 1609 to 1612 as a pupil of Giovanni Gabrieli, organist at San Marco, and again in 1628–9 when he revisited Venice. Master of Music to the Elector of Saxony in Dresden, Schütz was no exception to the general rule and, as other musicians of his time, had to live on a by-product of his genius – on his ability as an organizer and director of music. But the spiritual and material wilderness of Germany during the Thirty Years War (1618–48) is difficult to imagine, and Schütz's trouble was that for prolonged periods not only his musical activity but the whole organization of civil life was on the verge of disintegration. Famous in his forties and fifties, Schütz was all but forgotten when he died, thirteen years before the birth of Bach, whose greatest predecessor he had been.*

One may be amazed to learn that a conductor's worries in the seventeenth century started with the problem of obtaining strings for his players, and that even at this time certain guilds employed restrictive practices.

SCHÜTZ TO KAMMERSEKRETÄR LUDWIG WILHELM MOSER

Dresden, 3 July 1621

. . . as matters stand, I can not forebear to importune my most gracious Master with this present letter, it being my duty to report that not long since a sum of money was sent to Nuremberg from the Elector's exchequer here, wherewith to purchase strings for the Elector's orchestra from a wire-drawer of that place, by name Jobst Meuler, who manufactures steel strings for instruments, of such excellence that their like is impossible to be found elsewhere.

Now the aforesaid wire-drawer has indeed assured me in writing that he has the best will to give us satisfaction and prepare the strings; but that his fellow craftsmen will not give him leave to make anything out of the ordinary and better than they can do. Unless perchance a little order might be sent from our most gracious Master to the Town Council of Nuremberg, in which case he would surely be permitted.

Since, therefore, most gracious Herr Kammersekretär, I and my fellows in our profession set no less store by good strings than does a soldier, for example, by a pair of good pistols or other weapons, I trust you will not take it amiss that I trouble you in the matter.

And I hereby most humbly beg that without hesitation you obtain such a little order from our most gracious Master to the Nuremberg Council regarding the aforesaid Jobst Meuler, that he shall prepare the best strings for the Electoral Court in such quantity as may be ordered, and send it to me on the earliest occasion (by reason that a few days hence a messenger who understands these matters is to leave here for that place).

This is not only for the benefit of the whole orchestra but also to the advantage of our most gracious Elector and Master, inasmuch as he will receive good wares for the money. . . .

From the misery of his war-ridden country Schütz found a welcome temporary escape in a journey to Italy, where the new style – Monteverdi's 'seconda pratica' – was now in full flower. He was one of the first to bring back to Germany the modern innovations, all those new stimulations of dramatic style, instrumental music, progressing freedom of harmony. One must realize that compared with Venice, one of the most magnificent centres of art and music in Europe at that time, Germany – except for Munich and Vienna, its most southern outposts – was still at a primitive stage of musical development.

SCHÜTZ TO THE ELECTOR OF SAXONY

Venice, 3 November 1628

. . . Most gracious Lord, as is my most humble duty I am to inform you with my best obedience that although, according to your most gracious permission, I promptly set forth from Dresden on my journey to Italy, yet by reason that the passes in Germany, and more especially on the Venetian border, were closed, it was not until a few days since that I could make my way to Venice. As now, most gracious Lord, I live in hope that with God's help this my journey to gain further experience in my profession – paltry though it be – will in many ways be of marked service to me, it is no less my eager wish, and my most submissive and great trust, that your Illustrious Highness will not frown upon my absence, nor yet allow any other person to occupy or seek to obtain my place, which I have hitherto filled humbly to the best of my powers, but will maintain and keep it open for me until my near return, which shall, God willing, take place at your gracious command, most obediently and without fail.

Moreover, most gracious Elector and Lord, I have just grounds to thank your Illustrious Highness with all humility, for that you did most graciously consent and vouchsafe to maintain my established wages undiminished, by which means I have been able to begin my journey and continue it until now. But inasmuch as in the circumstances it would be very difficult and toilsome for me to carry out my plan at my own sole expense, seeing that already the journey hither, which occupied some ten weeks, has cost me no small sum, and that furthermore, more will be needful for the purchase of many new and excellent musical things: for as I perceive that since the time when I made my first visit to this place, this whole work is much changed, and the music used at princely tables, comedies, ballets and such performances has likewise been markedly bettered and increased, I have urgent cause most submissively to petition your Serene Highness, as a potentate blessed by God, and one to whom it will be but slight loss, at this time to be graciously pleased to grant your most humble servant an extra sum and give order for the same to the exchange in this place, assuring your Serene Highness in return, with all due devotion, that as my intention in coming hither was none other than to serve your reputation and fit myself the better for your service, so likewise in the future, and so long as God gives me life, I shall show your Serene Highness all due and becoming gratitude, more in the act, by my most submissive attendance upon you, than at present with further expenditure of words, by God's will, to my best endeavour at all times. . . .

With the war dragging on endlessly, Schütz applied again for leave of absence to make a journey to Copenhagen, where he had found a well-disposed patron in a prince of the Royal family, who later became the son-in-law of the Elector of Saxony. The following application was granted.

MOST HUMBLE PETITION TO HIS SERENE HIGHNESS THE ELECTOR OF SAXONY AND MY MOST GRACIOUS LORD

Dresden, 9 February 1633

. . . first to beg Your Serene Highness with my most humble devotion . . . graciously to permit me in the approaching Springtime to make the journey to Northern Germany for which I have several times humbly sought opportunity, to which end I would once again, in all obedience, bring to the notice of Your Serene Highness:

That while awaiting the outcome of the present ebb and flow of war I could well absent myself, since amid these events there is little need to set up an extensive ensemble; the company of players and singers is moreover somewhat weakened and reduced, some of them, owing to age and infirmity, being no longer able to appear, and others having departed to the war or on their own affairs, so that it would in any case be impossible to bring together a large orchestra or chorus.

That the orchestra as organized while I remain here (and which – according to present circumstances – may perhaps still suffice and be good) would nevertheless remain at your disposal and would not decline owing to my absence; likewise before my departure, with the knowledge of our Inspector, it would be put into good order and so left.

Also, that this my absence for a time would be a convenient means and good preparation for the future reformation and betterment of our *Collegii* (if the times will but permit of such a thing once more).

That the purpose of this my journey is again solely to escape for a while from the difficulties and impediments occasioned in our beloved fatherland by war and other circumstances, by which I too am affected, and in some place in Northern Germany to pursue my profession zealously and without disturbance of mind.

Moreover, in loyal obedience I cannot conceal from Your Serene Highness that a short while since, with no thought or striving on my part, the young elected royal Prince of Denmark enquired of me through Friedrich Lebzeltern [Agent of the Elector's Court] whether with your most gracious leave I could visit him for the better reformation and arrangement of his music, he assuring that he would remember it in my favour and would release me again whenever desired.

Now not only would this perhaps give pleasure to that renowned royal Prince, the beloved future son-in-law of our most gracious Lord, while to me such attendance upon him would likewise be something useful and profitable; but my absence for so short a time would be of no harm whatsoever to the Elector's music.

I therefore beg, and hope the more, that your Serene Highness may graciously receive this, my most submissive and perhaps not immodest petition. . . .

Between 1633 and 1645 Schütz made three visits to Copenhagen, where he organized the Court Chapel. In Dresden he tried persistently to save at least some remainders of his once numerous and excellent ensemble.

SCHÜTZ TO THE ELECTOR OF SAXONY

Dresden, 7 March 1641

. . . Although at the present time my most humble reminder (with respect to our now almost completely ruined orchestra) might, in view of the continued sad circumstances of our beloved fatherland, be regarded as untimely, even perhaps by Your Serene Highness, yet I hope to escape the reproach of unreasonableness and win your most gracious pardon; for even as the physician is in duty bound to tend a dangerous sickness before it takes a fatal turn, so must I succour our Corpus Musicum which now lies, as it were, at the last gasp. . . .

But Your Serene Highness, being of a lofty understanding, is well able to judge and determine unaided when and how far (the times being what they are) you may be graciously disposed to restore this work, and my most respectful petition is by no means directed towards securing the immediate and complete re-establishment of our Chapel, but, as I said, towards saving it from speedy and evident ruin and, as it were, to preserve a seed of your orchestra – the which, according to my humble ideas and reflections, could most conveniently be done by recruiting the following boys, bringing them together, feeding them and training them in music:

Firstly

Four choir- or singing-boys. . . .

Moreover

Four instrumentalist-boys. . . .

This, most gracious Elector, is in my humble estimate the proper and most befitting means by which Your Serene Highness can not only to some extent preserve your Court Chapel and enjoy a little music at your table, but also, when better times return—as please God they soon will – by adding a few good Italian or other instruments and as many good singers whenever you may be graciously pleased, you can complete and enlarge the Collegium Musicum, which, without the preparation I now most humbly propose and bring to your recollection, can scarce be hoped for.

There can be no doubt that Your Serene Highness will give gracious approval to my respectful proposal and put the same into effect; you will thus be giving further proof of the considerable prerogatives you possess; for not all potentates are pleased, like Your Royal Highness, to form and maintain orchestras at their Courts. Moreover, you will be showing Almighty God that duty and honour for which He himself gave order in His own praise and which have been rendered to Him in their pious gatherings by all godly potentates before and since the birth of our Lord and Saviour Jesus Christ; you will also be maintaining at your Court that Profession which sparkles brightly and shines far and wide in the midst of the seven free arts, no less than the sun among the seven planets. And who knows but that Your Serene Highness, among your present heavy cares of government, may in this manner be sometimes refreshed in spirit and the more richly blest by the good God with lasting health and other marks of prosperity befitting a prince? . . .

Schütz's worst time, however, came after the conclusion of the war, when the treasury was empty and the musicians did not get their salary. He made desperate efforts to save them from total destitution and demoralization, and the Chapel from total ruin. Prince Christian of Saxony, to whom the next letter is addressed, was the son of the Elector.

SCHÜTZ TO PRINCE CHRISTIAN OF SAXONY

Dresden, 14 August 1651

. . . Most gracious Lord: reluctant though I am to burden so illustrious a Prince with my repeated letters and reminders, yet I am compelled thereto by the continual comings and goings, hour after hour, the exceeding great lamentation, wretchedness and moaning of all the company of poor, neglected musicians of the Chapel, who are living in such distress as would draw tears from a stone in the ground. May God be my witness that their wretched condition and piteous lamentation pierces my heart, since I know not how to give them comfort and hope of some relief.

In former days one would scarce have thought it possible, but most of the company are firmly resolved and say that sooner than bring discredit upon their most gracious Lord by begging their bread, they will set out, compelled by dire necessity, and go their ways elsewhere; that it is impossible for them to remain and continue to endure what they have had to suffer for so long, they must perforce depart, leaving anyone who will to pay their debts. They have had enough of insults, no one will any longer give them credit for a groat, etc.

The duty I owe to my most gracious Elector and Lord obliges me, in view of this necessity, to submit the matter to the notice of Your Princely Highness, as our most gracious Inspector and Master, and to bring to your most gracious consideration that it would be a pitiful thing if the company, assembled with great pains and labour, were to be thus broken up and scattered.

I therefore submit to Your Princely Highness my most humble, earnest plea that you may compassionately solicit His Serene Highness, as your dearly beloved Father, to allow but a single quarter's salary to be paid to the company, that it may at least be held together.

And for this reason most graciously to inform me whether some little comfort or hope may be given them; that they may not be left in want and obliged to seek their bread elsewhere. But if Your Princely Highness should be unable to make some beneficial arrangement – though that is against all my hope – it would be impossible for me to hold them longer. In such case I shall have done my best and have no blame. . . .

SCHÜTZ TO THE ELECTOR'S SECRETARY, CHRISTIAN REICHSBROD

Dresden, 28 May 1652

. . . These 3 weeks past I have been unable to go out (because of the flux in my head which, if you will excuse me, later affected both my thighs and turned to erysipelas), but I had long ago agreed to this and now cannot conceal from you that the bass [Georg Kaiser, member of the Court Chapel], who from poverty again pawned his clothes a while ago, since when he has dwelt in his house in a state of brutishness, like a wild beast in the forest, is now again bestirring himself and informs me through his wife, that he must and will leave this place. . . .

Yet it would be infinite pity to lose so fine a voice from the Chapel. What matter that in other respects his disposition is none too good and that his tongue requires daily washing in the wine-tankard – it is only that so wide a gullet needs more moistening than several narrow ones, and even if the good fellow received his slender wages regularly, they would not stretch to great banquets; and with a right understanding of the fellow's management and housekeeping one should, to my mind, merely give him his small due at the proper time; but as long as this is not done, he cannot fairly be decried as a great spendthrift. . . .

In harness to the end – his numerous applications to be pensioned off were ignored – Schütz lived long enough to see at least the beginnings of a gradual recovery of the devastated country and of the Chapel, to which he had devoted so much love and work.

With a patron of unlimited power, a scramble for his favour will inevitably result, and such a situation is liable to expose questionable features of human nature. In France at the time of Louis XIV artistic activities were almost totally dependent on the King's will and support. One of his favourites, Jean Baptiste Lully (*1632–87*), *succeeded in snatching a Royal privilege for the performance of opera from its first holders, Robert Cambert and Pierre Perrin. The following letter of Lully to Colbert, the influential Minister of Finance, refers to this business. An efficient intriguer and string-puller, Lully was at the same time an artist of vision who established French opera with a distinctive style and organized the* 'Académie Royale de Musique' *which, as the Paris* 'Opéra', *has remained the most prominent musical institution in France ever since.*

LULLY TO JEAN-BAPTISTE COLBERT

Paris, 3 June 1672

Monseigneur,
Since I had the honour of speaking to you about the Royal Academy of Music, I have been daily subjected to further annoyances, of which I make bold to send you the latest, whereby you shall know, Monseigneur, that they make *false declarations* in everything, and in the first place when they say they obtained the Letters Patent from the King in the name of Perrin; and in the second place by declaring that I took the King by surprise, they who have presented several petitions to His Majesty and who knew his intentions better than I did. You know, Monseigneur, that I have followed no other course in this matter *than that which you prescribed to me*, and that at the beginning I believed they would follow the same. But they were careful not to submit themselves to your judgement, well knowing *that you would tolerate no imposture of the sort they have in mind* and which they intend to enforce in Parliament, *and with which you are more familiar than anyone in the world. . . .*

I hope, Monseigneur, that through your kindness the King will grant me the theatre in the Louvre, in which I would have work begun at once, despite the annoyances of the lawsuit, and would have the honour of waiting upon you with M. Quinault [Lully's librettist] to show you a project for the King's return, which I do not doubt will be brought to success, if it finds your approval. . . .

Having obtained the Royal privilege, Lully was able to open his theatre in the autumn of the same year. Very soon he found it necessary to make improvements to his premises.

LULLY TO JEAN-BAPTISTE COLBERT

July 1673

M. Colbert is most humbly begged to inform the King that the Royal Academy of Music requests His Majesty's permission to raise the ceiling of that part of the theatre in the Palais Royal which is above the stage, a thing which can be done without disturbing the roof of the said Palace or touching any of the apartments in the theatre. It also asks that certain beams which are broken and threaten to collapse, may be changed before work can begin, by reason that it would be unsafe to set up machinery there.

On either side of the proscenium there are two stone pillars which serve no purpose but, on the contrary, greatly encumber the space for the scenery. His Majesty is most humbly begged to grant permission to remove these and to use the stone to raise the walls, in the manner aforementioned. The whole on condition that the building and the measures proposed shall first be inspected by the officials of His Majesty's buildings and approved by Mons. Colbert. The Academy being at present under the necessity of paying for the subsistence of the Italian comedians and defraying the expense of building the new theatre, as well as the salaries and ordinary allowances of the Academicians, all this expense is so great that it most humbly begs His Majesty to consider that its establishment or its ruin depends entirely on a new play in the Palais Royal before the winter. . . .

This request too was granted.

Lully's success must have been extraordinary, if we may judge from the dedication of his opera 'Armide' (1686), addressed to the King. Referring as it does to an event of public notoriety, it can hardly have been an overstatement:

'Sire, of all tragedies set to music, this is the one with which the public has expressed the most satisfaction. It is an entertainment to which people flock in crowds and so far none has been seen to receive more applause. . . .'

His prestige was so enormous that half a century after his death a newcomer to opera in Paris, Jean-Philippe Rameau (*1683–1764*) *still had a tremendous uphill struggle before he got a chance of asserting himself in his great predecessor's citadel, the 'Académie Royale de Musique'. Even to be entrusted with a libretto – this was the aim of the following letter to a member of the Académie Royale – was a difficult task. And Rameau was already a well-known, respected composer at that time. His 'Traité de l'Harmonie', a momentous, widely acclaimed contribution to the theory of harmony which he had published some years before, had established his unshakable reputation as a 'learned musician'. After this, the aesthetic controversy on the respective merits of art and nature in music went on in Paris throughout the eighteenth century, with Jean-Jacques Rousseau, the philosopher and musician, as the foremost advocate of nature.*

RAMEAU TO A. M. HOUDART DE LA MOTTE

Paris, 25 October 1727

. . . Whatever reasons you may have, Sir, for apprehending that my music for the stage will not be greeted so favourably as that of a composer apparently more experienced in that style of music, permit me to contest them and at the same time to justify the prejudice I feel in my own favour, without claiming to derive from my learning any advantages other than those which you too will feel to be legitimate. Those who speak of 'a learned musician' ordinarily mean a man conversant with all aspects of the different combination of notes; but at the same time he is believed to be so absorbed in those combinations that to them he sacrifices everything – sentiment, common sense, wit and reason. Such a man is merely an academic musician, of an academy concerned with notes and nothing more; so that people do well to prefer to him the musician who sets less store by his erudition than by his taste. The latter, however, whose taste has been formed solely by comparisons within his own range of feeling, cannot excel in more than a few styles at most – I mean, in those related to his temperament. Is he naturally tender? Then he will well express tenderness; is his character quick, playful, frivolous, etc.? His music will be correspondingly so; but let him depart from these characteristics which are his by nature, and you will no longer recognize him. Moreover, since he draws everything from his imagination, with no help from art, by his recourse to various expressions, he at last wears himself out. In his first fire he was brilliant; but that fire diminishes each time he strives to rekindle it, and he ends by offering us nothing but repetitions and platitudes. . . .

Nature has not entirely withheld her gifts from me, and I have not devoted myself to forming combinations of notes so far as to forget their intimate connection with natural beauty, which by itself is sufficient to please, but which is not easily found in a soil which lacks seed and above all, which has made its last efforts. . . .

You need only come to hear for yourself what character I have bestowed upon the *Sauvages*, which appeared in the Théâtre Italien a year or two ago, and how I interpreted such titles as *Les Soupirs*, *Les Tendres Plaintes*, *Les Cyclopes*, *Les Tourbillons* (these being the swirls of dust stirred up by high winds), *L'Entretien des Muses*, a *Musette*, a *Tambourin*, etc.; you will then see that I am no novice in the art and above all that I do not appear to make a great display of learning in my productions, where I strive to employ the art that conceals arts; for in them I consider only people of taste, and learned men not at all, since there are many of the former and scarce any of the latter sort. . . . Here at least you have matter enough for reflection. . . .

With a different political structure in England, where a powerful aristocratic oligarchy had established itself beside the Crown and sometimes in opposition to it, the patronage of the aristocracy and the wealthy gentry became for the artist rather more important than that of the King. Already in the eighteenth century a gifted musician could make his fortune in London. George Frederick Handel *(1685–1759), who settled there in 1712, did so, having first made himself known as an operatic composer both in Germany and in Italy. For many years opera remained the centre of his activity, mainly in connection with a yearly season of some months, for which an ensemble of prominent singers, chiefly Italian, was engaged. Involved besides in the management of this enterprise, he became personally acquainted with its inevitable ups and downs. He had to travel to Italy to recruit singers and was confronted with all sorts of rivalry, from his Italian competitors as well as from his singers, from capricious or rebellious prima donnas of both sexes – or, worse than either, castrati – and finally was driven to bankruptcy. Reluctantly, he gave up opera in the end. The rest of his life was devoted to oratorio, in which his genius found its most mature fulfilment.*

In Handel's time, and for more than a century to come, operatic singers of the highest quality were only to be found in Italy.

Great singers have always commanded enormous fees and salaries, unlike great composers, but it is true that there has always been more public demand for the former than for the latter. The castrato Senesino, mentioned in the following letter, enjoyed a fabulous reputation. Considering the value of money at that time, a salary of 1,400 guineas for a six-month season is staggering. No wonder Senesino could retire in his middle fifties, a wealthy man.

HANDEL TO FRANCIS COLMAN
BRITISH AMBASSADOR TO THE COURT OF TUSCANY

London, 27 October 1730

Monsieur,

I have just been honoured with your letter of the 22nd last, from which I see the reasons that determined you to engage Sr Senesino on the footing of fourteen hundred Guineas, in which we acquiesce; and I most humbly thank you for the pains you have been good enough to take in this matter. The said Sr Senesino arrived here 12 days ago and I did not fail on presentation of your letter to pay him on account of his salary the hundred Guineas you had promised him. As for Sig^{ra} Pisani, we have not had her, and as the season is now far advanced and the operas will soon begin, we shall dispense with any other woman from Italy this year, having already arranged the operas for the company we have at present.

I am, however, much obliged to you for having thought of Sig^{ra} Maddalena Pieri, in case we had had absolute need of another woman to take men's parts, but we shall rest content with the five persons, having now found means of making up what was lacking.

It is to your generous assistance that the Court and the Nobility will in part owe the satisfaction of now having a company to their taste, so that it only remains for me to express to you my particular gratitude for this and to assure you of the most respectful attention, etc., etc.

In 1735 Handel ran into serious difficulties. 'A letter to a Friend in the Country' in a London newspaper of 20 March of that year, 'Old Whig: or, The Consistent Protestant', gives a graphic description of his circumstances.

'The late squabble at the Opera is pretty well adjusted. Parties were formed, and protests were just ready to be entered, to which many fair hands had threatened to subscribe: when by accommodating matters with Senesino all the ruffled passions were calmed, as if it had been by the melody of his voice. Farinelli [another famous castrato] surpasses everything we have hitherto heard . . . Handel, whose excellent compositions have often pleased our ears, and touched our hearts, has this winter sometimes performed to an almost empty pit. He has lately revived his fine Oratorio of 'Esther', in which he has introduced two concertos on the organ that were inimitable. But so strong is the disgust taken against him, that even this has been far from bringing him crowded audiences. . . . His loss is computed for these two seasons at a great sum. . . .

Handel's oratorios, which appealed to the Puritan, devoted to the Scripture and most of all to the Old Testament, found ever-increasing favour with his patrons. One of them, Charles Jennens, became one of his staunchest supporters and acquired merit by his arrangement of Milton's 'L'Allegro' and 'Il Pensieroso' for Handel's use, adding a third part, 'Il Moderato'. He also took a hand in the libretti of Handel's 'Messiah', 'Saul', and 'Belshazzar'. The composer's letters to him show the due submissiveness of a humble musician to his wealthy and influential patron, but his delight in Jennens's libretti was certainly genuine, and is borne out by the inspired music with which he reacted to them. It should be added that Handel's English never came up to the standard of his French, which had been a part of his upbringing.

HANDEL TO CHARLES JENNENS

London, 28 July 1735

Sir,
I received your very agreeable letter with the enclosed oratorio [probably *Saul*]. I am just going to Tunbridge, yet what I could read of it in haste gave me a great deal of satisfaction. I shall have more leisure time there to read it with all the attention it deserves. There is no certainty of my scheme for next season, but it is probable that something or other may be done, of which I shall take the liberty to give you notice, being extremely obliged to you for the generous concern you show upon this account. . . .

HANDEL TO CHARLES JENNENS AFTER THE FIRST PERFORMANCE OF 'MESSIAH'

Dublin, 29 December 1741

Sir,
It was with the greatest pleasure I saw the continuation of your kindness by the lines you were pleased to send me, in order to be prefixed to your oratorio *Messiah*, which I set to music before I left England. I am emboldened, Sir, by the generous concern you please to take in relation to my affairs, to give you an account to the success I have met here. The Nobility did me the honour to make amongst themselves a subscription for 6 nights, which did fill a room of 600 persons, so that I needed not sell one single ticket at the door. And without vanity the performance was received with a general approbation. Sig[ra] Avoglio, which I brought with me from London, pleases extraordinary. I have formed another tenor voice which gives great satisfaction. The basses and counter tenors are very good, and the rest of the chorus singers (by my direction) do exceeding well; as for the instruments, they are really

excellent, Mr Dubourg being at the head of them, and the music sounds delightfully in this charming room, which puts me in such spirits (and my health being so good), that I exert myself on my organ with more than usual success. I opened with the *Allegro, Penseroso & Moderato*, and I assure you that the words of the *Moderato* are vastly admired. The audience being composed (besides the flower of ladies of distinction and other people of the greatest quality) of so many bishops, deans, heads of the college, the most eminent people in the Law as the Chancellor, Auditor General, etc., all which are very much taken with the poetry. So that I am desired to perform it again the next time. I cannot sufficiently express the kind treatment I receive here, but the politeness of this generous nation cannot be unknown to you, so I let you judge of the satisfaction I enjoy, passing my time with honour, profit and pleasure. They propose already to have some more performances when the 6 nights of the subscription are over. . . .

HANDEL TO CHARLES JENNENS

London, 9 September 1742

. . . The report that the direction of the Opera next winter is committed to my care, is groundless. The gentlemen, who have undertaken to meddle with Harmony, cannot agree and are quite in a confusion. Whether I shall do something in the Oratorio way (as several of my friends desire), I cannot determine as yet. Certain it is that this time 12 months I shall continue my Oratorios in Ireland, where they are agoing to make a large subscription already for the purpose. . . .

HANDEL TO CHARLES JENNENS

London, 9 June 1744

. . . As you do me the honour to encourage my *Messiah* undertakings, and even to promote them with a particular kindness, I take the liberty to trouble you with an account of what engagements I have hitherto concluded. I have taken the Opera House in the Haymarket, engaged as singers Sig^{ra} Francesina, Mr Robinson, Beard, Reinhold, Mr Gates with his boys and several of the best chorus singers from the choirs, and I have some hope that Mrs Cibber will sing for me. . . .

Now I should be extremely glad to receive the first act, or what is ready, of the new oratorio [*Belshazzar*], with which you intend to favour me, that I might employ all my attention and time, in order to answer in some measure the obligation I lay under. This new favour will greatly increase my obligations. . . .

HANDEL TO CHARLES JENNENS

London, 19 July 1744

. . . At my arrival in London, which was yesterday, I immediately perused the act of the oratorio with which you favoured me, and, the little time only I had it, gives me great pleasure. Your reasons for the length of the first act are entirely satisfactory to me, and it is likewise my opinion to have the following acts short. I shall be very glad and much obliged to you, if you will soon favour me with the remaining acts. Be pleased to point out these passages in the *Messiah* which you think require altering. . . .

HANDEL TO CHARLES JENNENS

London, 21 August 1744

. . . The second act of the oratorio I have received safe and own myself highly obliged to you for it. I am greatly pleased with it, and shall use my best endeavours to do it justice. I can only say that I impatiently wait for the third act. . . .

HANDEL TO CHARLES JENNENS

London, 13 September 1744

Your most excellent Oratorio has given me great delight in setting it to music and still engages me warmly. It is indeed a noble piece, very grand and uncommon; it has furnished me with expressions, and has given me opportunity to some very particular ideas, beside so many great chorus. I entreat you heartily to favour me soon with the last act, which I expect with anxiety, that I may regulate myself the better as to the length of it. I profess myself highly obliged to you for so generous a present. . . .

HANDEL TO CHARLES JENNENS

London, 2 October 1744

I received the 3rd act with a great deal of pleasure, as you can imagine, and you may believe that I think it a very fine and sublime oratorio, only it is really too long; if I should extend the music it would last 4 hours and more.

I entrenched already a great deal of the music, that I might preserve the poetry as much as I could, yet still it may be shortened. The anthems come in very properly, but would not the words 'I will magnify thee, o God my King, and praise thy name for ever and ever',

'The Lord preserveth all them that love him, but scatters abroad all the ungodly', 'My mouth shall speak the praise of the Lord and let all flesh give thanks unto His holy name for ever and ever, Amen' conclude well the oratorio. . . .

When on his return journey from Italy in 1729 Handel visited his family in Halle, his birthplace, a humble church musician, Johann Sebastian Bach *(1685–1750), came there from Leipzig in order to meet his famous contemporary, of whom he had heard a great deal, He arrived too late; Handel had already left. So the two greatest musicians of their time, who were born in the same year and not very far from each other, never met. But they were opposites indeed, as divergent in their artistic attitudes as in their destinies. Handel lived in the great, open world, supported by the King and the nobility of the wealthiest country in Europe. Bach never crossed the close confines of a petty German residence or a church congregation. It is not easy to imagine the drabness and narrowness of a German provincial city in Bach's time. In the Thirty Years War one third of the population of Germany and nine tenths of her wealth had been destroyed, leaving a heritage of misery for generations. The patronage of numerous small Courts – Bach served at the Courts of the Duke of Weimar and of the Prince of Anhalt in Cöthen – was limited by lack of funds; and the Protestant Church, to which Bach's work was devoted from 1723 to his death, did not offer more than a modest living. Discipline was equally stern under the princes and their ministers and under the City Corporation of Leipzig, where Bach was Cantor, in charge of the Thomas-Schule and of music at the two main churches, St Thomas and St Nicolai.*

When he left service in Weimar to accept a better and more rewarding position in Cöthen, the price he had to pay was a prison sentence of some weeks, as we learn from a Weimar Court Secretary's report:

'On 6 November 1717 the quondam Concertmeister and organist Bach was confined to the County Judge's place of detention for too stubbornly forcing the issue of his dismissal, and finally on 2 December was freed from arrest with notice of his unfavourable discharge.'

The musician was a craftsman to his superiors and nothing more, and he had to do some odd jobs as well, as is born out by the following excerpts from the accounts of the Cöthen 'Capella':

12 September 1722: To the Capellmeister Bach for repairs to the Prince's cimbalo, *without the strings, 1 thaler.*

30 December 1722: The same for quilling the big clavecin, *including the strings, 1 thaler 8 groschen.*

20 March 1723: to the Capellmeister Bach, who had to quill this clavecin, *1 Thaler.*

Unfortunately little of Bach's personal correspondence has survived. The work he had on his hands was enormous, as composer, teacher, performer, and choir-master. An important part of his duties in Leipzig was the training and general supervision of the choir-boys of the Thomas Schule, *including the teaching of Latin. Add to this the demands of a large and growing family (twelve of his twenty children survived him), and it is no wonder that he found no time for correspondence, nor is it surprising that one does not know of any social contacts of his among the literary and University circles of Leipzig. What is available, apart from his gigantic output of music, consists mostly of official documents, which, in general, always have a safer chance of survival. Some of these are certainly of interest.*

BACH'S PLEDGE OF SERVICE TO THE LEIPZIG TOWN COUNCIL

5 May 1723

Undertaking of the Cantor at St Thomas's School

(1) That I shall set the boys the good example of an honourable, disciplined way of life, watch zealously over the school and faithfully instruct the boys,

(2) To the best of my ability, bring the music in both the parish churches of this town into a good state,

(3) Show all due respect and obedience to the honourable Council, watching over and furthering its honour and reputation in all places as well as may be; likewise, should a gentleman of the Council desire the boys to take part in a performance, that I shall permit them to go to him without opposition, but that apart from this I shall in no circumstances allow them to go into the country for funerals or weddings without the knowledge and consent of the Burgomaster in office and the headmaster of the school,

(4) Give due obedience to the inspector and headmaster of the school in all such matters as they may order on behalf of the honourable Council,

(5) Take no boy into the school unless he already has a grounding in music or unless he comes with the purpose of receiving instruction in the matter . . .,

(6) Instruct the boys zealously, not in singing only, but also in instrumental music, that the churches may not be burdened with unnecessary expense,

(7) In maintaining good order in the churches, so arrange the music that it shall not last over-long, and shall be of a style which will not

produce an *operatic* effect, but rather encourage the listeners to piety,

(8) Provide the New Church with good scholars,

(9) Deal with the boys in a friendly and circumspect manner, but should any refuse obedience, punish them *in moderation* or report them to the proper quarter,

(10) Be faithful in providing instruction in the school, and in all matters pertaining thereto,

(11) And if I should be unable to do this myself, arrange for it to be done by another able *subjectum* at no cost to the honourable Council or the school,

(12) Not go outside the town without the permission of the Burgomaster in office,

(13) At all funerals, according to custom, walk with and beside the boys as much as possible,

(14) and not accept any *Officium* at the University without the *Consens* of the honourable Council,

as I hereby, and by virtue of the foregoing, undertake and pledge myself faithfully to comply with the same and not to act in a contrary manner, on pain of the loss of my employment. In token whereof I have signed this undertaking with my own hand, etc., etc.

The first difficulty in Leipzig arose very early, owing to Bach's claim to the directorship of music in the University, which his predecessors had held. As we have learnt already, Bach was stubborn. In the end he applied to a higher authority, to the King who was well disposed towards him and whose intervention solved the problem in Bach's favour.

BACH TO FRIEDRICH AUGUST II, KING OF POLAND AND ELECTOR OF SAXONY

Leipzig, 14 September 1725

I beg Your Royal Majesty and Serene Highness to be graciously pleased to permit me to explain to you, with the most humble submission, that the Directorium of the music of the old and new worship at the honourable University of Leipzig, with the salary and customary perquisites, had always been combined with the office of Cantor of St Thomas, up to and including the lifetime of my *Antecessor*, but after his death, during the temporary vacancy, it was given to the organist at St Nicholas's, *Görnern*, and although when I took up my office the Directorium of the so-styled old worship was indeed again entrusted to me, the salary thereof was still withheld and, together with the *Directorium* of the new worship, allotted to the aforementioned Organist of St Nicholas's; and although I made proper application to the honourable university and strove for the restoration of the previous conditions, yet I could obtain no more than an offer of half the *Salarium*, which was formerly twelve guilders. . . .

I therefore present to Your Royal Majesty and Serene Highness my most humble petition and request that you may be pleased most graciously to command the honourable University of Leipzig to restore the former arrangements and to grant me the *Directorium* of the new worship, but more especially the full salary of the old one, and the perquisites due to both. . . .

Bach's character, determined, proud, and sometimes irascible, made him an unsuitable subordinate to a musically ignorant city authority. The results were more friction and, very soon, a desire for change. This is expressed in a letter to an influential friend, one of the rare specimens of Bach's informal private style of writing, pithy and straightforward, despite its quaint baroque paraphernalia. George Erdmann was Russian Plenipotentiary at Danzig.

BACH TO GEORGE ERDMANN

Leipzig, 28 October 1730

. . . Almost 4 years have now gone by since your Honour favoured me with a kind reply to my letter; and remembering that you were graciously pleased to ask for some news of my misfortunes, I herewith obediently comply with that request. You are well acquainted with my fate from youth up, until the change that took me to Cöthen as conductor. There I found a benevolent Prince, with a love and knowledge of music, and thought to pass the rest of my life in his service. But as it so fell out, the said Serene Highness married a Princess of Berenburg, and it seemed thereafter that the said Prince's inclination for music had somewhat cooled, especially as the new Princess appeared to be an *amusa*; and it pleased God that I should be offered a position here as *Directore musices* and *Cantore* at St Thomas's School. At first, indeed, I felt it most unbecoming to change from conductor to cantor. I therefore delayed my decision for some three months; but the post was so favourably described to me that in the end (particularly as my sons seemed disposed towards *studiis*) I took courage in the name of the All Highest and went to Leipzig, passed my examination and accepted the change. By God's will I have been here ever since. As, however, (1) I find that this service is not near so lucrative as it had been described to me, (2) many *Accidentia* [perquisites] of the post escaped me, (3) the place is very expensive and (4) the authorities are hard to please and care little for music, so that I am obliged to live amid almost continual vexation, envy and persecution, it seems that I shall be compelled, with your gracious assistance, to seek my *Fortune* elsewhere. Should your Honour know of or discover any *convenable station* for an old and faithful servant in that place, I would respectfully beg you to vouch me a gracious *Recommendation*; and I for my part shall make my best endeavour to give satisfaction for your gracious testimonial and intercession. My present post brings in about 700 thalers, and when there are a few more funerals than *ordinairement*, the perquisites increase proportionately; but when the air is wholesome, on the contrary, they diminish, this last year my *ordinaire* perquisites for burials declined by more than 100 thalers. In Thuringia I can make 400 thalers go further than twice as many hundred in this place, owing to the excessively high cost of living. . . . I have married again, my first wife having died in peace at Cöthen. From my first marriage, 3 sons and one daughter survive. . . . From my second marriage one son and two daughters. My eldest son is a *studiosus juris*, the other two still respectively frequent *primam* and *secundam classem*, and my eldest daughter is still unmarried. The children of the other marriage are still young, the eldest, the boy, being 6 years old. All of them however are born *Musici* and I can assure you that I am already able to form a concert *vocaliter* and *instrumentaliter* from my own family, as my present wife sings a very pretty *soprano* and my eldest daughter, too, joins in not badly. . . .

All the same, he stayed in Leipzig. His life seems to have been rather restless and dissatisfied and his relations with the Town Council a succession of minor and major conflicts and mutual recriminations. The essence of his work written for the church – his passion oratorios, cantatas, motets, choral preludes – was beyond the appreciation of those around him. This work remained buried among his manuscripts till it was rediscovered a century later. But it looks as if he had accepted with heroic resignation his isolation as an artist of unapproachable greatness. What he was fighting for, tenaciously and with bitter determination, was his due with respect to financial claims as well as to his position as head of music in the cathedral.

BACH TO THE LEIPZIG TOWN COUNCIL

Leipzig, 25 August 1733

Magnificent, most honourable, learned and wise, most honoured gentlemen and distinguished patrons.

May it please you to condescend to hear how Herr Johann Fredrich Eitelwein, merchant of this town, was married on 12 August of the present year out of town, and therefore believes himself entitled to withhold the fees due to us in such cases, and has made bold to disregard many friendly reminders from us. Whereas the said fees make up the greater part of our emoluments, and no one has hitherto endeavoured to withhold them from us. We are therefore compelled most dutifully to beg you, most magnificent and honourable gentlemen, for this reason to take us under your protection and by your decision and care to uphold us in our old rights and agreed *Salario*, and further to enjoin upon the said Herr Eitelwein that he remit to us our lawful shares of the marriage fees, to each his due proportion, together with the costs occasioned, in this instance, which we also claim, with all fitting respect and reverence.

Your magnificent and honourable gentlemen, our most honoured Lords and distinguished Patrons,
from your most dutifully devoted

Johann Sebastian Bach,
Director of Music and Cantor,
Johann Schneider, Organist,
M. Johann Matthis Gesner, Rector of St Thomas's School,
on behalf of the Alumni of that School

BACH'S APPLICATION FOR THE TITLE OF COURT COMPOSER TO THE KING OF POLAND AND ELECTOR OF SAXONY

[With the dedication of the Kyrie and Gloria of his Mass in B minor, presented in manuscript.]

Dresden, 27 July 1733

. . . With the deepest devotion I offer your Royal Majesty the present trifling example of the skill to which I have attained in Music, most humbly begging that you will not judge it by its bad composition, but in your world-famous clemency will look graciously upon it and deign to take me into your most mighty protection. I have for some years and until now held the office of Director of Music for the two parish churches at Leipzig, in which, however, through no fault of my own.

I have been exposed to sundry mortifications, and now, moreover, to a reduction of the emoluments pertaining to that function, which annoyances, however, might cease entirely if your Royal Majesty would be graciously pleased to bestow upon me some title in your Court Music, and to that end give order for a decree to be issued by the appropriate authority; the gracious acceptance of my humble petition will attach me to you in infinite veneration, and I offer myself in the most dutiful obedience, whenever your Royal Majesty may graciously require me, to show my unwearying zeal in the composition of music either for church or orchestra, and to devote my full power to your service. . . .

This petition was granted, but only after some years, owing to a long absence of the King. Meanwhile, however, another bitter feud had arisen, an open conflict, between the Cantor and the administrative director of the 'Thomas Schule', Ernesti. Once more, Bach had to apply to the King as supreme judge, while the Town Council took Ernesti's part, and it seems that the King mediated a peace between the two opponents, after two years of open war and mutual sabotage.

BACH TO THE LEIPZIG TOWN COUNCIL

Leipzig, 12 August 1736

May your Excellencies, etc., etc., be graciously pleased to permit me to report that whereas your honourable Council has given order respecting the School of St Thomas that it shall rest with the Cantor to select such of the boys as he deems fit to be *Praefects*, and that in making his choice he shall consider not only their voices, that they be good and clear, but also whether these *Praefects* (particularly he who sings in the first choir) will be able to direct the *Chori Musici* if the Cantor is ill or absent; and that this right has formerly and until now been exercised by the Cantors independently of the Administrative Director, and not otherwise; nevertheless the present Director, Magister Johann August Ernesti, has recently taken upon himself to replace the *Praefect* of the first choir without my knowledge or consent, and latterly appointed in this wise the then *Praefect* of the other choir, Krause, to be *Praefect* of the first-mentioned, and refuses to depart from this attitude despite all my friendly representations; but I cannot permit such a breach of the above mentioned school regulations and traditions, to the prejudice of my *Successores* and the detriment of the *Chori Musici*; I therefore humbly petition your Excellencies . . . graciously to vouchsafe to settle the difference which has thus arisen between the Director and myself in my *Officio*, and . . . to inform the Director, Mag. Ernesti, that in conformity with the school regulations and customs he shall from this time forth leave the appointment of the *Praefects* solely to me, and thus graciously to protect me in my *Officio*. . . .

BACH TO THE KING OF POLAND AND ELECTOR OF SAXONY

Leipzig, 18 October 1737

. . . In as much as Your Royal Majesty has been most graciously pleased to grant me the title of your Court Composer, I shall revere you all my life with the most humble thanks. As I therefore claim Your Royal Majesty's most gracious protection with the utmost confidence, I now venture to appeal to you most submissively in my present oppression.

My predecessors, the *Cantors* of St Thomas's School in this place, in conformity with the traditional government of the School, have always had the right to appoint the *Praefects* of its *Choris Musicis*. . . . This notwithstanding, however, the present Rector, Mag. Johann August Ernesti, has recently had the impertinence to appoint a *Praefect* without reference to me, and that, moreover, a *subject* very inexpert in *musicis*. And when, perceiving his weakness, and the confusion thereby occasioned in the choir, I found myself obliged to make a change and choose a more skilful *subjectum* in his stead, the said Rector Ernesti did not only resolutely oppose my intention, but also, to my great annoyance and humiliation, forebade all boys in the school, *sub poena relegationis*, to obey any of my arrangements. . . .

Therefore, with the deepest humility, I beseech Your Royal Majesty

(1) [to instruct] the Council of this town to maintain me undisturbed in my *jure quaestio ratione* with regard to the appointment of the *Praefectorum Chori Musici* and to protect me therein, and

(2) most graciously to command the *Consistorium* of this place that they require Rector Ernesti to apologize for his insults to me. . . .

Another manifestation of Royal favour is significant, not only because it was the most flattering distinction ever bestowed upon Bach, but because it became the source of an immortal work, called 'A Musical Offering'. Its history is well known. In May 1747, on a visit to Potsdam to his son Carl Philip Emanuel, a court musician to the King of Prussia, Frederick the Great, the old master was asked to take part in the King's chamber music, treated as a guest of honour, and invited to improvise on a theme given to him by his Royal host who, like many noble amateurs of his time, was no mean musician. Bach's reply to this act of favour was generous. He wrote a large set of compositions on the Royal theme – fugues, canons and a trio sonata –, had it printed (at his own expense, like all the music he ever published) and dedicated it to the King. The preface to this work is worth quoting as, for all its ceremonious formality, it is obviously sincere in its statements and in its appreciation of the theme, the majestic, austere beauty of which is wonderfully enhanced in Bach's exuberantly imaginative setting.

BACH'S PREFACE TO 'A MUSICAL OFFERING'

Most Gracious King,
With the most profound humility I dedicate to Your Majesty a musical work, the finest part whereof proceeds from your own exalted hand. With respectful gratification I still remember the special royal favour Your Majesty showed me some time ago, during my visit to Potsdam, when you yourself condescended to play for me on the harpsichord a theme for a fugue, and thereupon most graciously ordered me to perform the same forthwith in your exalted presence. It was my most humble duty to obey Your Majesty's command. I soon perceived, however, that for lack of the necessary preparation, the performance was not worthy of so excellent a theme. I thus decided, and at once pledged myself, to work out this right royal theme more fully, and then make it known to the world. The task has now been accomplished to the best of my ability, and with no other intention than the blameless one of extolling, albeit in a small point only, the fame of a Monarch whose might and strength in all the arts of war and peace, and also especially in music, deserve universal admiration and respect. I venture to add this most humble petition: may Your Majesty condescend to honour this trifling work by your gracious acceptance, and continue to vouchsafe your most exalted royal favour to

Your Majesty's
most humble, obedient servant,
the Composer

'Known to the world' – the narrowness of that world, in which Bach lived, is pathetically illustrated by a letter he wrote to a cousin, Cantor at Schweinfurt, who seems to have been anxious to make himself acquainted with this new work of the Cantor of St Thomas.

BACH TO JOHANN ELIAS BACH

Leipzig, 6 October 1748

Most noble, highly esteemed Cousin,
. . . For the time being I cannot oblige you with the copy of the Prussian Fugue [*A Musical Offering*] for which you ask, for *justement* the printer

has run out of copies today; for I had only 100 printed, most of which went gratis to good friends. Between now and the New Year, however, I shall have a few more printed; and if, cousin, you are still minded to have a copy, you need only inform me at your convenience sending a thaler at the same time, and it shall be despatched. . . .

In the eighteenth century the term 'learned music', which certainly applied to Bach's 'Musical Offering', was often used in a derogatory sense. His sons Wilhelm Friedemann, Carl Philip Emanuel, and Johann Christian, who became much more famous than he had been at any time of his life, had little sympathy with their father's venerable scholasticism. Carl Philip Emanuel's opinion on this is clearly expressed in a piece of kind advice to a younger colleague in Berlin.

CARL PHILIP EMANUEL BACH TO MUSIKDIREKTOR KÜHNAU

Hamburg, 31 August 1784

Dearest Friend,

The gift of your score gives me great pleasure. I thank you most cordially for it, and assure you of my true esteem and friendship. . . .

Permit me, *in true affection*, to teach you something for the future. In things intended for the press, and thus for the general public, you should be less ingenious and give more *sugar*. A pure style of writing, which you have, is sufficient. One must cure the ignorant of the mistaken prejudice which makes them believe that disciplined writing detracts from what is pleasing. . . .

THE VIENNA CLASSICS

From Gluck to Beethoven

What Carl Philip Emanuel calls 'sugar' – sweet lightness – is one of the chief features of that new style of the mid-eighteenth century, with which Johann Sebastian would never have any dealings. Another of its important features is 'the expression of the passions', frequently discussed in the aesthetic writings of the period, and this, across more than a century, links up with the main aims of Monteverdi. Christoph Willibald Gluck (*1714–87*), *the great reformer of opera, can hardly have known a bar of Monteverdi's music. But there is a deep affinity between his ideas and those of the Venetian master; their common ground is the heritage of ancient drama as conceived by the humanists and revived by the French classicists.*

Like his predecessor in the seventeenth century, Gluck was dependent on patronage. He found it in the highest quarters when he became music teacher to the Imperial family in Vienna. One of his high-born pupils, the Archduchess Marie Antoinette, married to Louis XVI, the luckless King of France at the time of the French Revolution, paved Gluck's way to the most distinguished operatic theatre in Europe, the 'Académie Royale de Musique' in Paris. There he became a celebrity and his works the focus of impassioned public discussion.

Gluck was the first great musician to realize the enormous importance of public opinion in promoting success and fame, and the first to carefully organize and cultivate his press relations. He was indefatigable in providing material for the public use of his supporters, formulating his artistic aims, always argumentative, disputing with his opponents, unceasingly aware of every tactical advantage to secure his position. Having produced 'Iphigenia en Aulide', 'Orfeo' and 'Alceste' in Paris with tremendous success in spite of a well-organized opposition, he found a rival in the Italian composer, Nicola Piccinni. The strife of the Gluckists and the Piccinnists, between the champions of the musical drama and of Italian melody, filled the newspapers and produced a flood of articles and pamphlets, and well-known writers such as D'Alembert, Marmontel, and De La Harpe threw themselves into the skirmish. When the director of the 'Académie Royale de Musique', Hébert, had the bright idea of having an opera on the same theme, 'Roland', written by each of the rivals, Gluck refused to be drawn into a position he considered undignified. Instead of 'Roland', which he left to Piccinni, he wrote 'Armide' and, two years after, 'Iphigénie en Tauride'. Both were hailed as masterpieces by his adherents and bitterly opposed by the Piccinnists. Le Blanc du Roullet, to whom the next letter is addressed, was secretary to the French embassy in Vienna and librettist of Gluck's 'Iphigenia in Aulis'.

GLUCK TO LE BLANC DU ROULLET

July 1776

I have just now, my friend, received your letter of 15 January, in which you urge me to continue working on the music of the Opera *Roland*; this is no longer possible, for when I learnt that the Management of the Opera, who were not unaware that I was doing *Roland*, had given the same work to be done by M. Piccinni, I burnt everything I had written so far, which was perhaps of little worth, and in that case the Public may be grateful to M. Marmontel for saving it from being obliged to listen to bad music. Moreover, I am no longer the right man for competition. M. Piccinni would have too much the advantage of me, for in addition to his personal merit, which is undoubtedly very great, he would have that of novelty, I having given Paris four works, good or bad, no matter; it wearies the imagination, and besides I have paved the way for him, he has only to follow me. I say nothing of the protection he enjoys. I am sure a certain Politician of my acquaintance will invite three fourths of Paris to dinner and supper to win proselytes for him, and that Marmontel, who is so skilled in making up Tales, will tell the whole Kingdom the tale of Sieur Piccini's unrivalled merits. Truly, I pity M. Hébert for having fallen unto the clutches of such persons, one who admires Italian Music to the exclusion of all else, the other a Playwright of allegedly Comic Operas. They will fool him to the top of his bent. I am really sorry for it, for M. Hébert is a gentleman, and that is why I am not departing from my intention to give him my *Armide*, but on the terms I described to you in my last letter, chief of which, I repeat, are that I am to be given at least two months, when I come to Paris, to train my Actors and Actresses; that I am to be at liberty to call as many rehearsals as I may consider necessary; that there shall be no alternative singer for any Role, but that another Opera shall be kept in readiness in case any Actor or Actress is indisposed. Those are my terms, or else I shall keep *Armide* for my own pleasure. I have written the Music in such a manner that it will not quickly become outmoded.

You tell me, my dear friend, in your Letter, that nothing will ever equal *Alceste*; but for my part I do not yet subscribe to your prophecy. *Alceste* is a complete Tragedy, and I admit that I believe it falls very little short of perfection; but you cannot imagine how many different shades and roads are available to Music; *Armide* is so different from *Alceste* that you would not think they were by the same composer. Indeed, I used what little sap was left in me to finish *Armide*; in it I tried to be more the Painter and the Poet than the Musician; well, you will be the judge, if it is to be heard. I confess I would like to end my career with that Opera. It is true that the Public will need at least as much time to understand it as they did to understand *Alceste*. There is a kind of delicacy in *Armide* which is not in *Alceste*; for I have found the way to make the characters speak in such manner that you will know beforehand by their style of expression whether it is Armide who is speaking, or a woman attendant, etc., etc. I must end, or you will think I have turned madman or quack. Nothing produces such a bad effect as praising oneself; that only befitted the great Corneille; but when Marmontel or I praise ourselves, people jeer at us and laugh in our faces. Indeed, you have good reason to say that the French Composers have been too much neglected; for unless I am much mistaken, I believe Gossec and Philidor, who know the cut of the French Opera, would serve the Public infinitely better than the best Italian Authors, if there were not this enthusiasm for all that seems novel. You also tell me, my friend, that *Orfeo* suffers by comparison with *Alceste*. But Lord! how can one compare the two works, which are in no way comparable? One may please better than the other; but have *Alceste* performed with your bad actors and any other actress than Mlle Le Vasseur, and *Orfeo* with the best you have, and you will see that *Orfeo* will tip the scales. The best things, badly performed, become all the more unbearable. No comparison can hold between two works of a different nature. If, for example, Piccinni and I were each to write an Opera on the theme of *Roland*, it would be possible to judge which of us had done best; but different Poems must necessarily produce different Music, each of which may be the most sublime of its kind in expressing the words; but there all comparison falls flat. I am almost afraid lest there be an attempt to compare *Armide* and *Alceste*, two such different poems, one of which is meant to cause tears and the other voluptuous sensations; were that to happen, I should have nothing left but to pray to God that the good city of Paris might recover its senses.

Farewell, my dear friend, I embrace you, etc. etc.

GLUCK TO J. B. SUARD

October 1777

Monsieur,

When I came to consider music not merely as the art of diverting the ear, but as one of the greatest means of moving the heart and exciting the affections, and in consequence took a new method, I began to concern myself with the stage, I sought for great and forceful expression, and above all I strove that all the parts of my works should be linked one to another. First of all I found I had against me the male and female singers and a great number of teachers; but all the men of wit and letters of Germany and Italy, without exception, made up for this by their praises and marks of esteem. It is not the same in France; for while there are men of letters in that country whose approval should indeed console me for this, there are also many who have declared against me.

It would appear that these gentlemen are more fortunate when they write on other matters; for, if I am to judge by the welcome the public has been good enough to extend to my works, that same public takes little account of their phrases or of their opinion. But what do you think, Sir, of the new attack just made on me by one of them, M. de La Harpe? This M. de La Harpe is a droll authority; he speaks of music in a way that would make every choir-boy in Europe shrug his shoulders . . . .

Et pueri nasum rhinocerontis habent.

Will you not say a brief word to him, Sir—you who have defended me against him with such great advantage? Ah, I beg you, if my music gives you some little pleasure, put me in a position to prove to my friends, the connoisseurs in Germany and Italy, that among France's men of letters there are some who, when speaking of the arts, at least know what they are talking about.

I have the honour to be, with great esteem and gratitude, Sir, your most humble and obedient servant,

The chevalier Gluck

GLUCK TO JEAN-FRANÇOIS DE LA HARPE, POET AND CRITIC

October 1777

. . . It is impossible for me, Sir, to resist the very judicious observations you have just made upon my operas in your *Journal de Littérature* of the 5th of this month; I find nothing, absolutely nothing, to object against them.

Until now I had been so simple as to believe that music was like the other arts in that all passions fell within its province and that it should give no less pleasure by expressing the heat of one enraged or the cry of one in grief, than by rendering the sighs of a lover.

I believed this maxim to be true in music as in poetry. I had persuaded myself that song, coloured through and through by the sentiments it was required to express, must change with them and take as many different accents as they had different shades; in short that the voice, the instruments, all sounds, even pauses, should be directed towards a single aim, that of expression, and that the union of words and singing should be so close that the poem would seem to be fitted to the music no less than the music to the song.

These were not my only errors; it appeared to me that the French language was lightly accented and had no fixed quantities like the Italian; I had been struck by another difference between the singers of the two nations. While I found the voices of the former to be softer and more pliant, the latter seemed to me to bring more vigour and action to their performance: I had concluded from this that the Italian style of singing was unsuitable for French voices. Thereafter, in looking through the scores of your old operas, despite the trills, cadenzas and other defects with which their airs seemed to me to be overloaded, I found in them sufficient real beauty to convince me that the French had their own resources to draw upon.

Those, Sir, were my ideas when I read your observations. But light immediately dispelled the darkness; I was confounded at perceiving that you had learnt more about my art in a few hours of reflection than I myself after practising it for forty years. You prove to me, Sir, that the man of letters can speak on any subject. I am now fully convinced that the music of the Italian masters is music *par excellence*, that it alone *is* music; that singing, if it is to please, must be regular and periodic, and that even in disordered moments, when the character who is singing, moved by a variety of passions, passes in succession from one to another, the composer must always preserve the same style.

I agree with you that of all my compositions, *Orfeo* alone is tolerable; I sincerely beseech the God of taste to forgive me for *deafening* my hearers with my other operas; the number of performances they have received and the applause the public has been good enough to bestow upon them do not prevent me from seeing that they are pitiful; I am so convinced of this that I wish to rewrite them; and as I perceive you to be in favour of tender airs, I shall place in the mouth of the angry Achilles a song so touching and so sweet that the whole audience will be moved to tears.

As for *Armide* I shall take good care not to leave the poem as it is at present, for, as you so justly observe, *Quinault's operas, though full of beauties, are designed in a manner very little suited to music; they are very fine poems, but very bad operas*: so even if they should become very bad poems, the only question being to make fine operas after your manner,

I implore you to make me acquainted with some versifier who can take *Armide* in hand and fit every scene with two airs. We shall agree together about the quantity and metre of the lines; so long as they have their full number of syllables I shall not concern myself with the rest. For my part I am working at the music, from which it goes without saying, I shall scrupulously banish all noisy instruments, such as the *timpani* and the trumpet; in my orchestra I wish only oboes, flutes, French horns and violins to be heard—with mutes, of course; all that will then remain will be to fit the words to the tunes, which will not be difficult, as we shall have taken our measurements beforehand.

The role of Armide will thus be no longer a *monotonous and wearisome bawling*, she will no longer be a *Medea, a sorceress*, but *an enchantress*; I am resolved that in her despair she shall sing you an air so *regular*, so *periodic*, that any fashionable young lady with the vapours shall be able to hear it without the least irritation of her nerves.

If some malicious-minded person should take it upon himself to say to me: Sir, you should note that Armide in a rage is not to express herself like Armide intoxicated with love, I shall reply that I am resolved not *to shock the ears* of M. de La Harpe, I am resolved not to *counterfeit nature*, I wish to *embellish* it, instead of causing Armide to *bawl*, I wish her to *enchant* you. Were he to persist, were he to point out to me that Sophocles, in the finest of his tragedies, was bold enough to bring Oedipus before the Athenians with bleeding eyes, and that the recitative, or species of intoned declamation in which that unfortunate King expressed his eloquent laments must undoubtedly have been delivered in tones of the most acute distress, my reply will be, again, that M. de La Harpe does not wish to hear the *cries of a man in pain*.

Have I not well grasped, Sir, the spirit of the doctrine with which your observations are imbued? I have given several of my friends the pleasure of reading them. 'You ought to be grateful,' said one of them, on returning them to me. 'M. de La Harpe gives you some excellent *hints*, he makes his statement of musical policy; do the same for him; procure his poetical and literary works and, in friendship for him, call attention to everything that does not please you in them. Many people claim that the sole effect of criticism in the arts is to wound the artist upon whom it falls; and in proof of this they declare that poets have never had more critics, or been more mediocre, than in our own day; but consult the journalists on this subject, and ask them whether anything is more useful to the State than newspapers. It may be objected that it is unbecoming in you, a musician, to decide questions of poetry; but would that be more surprising than to find a poet, a man of letters, uttering a despotic judgement on music?'

So said my friend; his reasoning seemed to me to be very sound; but despite my gratitude to you I feel, Sir, after fully considering the matter, that I cannot defer to it without incurring the fate of the dissertator who made a long speech on the art of war in the presence of Hannibal. . . .

GLUCK TO THE COUNTESS VON FRIES

Paris, 16 November 1777

Madame,

I have been so plagued about music, and am so much disgusted with it, that at present I would not write one single note for a louis; by this you may conceive, Madame, the degree of my devotion to you, since I have been able to bring myself to arrange the two songs for the harp for you, and have the honour to send them herewith. Never has a more terrible and keenly-contested *battaglia* been waged, than the one I began with my opera *Armide*. The cabals against *Iphigénie*, *Orfeo* and *Alceste* were no more than little skirmishes of light horse by comparison. The Neapolitan Ambassador, to ensure great success for Piccinni's opera, is tirelessly intriguing against me, at Court and among the nobility. He has induced Marmontel, La Harpe and several members of the Academy to write against my system of music and my manner of composing. The Abbé Arnaud, M. Suard and several others have come to my defence, and the quarrel grew so heated that from insults they would have passed to blows, but that friends of both sides brought them to order. The *Journal de Paris*, which comes out every day, is full of it. This dispute is making the Editor's fortune, for he already has more than 2,500 subscribers in Paris. That's the musical revolution in France, amid the most brilliant pomp. Enthusiasts tell me: Sir, you are fortunate to be enjoying the honour of persecution; every great genius has had the same experience. – I wish them to the devil with their fine speeches. The fact is that the opera, which was said to have fallen flat, brought in 37,200 *livres* in 7 performances, without counting the boxes rented for the year, and without the subscribers. Yesterday, at the 8th performance, they took 5,767 *livres*. . . . The pit was so tightly packed that when a man who had his hat on his head was told by the guard to take it off, he replied: 'Come and take it off yourself, for I cannot move my arms'; which caused laughter. I have seen people coming out with their hair bedraggled and their clothes drenched as though they had fallen into a stream. Only Frenchmen would pay so dearly for a pleasure. There are passages in the opera which force the audience to lose their countenance and their composure. Come yourself, Madame, to witness the tumult; it will amuse you as much as the opera. . . .

The essence of the dispute has remained the central problem of all opera – whether the drama or the music should predominate. It seems paradoxical that the German Gluck, taking unconditionally the side of the drama, appeared as the champion of national French opera, with Lully and Rameau as legitimate predecessors. If by nothing else, this is borne out by the fact that he could use for his 'Armide' a libretto written for Lully one hundred years before. The reader has to remember, however, that the greatest Austrian war-lord of history, Prince Eugène of Savoy, and the greatest of all Prussian heroes, Frederick the Great, spoke German only to their soldiers and servants; that in the Court Theatre of the popular Austrian Empress Maria Theresa the play was French and the opera Italian; that Handel was the most outstanding composer of Italian opera of the baroque period; that Gluck, the reformer of Italian and French opera, never wrote a German one; and that Mozart, who indeed put German opera on the map, had much less of Gluck than of Piccinni in his system.

When his last opera written for Paris, 'Écho et Narcisse', proved a failure, Gluck, feeling old and exhausted, retired from the field and returned to Vienna, where he spent his last years in modest comfort.

GLUCK TO M. GERSIN

Vienna, 30 November 1779

Sir,

I am very sensible of the honour you do me in sending me the plan of a tragedy for me to set to music; I find it well fitted to produce great effects, but you are no doubt unaware that I shall write no more Operas, and that I have finished my career; my age and the vexation I lately suffered at Paris in the matter of my Opera *Narcisse*, have disgusted me for ever with the writing of operas; it would be a pity, however, if you did not finish your work, for you will certainly find in Paris musicians of great merit who will be capable of satisfying you in all you desire.

I have the honour to be, with great esteem,

Sir,

Your most humble and obedient

Servant Gluck

Another letter of the old Gluck, addressed to one of the most revered German poets, shows how much he was already aware of the paramount importance of every detail of a dramatic performance. This is remarkable in view of the slovenly habits of a time when rehearsal was scanty and the quality of orchestral players very much a matter of chance.

GLUCK TO FRIEDRICH GOTTLIEB KLOPSTOCK IN HAMBURG

Vienna, 10 May 1780

. . . You are forever reproaching me because I send you no *explication* of how *Alceste* should be produced. I would have done so long ago, if I had found it *practicable*. So far as the singing is concerned, it is easy for any person of sensibility. She need only surrender to the promptings of her heart; but the instrumental accompaniments require so many observations that nothing can be done without my presence. Some notes must be long-drawn-out, others staccato, some played *mezzo forte*, others louder or softer, and I can make no attempt to indicate the *mouvement*. A little slower or faster, and a whole piece is spoilt. So I think, most esteemed friend, that you will find it much easier to render your new system of spelling familiar to the Germans, than I an Opera after my own method, especially in your region, where counterpoint receives more attention than all else, and imagination is unappreciated and deficient, while among you the greater number of musicians aspire only to be bricklayers, not architects. . . .

Josef Haydn (*1732–1809*) *has left only a modest number of letters. He had obviously no time to waste, nor the necessary impulse to convey and exchange views and thoughts. But his style, though homely enough, is not without a hint of the quality of definition and precision which makes his music so crisp and stimulating.*

Thrown onto the Vienna streets as an adolescent, inured to all the privations of life at starvation level, Haydn found the safety of employment in an aristocratic house a blessing well worth the lack of personal freedom it involved. For thirty years he remained in this employment, in charge of the music of Prince Esterházy at Eisenstadt, far out in the countryside of the Austro-Hungarian borderland. The most striking feature of Haydn's genius was his capacity for reacting with a creative impulse to everything that came his way. Deriving the utmost advantage from the modest resources at his disposal, he became a great master in circumstances in which any other might have become a drudge. The written instructions regulating his service have been preserved. They are of topical interest, because they give an impression of the conditions under which a musician in the eighteenth century had to live and to work. Here are some excerpts from this lengthy document.

'His Highness expects Mr Haydn to behave as an honourable officer of a princely establishment. To wit: to be always sober, to behave not rudely but politely and with consideration towards the musicians under his direction, and to be modest, quiet and honest in his conduct. Whenever there is music for His Highness, Mr Haydn will be responsible not only for his own but for his musicians' becoming appearance in proper livery, according to instructions with white stockings, white linen, well powdered, and either with pigtails or with hair-bags, but all in the same attire. . . .

'Mr Haydn will write at the order of His Highness such music as may be commanded; and he will make no communication of such music to others, still less have it copied for anybody else, keeping it solely at the disposition of His Highness; nor will he write for anybody else without His gracious permission. . . .

'Mr Haydn will appear every day, both in the morning and in the afternoon, in the "Antichambre", to receive his orders for the day regarding the music. And having done so, he will communicate them to his musicians and make sure that they arrive punctually according to order. . . .

'It is his duty to take care of all the instruments with the utmost conscientiousness, lest they be damaged or made unusable, and he will be responsible for same. He will duly instruct the singers, lest they forget in the country what they have learned in Vienna, with much work and expense, from distinguished masters.'

The Prince, a genuine lover of music, was well disposed towards Haydn. All the same, an artist of Haydn's productivity and diligence must have felt some mortification in receiving the following missive: 'The master of the music, Mr Haydn, is reminded to apply himself more assiduously to composition than he has done so far, especially with respect to pieces for the gamba [the "barytone", the Prince's favourite instrument], of which we have seen very little up to now; and, to show his zeal, he will hand in the first piece of every composition in a clean, tidy copy.' Haydn did apply himself; there are more than a hundred compositions for the barytone written for his master.

There are no letters of Haydn available from his earlier years at Eisenstadt and Esterház, the Prince's palace. His fame, spreading slowly but steadily through publication 'with gracious permission', of string quartets, symphonies, and sonatas, was already firmly established in the seventeen-eighties. And Haydn knew how to keep on the right side of his master.

HAYDN TO THE PUBLISHER ARTARIA IN VIENNA

Esterház, 27 May 1781

. . . As concerns the songs, I have prepared 14 of them with particular diligence, the number would long since have been complete, if I had

had the words for them. . . . I assure you that by reason of their varied, naturally beautiful and easy melodies, my songs will perhaps excel anything that has gone before: but as to whether you will take them, I am still in doubt, for in the first place I am asking 6 ducats for them, secondly 6 copies, and 3, that the following short dedication shall appear on the title-page:

ANTHOLOGY OF GERMAN SONGS
For the Harpsichord
Dedicated
With the greatest Respect
to
MADEMOISELLE CLAIR
by
Mr Joseph Haydn
Kapellmeister to Prince Esterházy

Between you and me, this Mademoiselle is the Divinity of my Prince. You will quite understand what an impression such things make! So if you will comply with this point, I shall not fail to finish in due course those that are still missing. But these songs must not appear until St Elisabeth's Day – that is, on the name-day of the aforesaid Beauty. . . .

Haydn occasionally visited Vienna when the Prince went there with his retinue, and such visits, sometimes lasting several months, were the highlights of his life. He met lovers of his music and devoted friends in the capital, and he frequently saw a young colleague who had settled there in 1781 and whom he found fascinating – Mozart. The latter in turn regarded Haydn as the only contemporary musician from whom he could still learn. But at that stage, in the seventeen-eighties, Haydn's situation as an exile in the country had already become irksome to him.

HAYDN TO PROVINZIALOBERVERWALTER ROTH IN PRAGUE

December 1787

. . . You ask me for an Opera buffa. With the greatest pleasure, if you would care to have an example of my compositions for singers to keep to yourself. But I can be of no service to you at the moment in presenting them on the stage in Prague for all my Operas are too closely connected with our company (at Esterház in Hungary), and elsewhere they would never produce the effect that I have calculated with that place in mind, It would be a quite different matter were I to have the supreme good fortune to compose an entirely new libretto for that Theatre [at Prague]. But that too would be very venturesome, since it is hard for anyone to stand beside the great Mozart.

For if I could but impress the matchless works of Mozart upon the souls of all music-lovers, and particularly of the Great, so deeply and with such understanding and sensibility as that with which I myself appreciate, and comprehend them, the Nations would vie with one another to possess such a treasure within their walls. Prague must hold the dear fellow – but reward him too; for without that, the history of great geniuses is melancholy and gives posterity little encouragement to further effort; on which account, alas, so many promising minds fall short of fulfilment. It angers me that the peerless Mozart has not yet been engaged at an imperial or royal court! Forgive me if I am carried away; but I am so fond of the man. . . .

HAYDN TO FRAU VON GENZINGER

Esterház, 9 February 1790

Dear Frau v. Genzinger,
Now – here I sit in my wilderness – deserted – like a poor orphan – almost without human company – sad – full of the memory of precious days gone by – yes, alas, gone by – and who knows when those pleasant days will return again? that charming company? wherein a whole circle shares One heart, One soul – all those fine musical evenings – which can only be remembered, not described in writing – where is all that enthusiasm? Gone – and gone for a long time. Your Grace must not be surprised that I have been so long in writing you my thanks! At home I found everything in confusion and for 3 days I did not know whether I was *Kapell-master* or *Kapell-servant*, nothing could comfort me, my whole apartment was in disorder, my Forte-piano, which I used to love, was out of order, disobedient, it rather vexed than soothed me, I got little sleep, even my dreams were a persecution, for when I dreamt that I was hearing an excellent performance of *le nozze di Figaro* that odious North wind woke me and almost blew my nightcap off my head. In 3 days I lost 20 pounds in weight, for the good Viennese titbits had already disappeared during the journey. Yes, yes, thought I to myself as I sat in my boarding-house, obliged to eat a piece off a 50-year-old cow instead of that delicious beef, an ancient mutton-stew with yellow turnips instead of the ragout with little dumplings, a slice of roast leather instead of the Bohemian pheasant, a so-called *Dschabl* or *Gros-Salat* instead of those

delicious, delicate oranges, tough apple-rings and hazelnuts instead of those pastries – and so forth. Yes, yes, thought I to myself, if only I had here all those titbits I could not manage to eat at Vienna! – Here at Esterház nobody asks me – do you take chocolate with milk or without, would you like coffee, black or with cream, what can I get you, my dear Haydn, would you like vanilla ice or a pineapple one? If only I had here a piece of good Parmesan cheese, especially on fast days to help the black dumplings and noodles down more easily, – this very day I ordered our porter to send me down a few pounds of it.

Forgive me, dearest lady, if on this first occasion I waste your time with such preposterous stuff in my wretched scribbling; forgive me as a man to whom the Viennese were too kind; but I am already gradually beginning to get used to country ways, yesterday I did some studying for the first time and it was quite in the Haydn manner.

You will certainly have been more diligent than I. The agreeable Adagio from the Quartet has, I hope, already been given its true expression by your lovely fingers. My dear Fräulein Peperl [daughter of Frau von Genzinger] will (I hope) often sing the Cantata and thus remember her Master, especially in clear expression and precise vocalization, for it would be a crime for such a beautiful voice to remain hidden in her breast, so I beg for a frequent smile, otherwise I shall take it amiss. I commend myself to Mons. François [her son] likewise for his musical talent. Even if he does sing in his dressing-gown it always goes well, I shall often send something new to encourage him. Meanwhile I kiss your hand again for all your kindness to me, and remain, my life long, with the greatest respect etc. . . .

HAYDN TO FRAU VON GENZINGER

Esterház, 14 March 1790

I beg your gracious pardon a million times for my tardiness in answering your two letters, which gave me so much pleasure. The cause was not negligence (from which sin Heaven will preserve me all my life), but the many matters I have to attend to for my most gracious Prince in his present sad situation. The death of his late wife so much depressed the Prince that we were all obliged to devote our energies to rousing him from his grief. For the first three evenings I therefore arranged large concerts of chamber music, but with no singing. But on hearing the first music, the poor Prince fell into such melancholy over my Favorit-Adagio in D, that I had a hard task to bring him out of it with other pieces.

By the fourth day we were already playing Opera, on the fifth a

Comedy, and finally, the daily performance as usual; at the same time I gave order for the study of the old Opera by Gassmann, *L'amor artigiano*, because our Master had remarked shortly before that he would like to see it. I wrote three new Arias for it, which I will send you by the next post, not because they are beautiful, but in order to convince you, gracious Lady, of my diligence. . . . It enraptures me to learn that my dear Arianna [Haydn's cantata, *Arianna a Naxos*] is winning applause at Schottenhof [the home of the Genzinger family]; I would just like to remind Fräulein Peperl to pronounce the words clearly, particularly in *Chi tanto amai*. . . .

HAYDN TO FRAU VON GENZINGER

Esterház, 27 June 1790

Now again, it oppresses me that I must remain at home. What I am losing thereby you can imagine for yourself. It is melancholy to be always a Slave: but Providence wills it so. I am an unfortunate creature! Always plagued with much work, very few hours of repose. . . .

In 1790 Prince Nicolaus Esterházy died. His successor dissolved the band and granted Haydn a comfortable pension. Taking advantage of his freedom, Haydn accepted the invitation of the impresario J.P. Salomon, which resulted in two journeys to London, in 1791 and 1794. Each time he spent a year and a half in England, made a modest fortune, and found himself at last a European celebrity. The most precious results of these journeys to England were his last twelve symphonies, written for London, and his two oratorios, 'The Creation' and 'The Seasons', both with libretti of English origin. They are Haydn's response to the overwhelming impression made on him by performances of Handel's oratorios.

HAYDN TO FRAU VON GENZINGER

London, 8 January 1791

. . . I hope, gracious Madam, that you will have received my last letter from Calais. I ought indeed to have sent a report as soon as I reached London, as I had promised, only I desired to wait for a few days that I might write of several matters together. I therefore report that on the first of this month, *viz*. New Year's Day, at half-past seven in the morning, after attending Mass, I went on board ship and, thanks be to the Almighty, reached Dover safe and sound at 5 o'clock in the afternoon. . . .

During the entire crossing I remained on deck, in order to sate my eyes with that monstrous animal, the sea. So long as there was no wind,

I was not afraid, but finally, as the wind grew ever stronger and I saw the high unruly waves breaking against the ship, I felt a little alarm, and with it a little nausea. However, I overcame it all and, *salva venia*, came safely into the harbour without vomiting. Most people were sick, and looked like ghosts. I took two days to recover. But now I am quite brisk and merry again, and am looking at London, that vast city which quite amazes me by its various beauties and wonders. I at once paid the necessary calls, visiting, among others, the Neapolitan Ambassador and our own. Both of them returned my call two days later, and four days ago I took my midday meal at the house of the former, but *notabene* at 6 o'clock in the evening. Such is the fashion here. . . .

My arrival made a great stir all over the town. For 3 days I was bandied about in all the papers. Everyone is curious to meet me. I have already been obliged to eat out 6 times, and might be invited every day if I would, but I must consider first my health and 2. my work. Except for the Mylords I receive no visitors until 2 o'clock in the afternoon, at 4 o'clock I eat at home with Mon. Salomon [the manager of Haydn's concerts]. . . . I have a small, convenient but costly lodging. My landlord is an Italian, and a cook as well, he serves me 4 very good meals, we pay 1 fl. 30 kr. each per day, without wine and beer, but everything is terribly dear. Yesterday I went to a big amateur concert, but I arrived rather too late, and when I handed over my ticket they would not let me in, but led me into a neighbouring room, where I had to remain until the piece then being performed in the hall was over. They then opened the doors and I was led, on the arm of the Manager, amid general hand-clapping, down the middle of the hall to the front of the pit, where I was gaped at and admired with a host of English compliments. People assured me that this honour had not been shown to anyone for 50 years. After the concert I was taken to another fine room next to the hall, where a large table enough to take 200 people stood ready for the whole company of amateurs, with a great number of places laid, and they desired me to sit at the head of it. Only, as I had that very day dined out and eaten more than usual, I refused this honour, with the excuse that I felt a little unwell, despite which, however, I had to drink in Burgundy wine to the harmonious health of all those present, who returned the toast, and then they allowed me to be driven home. All this was very flattering for me, yet I wished I might escape to Vienna for a little while, to work in greater quiet, for the noise in the streets, from all the various tradesfolk, is intolerable. True, I am as yet still engaged on symphonic work, because the libretto for the opera is not yet decided upon, but for the sake of quiet I shall have to take a room right outside the town. . . .

HAYDN TO FRAU VON GENZINGER

London, 17 September 1791

. . . Now, my dear, kind lady, what is your Fortepiano doing? Is some thought of Haydn's brought back to it at times through your fair hands? Does my dear Fräulein Pepi sometimes sing poor *Ariadne*? Oh yes, I can hear it from here, particularly in the last 2 months, for I am staying in the country, in a most beautiful district, with a Banker whose heart and family resemble those of the von Genzinger household, and where I live quite secluded. Withal I am, thanks be to God forever, in good health but for my usual rheumatism and working diligently, and every morning when I go for an early stroll in the woods, alone with my English grammar, I think upon my Maker, my family and all the friends I left behind me, among whom there are none I value more highly than you and yours. Indeed, I had hoped to enjoy your company sooner, only my circumstances – in short, Fate wills that I should remain in London another 8 to 10 months. Oh, dear lady, how sweet is the taste of a certain freedom! I had a kind Prince, but was at times dependent upon mean spirits. I often sighed for deliverance, now I have it after a fashion. And I acknowledge the benefit of it, although my spirit is oppressed with much work. The knowledge that I am not a bondsman makes up for all my toil. . . .

On 9 December of this year 1791 Mozart died in Vienna. The news reached London a fortnight later, to Haydn's great dismay.

HAYDN TO FRAU VON GENZINGER

London, 20 December 1791

. . . Now, dear lady, I would like to quarrel with you a little because you believe I prefer the city of London to Vienna and enjoy being here more than in my own country. I do not dislike London, but I could not bear to spend the rest of my days there, even if I could earn millions. The reason for this I will tell you by word of mouth. I am as happy as a child at the thought of returning home to embrace my good friends. My only regret will be at not including the great Mozart, if it be true, as I hope it is not, that he is dead. The world will not have such a talent again in a hundred years!

HAYDN TO FRAU VON GENZINGER

London, 17 January 1792

. . . I beg your forgiveness a thousand times, I acknowledge and confess that I should not be so negligent in keeping my promises, but if you only saw how I am pestered here in London to go to all the private concerts, which waste a great deal of my time, and the amount of work that is heaped upon me, you would feel the greatest sympathy for me. I never wrote so much in one year as in that which is just over; but then I am almost worn out, and after I reach home it will do me good to rest for a while. At present I am working for Salomon's concert and feel obliged to take all imaginable pains because our opponents, the Professional Concerts, have brought my pupil Pleyel here from Strasbourg to conduct for them. So there will be a musical war to the knife between master and pupil. All the newspapers began to talk of it at once, only it seems to me it will soon turn to an alliance because my credit stands too high. After his arrival Pleyel was so modest in his attitude to me that he has now won my affection. We are very often together and that is an honour, for him, and he knows how to appreciate his father. We shall make equal shares of our fame and both go home satisfied. . . .

HAYDN TO MICHAEL PUCHBERG, A FRIEND OF MOZART'S IN VIENNA

London, January 1792

. . . I was quite beside myself for a long while because of his [Mozart's] death, and could not believe that Providence would have so rapidly despatched an irreplaceable man to the other world, I only regret that he could not first have convinced the English, who are still in the dark, of what I had been daily preaching to them. . . .

With the great effort of his two oratorios, written in his late sixties, Haydn rose to the zenith, but also to the end, of his creative life, feeling suddenly exhausted and incapable of concentrated work. His last string quartet, begun at this time, remained unfinished. Practically his last work was a number of contributions to George Thomson's great collection of Scottish songs, to which Haydn's pupil, Beethoven, also contributed a number of items.

HAYDN TO HIS PUBLISHERS BREITKOPF & HÄRTEL IN LEIPZIG

Vienna, 12 June 1799

. . . Unhappily, my occupations multiply as my years increase; and yet it is almost as though, while my intellectual powers decline, my taste and urge for work grow stronger. Oh God, how much remains to be done in this glorious art, even by a man such as I have been! True, the world pays me many compliments every day, even seeing fieriness in my latest works; but no one will believe what toil and effort it costs me to produce them, for many are the days when my weak memory and the slackening of my nerves bring me so low that I sink into the most melancholy state, and am thus for many days thereafter in no condition to hit upon a single idea, until at length, Providence having put fresh courage into my heart, I can sit down again at the keyboard and begin to hammer away. And then it all comes back, thanks be to God. . . .

HAYDN TO ASSESSOR K. AND CANTOR D., UNKNOWN AMATEURS AT RÜGEN

Vienna, 22 September 1802

. . . You give me the sweetest assurance, which is the richest comfort in these hours of my already declining age, that I am often the enviable source from which you, and many families receptive to the feelings of the heart, draw your pleasure, your contentment, in the quiet of your homes. What happiness this thought gives me! Often, when I was wrestling with all kinds of difficulties which impeded my art, when often my mental and physical powers abated and it was hard for me to persist in the road my life had taken, a secret feeling whispered to me: 'There are so few happy, contented beings here below, they are everywhere dogged by grief and anxiety, perhaps your work may now and then become a spring from which the man who is careworn or overburdened with occupations can draw rest and refreshment for a few moments. . . .'

HAYDN TO THE PUBLISHER THOMSON IN LONDON

1805

My most valued Friend,
At last I am sending you all the remaining Scottish airs, which have given me a great deal of trouble because for some time I was very unwell. Yet for that I hope they will give you a little enjoyment,

though it is difficult for a man of seventy-three to please the public. Let the public decide as it may, I have done the best I could, dear friend in order not to displease you. . . .

Your most devoted and sincere friend
and servant,
Joseph

Our image of Wolfgang Amadeus Mozart (*1756–91*) *has been idealized by the dazzling light that radiates from his work. And a superficial look at the story of his life – the infant prodigy's triumphant progress through the capitals of Europe, the composer's early mastery, his happy family life, the acclaim of his operas in Vienna and Prague – may confirm a belief in the happiness of an artist of miraculous productivity and unrestricted joy in his work and its success. It is odd that the deep shadows of the Symphony in G minor, the pianoforte concertos in C minor and D minor, the String Quintet in G minor, hardly touched this general picture of Mozart, the favourite of the gods, the idol of Olympian brightness. Indeed, the man has disappeared behind the work that made him immortal. Against this conventional picture, however, a close-up of Mozart, the mortal, suffering man is unspeakably poignant. Such a close-up is offered in his letters. His style is unrefined, without the slightest touch of fastidiousness, sometimes even coarse, but his letters reflect a genuine urge for communication and they are not only topically interesting but infinitely attractive as expressions of his personality.*

Seen as a whole, Mozart's life unfolds like a tragedy of fate. In spite of everything Leopold Mozart, his ambitious, adoring father, did for him – he gave him a decent upbringing and as perfect an artistic training as any composer ever had – one cannot help seeing his father as an uncanny, dark force, looming over him, holding him down, striving to keep him in his grip, desperately sure of his own superior wisdom and his son's folly and lack of filial devotion. One must admit that the old man's assessment of the realities of a musician's living and chance of success was correct. What he never realized was his son's growing intolerance of leading-reins; nor was he conscious of how much of the opposition to the young genius may have been due to circumstances of his, Leopold's, own making, and how heavily the mature artist had to pay for the infant prodigy's easy success, the aggressive paternal pride and arrogance, the ill feelings aroused in a place of parochial narrowness such as Salzburg.

Two letters of Johann Adolf Hasse (*1699–1783*)*, one of the most prolific and successful operatic composers of the eighteenth century, who, as an old man, met the Mozarts in Vienna and in Italy in 1769 and 1771, may serve as a kind of preamble.*

HASSE TO THE ABATE GIAN MARIA ORTES IN VENICE

Vienna, 30 September 1769

. . . I have made the acquaintance of a certain Ms. Mozard, *Maestro di Capella* to the Bishop of Salzburg; he has wit and intelligence and is a man of the world, who I think knows what he is about, both in music and in other matters. This man has a daughter and a son. The former plays the harpsichord very well, and the latter, who cannot be more than twelve or thirteen years old, is already composing and conducting. I have seen compositions declared to be his which are assuredly not bad and in which I perceived no sign of a twelve-year-old boy; and I cannot well doubt that they are his own, for when I tested him at the harpsichord in various ways, he played me such things as are prodigious at that age and would be admirable even in a grown man. Now the father being wishful to take him to Italy to make him known, and having written me this, at the same time asking me for a few letters of introduction, I shall make bold to send him one for you. . . . But this letter is to have no further consequence than that you may permit him to make your acquaintance and deign to give him your customary wise advice, as you may deem useful for him and necessary in that country. The father says he will leave Salzburg on 25 October, so he can be there at the end of the month.

The said Ms. Mozard is a very polite and civil man, and the children are very well behaved. The boy is also handsome, graceful and full of good manners, so that when one knows him it is difficult not to love him. It is certain that if he makes due progress as he grows older he will be a prodigy, always provided that his father does not coddle him too much and spoil him by heaping him with exaggerated praise, which is the only thing I fear. . . .

HASSE TO THE ABATE GIAN MARIA ORTES

Vienna, 23 March 1771

. . . Young Mozard is certainly prodigious for his age, and I love him infinitely. His Father, so far as I can see, is equally dissatisfied everywhere; here, too, he used to make the same complaints. He idolizes his son a little too much, and therefore does his utmost to spoil him, but I hold such a good opinion of the boy's natural good sense, that I have hopes that despite his Father's flatteries he will not be spoilt, but will grow into a worthy man. . . .

At this time Dr Charles Burney, one of the founders of musical history, wrote in 'The Present State of Music in France and Italy' (1771): 'I must acquaint my musical reader that at the performance just mentioned [of the Philharmonic Society at Bologna] I met with Mr Mozart and his son, the little German, whose premature and almost supernatural talents astonished us in London a few years ago, when he had scarce quitted his infant state. Since his arrival in Italy he has been much admired at Rome and Naples; has been honoured with the order of the "Speron d'Oro" by His Holiness, and was engaged to compose an opera at Milan for the next Carnival.' It was on receipt of the same distinction, the papal Order of the Golden Spur, that Gluck assumed the title 'chevalier'. Leopold was wise enough not to let his son do the same; the neighbours in Salzburg would have looked askance at such presumption.

That they were not very kindly disposed to their somewhat overbearing fellow-citizen can be gleaned from another entry of Dr Burney, two years later (in 'The Present State of Music in Germany, the Netherlands and United Provinces'): 'The Archbishop and Sovereign of Salzburg is very magnificent in his support of music, having usually near a hundred performers, vocal and instrumental, in his service. The Mozart family were all at Salzburg last summer [1771]. The father has long been in the service of that Court, and the son is now one of the band [leader of the violins]. He composed an opera at Milan for the marriage of the Archduke [Ferdinand] with the Princess of Modena. By a letter from Salzburg, dated last November, I was informed that this young man, who so much astonished all Europe by his infant knowledge and performance, is still a great master of his instrument; my correspondent went to his father's house to hear him and his sister [Maria Anna, called 'Nannerl'] play duets on the same harpischord; but she is now at her summit, which is not marvellous; "and", says the writer of the letter, "if I may judge of the music which I heard of his composition, in the orchestra, he is one further instance of early fruit being more extraordinary than excellent."'

Considering the musicians' pitiless struggle for survival at a time of total dependence on noble patronage, one can easily realize how often competence was defeated or bypassed by flattery, pretence, or intrigue. Patrons were not always real experts; but they all had their human weakness, vanity, and prejudices. As the director of music of such a patron, a sovereign prince and ruler under the Imperial crown, Mozart's father had a great deal of experience and worldly wisdom. But his wariness may have been exaggerated by a rooted conviction that every colleague was a competitor, every competitor an unscrupulous enemy, and people in general rather ill than well disposed. He saw enemies everywhere and probably behaved accordingly. It is dismal to imagine how an adolescent of trusting, open-hearted disposition may have been influenced by such an attitude and by incessant admonitions to be on his guard.

LEOPOLD MOZART TO HIS WIFE

Milan, 29 December 1770

. . . God be praised, the first performance of the Opera [Mozart's *Mitridate*] took place on the 26th amid general applause. . . . Never in living memory was such curiosity over a first Opera to be seen in Milan as this time; because beforehand there was such terrible disagreement, and when two said that the Opera would be good, ten others sprang up at once who knew beforehand that it would be rubbish, others that it would be a hotch-potch, and others again that it would be barbaric German music. Here, moreover, patronage is no help towards approval of the opera, for everyone who goes there is determined to speak, shout, and criticize for his money, according to what he thinks of it. Patronage helped us, and was needful, so that the composition should not be impeded and no one should put a spoke in the Maestro's wheel while he was writing, and then during rehearsals, so that he should not be obstructed, and that the few ill-disposed members of the orchestra or the company of singers should not play any tricks on him. . . .

Not every mishap, however, is necessarily caused by intrigue; some are due to force of circumstance. The Archduke Ferdinand, for whose wedding in Milan young Mozart had been commissioned to write the Theatrical Serenade 'Ascanio in Alba' (1771), seems to have been very much impressed by the work and its composer, whom he intended to take into his service. But his mother, the Empress Maria Theresa, who ruled her lands as a thrifty housewife, blandly ruined a plan which might have been of momentous importance to Wolfgang's career. At the age of six, when invited to play for the Imperial family on his first visit to Vienna, the infant prodigy had sat on Her Majesty's lap. Now the Empress wrote to her son, the Archduke (12 December 1771):

'You ask my permission to take the young Salzburger into your service. I do not know as what, not believing that you need a composer or any useless people. Yet if it would give you pleasure I do not wish to prevent you. What I say is in order not to burden you with useless people; and never [give] titles to those sort of people as being in your service. That degrades the services, when these people roam about the world like beggars; in addition to this he has a large family. . . .'

So Wolfgang remained in the service of the Archbishop, but having had a taste of a freer, artistically more stimulating world, and most of all longing for opera, for which he felt destined, he became increasingly restless, chafing against the provincial narrowness of his duties in Salzburg. In the end,

Leopold consented to let his son try his luck and find a foothold in one of the larger centres of music, in Munich, Mannheim, or Paris. That journey became a momentous event in the inner development of Mozart. It marks the turning-point from apprenticeship to mastery. But it started under an unlucky star; its result was disappointment, disaster, and grief. He had his first serious love-affair that ended in bitter disillusion, and his first collision with his father's unbending will. For the first time the young musician found himself confronted by a callous world, every door closed after first seeming to welcome him, every enterprise frustrated. He learned the hard way to temper his optimism with scepticism. Becoming increasingly conscious of his immeasurable superiority as a musician, he could not but attribute every frustration to machinations or intrigues. What he never learnt was to assess the enormous component of indifference, shallowness, and selfishness in human affairs, the defenceless victim of which he remained for the rest of his life.

Having obtained leave of absence, Mozart, aged twenty-one, set out on his journey, escorted by his mother. Leopold was kept in Salzburg by his duties, but he was anxious to arm his son with good advice.

LEOPOLD MOZART TO HIS SON, WOLFGANG

Salzburg, 29 September 1777

. . . Now, turning to the matter of Munich, it might perhaps go well if you could but find occasion for the Elector to hear how much you can do. . . . You must blow your own trumpet before Count Seau [the intendant of the Elector's music], promising to compose all kinds of arias, etc., and ballets for his theatre without demanding payment. You must likewise be wonderfully civil to the courtiers, for every one of them has his say in the matter. . . . Perhaps you might give a concert in Count Seau's garden. If things begin to look hopeful you will need to prolong your stay at Munich. Make a good friend of Herr Woschitka [the Elector's valet], he has frequent occasion to speak with the Elector, and stands in great credit. Should you be required to do something on the *gamba* for the Elector, he [Woschitka] can tell you how it should be and show you what are the Elector's favourite pieces, so that you may come to know his taste. If you have not spoken with the Elector, or cannot do so, and are compelled to approach him by letter, Herr v. Belvall will advise you who should write the letter. Either by word of mouth or by letter you can make it known to the Elector and to Count Seau that, as concerns your skill in counterpoint, His Highness need only address himself to Padre Maestro Martini at Bologna or to Herr Hasse at Venice in order to hear those gentlemen's opinion of you, and if you find it needful I shall send you the 2 diplomas by which in your 14th year you were already declared Maestro di Cappella of the Academies of Bologna and Verona. . . .

MOZART TO HIS FATHER

Munich, 29 September 1777

. . . Today I waited upon Prince Zeil, who said to me as follows, in the most civil manner: 'I think we shall not be able to do much here. At dinner at Nymphenburg I spoke privately with the Elector. He said to me, "It is still too soon, he should go away, visit Italy and make himself famous. I refuse him nothing, but it is still too soon."' So there we have it. . . . The Bishop at Chiemsee likewise spoke quite alone with the Electress, who shrugged her shoulders and said she would do her best, but she very much doubted. . . . Count Seau asked Prince Zeil, after he had told him of all this, 'Do you not know, has Mozart really not so much of his own that with a little extra help he could remain here? I should like to keep him. . . .' I enjoy being here; and to my mind, if I could only stay here for a year or two I might profit and gain merit by my work and thus be rather sought out by the Court than have need to seek them. . . .

MOZART TO HIS FATHER

3 October 1777

Tomorrow the Court departs, and will not return before the 20th. Had it remained here I could have taken further steps and would have remained here a while longer; but as it is, I hope to resume my journey with Mama next Tuesday. . . .

After a stay of some weeks in Augsburg with the family of Leopold's brother, the travellers proceeded to Mannheim, where the Elector Palatine maintained one of the best orchestras to be found in Europe at that time, known as the 'Mannheim Orchestra'. There young Mozart found kind, appreciative friends, among them the director of the orchestra, Christian Cannabich.

MOZART TO HIS FATHER

Mannheim, 29 November 1777

. . . Last Tuesday . . . I went in the morning to Count Savioli and asked him if it would not be possible for the Elector to keep me here this winter? I would like to teach the young Counts. He said yes, I shall propose it to the Elector; and if it rests with me, it will certainly come about. In the afternoon I visited Cannabich and as it was on his advice that I had gone to the Count, he asked me at once if I had done so. I related everything to him. He said to me, I shall be very happy if you spend the winter with us, but I should be still happier if you were remaining here, and that in the Elector's service. I said I desired nothing better than to be always near him, but how it might be permanent I really could not tell, they have already two Kapellmeisters [Cannabich and Vogler], so I did not see what I could be, for I should not wish to come after Vogler! Nor shall you, said he, no one belonging to the music in this place is under the Kapellmeister, or even under the Intendant. The Elector might make you his composer of chamber music: only wait, I shall speak of it to the Count. The Thursday following there was a great concert. When the Count saw me he asked me to excuse him for not having spoken yet, because these were the gala days. So soon as the Gala should be over, however, *viz.* on Monday, he would assuredly speak. I allowed three days to go by, and hearing not a word, I then waited on him to ask for information. He said, my dear M. Mozart (this was on Friday, *viz.* yesterday), today was a hunting day, and therefore it was impossible for me to question the Elector; but tomorrow about this time I shall certainly be able to give you an answer. To say the truth, at this I departed a little angry, and therefore resolved to take my 6 easiest variations on the Fischer Minuet (which I had written here for this very purpose) to the young Count, and thus have an opportunity to speak with the Elector myself. You cannot imagine how pleased the governess was when I arrived. I was received with great politeness. When I brought out the Variations and said they were for the Count, she said, Oh that is fine, but you surely have something for the Comtesse as well? Not yet, said I, but if I remain here long enough to have time to write something, I shall. Apropos, said she, I am glad you are to stay here all winter. 'Well, if he has said so, then it has been said by him who can say it. For without the Elector I naturally cannot remain here.' I told her the whole story, and we agreed that I should come back next day (that is, today) at 4 o'clock and bring something with me for the Comtesse. She will speak to the Elector before I come, and I shall meet him again. I went there today, but he had not come today. But tomorrow I shall go there again; I have written a Rondeau for the Comtesse; have I not now good reason to remain here and await the outcome? Ought I to go away now, when the biggest step has been taken? – Now I have an opportunity to speak to the Elector himself. I think I shall most likely spend the winter here. For the Elector is fond of me, sets great store by me, and knows what I can do. . . .

Once again a hopeful beginning petered out in polite excuses and non-commital expressions of good will. Very soon, however, the young musician was aglow with new plans: a pretty young singer, daughter of one of the Mannheim musicians, had conquered his heart.

MOZART TO HIS FATHER

Mannheim, 17 January 1778

Next Wednesday I am going for a few days to Kirchheim-Poland to visit the Princess of Orange; so much good has been said of her to me here that at last I have made up my mind. . . . At the very least I shall receive eight Louis d'or; for as she is unusually fond of singing, I have four arias transcribed for her, and I will give her a Symphony too, for she has a quite elegant orchestra and gives a concert every day. I shall be at no great expense for the copying of the arias, for a certain Herr Weber, who is to go there with me, has copied them for me. He has a daughter who sings admirably, with a beautiful, pure voice, and is only 16 years old. She lacks nothing but action, and then she can play the Primadonna on any stage. . . .

MOZART TO HIS FATHER

Mannheim, 2 February 1778

. . . The first thing is for me to write to you how matters went with me and my worthy friends at Kirchheim-Poland. We left here on Friday morning at 8 o'clock . . . by four o'clock we had reached Kirchheim-Poland. The very next morning Herr *Konzertmeister* Rothfischer called on us; he had already been described to me at Mannheim as a thoroughly honest man; and so I found him. That evening we went to the Court, this was Saturday, and Mlle Weber sang 3 arias. I will pass over her singing – which in one word was excellent! – true, in my last letter I spoke of her merits; but I cannot close this one without saying more about her, for only now have I really come to know her and thus to perceive her full powers. . . . Next day, Monday, there was music again, and again on Tuesday, and again on Wednesday; Mlle Weber sang 13 times in all, and twice played the clavier, for she plays it not at all badly. What most astonished me was that she reads music so well; just imagine, she played my difficult Sonatas prima vista, slowly but without missing a note. On my honour, I would rather hear my Sonatas played by her than by Vogler. I played 12 times in all, and once, upon request, played the organ in the Lutheran Church, and I offered the Princess 4 Symphonies, and received no more than seven Louis d'or in silver, and my poor dear Weberin five. I should truly never have expected that, I had never hoped for much, but at the very least, eight for each of us. Basta; we have lost nothing by it; I am still 42 fl. to the good. . . .

MOZART TO HIS FATHER

4 February 1778

. . . I am here very conveniently finishing the music for De Jean, and then I shall receive my 200 fl. I can remain here as long as ever I wish, and am at no cost either for board or lodging. Meanwhile, Herr Weber will busy himself to obtain concert engagements where he can for himself and me. And then we shall travel together; when I travel with him, it is just as though I were travelling with you. That is why I am so fond of him, for except in appearance he is just like you and has just your character and way of thinking. . . . I must confess I was truly delighted to travel with them. We were cheerful and merry. I heard a man talk like you, I did not need to concern myself with anything, whatever was torn I found it mended, in short I was served like a prince. This unfortunate family is so dear to me that I wish nothing more than to make them happy; and perchance I may. My advice is that they should go to Italy. And I would therefore ask you to write, the sooner the better, to our good friend Lugiati and enquire of him how much, and what is the most, that is paid to a Primadonna at Verona. The more the better, one can always come down. . . . Perhaps one could also have the Ascenza [the Ascension Day Opera] at Venice. I will stake my life on her singing, that she will assuredly do me credit. In this short time she has already profited greatly from me, and how much more will she not have profited by then? I have no anxiety as to her acting. If it comes about then we – Mr Weber, his 2 daughters and I – will have the honour, dear Papa and dear Sister, to visit you for 2 weeks on our way, my Sister will find a friend and comrade in Mlle Weber, for she has the same reputation here as my sister at Salzburg by reason of her good behaviour, her Father the same as my father, and the whole family like the Mozarts. . . . I beg you to do your utmost that we may go to Italy. You know my greatest desire – to write Operas.

At Verona I shall gladly write an opera for 50 zecchini, only that she may win fame by it; for unless I write it, I am afraid she will be victimized. By that time I shall already have made so much money by other journeys we intend to make together that it would do me no harm. I believe we shall go to Switzerland, perhaps also to Holland, only write to me soon about it. If we stay long in one place, the other daughter, who is the eldest, will be most useful to us, for then we can run our own household, since she can cook as well. . . . I beg you will answer me soon; do not forget my wish to write operas. I envy everybody who writes one. I could weep from sheer vexation when I see or hear an aria. But Italian, not German, serious, not buffa. . . .

Mozart's mother adds:

5 February 1778

My dear husband, you will have perceived from this letter that when Wolfgang makes new acquaintances he straightway wishes to give them his heart's blood. It is true she sings incomparably, but one must never set aside one's own interests. . . .

LEOPOLD MOZART TO HIS SON

Salzburg, 12 February 1778

My dear Son,

I read your letter of the 4th with amazement and horror. . . . Your journey arose out of 2 intentions: either to seek a good permanent service; or, should that plan go awry, to betake yourself to some large place where large profits are to be found. Both had the object of succouring your Parents and helping your dear Sister, but above all else, of winning Fame and Honour for yourself in the world. . . . It depends entirely on your own reason and manner of life whether you wish to die a musical hack, forgotten by the whole world, or a famous *Kapellmeister* of whom posterity will still continue to read in books – whether in sheep-like subjection to some hussy, with a roomful of starveling children, on a straw pallet, or after a Christian life, in happiness, honour and enduring fame, with good provision for your family, and respected by all. Your journey took you to Munich. You know the purpose – there was nothing to be done. . . . At Augsburg, too, you had your little ploys and much merry dalliance with my brother's daughter, who was also required to send you her portrait . . . suddenly there comes your new acquaintance with Herr Weber: and all that went before is forgotten; now that family is the most estimable, most Christian of families, and the daughter is the chief performer in the tragedy to be staged between your family and hers, and all you have imagined, without sufficient reflection, in the confusion into which your heart – open to all comers – has thrown you, is so right and so unfailingly possible, as though it were the most natural course that events could take.

You propose to take her to Italy as a Primadonna. Tell me if you know any Primadonna who has appeared on the stage in Italy as a Primadonna, without having already sung in public many times in Germany. . . . I will allow that Mlle Weber sings like Gabrielli, that she has a voice strong enough for the Italian theatre, that she has the proper stature for a Primadonna, etc.: but it is still ridiculous that you are ready to vouch for her acting. It needs something more than that. . . . Not only women, but men with experience of the stage tremble at their debut in a foreign country. . . . What impresario would not laugh if one should seek to recommend to him a girl of 16 or 17, who has never set foot on a stage before? Your proposal (I can scarce write the word, when I think of it), the proposal to travel about with Herr Weber and N.B. two daughters, almost drove me out of my mind. Dearest Son! How can you allow yourself to be deceived even for an hour by such an abominable notion? Your letter is written exactly in the manner of a novel. . . .

Be off with you to Paris! and go soon! Win great people to your side – aut Caesar aut nihil – the very thought of seeing Paris should have protected you from all fleeting ideas. *From Paris, the name and fame of a man of great talent spreads to all the world, there the aristocrats treat men of genius with the greatest condescension, esteem and politeness – there one sees an elegant mode of life, which makes a quite astonishing contrast to the coarse manners of our German courtiers and ladies, and there you can gain a real command of the French language. . . .*

LEOPOLD MOZART TO HIS SON

23 February 1778

. . . If I could bring you to a more composed behaviour, or even to longer reflection when you are in the heat of these ideas of yours, I should make you the happiest man in the world. But I see that nothing comes before its time – yet in the matter of your talent, everything came before the time. Moreover, in scientific matters you understood everything with the greatest of ease. Why should it not be possible to learn to understand people? To divine their intentions? To close your heart from the world? And to reflect well upon every matter and in especial N.B. not always to fasten upon the favourable aspect of things, or the side which is propitious to you or to the purposes you have at the back of your mind? Even those who do not yet know you will read in your face that you are a genius. But when flatterers praise you to the skies, intending to use you for their own ends, you open your heart to them with the greatest ease and take their every word for gospel. . . . And to capture you the more certainly, the women take a hand in it – if you do not resist that, you will be unfortunate to your dying day. . . .

Wolfgang obeys with a heavy heart, tearing himself away from Mannheim, his love and his dreams, and travels to Paris, accompanied by his mother. His father has provided him with a huge list of addresses of influential people to be seen, a generous supply of instructions on how to set about the task of conquering Paris, and innumerable warnings of what to avoid in order not to get involved in the Paris squabbles. 'Should Gluck, should Piccinni be there, avoid meeting them as much as possible; do not make friends with Grétry either' [one of the prominent French operatic composers]. 'De la politesse, et pas d'autre chose.' ('Be polite, and no more.') 'With high dignitaries you may speak quite openly, but with all the others play the Englishman, I implore you – do not give yourself away. . . . Do not let even your friends know when you have got money.'

Wolfgang obediently does as he has been told. He pays his visits, offers his services, tries to be obsequious to the grandees, but his natural pride is inhibiting; he is certainly no diplomat, and one can read between the lines of his letters that he has already lost faith in the ultimate success of his enterprise and that a feeling of exasperation is growing in him. He has found some pupils, but has to fight for his fees. He writes a symphony – the 'Paris', No. 32 – and gets it performed. This, however, was the only positive result of frantic efforts, and the worst catastrophe burst upon him like a thunderbolt.

MOZART TO HIS FATHER

Paris, 24 March 1778

. . . Our journey lasted for 9½ days. We thought we would not be able to endure to the end. In all my life I have never suffered such boredom. You can easily imagine what it was like to leave Mannheim and so many dear and kind friends. . . . We departed on Saturday the 14th, and on the previous Friday there was yet another concert at Cannabich's, at which my Concerto for 3 pianos was played. . . . Mlle Weber sang 2 of my arias, *Aer tranquillo* from *Re Pastore* and the new one, *Non so d'onde viene*. With this latter, my beloved Weberin did surpassing honour to herself and me. The whole company declared that they had never been so moved by an aria as by that one. . . .

MOZART TO HIS FATHER

Paris, 5 April 1778

. . . I am now about to compose a Symphonie concertante for Flute – *Wendling*, Oboe – *Ramm*, French horn – *Punto*, and Bassoon – *Ritter*.

Punto plays magnifique. I have this moment returned from the Concert Spirituel. Baron Grimm and I often give vent to our musical spleen about the music here. N.B.: between ourselves. For in public it is bravo, bravissimo, and one claps until one's fingers smart. . . .

Now I must again beg you, my dearest Papa, not to distress yourself so greatly or be over-anxious, since you now have no cause. For now I am in a place where money is certainly to be made, though at the cost of terrible pains and toil; but I am ready to do everything to give you pleasure. What most angers me in the matter is that the French have improved their goût only to the extent that they can now listen to good things as well. But have they perceived that their own musique is bad, or at least noticed a difference – not a bit of it!

Leopold's main hope is the favour of an influential patron, Baron Grimm, ambassador in Paris of a small German principality, a friend of Diderot and Rousseau and a staunch supporter of Gluck.

LEOPOLD MOZART TO HIS SON

Salzburg, 6 April 1778

. . . Now I most strongly advise you to win the favour, love and friendship of Herr Baron von Grimm, or rather to retain them, by a *complete, childlike confidence*, asking his advice in all matters and not acting on your own whim or on preconceived notions, and in everything to consider *your own* interest and thus the *general interest of us all*. The style of life in Paris is very different from the German, and the French manner of polite address, of paying compliments, of asking for patronage, introducing oneself, etc., is something quite of its own, so that in the old days Herr Baron Grimm used to give me hints, and I asked what I should say and how I ought to say it. . . .

MOZART TO HIS FATHER

Paris, 1 May 1778

. . . M. Grimm gave me a letter (to the Duchesse de Chabot) and I drove thither. The contents of the letter were chiefly to recommend me to the Duchesse de Bourbon, who was at the time in a convent, and to introduce me again to her. . . . There I was obliged to wait for half an hour in a large, ice-cold, unheated room with no fireplace. At last the D. de Chabot arrived, with the greatest civility, and asked me to make the best of the piano, as none of hers was in tune; I could try for myself. I said I should be delighted to play something, but at present it was impossible, because my fingers were numb with cold; and asked her at least to have me conducted to a room with a fire in the grate. 'O oui, Monsieur, vous avez raison', was the only reply. She then seated herself and sat drawing for a full hour, in the company of other gentlemen, all sitting in a circle round a big table. Thus I had the honour to wait for a whole hour. The windows and doors were open. Not only my hands, but my whole body and feet were cold; and my head soon began to ache as well. So there was altum silentium. And I did not know what to do all this long time, for cold, headache and tedium. I often said to myself that if it were not for M. Grimm, I would go away again that very moment. At last, to cut it short, I did play on the miserable, wretched pianoforte. But the most vexatious thing of all was that Madame and all the gentlemen never paused in their drawing for a moment, but went on as before, so that I was obliged to play to the chairs, table and walls. In these hateful circumstances my patience deserted me – so I began the Fischer Variations, played half of them, and stood up. There came a shower of éloges. I, however, said the only thing there was to say, namely that I could do myself no credit with this instrument and should very much like to choose another day, when there was a better one there. But she would not give way, I had to wait for half an hour longer, until her husband came. But he sat down beside me and listened with all his attention – and at this I forgot all about cold and headache, and played, in spite of the wretched clavier – as I play when I am in the right humour. Give me the best instrument in Europe, but listeners who understand nothing or do not wish to understand and who do not feel with me in what I am playing, and all my pleasure is spoilt. I told M. Grimm all about it afterwards. You write that I am to be good about calling on people, so as to make fresh acquaintances and renew the old ones. But that is not possible. On foot it is always too far or too muddy, for the dirt in Paris is beyond description. To go by carriage means the honour of spending 4 or 5 livres a day, and *in vain*, for people greet one politely and that is all; they appoint such and such a day for me to come and play; I play, then they all cry O *c'est un prodige, c'est inconcevable, c'est étonnant*. And so farewell. I spent enough money so on coach hire in the beginning – and often in vain, for I found the people were not at home. No one who is not here would believe how vexatious it is. In general, Paris is much altered, the French have much less politesse than fifteen years ago. They now border closely upon insolence, and they are abominably arrogant. . . .

As to the Symphonie Concertante there is again some shillyshallying. But I think there is again something else behind it. For here again I have my enemies, but where have I not had them? But that is a good sign. I had to write the Symphonie in the greatest haste, I worked diligently, and the four performers were and are still quite enamoured of it. Le Gros had it four days for copying, but I found it always lying in the same place. At last, the day before yesterday I could not see it – but searched under all the music – and found it hidden. Did nothing, just the same. Asked Le Gros, apropos, have you given the Symph. Concertante to be copied yet? – no – I forgot. Since I naturally cannot order him to have it copied and performed, I said nothing. . . . If there were any place here where people had ears and feeling hearts, and understood something of music, however little, and had taste, I would laugh heartily at all these things. But so far as concerns music, I am among brute beasts. . . . Well, here I am and I must endure it, for your sake. I shall thank Almighty God if I escape with my taste unspoilt. I pray God daily for grace, that I may persevere steadfastly here; that I may do honour to myself and the whole German nation, since all is for His greater honour and glory, and that He will permit me to be fortunate, and to make a great deal of money, so that I may help you out of your present afflictions. . . .

MOZART TO HIS FATHER

Paris, 14 May 1778

I think I told you already in my last letter, that the Duc de Guines, whose daughter is my pupil in composition, plays the flute incomparably, and she the harp magnifique; she has great talent, and genius, especially an incomparable memory, for she plays all her pieces, and she really knows 200, by heart. She greatly doubts, however, whether she also has a gift for composition – especially in the matter of invention; but her father, who (between ourselves) is a little too much enamoured of her, says she most certainly has ideas; that it is only bashfulness – that she has too little confidence in herself. Well, we must see. If no ideas or inventions come to her (for at present she indeed has none at all) then it is all in vain – for God knows I cannot give her any. . . .

MOZART TO HIS FATHER

Paris, 3 July 1778

. . . My dear Mother is very ill – she had herself bled, as was her custom, and it was very needful; and she felt quite well afterwards – but a few days thereafter she complained that she was cold, and then at once of fever; then she had diarrhoea, headache . . . but as she grew worse and worse – could scarce speak, lost her hearing so that we were obliged to shout – Baron Grimm sent his doctor here. She is very weak, still has fever, and her mind wanders. I am told I may have hope, but I have not much – for a long time now I have been day and night between fear and hope – but I have given myself up entirely to the will of God – and hope that you and my dear Sister will do so likewise; for how else can one be calm? – I mean, calmer, for to be entirely so is not possible. . . .

I had to compose a symphony for the opening of the Concert Spirituel. It was performed on Corpus Christi Day, amid general *applauso*. I hear, too, that a report on it has been printed in the Courier de l'Europe. So it pleased uncommonly. At the rehearsal I was in great fear, for never in all my life had I heard worse playing. You cannot conceive how, twice over, they blundered and scratched through it – I was truly most alarmed – I would gladly have rehearsed it once again, but as so many things are always being rehearsed there was no time left; and I had to go to bed with a faint heart and a wrathful, discontented mind. The following day I had determined not to go to the Concert at all; but the evening was fine, and at the last I went – resolving that if matters should go as badly as at the rehearsal, I would assuredly make my way to the Orchestra, to Herr Lahousé, the *1. Violin*, snatch his violin from him and conduct the thing myself. I prayed God for grace, that it might go well, since all is for His greater honour and glory, and ecco, the Symphony began. Raff was standing beside me, and in the very middle of the first Allegro was a passage I was certain must please them, all the audience were carried away by it – and there was a great applaudissement – but as I knew while I was writing it how strong an effect it would make, I had brought it in again at the end – and now there were cries of 'da capo!' The Andante also pleased, but especially the last Allegro; for as I had heard that here all last as well as first Allegros begin with all the instruments playing together and generally unisono, I began with the 2 violins alone, *piano* for 8 bars – then at once a *forte* – the audience (as I had expected) went *sshh* . . . at the *piano* – then came the *forte* at once – and no sooner did they hear the *forte* than they began to clap. So in my delight I went straight after the Symphony to the Palais Royal – ate a delicious ice-cream – recited the rosary as I had promised – and went home. . . .

MOZART TO HIS FATHER

Paris, 9 July 1778

Monsieur, mon très cher Père,
I hope you will be prepared to hear with fortitude some of the saddest and most painful news. My last, of the 3rd, will have put you in a state

where you would not expect good news – on that same day, the 3rd, at 21 minutes past 10 at night, my mother fell asleep blessedly in the Lord. When I wrote to you she was already enjoying heavenly bliss – for all was over by then – I wrote to you in the night – I hope you and my dear Sister will forgive me this small and very needful deceit – for after judging from my pain and sorrow what yours must be, I could not find it in my heart to surprise you at once with this dreadful news. . . .

You write that it is long since you heard anything concerning my composition pupil, and I believe it is so; for what should I write to you about her? She is not a person for composition, all pains are wasted on her. For one thing, she is heartily stupid, and moreover, heartily lazy. As to Noverre's ballet, I never wrote but that he would perhaps do a new one – he has just presented half a ballet, and I wrote the music for that [*Les Petits Riens*]. I mean that there are 6 pieces by others in it, consisting merely of old, wretched French airs; the Symphonie and Contredanses, 12 pieces in all, are by me. This ballet has already been given 4 times with great applause. But I shall do nothing more whatsoever unless I know beforehand what I am to get by it – for this was only a token of friendship for Noverre. . . .

MOZART TO HIS FATHER

Paris, 31 July 1778

. . . The daughter of the Duc de Guines is about to be married and will not continue [her lessons] (which for my reputation's sake gives me no great vexation); I lose nothing from her, for the Duke pays no more than everyone pays here. Just conceive, the Duc de Guines, to whose house I went daily and was obliged to stay 2 hours, allowed me to give 24 lessons (whereas one is always paid after the 12th), went away to the country, came back after 10 days without sending me word (if I had not had the curiosity to make enquiries for myself, I should not yet know that they were here), and at last the Gouvernante brings out a purse and says to me: excuse me if I pay you for only 12 lessons this time, I have not money enough – that is noble! – and counted me out 3 Louis d'or – and added: I hope you are satisfied – if not please tell me so. This M. le Duc was thus a man without a spark of honour – and thought, this is a young fellow, and a stupid German into the bargain – as all French people say of the Germans – and so he will be quite delighted with this. But the stupid German was not delighted – indeed he did not accept – thus he wanted to pay me only one hour out of 2 – and this from *égard*, for he has already had a Concerto for Flute and Harp from me 4 months ago, and has not yet paid me for it – so I am only waiting until after the wedding, and then I shall go to the Gouvernante and demand my money. . . . I shall now do my very best to make my way here with pupils and to earn as much money as possible – I do so now in the fond hope that a change may soon come about, for I cannot conceal from you, but must confess, that I shall be delighted to be released from this place; giving lessons is no joke – it is very fatiguing; and unless one takes *many*, one does not earn much money. You must not think this is laziness – No! – but because it is quite contrary to my genius and my real way of life. For you know that I bury myself, as it were, in music – that my head is full of it all day long – that I love pondering – studying – reflecting. But my way of life here prevents me from doing so – true, I shall have a few free hours, but I shall need those brief hours rather for rest than for work. . . .

LEOPOLD MOZART TO HIS SON

Salzburg, 13 August 1778

. . . Baron v. Grimm wrote to me on 27 July. His letter both pleased and displeased me. It *pleased* me because I learnt from it that you are well; and because he wrote that you had been most exact (of which indeed I had no doubt) in all filial duties towards your late dear mother. But it *displeased* me because he . . . was in great doubt as to whether you could now find success or happiness or even, said he, make a living for yourself, in Paris. He said: 'He is *zu treuherzig*, too indolent, too easily deceived, too little concerned with the ways that lead a man to fortune. Here, to make his way, a man must be crafty, enterprising, bold. For his own sake, I would wish him half as talented and twice as astute, I should then have no anxiety for him. Be that as it may, there are only two ways open to him here. The first is to give piano lessons; but even apart from the fact that to find pupils requires great activity and a considerable touch of the mountebank, I do not know if his health would permit him to sustain that profession, for it is very tiring to run all over Paris and wear oneself out in talking and explaining. And then it is a profession he would not relish, for it would prevent him from composing, which is what he loves above all. He might therefore devote himself entirely to that; but in this country the general public knows nothing about music. In consequence, everything depends on names, and the merit of a work can be judged by only a very few people. At the present moment the public is ridiculously divided between Piccinni and Gluck, and all the arguments one hears about music are pitiful. It is thus very hard for your son to succeed between these two parties.'

All this is true in its way. Only the last matter depends in great part upon good luck and chance. And precisely because there are two parties, a third can hope for more applause than if the whole public were absorbed with one composer. For my part, I consider that the hardest thing is to have an opera commissioned: and that indeed requires *going about, pushing, employing any and every means, seeking friends*, etc.: and now of course matters are at a climax – for Piccinni and Gluck will do anything to prevent the thing, and it seems to me almost impossible that you should secure such a commission. . . . He also writes to me: 'You see, mon cher maître, that in a country where so many mediocre and even execrable musicians have made huge fortunes, I greatly fear that your son may not even be able to earn a living. . . . I have given you this faithful report, not in order to distress you, but so that we may together decide upon the best possible course. . . .'

Leopold, judging the situation realistically and cutting his losses, succeeds in securing his son's reappointment in Salzburg, even with improved conditions. Wolfgang has had enough; he gives up the hopeless struggle and consents to return to the hated service of the Archbishop. Yet on his return journey he stops once more at Munich, ostensibly to try once more to find useful contacts, but in fact for the sake of meeting his 'dear Weberin' again. The main body of the Mannheim Orchestra, on the succession of the Elector Palatine to the throne of Bavaria, has moved to Munich, and so has the Weber family. Aloysia, however, is irreconcilable; she does not care any more for a lover who has abandoned her. Mozart's high opinion of her talent, by the way, proved justified: she became a famous singer and he met her again in Vienna, some years later, as Mme Lange. Mozart's fate, as we shall see, remained closely linked with the Weber family.

The most momentous event of the following years of Mozart's life was the 'scrittura' (commission) of an opera for the Court Theatre in Munich. 'Idomeneo', his first great operatic masterpiece, performed for the first time on 29 January 1781, was a landmark in his artistic development.

His early operatic experience proved a tremendous asset, on this occasion as well as later in Vienna. He had an infallible feeling for the stage, and he certainly knew more about it than the librettist of 'Idomeneo', Abbé Varesco in Salzburg, who had made it up from a French original. With only parts of the music sketched, Mozart, once more on leave of absence, travelled to Munich in November 1780, to finish his work in close contact with the singers at his disposal.

MOZART TO HIS FATHER

Munich, 8 November 1780

My dearest Father,
I arrived safely and gladly! – safely, because we met with no unpleasant incidents on the way, and gladly because we could scarce wait for the end of a journey which, though short, was very painful; – for I assure you not one of us could get a moment's sleep all night – the coach was like to have shaken body and soul apart! – and the seats! – hard as stones! – From Wasserburg onwards I really thought I should not get my behind to Munich in one piece! – it was bruised all over – and, I suppose, fiery red – For two whole stages I sat with my hands on the cushions, holding my behind off the seat – but enough of that, it is over now! – but in future as a rule I shall rather travel on foot than by mail-coach! . . .

I have only one request to make to the Herr Abate [Varesco]: for my purposes I should like a slight change to be made in Ilia's aria in Act 2, Scene 2 – *se il padre perdei in te lo ritrovo*; that stanza could not be better – but then comes what to me always seems unnatural, N.B. in an aria, namely an aside. In dialogue such a thing is quite natural – the actor looks away and says a few rapid words – but in an aria – the singer must repeat the words more than once – it makes a disagreeable effect. . . . We have agreed among ourselves to present an *Aria andantino* here, for 4 wind-instruments – Flute, Oboe, Horn and Bassoon – and please may I have it as soon as possible. . . .

MOZART TO HIS FATHER

Munich, 6 December 1780

. . . The effect of the air and water in this town upon Mme and Mlle Cannabich is such that their necks are slowly becoming thicker and thicker; in the end it might even turn to goitre – God be with us! – true, they are taking a kind of powder, or what have you – that is not what it is called. – No; but it does not really serve – so I took the liberty of recommending those 'Goitre pills', as they are called, disclosing (to give greater value to them) that my sister had had 3 goitres – and yet in the end, thanks to these excellent pills, had been completely cured – if they can be made up here, please send me the prescription – but if they are only made at Salzburg, then please send me a few hundredweight of them, to be paid for cash down, by the next mail coach. . . .

This afternoon we are to rehearse the first and second Acts in the

Count's room, as before – after that we shall rehearse only the third Act in the room and then go straight on to the stage. . . . Have no anxiety about the so-called *Populare*, for in my opera there is music for all worthy folk – only not for asses' ears. – Apropos: how do matters stand with the Archbishop? It will be six weeks on Monday since I left Salzburg, you know, dear Father, that I am there only for your sake – for – by God, did it rest with me – before I left the place this time I would have wiped my tail with the latest Decree – for upon my honour, I find, not Salzburg itself, but the Prince – the proud Noblesse – every day more intolerable – so I would wait with pleasure for a letter to say he had no further use for my services – and indeed, with the exalted patronage I now enjoy here I should be secure enough, for the present and for the future – except in the case of death, against which there can be no security. . . . But for your sake, anything in the world – and I should find it yet easier if one could only now and then go away for a little while, to recover one's breath. You know how hard it was to get away this time . . . it almost makes one weep to think of it. . . .

MOZART TO HIS FATHER

Munich, 27 December 1780

. . . The last rehearsal went most admirably. It was held in a large room at Court, the Elector was there as well – This time we rehearsed with the full orchestra (I mean, as many as are accommodated in the Opera House). After the first Act the Elector called to me loudly Bravo. And when I went to kiss his hand, he said: *This Opera will be charmant; it will certainly bring you honour.* As he did not know whether he could stay till the end, we were obliged to perform the Aria with obbligatos for wind-instruments and the thunderstorm for him at the beginning of the second Act. After this he again expressed his approval to me in the kindest fashion and said laughingly: *one would never suppose such a small head could contain such great things.* And the next morning at his *levée* he praised my opera highly. . . .

MOZART TO HIS FATHER

Munich, 30 December 1780

A Happy New Year! Forgive me if I write very little this time – for I am now over head and ears in work – I have not quite finished the third Act yet – and besides, as there is to be no extra ballet but only a divertissement contained in the opera, I have the honour of writing the music for that as well. I am, however, very glad of this, for the music will thus be all by *one* composer. The third Act will be *at least* as good as the first two – but I believe it will be infinitely better and that it may justly be said that *finis coronat opus*. The Elector was so pleased the other day at the rehearsal that as I told you in my last letter, he praised my opera highly the next morning at his *levée* – and again at Court that evening. And I also learnt from a very reliable source that, on the evening after the rehearsal itself, he spoke of my music to everyone who approached him, and these were his words: *I was quite surprised – no music had ever impressed me so much before; it is magnifique music. . . .*

MOZART TO HIS FATHER

Munich, 3 January 1781

My head and hands are so full of the third Act that it would be no wonder if I turned into a third Act myself. It is costing me more trouble by itself alone than a whole Opera – for there is scarce a scene in it that is not extremely interesting. . . .

MOZART TO HIS FATHER

Munich, 18 January 1781

. . . The rehearsal of Act III went most excellently. It was declared to excel the first two Acts by far. Only the libretto here is too long and therefore the music also (as I have always said). So Idamante's Aria *No, la morte io non pavento* has been taken out – in any case it came in clumsily there – though people who have heard it sung are lamenting its loss – and so has Raaff's [Idomeneo's] – over which people are lamenting still more – but we must make a virtue of necessity. The Oracle's speech likewise is still much too long – I have shortened it – there is no need for Varesco to know any of this, for it will all be printed as he wrote it. . . . Meanwhile, tell Varesco from me that he will not receive a farthing more from Count Seau than was agreed – for the changes he made for me, not for him – and moreover he should be obliged to me, as it was done for the sake of his reputation – there is much more that should be changed – and assure him that he would not have come out of it so well with any other composer as with me. . . .

The unqualified success of 'Idomeneo' remained a local event and Mozart's fond hopes of a permanent appointment in Munich evaporated. His impatience with the conditions of service in Salzburg grew out of control; on the next occasion it blew up to a crisis that shattered Leopold's cautious plans and marked the end of his paternal authority. In March 1781 – a few months after the success of 'Idomeneo' – the Archbishop took his retinue, including Wolfgang, to Vienna on a state visit. We learn from Mozart's letters what happened there.

MOZART TO HIS FATHER

Vienna, 4 April 1781

... I told you in a recent letter that the Archbishop is a great hindrance to me here, for through him I have lost at least 100 ducats that I could certainly make by a concert in the theatre ... I can truthfully say that yesterday I was really pleased with the Viennese public. I played in the concert for the widows at the Kärtnertor Theatre, and had to go right through the piece again because there was no end to the applause. Now that the public has come to know me, how much do you think I could earn if I gave a concert for my own benefit? But our Archbooby will not allow it – he will not have his people make profit, only loss – but with me he will not succeed in this; for if I have 2 pupils here, I am better off than at Salzburg – I have no need of board and lodging from him – now only listen: Brunetti said today at dinner that Arco had given him a message from the Archbishop *to tell us* that we were to receive the money for our coach-fares and to leave by Sunday; adding, that anyone who wished to remain here – how reasonable of him! – might do so, but at his own expense, for he would no longer receive board and lodging. When they asked me what I meant to do, I answered: *I still do not know that I am to leave – for until Count Arco tells me so himself, I shall not believe it – and I shall tell him then what are my intentions – curse him.* ... Oh, I shall certainly make a fool of the Archbishop, it will be delightful. ...

P.S. I assure you that this is a splendid place – and for *my métier* the best place in the world; everyone will tell you that – and I am happy to be here; consequently I am putting my time to good use, so far as my powers permit me. Be assured that my only purpose is to make as much money as possible: for next to good health, that is the best of all. – Think no more of my follies, I have for long heartily regretted them – loss sharpens the wits – and I now have other thoughts. ...

Brunetti was a violinist in the Archbishop's band, Count Arco, the Archbishop's Chamberlain.

MOZART TO HIS FATHER

Vienna, 8 April 1781

. . . Today we had – for I am writing at 11 at night – a concert, at which 3 pieces by me were played. I mean, new ones; the Rondeau of a concerto for Brunetti – a sonata with violin accompaniment, for myself – which I composed last night between 11 o'clock and midnight – but so as to be ready in time, I wrote out only the accompaniment – Brunetti's part, and kept my own in my head – and then a Rondeau for Ceccarelli [castrato soprano], which he had to repeat. – Now I will ask you for a letter as soon as possible, with fatherly, and therefore the friendliest possible advice on the following subject: we are now told that we are to leave here for Salzburg two weeks hence – I can remain here, not only without loss, but to my own *benefit* – so I have it in mind to ask the Archbishop's permission to allow me to remain here. – Dearest Father: I am indeed very fond of you, as you may see from this, that for your sake I deny all my own wishes and desires – but for you, I swear to you on my honour that I should not lose a moment before resigning my post – giving a big concert, taking four pupils, and certainly prospering so well here at Vienna that within twelve months I should be earning at least a thousand thalers a year . . . I am still young, as you say, that is true, but to drag through one's youth in idleness in such a beggarly place is sad enough – and a waste withal – so I beg you for your fatherly and benevolent advice – but soon, for I must announce my intentions – for the rest, only trust me – I think more sensibly nowadays. . . .

MOZART TO HIS FATHER

Vienna, 11 April 1781

. . . On Sunday week, that is the 22nd, Ceccarelli and I are to leave for home. When I reflect that I shall be leaving Vienna without at least 1,000 fl. in my pocket, my heart aches; for the sake of an ill-disposed Prince who pays me only a lousy 400 gulden and torments me to boot, am I really to kick away a thousand gulden? For I should most certainly make that much if I gave a concert. When we held our first big concert here in the house, the Archbishop sent the three of us 4 ducats each. At the last one, for which I had composed a new Rondeau for Brunetti, a new Sonata for myself and a new Rondeau for Ceccarelli, I received nothing at all. But what makes me almost desperate is that on the same evening when we had this filthy concert, I was invited to Countess Thun's house, and thus could not go, and who was there? *The Emperor*. Adamberger and Mme Weigl were there and received 50 ducats each! – and what an opportunity! After all, I cannot send a message to the Emperor that if he wishes to hear me he must lose no time, because I am leaving on such and such a day. One always has to wait for such things. And I cannot and will not remain here unless I give a concert. Indeed, I should be better off here if I had only two pupils, than I am at home. But – with 1,000 or 1,200 fl. put by, one need not accept the first offer, and can therefore demand better terms. But he will not permit that, the heartless monster – so I must call him, for such he is, and that is what all the noblesse call him. Enough of that; Oh, I hope to learn on the next mail day whether I am still to bury my youth and my talent in Salzburg. . . .

MOZART TO HIS FATHER

Vienna, 9 May 1781

Mon très cher Père,
I am still bursting with fury! – and you, my dearest, most beloved Father, are certainly in the same case – my patience has been tried for so long, but at last it has given way; I am no longer so unfortunate as to be in Salzburg's service – today was my lucky day; listen.

Twice already that – I really do not know what to call him – had thrown the grossest *sottises* and *impertinences* in my face, of which, to spare your feelings, I said nothing in my letters . . . he called me a knave, a dissolute rascal – told me to be off – and I endured it all, though I felt that your honour as well as mine was being attacked – but you would have it so – and I remained silent. Now listen: a week ago the messenger arrived without warning and told me I must leave then and there. The others had all been told what day they were to go, only I not – so in haste I crammed everything into my trunk, and old Madame Weber was so kind as to invite me to her house – where I have a pretty room, and am with obliging people, who give me a helping hand over all the matters one so often requires in a hurry (and cannot get done when one lives alone). I had fixed my departure for Wednesday (that is, today, the 9th) by the *ordinaire*, but that did not give me time to collect the money that is still owing to me, and I therefore put off my journey until Saturday. Today when they saw me appear, the valets told me that the Archbishop wished to send a package by me. I asked if it were a pressing matter, whereupon they said yes, it was of great importance. So to my regret I shall not have the gratification of serving His Grace, for (owing to the reasons given above), I cannot leave until Saturday. . . . When I went into his room – N.B. I must tell you first of all that Schlaucher advised me to give the excuse that the Ordinaire was already full – he would think that a sounder reason – when I went into his room it began thus: Arch: 'Well, young fellow, so when are you leaving?' I: 'I had meant to leave tonight, but all the seats were already taken.' Then it all came out in one breath: I was the most dissolute fellow he had ever known – no one served him so badly as I – he advised me to leave today after all, or he would write home to have my salary stopped – I could never get a word in, he blazed away so fast – I listened coolly to it all – he lied to my face, saying my salary was 500 fl. – called me scoundrel, rascal, knave, booby – oh, I cannot bear to repeat it to you. – At last, when my blood was really up, I said: 'So Your Grace is not satisfied with me?' 'What, do you threaten me, you booby – oh, you booby! There is the door, look, I will have nothing more to do with such a miserable scoundrel.' At last I said: 'Nor I with you.' 'Then be off!' As I went out, I said: 'There will be no going back on this; tomorrow you shall have it in writing.' Now tell me, dearest Father, did I not say that too late rather than too soon? Now listen – I value my honour above all else, and I know it is so with you as well.

You need have no anxiety for me – I am so sure of my position here, that I would have resigned even without the least cause – now that I have had cause, and that 3 times over, I have no further merit in doing so; au contraire, I had twice played the coward and I positively could not do it a third time. . . . For the rest, I beg you to be cheerful, for my good fortune is about to begin, and I hope mine will be yours as well. Write to me privately that you are glad of it, as indeed you may well be – but in public berate me soundly, so that no blame shall be laid on you. . . .

After the occurrence described in this last letter, Wolfgang tried in vain to tender his formal resignation as a member of the Archbishop's retinue; in the end he got his dismissal informally.

MOZART TO HIS FATHER

Vienna, 9 June 1781

Mon très cher Père,

Well, Count Arco has managed things to perfection! – so that is the way to persuade people, to win them over – to refuse petitions out of congenital stupidity, not to say a word to your master for lack of spirit and love of sycophancy, to keep a man hanging about for four weeks and at last, when he is obliged to present the petition himself, instead of at least arranging for his admittance, to throw him out and give him a kick in the pants. . . . I wrote three petitions, handed them in 5 times, and each time had them thrown back at me. . . . At last, when the petition was sent back to me in the evening through H. von Kleinmayer (whose duty it is, here at Vienna), and as the Archbishop was to leave on the following day, I was quite beside myself with rage – wrote another petition, in which I disclosed to him that I had had a petition in readiness for the past 4 weeks and that, though why I did not know, I had been kept dancing with it for so long that I was now obliged to present it to him myself, and at the last moment. With this petition I received my discharge in the handsomest manner – for who knows if it was not done at the Archbishop's order? . . .

Seeing all the reasons why I left (with which you are well acquainted) no father could think of being angry with his son; rather, if he had *not done it*. . . . That you should make a comparison between me and Madame Lang [Aloysia Weber, Mozart's 'beloved Weberin' at Mannheim] absolutely astonishes me, and it distressed me for the whole day. That girl was a burden to her parents so long as she was unable to earn any money for herself – but no sooner had the time come when she could show her gratitude to them (N.B.: her father died before she had earned a farthing here) she deserted her poor mother, attached herself to an actor, married him – and her mother gets *nothing* from her! . . . I beseech you, dearest, most beloved Father, write me no more such letters – I entreat you, for they only irritate my mind and disturb my heart and spirit – and as I must now be always composing, I need a cheerful mind and a tranquil spirit. . . .

However indignant one may feel at the Archbishop's and his Chamberlain's brutality, boorishness, and inability to distinguish between an artist and a flunkey, one cannot help admitting that Mozart would have been a trying servant for any master. Born too late, he was too sensitive, too self-conscious as a personality, to submit humbly, as Haydn had done, to the iniquities of a social system that was already heading towards the cataclysm of the French Revolution. Quite apart from that, Mozart's reactions were always prompted by his creative instinct rather than by a cool appreciation of facts. Behind the fateful decision that made him free, but also left him totally unprotected in a ruthlessly competitive world, the mirage of 'The Marriage of Figaro', 'Don Giovanni', 'The Magic Flute' appears, that galaxy of peerless works in which Mozart's genius found its most sublime manifestation. In Vienna, with its musical and social background, he became the supreme artist whom we adore. In Vienna he found his beloved wife, Konstanze, the joys and sorrows of family life, and a nightmare struggle for existence with few parallels in the lives of other great benefactors of mankind.

From the first, Mozart's expectation of success proved justified. He found pupils in the high aristocracy, was acclaimed both as composer and virtuoso and secured a commission for a German opera, to be written for the Court Theatre. The 'Singspiel', still a new venture on the German stage, was near to the heart of the Emperor Joseph II, who had succeeded Maria Theresa in 1780 as ruler of Austria. 'Die Entführung aus dem Serail' – known on the English stage as 'Il Seraglio' – became Mozart's first popular success. Joseph, a lover of music and even a connoisseur like many of his Hapsburg ancestors, remained Mozart's most important patron. Two more of Mozart's operas, 'The Marriage of Figaro' and 'Così fan tutte', were commissioned for Joseph's Court Theatre, and after Gluck's death in 1787 Mozart inherited his honorary post as Composer to the Court ('Kammer-Compositeur'), a sinecure with a salary of 800 fl. (about £80). 'Too much for what I do in return, too little for what I could do', was Mozart's comment. It is true that Joseph was as thrifty as his mother, and the Austrian treasury had been in a poor state ever since the disastrous Seven Years War.

Totally unlike Gluck, who always complained about the vanity and presumption of singers, Mozart regarded them as his best allies, and he knew how to make the best of their individual peculiarities. This is one of the secrets of the marvellous vocal impersonation of his characters.

MOZART TO HIS FATHER

Vienna, 16 June 1781

. . . Now concerning the Theatre. I think I told you in my last letter that Count Rosenberg [Intendant of the Imperial Theatre], when he went away, gave instructions to Schröder to find a libretto for me. It is indeed already written, and Stephani (the younger) as superintendant of the Opera has it in hand. . . .

MOZART TO HIS FATHER

Vienna, 1 August 1781

. . . The day before yesterday the younger Stephani gave me a libretto to compose. I must confess that however badly he may behave to other people, as to which I know nothing, he is a very good friend to me. The libretto is quite good, the subject is Turkish and it is called *Bellmont und Konstanze*, or *Die Verführung aus dem Serail*. I shall write the overture, the chorus in the first Act, and the final chorus like Turkish music [using cymbals and triangle]. . . . It gives me such pleasure to work on this libretto that the first aria for Cavalieri [Konstanze] and the one for Adamberger [Belmonte], and the trio that concludes the first Act, are finished already. It is true that time is short; for it is to be performed in the middle of September – but the circumstances connected with the time when it is to be performed – and all other considerations in general – raise my spirits so much that I hurry to my desk with the greatest eagerness and remain sitting there with the greatest enjoyment. . . .

MOZART TO HIS FATHER

Vienna, 8 August 1781

I must write in a hurry, for I have this very moment finished the Janissaries' chorus. . . . Adamberger, Cavallieri and Fischer [Osmin] are highly satisfied with their Arias. . . . Yesterday I dined at Countess Thun's, and I am to do so again tomorrow – I have played her what is already finished. At the end of it she told me that she would stake her life that what I had written so far was certain to please – At this point I heed *no one's praise or blame* – until people have heard or seen the thing in full; but follow *my own instinct* alone.

MOZART TO HIS FATHER

Vienna, 26 September 1781

. . . The Opera at first opened with a monologue, and then I asked Herr Stephani to turn it into a little ariette, and that instead of the two chatting together after Osmin's little song there should be a duet. As we intended the role of Osmin for Herr Fischer, who has an admirable bass voice (though the Archbishop told me he sang too deep for a bass, and I assured him he would sing higher the next time), we must make good use of him, especially as he is a favourite with the public here. But in the original libretto Osmin had only one little song and that was all, except the Trio and the Finale. Now he has been given an aria in Act I and is to have another in Act II. I sketched out the whole aria for Herr Stephani; and the better part of the music was already written before Stephani knew anything about it. . . . In this way Osmin's rage becomes comic, because I use Turkish music for it. In composing the aria I have brought out his beautiful, deep notes (notwithstanding the Salzburg Midas). The *Drum beim Barte des Propheten* ['Therefore by the beard of the Prophet. . . .'], etc., is, indeed, in the same tempo, but with hurried notes; and as his rage is constantly increasing the allegro assai – coming in totally different time and a different key, and when people suppose the Aria to be already finished – will produce the most striking effect; for when a man is in such a violent rage he oversteps the bounds of order, moderation and propriety, he forgets himself – so the music too must forget itself. But since the passions, whether violent or no, must never be expressed so strongly as to disgust, and music, even in the most frightful situations, must never offend the ear, but is even then to give pleasure, and consequently must always remain musical, I did not choose a key in discord to F (the key of the aria), but one in harmony with it – not the nearest, D minor, but the one beyond that, A minor. As to Belmonte's Aria in A major – *O wie ängstlich, o wie feurig* ['O how anxious, O how ardent . . .'] – do you know how that is expressed – the throbbing, loving heart is likewise shown at once – by the 2 violins playing octaves. This is the *favourite aria* of everyone who has heard it – myself included – and was written especially to suit Adamberger's voice. . . .

The Janissaries' chorus is everything one could wish for a Janissaries' chorus – short and merry – and just the thing for the Viennese. In Konstanze's arias I have made some slight concessions to Mlle Cavalieri's flexible larynx . . .

All you have of the Overture is 14 bars. It is quite short – alternating continually between forte and piano; the Turkish music comes in at every forte – It modulates on through different keys – and I do not think anyone will be able to fall asleep while it lasts, even should he have had no sleep the night before. . . .

For technical reasons, the performance of 'Entführung' had to be postponed until the following summer. Meanwhile another incident took place which finally broke father Mozart's power over his son.

MOZART TO HIS FATHER

Vienna, 15 December 1781

Dearest Father,
You ask me for an explanation of the words with which I ended my last letter! Oh, how gladly would I have opened my heart to you long since; but I held back lest you should reproach me for *thinking of such a thing unseasonably* – although thinking can never be unseasonable. . . . To marry! – You are alarmed by the idea? But I entreat you, dearest, most beloved Father, to listen to me! I was obliged to disclose my intentions to you, now permit me also to disclose my reasons, which indeed are forcible ones. Nature's voice speaks within me as loudly as in any other man, and perhaps louder than in many a tall, strong lout. I cannot lead the same life as most young men do nowadays. Firstly, I have too much religion, secondly, too much love of my neighbour and sense of honour, to be able to seduce an innocent girl, and thirdly, too

much horror and disgust, dread and fear of diseases, and too much regard for my health, to be running after whores. Thus I can swear that until now I have had no dealings of this kind with any woman. If it had happened I would not conceal it from you, for it is always natural enough for a man to err, and to err *once* would be mere weakness – though I would not trust myself to promise that I should be satisfied with a single error if I once indulged myself in this respect – but I can stake my life on this assurance to you. I am well aware that this reason, powerful though it always is, has not sufficient weight. But my temperament is more disposed towards a tranquil, domestic life than towards rowdiness; moreover from youth up I have never been accustomed to attend to my own affairs, such as linen, clothes, etc. – and I can think of nothing more necessary to me than a wife. I assure you that I am often put to needless expense because I do not give heed to anything – I am quite persuaded that with a wife (and the same income I have by myself) I should manage better than I do as it is. And how many needless expenses would be saved! One incurs others in their stead, that is true – but one knows what they are, one can allow for them – in short, one leads a well-ordered life. In my eyes a bachelor is only half alive – my eyes are like that, I cannot help it. I have considered and reflected sufficiently on the matter, and my mind is made up. But who then is the object of my love? Do not be alarmed again, I implore you; but surely she is not a Weber? – Yes, a Weber – but not Josepha – not Sophie. – It is *Konstanze*, the middle one. I never met such different natures in any family as in this one. The eldest daughter is a lazy, coarse, perfidious creature and as sly as a fox. Madame Lange [Aloysia, his former love] is a false, malicious creature and a coquette. The youngest – is still too young to be anything at all – is nothing more than a kind-hearted but too frivolous girl! May God preserve her from seduction. The middle one, however, namely my dear, kind Konstanze, is the martyr among them, and perhaps for that very reason the most warm-hearted, the cleverest, and in short the best of them all. She attends to everything in the house, and yet can do nothing right. Oh, dearest Father, I could fill whole pages if I were to describe to you all the scenes the two of us have witnessed in that house. . . . She is not ugly, but she is far from beautiful. Her only beauties are a pair of little black eyes and a lovely figure. She has no wit, but enough good sense to be able to carry out her duties as wife and mother. She is not inclined to extravagance . . . and most of what a woman needs she can make for herself, and she dresses her own hair every day as well – understands housekeeping, has the kindest heart in the world – I love her, and she loves me with all her heart. Tell me, could I wish myself a better wife?

I should tell you too that when I left [my service] I was as yet not in love with her – that was born of her tender care and waiting upon me (while I was living in their house).

All I wish for now is to obtain a little security (and praise be to God I have real hope of that as well), and then I shall certainly ask for her hand, so that I may rescue the poor girl – and myself at the same time – and, I may say, make us all happy – for you will surely be so if I am? And half the *security* I earn, shall go to you. . . . Now you will sympathize with your son!. . . .

MOZART TO HIS FATHER

Vienna, 22 December 1781

. . . Meanwhile, I will only tell you that at dinner just recently, the Emperor, after praising me most highly, concluded with the words: *C'est un talent décidé.* And the day before yesterday I played at Court. Another pianist has arrived here, an Italian called *Clementi*. He too was summoned to Court. Yesterday 50 ducats were sent to me from there, which I needed very badly at the moment. . . .

Mozart was severely critical of his colleagues, which may not have endeared him to them. He frequently complained about the favour Salieri, the master of the Court Chapel, enjoyed at the Court, and he certainly did not appreciate Clementi, who must have been an extraordinary virtuoso.

MOZART TO HIS FATHER

Vienna, 12 January 1782

. . . Clementi plays well where the right hand comes into use. His strongest passages are thirds. For the rest he does not possess a jot of feeling or taste, in short he is a mere technician. . . .

MOZART TO HIS FATHER

Vienna, 10 April 1782

. . . Regarding what you say about the rumour that I shall quite certainly be taken into the Emperor's service, the reason why I have not written to you about it myself is that – for my part I have not heard a word about it. What is certain is that the whole town is full of it and a host of people have already congratulated me. . . . Things have gone so far that the Emperor has it in mind, and that without my having taken a single step in the matter. . . .

MOZART TO HIS FATHER

Vienna, 20 July 1782

Mon très cher Père,
I hope you duly received my last letter, in which I told you of the favourable reception of my Opera [*Die Entführung*]. Yesterday it was given for the 2nd time; would you believe it, the cabal was even worse yesterday than on the first night? They hissed right through the first Act. But they could not prevent the loud cries of 'Bravo' at the end of each aria. I pinned my hopes on the final Trio – but then, by ill-luck, Fischer [Osmin] broke down – with the result that Dauer [Pedrillo] followed suit – and Adamberger could not by himself make up for all the rest – so that the whole effect was lost and this time it was *not encored*. I was beside myself with rage, and so was Adamberger – and declared at once that I would not permit the opera to be given again without a short rehearsal beforehand (for the singers). In the 2nd Act both Duets were encored, as at the first performance, and so was Belmont's Rondeau, *Wenn der Freude Tränen fliessen* ['When tears of joy flow . . .']. The theatre was almost more crowded than on the first night. By the day before there was not one reserved seat to be had, either in the *Noble Parterre* or in the 3rd balcony; and not one box either. At the two performances, the Opera took 1,200 fl. . . .

MOZART TO HIS FATHER

Vienna, 27 July 1782

. . . Yesterday, in honour of all Nannerls [it was his sister's name-day], my opera was given for the third time, amid universal Applauso. And in spite of the appalling heat the theatre was again packed to the doors. There is to be another performance next Friday – but I have protested, for I will not allow it to be whipped up after this fashion. I must say that people have really gone mad about this opera. It does one good, all the same, to receive such applause. . . .

Dearest, most beloved Father! I must implore you, by all you hold dear in the world, to give your consent to my marriage with my dear Konstanze. Do not think that it is simply for the sake of getting married – if that were all, I would gladly wait – but I can see that it is absolutely necessary, for my honour and the honour of my betrothed, and for my own health and spirits. My heart is troubled and my mind bewildered – how can one think and work sensibly in those circumstances? Why is this so? Because most people believe we are already married – the mother is furious about it – and the poor girl and I are being tormented to death. This could so easily be remedied. . . . I await your consent with longing, dearest Father – I await it confidently – my honour and my reputation depend upon it – do not too long deny yourself the happiness of soon embracing your son and his wife. . . .

MOZART TO HIS FATHER

Vienna, 31 July 1782

. . . Meanwhile you will have received my last letter; and I do not doubt that in your next letter I shall receive your consent to my marriage; you could find no objection to it – and indeed you have none, as your letters show me! – for she is a good, honourable girl of good parentage – I am in a position to support her – we love each other – and want each other. . . . So there is no reason for delay – it would be better for my affairs to be put into proper order and for me to be made an honest man! God will always reward it; and I wish to have no cause to reproach myself. . . .

MOZART TO HIS FATHER

Vienna, 7 August 1782

Mon très cher Père,

You are very much mistaken in your son, if you believe him capable of dishonest conduct. My dear Konstanze, now (thank God) my lawful wife, had long since learnt from me what were my circumstances and what I could expect from you. But her friendship and love for me were so great that she willingly, with the greatest joy, sacrificed her whole future to my prospects. . . . And so it came about that having looked in vain on two post-days for a reply [from you], and the wedding being fixed for the day (when I was certain to be completely informed), being already quite assured of your consent and comforted, I was married, with God's blessing, to my beloved. . . . I now have only to ask your forgiveness for my too hasty trust in your fatherly affection; this frank confession on my part gives you fresh proof of my love of the truth and my horror of lies. . . . You will rejoice in my happiness, when you come to know her! and if in your opinion as in mine, a well-meaning, honest, virtuous woman is a happiness to her husband. . . .

My opera was given again yesterday (and this at Gluck's request); Gluck paid me many compliments on it. Tomorrow I am to dine with him. . . .

MOZART TO HIS FATHER

Vienna, 21 December 1782

. . . On the 10th my Opera was again performed, amid universal applause, this being the 14th time, and the house was as full as the first time – or rather, as it has always been. Count Rosenberg himself, at Galitzin's, has been seeking to persuade me to compose an Italian opera; I have already given an order for the newest libretti for *opere buffe* to be sent from Italy so that I may choose one, but have received nothing as yet . . . .

MOZART TO HIS FATHER

Vienna, 12 March 1783

. . . Yesterday my sister-in-law Lange had her concert at the theatre, and I too played a concerto. The theatre was crowded; and the audience again gave me such a splendid reception that I could not help but feel really gratified. I left the stage, but they would not stop clapping, and I had to play the Rondeau again; there was an absolute tempest of applause. This is a good omen for my own concert, which I am to give on Sunday, 23 March. I also gave my Symphony from the Concert Spirituel [the *Paris Symphony*, No. 32]. My sister-in-law sang the Aria *Non sò d'onde viene*. Gluck had the box next to the Langes', where my wife was sitting too. He could not praise the Symphony and the Aria enough, and invited all four of us to dine with him next Sunday. . . .

'Academies', public subscription concerts with orchestra, became an important source of income for Mozart during the early years of his married life. In a letter to his father (10 February 1784) he includes a list of 174 aristocratic subscribers to such an 'Academy', and he continues:

MOZART TO HIS FATHER

10 February 1784

. . . I by myself have some thirty more than Richter and Fischer together, for on the last three Wednesdays in Lent, beginning on 17 March, I am to give three subscription concerts at the Trattner Hall; the price for all three concerts is 6 fl. I shall give two concerts in the theatre this year; so you can easily imagine that I must play new things, and that means composing them. The whole morning is given over to my pupils, and nearly every evening I have to play [he lists 22 events, from 26 February to 3 April]. . . . Have I not enough to do? I do not think I shall get out of practice in these circumstances. . . .

MOZART TO HIS SISTER, NANNERL, ON THE EVE OF HER WEDDING

Vienna, 18 August 1784

Ma très chère soeur,

Potz Sapperment! It is high time I wrote to you, if I wish my letter to find you still a Vestal! Another few days and good-bye to that.

My wife and I wish you all good fortune and happiness in your change of condition and are only heartily sorry that we cannot have the pleasure of being present at your wedding. . . . Our one regret now is for our dear father, who will be left all alone! True, you will not be far away and he can often drive out to visit you – but now he is tied again to that cursed chapel! Were I in Father's situation, however, this is what I should do: I should ask the Archbishop to allow me to retire (as a man who has served so long already) – and once I had been granted my pension I would go to my daughter at St Gilgen and live there in peace; if the Archbishop refused my request, I would ask for my dismissal and go to my son in Vienna. . . .

And now I send you 1,000 more good wishes from Vienna to Salzburg, especially that the pair of you may live as happily together as we two; this leads me to bring out a little piece of advice from my poetical brain-box: now do but listen:

The married state will teach you more
Than you had clearly known before.
'T'will by experience show to you
What Mother Eve first had to do
That ever Cain could come to life.
But Sis, the duties of a wife
Are heartfelt pleasure and not strife;
Trust me, they'll not prove burdensome.
Yet this world can't be always fun.
Marriage brings many joys, indeed,
But cares come too, with equal speed.
So when your husband for an hour
Frowns on you with a mien that's sour,
Though faults you've not committed one,
Tell yourself these are mannish flights
And murmur, Lord, thy will be done
By day – and mine o' nights.

Your candid brother
W. A. Mozart

LEOPOLD MOZART TO HIS DAUGHTER AT ST GILGEN

Vienna, 16 February 1785

... That your brother has a fine lodging, well appointed for housekeeping, you may conclude from his paying a rent of 460 fl. On the Friday, at 6 o'clock in the evening, we drove to the first of his subscription concerts, where there was a great assembly of people of rank. ... The concert was matchless, the orchestra most excellent; apart from the symphonies, a singer from the Italian Theatre sang 2 arias. Then came a new and most excellent piano concerto by Wolfgang, on which the copyist was still at work when we arrived; and your brother did not even have time to play the Rondeau through once, because he was obliged to look over the parts. ...

On Saturday Herr *Joseph Haydn* and the two Baron Tinti visited us, the new quartets were played, but only the 3 new ones, which he has composed in addition to the other 3, which we already have – it is true they are a little easier, but most excellently composed. Herr Haydn said to me: 'I say to you before God, on my word of honour, *your son is the greatest composer whom I know personally or by name*; he has taste and the greatest skill in composition as well.' On Saturday evening at the theatre there was a concert for the Italian singer, Mme Laschi, who is now returning to Italy. ... Your brother played a magnificent concerto which he had composed for Mlle Paradis for Paris [B flat major, K. No. 456]. ... When your brother went away the Emperor waved to him with his hat, calling out: *bravo Mozart.*

The six string quartets mentioned above were dedicated to Haydn.

Leopold's report is interesting in more than one respect. It reflects the old man's keen satisfaction with his son's success and reputation, but betrays at the same time a certain anxious misgiving at his expensive way of living.

There is a well-known legend of the overture to 'Don Giovanni' having been written the night before the first performance. Whether this is true has never been established, but the passage in Leopold's letter that refers to a pianoforte concerto by Mozart – it was the Concerto in D minor, one of his most outstanding masterpieces – shows that an occurrence of that kind was quite possible and much in keeping with Mozart's uncanny facility as well as with the easy-going performing habits of his time.

These were Mozart's prosperous years, a period of unparalleled productivity, culminating in 'The Marriage of Figaro', performed in Vienna and in Prague in 1786, 'Don Giovanni', performed in Prague in 1787 and in Vienna in 1788, and 'Così fan tutte', performed in Vienna in 1790. After 1787, however, Mozart found it increasingly difficult to make ends meet. The success of his works at a time of unprotected copyright brought hardly any financial reward, apart from a modest commission fee; pupils and subscribers dwindled and expenses were rising with a growing family, the birth and death of children, and frequent illness.

In 1785 Mozart had joined the society of freemasons. The last letter he wrote to his father, who died in May 1787, is tinged with masonic thought, but perhaps also with a presentiment of an early death – not totally inexplicable, considering the excessive strain of working under continuous pressure and the exhaustion he must have felt at times.

MOZART TO HIS FATHER

4 April 1787

. . . As death, strictly speaking, is the true goal of our lives, I have for some years past been making myself so familiar with this truest and best friend of man that its aspect has not only ceased to appal me, but I find it very soothing and comforting! And I thank my God that He has vouchsafed me the happiness of an opportunity (you will understand me) to recognize it as the *key* to our true bliss. I never lie down to sleep without reflecting that (young as I am) I may perhaps not see another day – yet none of those who know me can say that I am morose or melancholy in society – and I thank my Creator every day for this happiness and wish from the bottom of my heart that all my fellow men might share it. . . .

MOZART TO HIS SISTER

Vienna, 19 December 1787

. . . You may perhaps know already that I composed *Don Juan* at Prague and that it won the greatest possible applause – but perhaps you do not know that His Maj. the Emperor has now taken me into his service. I am sure the news will be welcome to you. . . .

The appointment as 'Kammer-Compositeur', mentioned before, was a great satisfaction to Mozart; but it by no means solved his financial problems. Twenty letters of his to a wealthy fellow-mason and lover of music, Michael Puchberg, have been preserved. Punctuating the last three years of his life, they give a pathetic impression of an ever-increasing agony of distress. Here are a few of them.

MOZART TO HIS FRIEND MICHAEL PUCHBERG

June 1788

Dearest Brother,
Your true friendship and brotherly love embolden me to ask you for a great favour: I still owe you 8 ducats – and not only am I unable at the moment to repay them, but my confidence in you is so great that I venture to beg you to help me, only until next week (when my concerts at the Casino begin), with the loan of 100 fl.; the subscription money cannot fail to be in my hands by that time, and I can quite easily repay you 136 fl., with my warmest thanks. . . .

MOZART TO MICHAEL PUCHBERG

17 June 1788

. . . The firm belief that you are my true friend, and that you know me as *an honourable man*, encourages me to open my heart to you completely and to make you the following request. . . . If, out of love and friendship for me, you would help me for 1 or 2 years with 1 or 2 thousand guilders at a suitable rate of interest, you would be doing me the service of a lifetime! You yourself will assuredly find it *sound* and *true* that for me it is hateful, indeed impossible, to live in dependence upon irregular earnings! – unless one has something in reserve, at least to cover necessaries, it is impossible to put order into one's affairs – *nothing* can be done with nothing. If you will do me this kindness, I shall *primo* (being thus provided) be able to make necessary payments *when they are due* and therefore more easily, whereas I now continually delay and must then often pay out at once all I have received, and that at the most inconvenient moment. *Secondo*, I shall be able to work with an easier mind and a lighter heart, and thus earn more. As for security, I do not believe you will have any doubts! You know pretty well how I stand and are acquainted with my principles! As for the subscriptions you need have no anxiety; I am now extending the time by a few months; I have some hope of finding more supporters abroad than here. . . .

Now I look forward eagerly to your reply – and truly, to a *favourable reply*; and I do not know, but I take you for *a man* who, *like myself*, when he can do so, will surely assist his friend, if he is a *true friend*, his brother if *indeed his brother*. Should you perhaps be unable to spare such a sum at once, I entreat you to lend me until tomorrow *at least* a *couple of hundred guilders*, for my landlord in the Landstrasse was so insistent that I was obliged to pay him on the spot (to avoid unpleasantness), which has greatly upset my finances. . . .

MOZART TO MICHAEL PUCHBERG

Vienna, July 1788

Dearest Friend, and Brother in the Order,
Amid my toils and anxieties I have brought my affairs to such a pass that I must needs raise a little money on these 2 pawnbroker's tickets. I implore you by our friendship to do me this favour, but it must be done instantly. Forgive my importunity, but you know my circumstances. Ah, had you but done as I asked you! If you do it even now, all will go as I wish. . . .

A journey to Berlin by way of Prague, Dresden, and Leipzig resulted in a commission by the King of Prussia, Frederick William III, for a set of string quartets, and Mozart was able to bring home 100 Friedrich d'ors. But this did not solve the burning problem. On his journey he wrote the most tender letters to Konstanze, from whom he found himself separated for the first time since their marriage.

MOZART TO HIS WIFE

Dresden, 13 April 1789

. . . Dearest little wife, if only I also had a letter from you already! – if I tried to tell you all the things I do with your dear picture, I think you would often laugh – for instance, when I take it out of its case, I say Good-day to you, Stanzerl! Good-day to you, little rogue – pointed-nose – scrap of nothing! and when I put it back again I slip it in little by little saying all the time, Stu! – Stu! – Stu! [term of endearment]. But with the special emphasis that this most meaningful word demands, and at the last moment, quickly, Good-night, little Mouse, sleep well! – Now I think I have written something foolish enough (at least to the world), but to us, because we love each other so dearly, it is not foolish at all. This is the 6th day since I parted from you and, by heaven, it already seems like a year. . . .

From the summer of 1789 Mozart's desperate cries for help were increasing in frequency. Puchberg did help, at least occasionally, and in the end Mozart owed him 1,000 florins. At the time of the following letters he was writing the music of 'Così fan tutte', the graceful lightness and beauty of which offers a fascinating illustration of the artist's capacity for isolating himself from the surrounding world and from all his worries. Besides, he never spurned a commission that came his way, turning even a piece for a wretched mechanical organ into a finished work of art.

MOZART TO MICHAEL PUCHBERG

Vienna, 12 July 1789

. . . God! I am in a situation in which I would not wish to see my worst enemy; and if you forsake me, dearest friend and brother, I am lost – by my misfortune, not my fault – and my poor wife and child as well. . . . I need scarce repeat to you that this unhappy illness [of Konstanze] is impeding all my efforts to earn money; but what I must tell you is that despite my wretched circumstances I resolved to give subscription concerts in my house . . . but in that, too, I have failed; fate is alas so unfriendly to me, *though only in Vienna*, that I can earn nothing whatever I do; 14 days ago I sent round a list, and the one and only name it bears is *Swieten* [Baron van Swieten, one of Mozart's chief supporters in Vienna]. . . . Since it now appears that the health of my dear little wife is improving daily, I should nevertheless have been able to set to work again, if this blow, this new heavy blow, had not fallen. . . . Meanwhile I am writing 6 easy piano sonatas for Princess Friederika and 6 quartets for the King [both commissions from Berlin]. . . . Only reflect that without your support, your friend and brother will lose his honour, his tranquillity and perhaps his life. . . .

MOZART TO MICHAEL PUCHBERG

Vienna, 20 February 1790

. . . I entreat you, dearest friend, to send me a few ducats *if you are able*, only for a day or two, for the matter is one that will not brook delay but must be settled instantly. . . .

In 1791, the last year of his life, the bulk of Mozart's output grew to heroic dimensions. In midsummer he interrupted his work on 'The Magic Flute', written for his friend and fellow-mason Schikaneder, director of the suburban 'Freihaus-Theatre' in Vienna, in order to compose the music to 'La Clemenza di Tito', commissioned for Prague. At the same time, before setting out for Prague, he accepted a commission for a Requiem from a stranger, who in the end turned out to be the agent of a noble amateur who wanted to pass it off as his own work. Back in Vienna after the performance of 'Titus', he finished 'The Magic Flute', the first performance of which, on 30 September, was the greatest success of his life. At that time, however, he must have been conscious of having burned his candle at both ends. Puzzled by the mysterious stranger who had ordered the Requiem, he became obsessed with the idea of writing it for himself.

The last letters of Mozart of which we know are happy reports of the success of 'The Magic Flute' to his wife Konstanze, who was taking the waters at Baden, a health resort near Vienna. Emanuel Schikaneder, the director of the 'Freihaus-Theater', where 'The Magic Flute' was being performed, played the part of Papageno.

MOZART TO HIS WIFE

7–8 October 1791

. . . I have just come home from the Opera; it was as full as ever. – The Duetto *Mann und Weib*, etc., and the *Glöckchenspiel* in Act I were encored as usual – so was the boys' trio in Act 2 – but what pleases me most is the quiet approval! – one can see clearly that this opera is steadily increasing in popularity. . . .

The most curious thing about it is that on the very evening when my new opera was performed for the first time amid so much applause, that same evening at Prague *Tito* was performed, for the last time, also with extraordinary success – every item was applauded. . . .

I went onto the stage for Papageno's aria with the *Glöckchenspiel*, because today I felt an impulse to play it myself. I played a joke on Schikaneder [Papageno]: where he has a pause, I played an arpeggio – he started – looked off-stage and saw me. When the second pause came, I did nothing – so he waited and would not go on. I guessed what he was thinking and played another chord – whereat he hit the *Glöckchenspiel* and said *hold your tongue* – at which everybody laughed – I think this joke made many people notice for the first time that he does not play the instrument himself. . . .

Mozart fell seriously ill soon after. In bed, he worked on the 'Requiem' to his last breath. He died on 5 December. The nature of his illness has remained a mystery among experts, but in his state of nervous tension and exhaustion any acute illness might have proved fatal, in view of the empirical and primitive nature of medicine at that time.

Using whatever sketches were left, Mozart's faithful pupil Süssmayer completed the score of the 'Requiem', in order to secure the fee for Konstanze, who was left destitute with two children.

Mozart had a pauper's burial.

His fame spread rapidly after his death.

Five years later, Europe would have been at his feet.

A comparison of Ludwig van Beethoven *(1770–1827) with his great predecessors Haydn and Mozart reveals more than a striking contrast of characters; two periods of history are confronted, and the music of their greatest representatives reflects a radical change in the cultural climate. The most obvious external cause of this change was the gradual decay of the aristocratic prerogative of wealth and power. With this the maintenance of music, hitherto an expensive hobby of noble patrons, was left to an anonymous community of citizens.*

Beethoven, living in a time of transition, had undeniable advantages from both sides. Aristocratic patronage was not only instrumental in his early career, but maintained him throughout his life without, however, encroaching upon his personal liberty. Firmly established as a composer of high reputation before he was thirty, he could demand fees from publishers as no composer before, received more commissions than he could cope with, and was able to maintain his independence. In 1808, moreover, when King Jérôme of Westphalia made him a tempting offer of a highly paid position in Kassel, three of his most exalted patrons, Archduke Rudolph, Prince Lobkowitz, and Prince Kinsky, combined in awarding him a considerable annual pension in order to keep him in Vienna.

Beethoven's letters are of extraordinary interest because they are written without any restraint. Sometimes rude, often moody, often offensive, never able to control his temper or his passion, Beethoven writes in a style of the most impulsive directness. Two letters to a respected contemporary illustrate amusingly his manner of flaring up and immediately regretting it.

BEETHOVEN TO JOHANN NEPOMUK HUMMEL, COMPOSER AND PIANIST

Vienna, 1799

Never come near me again! you are a faithless cur, and may the hangman take all faithless curs. [Beethoven here uses the insulting 'er' for 'you'.]

Beethoven

BEETHOVEN TO HUMMEL, ONE DAY LATER

My dearest Nazerl,

You are an honest fellow and I now perceive you were right; so come to see me this afternoon; Schuppanzigh will be here too, and the pair of us will scold you, cuff you and shake you to your heart's content. [Beethoven here uses the familiar and affectionate 'Du'.]

A warm embrace from

your Beethoven
also known as Little Dumpling

Here are another two letters, referring to a similar incident; the innocent victim was one of Beethoven's closest and earliest friends, Stephan von Breuning. All the impulsiveness and directness of feeling which is so overwhelming in his music is expressed in such letters, and also his brooding, sullen loneliness.

BEETHOVEN TO FERDINAND RIES, A PUPIL AND FRIEND

Baden, 24 July 1804

. . . I expect you were surprised at the von Breuning business; believe me, my dear fellow, my outburst of rage was only the result of many previous unpleasant incidents with him. I have the capacity to hide my feelings and restrain myself in a great many circumstances; but if someone irritates me at a moment when I am more disposed to anger, I explode more violently than anyone. . . . No, he will never recover the place he once held in my heart. . . .

BEETHOVEN TO STEPHAN VON BREUNING IN VIENNA

1804

Behind this picture [a miniature portrait of Beethoven by Hornemann, 1802], my dear, beloved Steffen, let all that once passed between us be hidden for ever. I know I wounded your heart. My own agitation, which you must certainly have perceived, punished me sufficiently for it. What turned me against you was not malice – no, in that case I should no longer deserve your friendship; passion on your side and on mine – but I was full of distrust of you. . . . My portrait has long been intended for you; as you know, I always intended to give it to somebody – and to whom could I present it with the warmest affection but to you, my faithful, kind, noble Steffen? Forgive me if I caused you pain; I myself suffered no less; not seeing you for so long, I felt keenly for the first time how dear you are to me and ever will be. . . .

In 1800, at the age of thirty, Beethoven was already regarded as one of the most outstanding composers of his day. He was admired as a virtuoso of fascinating powers, and generously patronized by Vienna's high aristocracy. By the turn of the century, however, the dark fate under which he was doomed to suffer for the rest of his life had already fallen upon him.

BEETHOVEN TO HIS FRIEND CARL AMENDA

Vienna, 1 June [1800]

... Your Beethoven is living most unhappily at odds with Nature and his Creator; several times already I have cursed the latter for exposing His Creatures to the most trifling accidents, whereby the finest flowers are often destroyed and broken. You must know that the noblest part of me, my hearing, has greatly declined; while you were still with me I already had some inkling of this, but said nothing; and now it has grown steadily worse. Whether it is curable remains to be seen; they say it is caused by the condition of my bowels. In that respect I am almost completely cured. As to whether my hearing will now improve as well, I indeed hope so, but faintly: such diseases are the most persistent. How sad my life will be henceforth, deprived of all I love and value, and withal surrounded by such miserable, selfish people. ... I must say I find Lichnowsky the staunchest of all; since last year he has made me an allowance of 600 fl.; thanks to that and to the ready sale of my work, I need have no anxiety about making both ends meet. Everything I write now I could sell 5 times over at once. ...

How happy I should now be, if only my hearing were unimpaired. ... Melancholy resignation, in which I must now take refuge; I have indeed resolved to disregard all this, but how shall I be able to do so? ... *I beg you to keep the matter of my hearing a great secret and not to confide it to anyone whatsoever....*

BEETHOVEN TO HIS FRIEND DR FRANZ WEGELER IN BONN

Vienna, 29 June 1800

... You ask about my circumstances; well, as it happens they are not so bad. Since last year, *Lichnowsky* – who, incredible as you may think it, has always been and still is my warmest friend (there have, indeed, been some slight disagreements between us, but these perhaps only strengthened our friendship) – has made me a guaranteed allowance of 600 fl., on which I can draw until I find a suitable post; my compositions are bringing in a deal of money, and indeed I have almost more commissions than I can satisfy. Moreover, for each work I can have six or seven publishers, or even more if I choose to concern myself with the business; they no longer make agreements with me; I state my terms and they pay up. ... But now that envious demon, my bad health, has played me a scurvy trick, namely: for the last three years my hearing has grown steadily weaker, and the first cause of this is said to be my bowels, which as you know were already troublesome in the old days, but grew worse after I came here, for I was afflicted with constant diarrhoea which made me extremely weak. . . . Last winter I was in a really poor way . . . until about four weeks ago, when I went to *Vering*. . . . He has almost put a stop to the violent diarrhoea; he ordered me to take warm baths of Danube water, to which I must always add a little bottleful of tonic stuff, gave me no medicine at all until, some four days ago, he prescribed stomach pills and an ear-wash; and, as a result, I certainly feel stronger and better in health – except for my ears, which hum and sing all day and all night. I really lead a wretched life, for nearly two years I have been avoiding almost all company, because I simply cannot tell people I am deaf. If I had any other profession it would be easier, but in my profession this is a terrible situation; and as for my enemies – of whom I have no small number – what would they say about it! . . . If I am at a certain distance from instruments or singers, I cannot hear the high notes; in conversation it is astonishing that there are still people who have never noticed it; I am usually absent-minded, and they put it down to that. Moreover, I can often scarcely hear a person who speaks in a low voice – the tone, yes, but not the words; yet if anyone shouts I find it insupportable. What will happen next, heaven only knows. *Vering says there will certainly be an improvement, if not a complete recovery.* Often already I have cursed my life; Plutarch has taught me resignation. If it proves otherwise I shall brave my fate, though at times I shall be the most unhappy of God's creatures. . . . Resignation! What a miserable refuge, yet it is the only one left for me. . . .

With his increasing deafness, Beethoven's urge for communication became more and more concentrated on his creative activity. His letters rarely contain anything more than information on practical matters, business transactions, problems of daily life, and copious invective whenever his personal wrath is aroused. Business letters always have a better chance of survival than private ones, and a great many letters to his publishers have been preserved. They are instructive in many ways. From the following, for example, one learns that a dedication was not always a mere act of homage, but a business proposition: the person honoured by a dedication acquired an exclusive right to the work concerned, restricted by agreement to a term of a year or two. Most of Beethoven's earlier works were published only after such an interval and all his earlier symphonies and concertos were first performed by the private orchestras of such liberal patrons as Prince Lichnowsky, Prince Lobkowitz, or Prince Kinsky, to whom they were dedicated. The unnamed lady mentioned in the following letter had obviously suggested a Revolution Sonata, but Beethoven, always ready to accept a commission, was by no means amenable to any further guidance. Although an incarnate republican and a stern critic of the reactionary Austrian government, he was no Don Quixote.

BEETHOVEN TO THE PUBLISHER HOFMEISTER IN LEIPZIG

Vienna, 8 April 1802

Gentlemen, have you all gone out of your minds? To suggest that I should compose *such a Sonata*? When the revolutionary fever was at its height, there might have been something in it; but now, when everyone is trying to get back on to the old track, and Buonaparte has concluded his Concordat with the Pope – such a sonata as that? If it were to be *Missa pro Sancta Maria a tre voci*, or a *Vesper*, etc., I would pick up my brush at once – and write a *Credo in unum* in big semi-breves. But good God – such a sonata as that, in this dawn of a new Christian epoch – hoho, leave me out, it won't come about! Now, in the quickest time, my answer: the lady may have a sonata by me; and from the aesthetic standpoint, generally speaking, I will follow her plan – though not as regards the keys; the price will be 5 ducats: that will entitle her to keep it for her own enjoyment for a year, neither I nor she being allowed to publish it; at the end of the year, the sonata becomes my sole property – i.e. I can and shall publish it, and she – if she feels it would be an honour – can always ask me to dedicate it to her. . . .

One can appreciate Beethoven's intolerance of criticism. His music, fascinating to connoisseurs and amateurs right from the beginning, spread rapidly, and publishers found sufficient immediate profit in printing it to accept the risk involved in the prevailing anarchy of copyright. But critics were not easy to please. One of Beethoven's publishers, Breitkopf and Härtel in Leipzig, who issued the only serious German music magazine of that time, the 'Allgemeine Musikalische Zeitung', seems to have found it occasionally quite convenient to put such a pretentious composer in his place. They must have known better than Beethoven did himself how little harm such critical pinpricks could do to the sale of a work of an already famous composer.

It is not without interest, by the way, to learn that at a time when publishers found it already profitable to print Bach's music, his last surviving daughter was totally destitute, living on public charity.

BEETHOVEN TO THE PUBLISHERS BREITKOPF & HÄRTEL IN LEIPZIG

Vienna, 22 April 1801

. . . Advise your critics to show greater caution and prudence, particularly in considering the work of young composers; this may have a discouraging effect upon many who might otherwise prove successful. For my part, I assuredly do not consider myself so near to perfection as to brook no reproof; yet your critic's outcry against me was at first so humiliating that when I began to compare myself with others I could hardly object to it, but remained quite calm and thought 'they do not understand'. I was the better able to keep calm about it when I observed how men were praised to the skies who count for very little among the better people over here – and have almost disappeared here, however worthy they might otherwise be. But now *pax vobiscum* – peace between you and me – I would never have mentioned it at all if you had not done so yourselves. . . .

When I visited a good friend of mine the other day and he showed me what had been collected for *the daughter of the immortal god of harmony* [J. S. Bach's youngest daughter, Regina Susanna, 1742–1809], I was amazed that Germany, and especially *your Germany*, should have raised so small a sum for a person I honour for her father's sake. . . .

BEETHOVEN TO BREITKOPF & HÄRTEL

September 1803

. . . Please give my humble thanks to the editor of the *Musikalische Zeitung* for his kindness in permitting the insertion of such a flattering report on my Oratorio [*Christ on the Mount of Olives*] . . . it presumably shows their impartiality – towards me – I do not mind if that makes the *M.Z.* happy.

How much magnanimity is expected of a real artist – sometimes in vain, it is true; but on the other hand, how abominably, how meanly and with what alacrity people attack us. . . .

BEETHOVEN TO BREITKOPF & HÄRTEL

Vienna, 5 July 1806

. . . I hear the *Musikalische Zeitung* has been hard on the symphony [the *Eroica*] which I sent you last year, and which you returned to me. I have not read it; if you think you are doing me harm with it, you are mistaken; on the contrary, you bring discredit on your paper—the more so since I too have made no secret of the fact that you returned this symphony to me, with other compositions. Remember me most kindly to Herr v. Rochlitz [the critic of that magazine], I hope his bad blood against me has somewhat cooled. . . .

BEETHOVEN TO BREITKOPF & HÄRTEL

Vienna, 9 October 1811

. . . You may give my oratorio, *Christ on the Mount of Olives*, and anything else as well, to whatever critic you choose. I am sorry I wrote to you at all about the wretched article; who can possibly enquire about such criticism when he sees the most wretched scribblers being praised to the skies by equally wretched critics, and how harshly, in general, they deal with works of art – as they must, because of their clumsiness, which prevents them from immediately finding the proper measure, as the shoemaker finds his last. . . . And now, criticize as long as you choose, I wish you joy of it; even if it sometimes irritates me slightly, like a gnat-bite, it ends by turning into a great joke; cri-cri-cri-cri-cri-ti-ti-ci-ci-ci-ci-ze-ze-ze—*not to all eternity, for that you cannot do*. And so God be with you! . . .

Pirated editions of Beethoven's music, proof of its popularity, were abundant. He tried occasionally to uphold the interests of his legal publishers by a public declaration. This was all he could do. The first legal provision against unauthorized re-publication came in Napoleonic France, and it is to this that Beethoven refers in his protest against a pirate publisher in Mainz, at that time under French occupation.

NOTICE PUBLISHED BY BEETHOVEN IN THE 'WIENER ZEITUNG'

22 January 1803

To all Music-lovers

I hereby inform the public that my Quintet in C Major [Op. 29], which I myself announced long ago, has now been published by Breitkopf & Härtel at Leipzig, and at the same time I declare that I have no connection whatsoever with the edition of this Quintet which was brought out at the same time by Messrs. Artaria and Mollo at Vienna. My principal reason for making this declaration is that this edition is full of errors, incorrect, and quite useless to a player, whereas Messrs. Breitkopf & Härtel, the legal owners of this Quintet, have done everything necessary to produce the work in the finest possible form.

Ludwig van Beethoven

NOTICE PUBLISHED BY BEETHOVEN IN THE 'INTELLIGENZBLATT ZUR ALLGEMEINEN MUSIKALISCHEN ZEITUNG'

Leipzig, November 1803

Herr Carl Zulehner, an engraver at Mainz, has announced an edition of my complete works for pianoforte and strings. I consider it my duty to make it publicly known thereby to all music-lovers that I have not the least connection with this edition. I would never have offered to participate in a collected edition of my works, an undertaking I regard in any case as premature, without first consulting the publishers of the individual works, and taking steps to ensure the accuracy which is lacking in the editions of several of them. I must also point out that no pirated edition of my works can ever be complete, for several new works will shortly appear in Paris, and Herr Zulehner, as a French subject, will not be allowed to engrave copies of these. . . .

In one case Beethoven tried to forestall a critical reprimand by personally reporting to his publisher an unfortunate incident in one of his 'academies' in Vienna. At the time he was perhaps not quite conscious yet of his decline as a performer, owing to his growing infirmity and consequent lack of aural control.

BEETHOVEN TO BREITKOPF & HÄRTEL

Vienna, 7 January 1809

. . . It is possible that articles reviling my last concert may again be sent from here to the *Musikalische Zeitung*. I certainly do not wish everything hostile to me to be suppressed; but it must be realized that no one has more personal enemies here than I; which is not difficult to understand, since the musical situation here is becoming worse and worse. . . . I had to give my concert, on which occasion obstacles were put in my path by people in every quarter of the musical world. . . . Although, through no fault of mine, several mistakes occurred, the public gave an enthusiastic welcome to everything – despite which scribblers from this town will certainly not fail to send more of their paltry attacks on me to the *Musikalische Zeitung*. What chiefly angered the musicians was that when they made careless mistakes in the simplest, most straightforward passages in the world, I suddenly stopped them and shouted *play that again* – which had never happened before; at which the audience showed its delight. . . .

There is another account of this event in a diary of a musical journey by Johann Friedrich Reichardt (*1752–1814*). *Reichardt was a competent musician and spirited writer, and a friend of Goethe, whose 'Claudine von Villa Bella' he set to music, very much to the poet's satisfaction. One gathers from this account the enormous vogue Beethoven enjoyed in Vienna at the time, the lively interest in music among the aristocracy, and the hardships to be endured when going to a theatre during winter.*

FROM REICHARDT'S 'VERTRAUTE BRIEFE, GESCHRIEBEN AUF EINER REISE NACH WIEN' (1808–9)

Vienna, 25 December 1808

Last week, when all the theatres were closed and the evenings given over to public music recitals and concerts, my zeal and my determination to hear everything placed me in a considerable dilemma. This was particularly so on the 22nd, when the Viennese musicians were giving their first great concert of the season at the Burgtheater in aid of their large and admirable foundation for widows, while *Beethoven* was giving a concert for his benefit at the big theatre in the suburbs ['Theater an der Wien'] with a programme consisting entirely of his own compositions. I could not possibly miss that, so I gratefully accepted Prince von Lobkowitz's kind offer to take me out there and give me a seat in his box. There, in the bitterly cold theatre, we held out from half-past six until half-past ten, and discovered yet again that it is easy to have too much of a good thing – let alone a powerful thing. But neither I nor the exceedingly kindhearted and tactful Prince – whose box was in the first tier, quite close to the stage, where the orchestra was placed with Beethoven conducting it – felt we could leave the box before the very end of the concert, though many faulty performances put a great strain on our patience. Poor Beethoven depended on this concert of his for the only clear profit he could make and keep in the entire year, and in arranging it and carrying it out he had met with strong opposition and only weak support. The singers and orchestra had been scraped together at random, and some of the pieces – all of which were full of the greatest difficulties – had not been played right through even once at rehearsal. Nevertheless you will be astonished to hear how many compositions by that fertile genius and tireless worker were performed during the four hours.

First came a *Pastoral Symphony*, or reminiscence of country life. . . . Each movement was a very long, perfectly constructed piece full of vivid description and brilliant ideas and figures; so that this Pastoral

Symphony lasted longer by itself than the time allowed for an entire Court concert with us [at Kassel].

Next came . . . a lengthy *Italian Scene* [the aria *Ah perfido*] sung by Mademoiselle Killitzky, the beautiful Bohemian with the lovely voice. In such terrible cold, the beautiful girl cannot be blamed for the fact that on this occasion her voice shivered rather than sang; for we ourselves were shivering as we sat, swathed in furs and cloaks, in our closed-in boxes. . . . A *Gloria* [from the Mass in C major] with choral singing and solos, which, however, was unfortunately very badly performed. . . . A new and tremendously difficult *Pianoforte Concerto* [No. 4, G major] which Beethoven played amazingly well at top speed. He positively sang the Adagio – a masterly piece of beautiful, continuous melody – on his instrument, with deep, melancholy feeling which flooded through me, too, as he played. . . . A vast, very elaborate over-long Symphony [the Fifth] . . . a *Heilig* [the *Sanctus* from the Mass in C major], also with choral singing and solo parts, which, like the *Gloria*, was unhappily quite spoilt in performance. . . . A long Fantasia, in which Beethoven displayed all his virtuosity, and finally, by way of conclusion, another Fantasia [the Choral Fantasia, Op. 80], where the orchestra soon joined in, and finally even the chorus. This strange idea came to grief in its execution, for the orchestra fell into a state of such complete bewilderment that Beethoven, possessed by the artist's sacred fire, forgot his audience and his surroundings and suddenly shouted 'Stop there and take it again from the beginning!' You can imagine how I and all his other friends suffered for him. At that moment I even wished I had had the courage to leave earlier. . . .

That morning I had already heard, at Schuppanzigh's house, three beautiful quartets by Haydn, Mozart and Beethoven. . . .

31 December 1808

. . . Again I spent a musical evening in two sections. First a quartet at Countess Erdödy's house. Beethoven gave a virtuoso performance, full of enthusiasm, of the new trios he composed recently [Op. 70], one of which contained a divine *cantabile* movement (in 3/4 time in A flat major) [Op. 70, No. 2, 3rd movement] such as I never heard before in his work; it is indeed the most charming, graceful thing I ever heard; it melts and elevates my soul whenever I think of it. . . .

8 January 1809

. . . A string quartet evening at Schuppanzigh's, where a very beautiful quartet by Romberg, one by Mozart and a quartet by Beethoven – highly original, and particularly well executed – were performed. . . .

And the same evening (at Prince Lobkowitz's house) a grand concert at which Archduke Rudolf, the Emperor's brother, played several very difficult compositions for the fortepiano, some by Prince Louis Ferdinand and others by Beethoven, with great skill, accuracy and tenderness. . . .

15 January 1809

An evening of really grand music at Countess Erdödy's, where Beethoven again played new, magnificent things and improvised wonderfully. . . .

In general, performing was more or less an act of improvisation, with insufficient rehearsal time and a scarcity of competent orchestral players. The composer must have suffered agonies at the performance to which he refers in his letter to Sebastian Meyer, the first Pizarro in Beethoven's 'Leonore', the original version of 'Fidelio'.

BEETHOVEN TO SEBASTIAN MEYER

April 1806

. . . I wish you would beg Herr v. Seyfried to conduct my opera today; I would like to watch and listen to it myself today from a distance; at least that will not try my patience so sorely as when I have to listen to my music being mangled at close quarters! I can never help thinking it is done on purpose to upset me. I say nothing about the wind instruments; but that all pp, crescendo, all decresc. and all *forte* ff passages should be deleted from my opera! Yet none of them is played. I shall lose all interest in composing if it is to sound like *that*. . . .

In 1813 – five years after Reichardt's visit – Louis Spohr (*1784–1859*) *settled in Vienna where he frequently met Beethoven. Spohr has left an autobiography which contains valuable information on the musical life of his time. His description of Beethoven as a performer gives a pathetic impression of the great man's misery.*

FROM SPOHR'S 'SELBSTBIOGRAPHIE'

Beethoven's new compositions gave exceptional pleasure, especially the Symphony in A major (the Seventh); the wonderful second movement was encored; on me too it made a deep and lasting impression. The performance was quite masterly, despite Beethoven's hesitant and often comical conducting.

One could see quite clearly that the poor deaf Master could no longer hear the *piano* passages in his music. But this was particularly obvious at one point in the latter half of the first *Allegro* in the symphony. Here there are two pauses, in close succession, the second of them being followed by a *pianissimo*. Beethoven must have overlooked the fact, for he began to beat time again before the orchestra had even come to this second pause. Thus, without knowing it, he was already ten or twelve bars ahead of the orchestra by the time they resumed playing – *pianissimo*, of course. In order to indicate this [the *pianissimo* passage] in his own way, Beethoven had crawled right underneath the music-stand. During the *crescendo* that followed, he came back into view, gradually straightening up, and at the moment when, by his reckoning, the *forte* was due to begin, he leapt into the air. As no *forte* came, he looked round him in alarm, stared at the orchestra with amazement because it was still playing *pianissimo*, and only found his place again when the long-expected *forte* at last began and he could hear it. Fortunately it was not during the performance that this comical scene took place. . . .

By the time I made his acquaintance, Beethoven had ceased to play the piano either in public or at private gatherings, and my only opportunity of hearing him was when I once chanced to call at his house during the rehearsal of a new trio (D major, 3/4 time) [Op. 70, No. 1]. It was not a treat; for one thing the piano was badly out of tune – something that did not disturb Beethoven because in any case he could not hear it – and for another thing his deafness had robbed him of nearly all his once-celebrated virtuosity. At *forte* passages the poor deaf fellow banged the keys so vigorously that the strings twanged, while in the *piano* passages he played so softly that whole groups of notes went unheard and one lost the thread unless one could look into the music at the same time. The thought of his hard fate plunged me into deep depression. It is a great misfortune for anyone to be deaf, so how can a musician endure it without despair? I was no longer puzzled by Beethoven's almost perpetual melancholy. . . .

It was fortunate, in the circumstances, that Beethoven did not accept the offer of an appointment to the Court at Kassel. It would not have lasted anyway, as the 'merry King Jérôme', brother of Napoleon, lost his kingdom in 1813. But Beethoven did not enjoy for very long the full value of the handsome pension his patrons had offered him to keep him in Vienna. Wars and defeats had ruined the Austrian exchequer, resulting in 1810 in a state bankruptcy – the euphemism 'inflation' did not yet exist – that reduced the value of Austrian currency to a fifth. His patrons, however, indemnified him for at least a part of his loss.

BEETHOVEN TO BARON IGNAZ VON GLEICHENSTEIN

[*1809*]

. . . I have received a splendid offer to become *Kapellmeister* to the King of Westphalia – I should be well paid, say how many ducats I want, etc. – I would like to talk it over with you – so come and see me, if you can, this afternoon about half-past three. . . .

BEETHOVEN TO BREITKOPF & HÄRTEL

Baden, 21 July 1810

. . . Last year, before the French came, my 4,000 fl. was worth something; this year it is not even worth 1,000 fl. Convention money. . . . My final aim is not, as you think, to become a musical miser, composing only in order to grow rich – heaven forfend! But I like to be independent. . . . You, being more humane and cultivated than any other music publishers, should also make it your aim not merely to pay the artist a pittance, but to put him in a position where he can develop, in tranquillity, what he has in him and what other people expect of him. . . .

While taking infinite care with the minutest detail in the actual composition of his music, Beethoven was physically incapable of controlling his nervous impatience in the act of writing it down. His wild, erratic, sometimes almost unreadable handwriting was the despair of his copyists and engravers, as it has remained a source of despair to editors. His manuscripts abound in inconsistencies and errors. He complained frequently of misprints to his publishers; in one case, however, he was ready to admit ruefully his own mistake.

BEETHOVEN TO BREITKOPF & HÄRTEL

26 July 1809

. . . Here you have a good batch of printer's errors, to which my attention was drawn by a kind friend – for I have never in my life concerned myself with any of my work once it was finished (namely, in the violoncello sonata) [A major, Op. 69]. I shall have the list written out or printed here and announce in the magazine that anyone who has bought the piece can come for a copy. . . .

BEETHOVEN TO BREITKOPF & HÄRTEL

Vienna, 3 August 1809

. . . This will give you a laugh at my composer's scruples! Only imagine – I discovered yesterday that in correcting the mistakes in the cello sonata I had put in fresh mistakes of my own. . . . This will show you that I am really in a state where one can only say 'Lord, into thy hands I commend my spirit. . . .'

BEETHOVEN TO BREITKOPF & HÄRTEL

Vienna, 6 May 1811

. . . Mistakes – mistakes – you yourselves are one great mistake – I have to keep my copyist and myself perpetually on the rush if I am to prevent my published work from consisting solely of mistakes: the Leipzig *Musiktribunal* seems unable to produce a single decent proof-reader, and at that, you send off the work even before you receive the corrected proofs! In major works with [printed] single parts the bars should at least be counted. But one can see from the Fantasia, etc., what happens: and if you look at the piano reduction of the *Egmont* overture, you will see that a whole bar has been left out. . . .

Beethoven adored Goethe, with whom he came into personal contact through a common friend, Bettina Brentano. The two great contemporaries actually met in the Bohemian health resort of Teplitz in 1812, not without some mutual disappointment. Goethe, more than twenty years older, an acting Cabinet Minister to a sovereign prince, was accustomed to punctilious observance of Court etiquette, whereas Beethoven could never suppress his deep-rooted republican feelings.

BEETHOVEN TO BETTINA BRENTANO

Vienna, 10 February 1811

. . . If you write to Goethe about me, try to find all the words that will assure him of my deepest respect and admiration; at this very moment I am writing to him myself about *Egmont*, which I set to music from sheer love of his poems, which make me happy; but who can ever give enough thanks to a great poet, the most precious jewel a nation can possess? . . .

BEETHOVEN TO BREITKOPF & HÄRTEL

Franzensbrunn bei Eger, 9 August 1812

... Goethe greatly relishes the Court atmosphere – more than beseems a poet. There is not a great deal to be said about the absurdity of the virtuosi at this place, if poets, who should be regarded as the nation's foremost teachers, can forget everything else for the sake of this glitter. ...

GOETHE TO FRIEDRICH ZELTER

Karlsbad, 2 September 1812

... I made Beethoven's acquaintance at Teplitz. His talent amazed me; but unfortunately he is a completely untamed personality, who indeed is not mistaken in finding the world detestable, but who certainly does not make it more enjoyable, either for himself or for other people, by saying so. But he is much to be excused, and much to be pitied because he is losing his hearing – which is perhaps less damaging to the musical side of his being than to the social side. He is of a laconic disposition anyway, and this defect is making him doubly so. ...

A few years later the only communication with Beethoven was by way of conversation books, in which interlocutors had to write down what they wished to say. His domestic situation became more and more problematic with his increasing helplessness, and he became irritable and suspicious. His servants had no easy life with their master, and vice versa. Some friends of his were helpful in lending him a hand on occasion, but it was no easy job to get on with him. Schindler, his devoted 'famulus' during the last years of his life and his first biographer, was made to suffer all kinds of humiliations and insults.

BEETHOVEN TO MME NANETTE STREICHER

[*1816*]

... The kitchen-maid seems more serviceable than the previous one – the bad one with the beautiful face, who is keeping well out of the way; a sign that she had no hope of a good reference, though I had intended to give her one. Now there is another vacancy on the domestic staff; so I beg you to give the most careful consideration to it – a good cook, to ensure good digestion – but she should in any case be able to deal with mending (no finery) shirts, etc., and have as much sense as is required to provide for the needs of our household adequately but with due care for my purse. The new kitchen-maid pulled a somewhat wry face when told to carry wood, but I hope she will remember that our Saviour had to drag His cross even on Golgotha. . . .

BEETHOVEN TO MME STREICHER

1817 (?)

. . . Thank you for taking an interest in me – meanwhile, today, I have had a great deal to put up with from that girl N. – but I threw half a dozen books at her head by way of New Year's greeting. . . .

BEETHOVEN TO MME STREICHER

1817

. . . Miss N. is a changed woman since I threw those half-dozen books at her head. Something of them must have penetrated by chance into her brain or her evil heart – at least we have a bosomy deceiver in her. . . . Yesterday morning she began her devilry again; I made short shrift of it and hurled my heavy armchair at B. – the one that stands beside my bed; after that I had peace for the whole day. . . .

BEETHOVEN TO HIS FRIEND NIKOLAUS VON ZMESKALL

Nussdorf, 23 July 1817

. . . What does one pay nowadays to have a pair of boots mended? I have now to settle up for this with my servant who has to walk a lot. Incidentally, I am in despair at being condemned by the state of my hearing to spend the greater part of my life with that most infamous section of humanity and to some extent to be dependent on them. . . .

BEETHOVEN TO NIKOLAUS VON ZMESKALL

1817 (?)

. . . I am already in trouble again over a servant, and have probably even been robbed – on the 4th I gave him a fortnight's notice, but he drinks, stays out for whole nights, and is so shockingly rough and impudent that I would rather get rid of him earlier; so I should like to pay him his fortnight's wages and send him away at once. . . .

BEETHOVEN TO ANTON SCHINDLER

[*1824*]

. . . I do not accuse you of behaving badly over the *Akademie*, but imprudence and headstrong behaviour have spoilt many things; and in general I have a kind of fear of you, a feeling that one day you may bring some great misfortune upon me. When a sluice is full, it often opens suddenly, and that day in the Prater I felt you were touching on many of my sore points; on the whole I would much rather try to repay your services to me more often with a small present, than by having you at my *table*, for I confess that disturbs me too much in many ways; if I am not looking cheerful, you proclaim at once 'bad weather again today'. For, being commonplace yourself, you must needs fail to appreciate the uncommon. In short, I am too fond of my liberty. I shall certainly invite you often – but as a permanent arrangement it is impossible, for it upsets the whole order of my existence. . . .

Franz Grillparzer, who wrote an operatic libretto for Beethoven – 'Melusine', later set to music by Conradin Kreutzer – gives a colourful description of the master during this last period of his life.

FROM GRILLPARZER'S 'ERINNERUNGEN AN BEETHOVEN'

. . . A few days after this, Schindler – who was then Beethoven's man of business and later wrote his biography – called on me on behalf of his lord and master, who he said was unwell and would like me to visit him. I dressed, and we went at once to Beethoven's house – he was then living in the suburb of Landstrasse. I found him lying in dirty night attire on an untidy bed, with a book in his hand. At the head of the bed was a small door which, as I subsequently discovered, led into the larder, on which Beethoven kept an eye, so to speak. For later on a kitchen-maid came out with butter and eggs, and even in the midst of our lively conversation he could not refrain from throwing a sharp glance to discover what quantities she had brought. This gave one a sad idea of the disorder of his domestic life. . . .

In 1816 Beethoven adopted his nephew Karl van Beethoven whose father, Beethoven's brother Karl Kaspar, had died and whose mother had earned the composer's violent dislike and disapproval. He used to call her 'the Queen of the Night', as a personification of the evil principle. Karl, a good-natured but weak character, became the helpless object of bickering and litigation between the mother and the doting, violently and passionately emotional uncle, to whom he caused endless trouble and worry and who, blowing hot and cold, impatient, capricious, and tyrannical, was certainly no pedagogue.

BEETHOVEN TO THE COUNTESS MARIE ERDÖDY

Vienna, 13 May 1816

... My brother's death was the cause of great grief to me, and then of a great struggle to rescue my nephew, whom I love, from his depraved mother; in this I succeeded; but the best I could do for him here was to put him into a boarding-school; so that he does not live with me – and what is a boarding-school in comparison with the direct, sympathetic care of a father for his son? For as such I now regard myself, and I am racking my brains to find some means of having my beloved treasure closer at hand, so that I can influence him more rapidly and to better advantage. But it is so difficult for me! Moreover, for the past 6 weeks I have been in precarious health, so that I often think of death, though not with dread; it would only be for my poor Karl that I should be dying too soon. . . .

BEETHOVEN TO GIANNATASIO DEL RIO, HEAD OF A PRIVATE BOARDING-SCHOOL IN VIENNA

[*February 1816*]

. . . I am delighted to inform you that tomorrow I shall at last be bringing you the dear pledge that has been placed in my care. For the rest, I would ask you once again to allow his mother no say whatsoever as to how or when she is to see him; I will discuss all this more fully with you tomorrow. . . . You will even need to keep an eye on your servants to some extent, for once already she bribed my own man, though that was in different circumstances. . . .

BEETHOVEN TO GIANNATASIO DEL RIO

[*1816*]

. . . With regard to the mother, I entreat you, even if you have to pretend that he is too busy, not to let her approach him at all; no one is better qualified than I to know and appreciate that this alone would go far to upset all my carefully thought-out plans for the boy's welfare. . . .

BEETHOVEN TO GIANNATASIO DEL RIO

1816 (?)

. . . Under no pretext is Karl to be taken out of the school without his guardian's permission; nor may his mother ever visit him there. Should she wish to see him, she must apply to his guardian, who will make the necessary arrangements. . . .

Last night this *Queen of the Night* was at the Artists' Ball until 3 o'clock in the morning; not only mentally but physically in the nude. . . . Oh horror – and are we to entrust our treasure to such hands even for an instant? No, assuredly not. . . .

BEETHOVEN TO GIANNATASIO DEL RIO

14 November 1816

. . . I wish to know the effect of my behaviour towards Karl since your recent complaints. Meanwhile I have been very touched to discover that he has such a keen sense of honour; before we left your house I made allusions to his laziness; and we went away together in an unusually grave mood; he pressed my hand timidly, but I made no response. At table he ate scarcely anything, and declared that he was very unhappy; but I could not persuade him to say why. At last, while we were out walking, he explained that he was unhappy because he had not been able to work as diligently as he used. I now spoke as I should on the point, in a kinder tone than before. This certainly shows delicacy of feeling, and it is these traits which encourage me to think that all will be well. . . .

BEETHOVEN TO COUNTESS MARIE ERDÖDY

Heiligenstadt, 19 June 1817

. . . My hearing has deteriorated and I, who was already incapable of looking after myself and my own needs, find my cares increased owing to my brother's child. I have not even found decent accommodation here; since it is hard for me to look after myself, I turn first to one person, then to another, and everywhere I am neglected and preyed upon by miserable wretches. . . .

BEETHOVEN TO HIS NEPHEW KARL

4 October [*1825*]

. . . I wish you may not feel ashamed of your unkindness to me; I am suffering, that is all I can say. . . . Rest assured that you will never have anything but kindness from me; but can I not desire the same of you? Even if you see me in a rage, you must ascribe it to my great anxiety about you, because you may easily fall into danger. . . . I hope at least to have a letter from you tomorrow, do not alarm me, oh, think how I suffer. . . .

BEETHOVEN TO HIS NEPHEW

Baden, 5 October 1825

My dear Son,

I beg you, no more of this! – only come to my arms, you shall not hear a single harsh word. Oh God, do not go away in your misery – you shall find the same loving reception as always – and we shall have an affectionate talk about plans for the future; I give you my word of honour that you need fear no reproaches from me – for they would in any case be fruitless now – only the most loving care and help. . . .

BEETHOVEN TO HIS NEPHEW

[*Summer 1826*]

. . . If only because you did at least follow me, all is forgiven and forgotten; I will speak further about it when we meet. Today quite calm. Never suppose that I have any other thought than for your welfare, and judge my actions in that light – I beg you to take no step that would make you unhappy and shorten my life. I did not get to sleep until about 3 o'clock, for I was coughing all night. I embrace you warmly, and am convinced that you will soon cease to *misjudge* me; in that light, too, I regard your conduct of yesterday. . . .

BEETHOVEN TO THE PHYSICIAN DR A. SMETANA IN VIENNA

[*August 1826*]

. . . There has been a terrible misfortune; Karl has accidentally injured himself. I hope it may still be possible – for you at any rate – to save him. If only you come quickly. Karl has a bullet in his head – how, you shall hear at once – only come quickly, for God's sake, quickly. . . .

The catastrophe mentioned in the last letter – the attempted suicide of the poor, desperate boy – was fortunately not fatal.

The last years of Beethoven's life were beset by ill health. The great works he finished during these years – the 'Choral Symphony', the 'Missa Solemnis', the last five string quartets – are monuments of heroism as much as they are achievements of unfathomable depth and greatness. His impetuous urge to create, to fulfil his destiny, is wonderfully expressed in some letters.

BEETHOVEN TO THE PUBLISHERS B. SCHOTTS SÖHNE AT MAINZ

17 September 1824

. . . The quartet, too, will certainly reach you by mid-October [E flat major, Op. 127]. I am overwhelmed with work and in poor health, so people must be a little patient with me. I am here [at Baden] on account of my health; but it has already improved, Apollo and the Muses will not yet allow me to be handed over to the bony Reaper, for I am still so much in their debt, and before I depart to the Elysian Fields I must leave behind me what the spirit has endowed me with and orders me to complete. I feel as though I had written a few notes at most! I wish you all success in your efforts on behalf of the arts; it is these, together with science, that give us inklings of a higher existence and the hope of attaining it. . . .

Some months after Karl's attempted suicide Beethoven fell gravely ill. He struggled with his customary courage and determination, but his strength was sapped and he could leave his bed no more. A generous gift from his friends in London was the last pleasure of his life.

BEETHOVEN'S BROTHER JOHANN TO SCHOTT AT MAINZ

Vienna, 4 February 1825

I am enclosing the seven works by my brother in a fair copy which he has just checked and corrected, so that they are ready for the engraver; all the works in your possession, namely the great Mass (Missa Solemnis), the Symphony (the Ninth) and the works enclosed herewith should therefore not be sent to my brother for correction of the proofs, but to the well-known, capable Mr Gottfried Weber, thereby ensuring that publication will not be too much delayed. I have no doubt that he will, out of affection for the composer and his works, gladly make the corrections. . . .

Below this letter there is a remark written by Gottfried Weber, a well-known theoretician and writer, to whom it was forwarded by the publisher. It runs as follows:

I cannot possibly undertake these corrections and do not want to become Mr Beethoven's proof-reader. The damned presumption of the tomfool!

BEETHOVEN TO HIS FRIEND MAX STUMPFF IN LONDON

Vienna, 8 February 1827

. . . Unhappily I have been lying ill with dropsy ever since 3rd December. You can imagine to what straits this is reducing me. In the ordinary way I live solely on what I earn by my works, trying to make as much as possible out of them for myself and my dear Karl. But for the past two and a half months, alas, I have not been able to compose a note. My income is enough to cover the rent, with a few hundred florins left over. Remember that it is impossible to say as yet how long I shall take to recover from my illness, and even then I shall not be able to bestride Pegasus and soar at once into the air with all sails spread. The doctor, the surgeon and the apothecary will all have to be paid – I well remember that several years ago the Philharmonic Society proposed giving a benefit concert for me. It would be a happiness to me if they would return to this project, for then I might still, perhaps, be rescued from all my present embarrassments. . . .

BEETHOVEN TO IGNAZ MOSCHELES IN LONDON

Vienna, 18 March 1827

. . . I can find no words to describe the feelings with which I read your letter of 1st March. I am moved to the depths of my soul by the noble conduct of the Philharmonic Society, with which they almost anticipated my request. . . . Please tell those estimable men that when God has restored me to health I shall try to express my gratitude through works as well, and that I leave the Society to decide what I am to write for them. . . . May heaven very soon restore me to health, and I will show the noble-minded Englishmen how greatly I appreciate their sympathy with me in my sad fate. . . .

I was obliged to draw the whole of the 1,000 florins [£100] at once, for I was just then in the unpleasant position of having to raise money.

I shall never forget their noble behaviour, and I shall very soon be conveying my particular thanks to Sir Smart and Mr Stumpff. . . .

This was Beethoven's last letter, not written in his hand, but dictated. He died a week later.

THE ROMANTIC TWILIGHT

From Schubert to Schumann

It is an odd fact that Beethoven probably never met the greatest musician among his younger contemporaries, Franz Schubert (*1797–1828*), *although they both lived in Vienna. Schubert adored him, but kept at a safe distance, and Beethoven, deaf and often surly, was not easy to approach. The great and mighty, who had patronized Beethoven ever since his first appearance, knew nothing of Schubert who was too humble to approach them and whose supporters and friends belonged to the intelligent, musically active middle class. When he died, Schubert was hardly known outside Vienna.*

The obscurity in which he lived is illustrated ironically by a letter of a namesake of his, a certain Franz Schubert (he is sometimes called 'François') of Dresden, who enjoyed some reputation as a songwriter, to Messrs Breitkopf and Härtel in Leipzig. Schubert of Vienna had submitted to these same publishers his ballad 'Der Erlkönig', which they turned down, and his manuscript was returned by error to Franz Schubert in Dresden.

FRANÇOIS SCHUBERT TO BREITKOPF & HÄRTEL

Dresden, 18 April 1817

Dear Friend,

. . . I must also inform you that some 10 days ago I received your esteemed letter enclosing a manuscript, *Goethe's Erlkönig*, which purported to be by me, to my greatest astonishment – for I can assure you that I never composed this cantata. I will keep it in my custody in order to find out if possible who was so uncivil as to send you such wretched stuff, and also who is the fellow who thus takes my name in vain. For the rest I am much obliged to you for kindly sending it to me, and remain, with great esteem,

Your most obliged friend and brother,

Franz Schubert,
His Majesty's Composer of sacred music

Immensely sociable, the heart and soul of a circle of friends who were devoted to each other like brothers, Schubert found his urge for communication satisfied in daily personal contact. Letters were rarely exchanged. This is one reason why only a modest number of his letters has been preserved. Another may be that he was obviously not fond of writing. His pleasure in putting his thoughts into words is noticeably allayed by the need to express himself, as it were, in an unfamiliar idiom. He writes a correct German, in contradistinction to Beethoven, whose style is rough and often clumsy. But Schubert's mother tongue was the homely Viennese dialect, certain features of which would involuntarily penetrate occasionally into his otherwise punctiliously correct style of writing just as features of a typically Viennese idiom are to be found everywhere in his music. It is as if verbal expression seemed an unnecessary bother to him; whatever he had to tell, he put into his melodies. Robert Schumann, *who fell in love with Schubert's music, has characterized it most succinctly in this respect.*

SCHUMANN TO FRIEDRICH WIECK

Heidelberg, 6 November 1829

. . . Schubert is still my 'one and only Schubert', especially as he has everything in common with my 'one and only Jean Paul'; when I play Schubert I feel as though I were reading a novel by Jean Paul composed in music. . . . No music except Schubert's is so psychologically remarkable for the development and association of ideas and the impression of logical transition that it conveys; moreover, very few composers have been so successful in imprinting a single individuality upon such a variety of tone-pictures, and fewer still have written so much for themselves and their own heart. Where other people keep diaries in which they record their momentary feelings, etc., Schubert simply kept sheets of music by him and confided his changing moods to them; and his soul being steeped in music, he put down notes when another man would resort to words. . . .

There is a letter of Schubert, written at the age of fifteen when he was a choirboy in the Court Chapel in Vienna. Already it shows his irresistible personal charm. Just as one may see in a child's portrait the soft outlines of the familiar features we know from later pictures, so Schubert's early compositions, dating from the same time as this letter, already reveal the unmistakable fingerprints of the mature artist.

SCHUBERT TO HIS BROTHER FERDINAND IN VIENNA

24 November 1812

. . . I shall come straight out with what I have in mind, for this will bring me the sooner to my purpose and you will not be kept in suspense by my beating about the bush. For a long time I have been thinking over my circumstances, and have concluded that while on the whole they are good, yet in certain respects they might be better. You know by experience that now and then a fellow has a fancy to eat a roll of bread and an apple or two – especially when he has not had much of a midday dinner and can only look forward to a scanty supper 8½ hours later. This desire, which I have often felt keenly, is becoming more and more importunate, and willy-nilly I must find some way of changing the situation. My beggarly allowance from our respected father is scattered to the winds in the first few days, and what am I to do for the rest of the time? 'They who put their trust in thee shall not perish' (St Matthew, Chap. 3 v. 4). And I think so too. How would it be if you were to send me a few shillings a month? You would not even feel it, for then I should think myself happy in my retreat and be satisfied. As I said before, I base myself on the words of the Apostle Matthew, who also says 'He that has two cloaks, let him give one to the poor', etc. Meanwhile, I hope you will listen to the voice, which is ceaselessly calling on you,

of your
affectionate, impoverished, hopeful
and – I repeat – impoverished brother,
Franz

One may hope that the boy's modest wish was granted. It may be added that his solemn quotations from St Matthew are spurious, and probably intended to amuse his loving brother. In one respect this letter is already typical of Schubert's whole life: he was usually penniless. His friends – Schober, Spaun, the painters Kupelwieser and Schwind, the playwright Bauernfeld, the poet Mayrhofer – would help occasionally, although they were not wealthy either. The only appointment Schubert ever held, after having given up the drudgery of a humble schoolmaster in a suburban school in Vienna, was as piano-teacher to the daughters of a Hungarian magnate, Count Esterházy, on whose estate at Zseliz in western Hungary he spent the summer months of 1818 and 1824. This was his only contact with high aristocracy. His letters from Zseliz read much as if they were written by an exile, although one discerns no resentment against being treated as a servant.

SCHUBERT TO A NEW FRIEND, JOSEF HÜTTENBRENNER

Vienna, 21 February 1818

. . . I am delighted that you like my songs. As a token of warm friendship I am sending you another herewith – which I have just written, at midnight, at Anselm Hüttenbrenner's house [Josef's brother]. I wish I could carry our friendship further, over a glass of punch. Vale.

Meaning to sprinkle sand on the thing, and being in a hurry and rather drowsy, I have just picked up the inkpot and, with perfect composure, emptied it over the page. What a disaster! . . .

SCHUBERT TO HIS FRIENDS IN VIENNA

Zseliz, 8 September 1818

Dear Schober, Dear Senn,
Dear Spaun, Dear Streinsberg,
Dear Mayrhofer, Dear Wayss,
Dear Weidlich,

. . . I was attending an auction of cows and oxen when your fat letter was handed to me. I broke the seal, and gave a loud cry of joy when I saw the name of Schober. . . . No one here has any feeling for true art, except (if I am not mistaken) the Countess now and then. So I am alone with my beloved, and must conceal her in my room, in my piano, in my bosom. Though this often grieves me, on the other hand it elevates me in proportion. So do not be afraid that I shall stay away any longer than is strictly necessary. Meanwhile, I have produced several songs, which I hope have turned out very well. . . .

Our castle is not particularly large, but built in a very elegant style. It stands in a beautiful garden. I am lodged in the estate manager's house. It is fairly quiet, except for about 40 geese, which sometimes strike up such a chorus of cackling that one cannot hear oneself speak. The people here are all most kindly. It is rare to find an aristocrats' household living in such harmony as this one. The estate manager, a Slavonian, is a worthy man with a high opinion of his erstwhile talent for music. Even now he can play two German dances in 3/4 time on the lute like a virtuoso. His son, who is a philosophy student, has just arrived for the holidays, I should like to make friends with him. His wife is like all women who wish to be thought genteel. The comptroller is the right man in the right place, with a shrewd eye for his pockets and money-bags. The doctor is really clever, but though only 24 he is as fussy about his health as an old lady. Something most unnatural there. The surgeon is my favourite, a respectable old man of 75, always serene and cheerful. May God grant us all such a happy old age. The Justice is a very natural, worthy man. One of the Count's companions, a merry old fellow and a good musician, often comes to keep me company. The cook, the lady's maid, the housemaid, the children's nurse, the steward, etc., and the 2 equerries, are all pleasant people. The cook is somewhat dissolute, the lady's maid 30 years old, the housemaid very pretty, often keeps me company, the children's nurse a kindly old soul, the steward my rival. The 2 equerries are much more at home with horses than with people. The Count is rather rough, the Countess haughty but more sensitive, the young Countesses are nice children. So far I have been spared the roast. I can think of no more to say. Knowing me as you do, I need hardly tell you that with my natural sincerity I get on very well with all these people. . . .

Schubert's brother Ferdinand, the benefactor to whom he had applied as a starving choirboy, was in charge of a church choir in Vienna. On one occasion he could not resist the temptation of appropriating a mass by his brother Franz and ruefully confessed to him the sin of having performed it under his own name. Here is Schubert's touching answer.

SCHUBERT TO HIS BROTHER

Zseliz, 29 October 1818

Dear brother Ferdinand,

For the sin of your appropriation I had already forgiven you in my first letter. So your long delay in writing can have no other reason than, perhaps, your tender conscience. You liked the funeral mass, it made you weep, and perhaps at the same point where I myself wept; dear brother, that is my greatest reward for the gift, you need not mention any other.

If only I were not getting to know the people around me better every day, I should be as contented here as I was at first. But now I perceive that I am really alone among them all, except for a couple of genuinely good-natured girls. . . .

The local parson, who is a big old so-and-so, as stupid as an arch-ass and as coarse as a buffalo, preaches sermons that put the much-revered Pater Nepomucene into the shade. It is a joy to listen to him hurling epithets such as 'carrion', 'canaille', etc., from the pulpit, or bringing out a skull and saying 'Take a look at this, you cross-eyed dullards, that's what you will all look like one day', or 'Yes, a lad goes with his hussy to the tavern, dances all night, then they go tipsy to bed and when they get up there are three of them', etc. . . .

Some years later, the happy circle of friends had largely dispersed, and Schubert, stricken by an illness of which we know nothing definite, seems to have been frequently in an elegiac mood. His attempts to gain a foothold in opera failed, mainly owing to the indifferent quality of the librettos on which he wasted a profusion of precious music. Half-hearted efforts directed towards getting a musical appointment of one kind or another did not succeed either.

Schubert remained a Bohemian, poor as Job, creating a musical treasury of which the world knew nothing, and which only slowly and gradually came into the light of publicity, long after his death.

SCHUBERT TO HIS FRIEND LEOPOLD KUPELWIESER IN ROME

[*Vienna*] *31 March 1824*

. . . In short, I feel I am the wretchedest, most unhappy creature in the world. Picture a man whose health will never entirely recover and who in his despair about it makes matters worse and worse instead of better – picture, I say, a man whose brightest hopes have come to nothing, to whom the joys of love and friendship can offer only the greatest pain, whose enthusiasm (at least stimulating) for beauty is in danger of dying away, and ask yourself if he is not a wretched, unhappy creature. 'My peace has gone, my heart is heavy' [from Margaret's Spinning-wheel Song in Goethe's *Faust*], so might I now sing every day, for every night I go to bed hoping that I shall not wake again, and each morning only brings back the grief of the day before. So I spend my days, joyless and friendless, except that Schwind sometimes visits me and brings a ray of sunshine from the happy times gone by. As you probably know already, our society (Literary Society) has committed suicide through over-indulgence in beer-drinking and sausage-eating by the rude mob; it is to be wound up in two days' time – though for my part I have hardly been to one meeting since you left here. Leidesdorf [one of Schubert's publishers], whom I have come to know very well, is indeed a really good man with great depth to him, but so melancholy that I almost fear I have been far too much affected by him in this respect; besides, his affairs and mine are going badly so that we never have any money. Your brother's libretto (it was not very judicious of him to leave the theatre) was declared to be good for nothing, with the result that my music was not wanted either. Castelli's libretto, *Die Verschworenen* [*The Conspirators*], has been set to music in Berlin by a local composer and received with applause. So I seem to have composed two more operas to no purpose.

. . . The latest news in Vienna is that Beethoven will be giving a concert at which his new symphony [the Choral Symphony], 3 pieces from his new Mass [*Missa Solemnis*] and a new overture are to be performed. God willing, I have a mind to give a similar concert in the coming year. . . .

SCHUBERT TO HIS BROTHER FERDINAND

Zseliz, 16–18 July 1824

. . . Lest these lines should mislead you into supposing that I am unwell or melancholy, I hasten to assure you of the contrary. The happy time is, of course, gone by in which we saw every object haloed by youth; now comes the unpleasant recognition of miserable reality, which (thank God) I try to spare myself as far as possible by the exercise of my imagination. We suppose that happiness attaches to any place where we were once happy, whereas it is only within ourselves, and so I was at first disappointed here – a repetition of the experience I had before at Steyr; but I am now better able to find happiness and tranquillity within myself than I was then. You will see evidence of this in the fact that I have already composed a long sonata and Variations on a theme of my own, both for piano duet. The Variations are winning quite exceptional applause. . . .

SCHUBERT TO HIS FRIEND FRANZ VON SCHOBER

Zseliz, 21 September 1824

. . . I hear you are not happy? must sleep off the intoxication of your despair? So Schwind wrote to me. Although this greatly saddens me I am not at all surprised to hear it, for such is the fate of almost all rational men in this miserable world. And what have we to do with happiness, we for whom unhappiness is the one remaining incentive? If only we were together, you, Schwind, Kuppel and I, I could make light of all misfortune. But we are separated, each in his own corner, and that is the real cause of my unhappiness. I could cry with Goethe: 'Wer bringt nur eine Stunde jener holden Zeit zurück!' ['Who brings back one hour of that lovely time past'.] The days when we sat together in intimate companionship and each showed his artistic offspring to the others with maternal bashfulness, waiting, not without anxiety, for the frank verdict that affection would pronounce. Those days when one fired the other with his own enthusiasm and all were inspired by the same striving after beauty. Now I sit here alone, in the depths of Hungary, whither I unfortunately allowed myself to be lured for the second time, without even *one* person with whom I can exchange an intelligent word. . . .

A trip to Upper Austria and Salzburg with his friend and favourite interpreter, the singer Michael Vogl, was a happy interlude and one of the rare occasions when Schubert was able to enjoy the happiness of his suggestive power as an artist. His descriptions of the journey are picturesque indeed. In one of his letters his outspoken pacifist feelings are remarkable, considering the emotional nationalism of the wars of liberation from Napoleon one decade before and the immense nimbus of the Tyrolese resistance movement against the Bavarians, who in 1809 had been allies of the French usurper.

SCHUBERT TO HIS PARENTS IN VIENNA

Steyr, 25 July 1825

... My new songs from Walter Scott's *Lady of the Lake*, in particular, gave a great deal of pleasure. People were also much surprised at my piety, which I have expressed in a hymn to the Holy Virgin [*Ave Maria*]; this seems to impress everyone and induce devout feelings. I think the reason is that I never force the devout sentiment and never compose hymns or prayers of this kind except when I am involuntarily overwhelmed by it, so that it is usually a real, genuine devoutness. ... At Steyereck we stayed with Countess Weissenwolf, who is a great admirer of my humble person, has all my compositions, and sings many of them very prettily. The Walter Scott songs made an exceedingly favourable impression on her, and she showed it at once, as though she would be by no means displeased to have them dedicated to her. But I am planning to handle the publication of these songs differently from the usual method, which attracts so little attention; for these will be headed by Scott's honoured name and are therefore likely to awaken greater curiosity, and if the English words are given as well they would make me better known in England too. If only it were possible to do honest business with the ..... dealers; but the State, in its wisdom and benevolence, has so arranged matters that artists must always remain the slaves of those miserable hucksters. ...

SCHUBERT TO HIS BROTHER

12 September 1825

... The inscriptions on the city [Salzburg] gates proclaim the vanished power of its priestly rulers. ... One goes past the house of Theophrastus Paracelsus, with its wonderfully decorated façade, and crosses the bridge over the Salzach, which foams beneath, dark and turbid. The town itself made a somewhat gloomy impression on me, for the weather was overcast, so that the old buildings looked still more melancholy; and the fortress that crowns the highest peak of the Mönchsberg frowns down into all the narrow streets with a spectral greeting. ... Herr Pauernfeind, a merchant acquaintance of Herr v. Vogl, took us to visit Graf von Platz, the President of the *Landrechte*, whose family already knew us by name and welcomed us most kindly. Vogl sang several of my songs, whereupon we were invited for the following evening and asked to present our wares to a select circle, who were all particularly impressed by the *Ave Maria* I mentioned in my first letter. The way Vogl sings and I accompany him, so that at such moments we seem to be at *one* with each other, is something quite new and unprecedented to these people. Next morning we climbed to the top of the Mönchsberg, from which one overlooks a great part of the town, and I was amazed at the number of magnificent buildings, palaces and churches. But the place is largely deserted, many of the buildings stand empty, many others have only one, or at most two or three families living in them. In the public squares, which are many and handsome, there is so little traffic that grass grows between cobblestones. . . .

SCHUBERT TO HIS BROTHER

Steyr, 21 September [*1825*]

. . . A few hours brought us to Hallein, which is certainly a remarkable town, but excessively dirty and sinister. . . . It was impossible to persuade Vogl to visit the Salzberg with its salt-mines; his mighty spirit, spurred on by gout, was striving towards Gastein like a traveller towards a spark of light on some murky night. So we drove on past Golling, whence we could already see the first high, impassable mountains whose fearsome gorges are traversed by the *Lueg Pass*. Having slowly scrambled up a high mountain, with other terrible mountains towering in front of our noses and to either side, as though the earth had planks nailed all over it in this district, we reached the top and suddenly found ourselves looking down into a frightful gorge, so that for a moment our hearts quailed. . . . Amid this terrible scenery, man has tried to perpetuate his even more terrible bestiality. For it was here, where the Salzach, foaming far, far below, bars the way to the Bavarians on one side and the Tyrolese on the other, that that horrible slaughter took place, when the Tyrolese, hidden among the rocky peaks, fired down with devilish yells of glee at the Bavarians who were trying to capture the pass, and those who were hit went hurtling into the depths without ever discerning whence came the shots. This most disgraceful proceeding, which lasted for days and weeks, is commemorated by a chapel on the Bavarian side and a red cross in the cliffs on the Tyrolese side, partly to mark the spot and partly to proffer an atonement in these sacred symbols. Oh glorious Christ, to how many infamous deeds must you lend your emblem! Yourself the bitterest memorial to human infamy, they set up your image as though to say: 'Behold, we trampled Almighty God's most perfect creation beneath our insolent feet, and should we shrink from destroying, with a light heart, the vermin we call our fellow men?' . . .

The illness that ended Schubert's life in his thirty-second year was probably an attack of typhoid fever. Here is his last letter.

SCHUBERT TO FRANZ VON SCHOBER

Vienna, 12 November 1828

Dear Schober,
I am ill. For the last 11 days I have taken nothing to eat or drink; I can only totter feebly from my arm-chair to my bed and back. Rinna is treating me. If I do take any nourishment my body rejects it again at once.

In kindness, let me have some books to ease this desperate situation. Those of Cooper's I have read are *The Last of the Mohicans, The Spy, The Pilot* and *The Settlers.* If by chance you have anything else by him, I do beseech you to leave it for me with Frau v. Bogner at the coffee-house. My brother, who is the soul of conscientiousness, will bring it to me in the most conscientious manner. Or anything else instead.

Your friend
Schubert

The Austrian poet Franz Grillparzer wrote an epitaph on him: 'Here lie rich treasure and still fairer hopes'. This was the opinion generally held of Schubert in Vienna, where after his death, in point of fact, nobody bothered much about the 'rich treasure'. Schumann and Liszt were the first to realize the immense greatness of this humble musician and were instrumental in promoting his posthumous fame.

During the first half of the nineteenth century the social conditions of music passed through a development which completely changed the musician's position in society and his whole manner of living. The crisis of the French Revolution and the Napoleonic Wars removed the main factor which for some centuries had sustained musical activities – aristocratic patronage. During the period of transition it could still maintain an artist such as Beethoven, but in the twenties the aristocracy had lost a great deal of its ancient privilege and was already finished as an active element in musical life. The immediate result was a kind of vacuum. Everything pertaining to the constitution of self-

supporting musical bodies, such as operatic enterprise, orchestras, conservatories, had to be more or less improvised, and everything dependent on such organizations created specific problems which, lacking any planned approach, could be solved only by trial and error. This explains the problematic situation in which the composer found himself at a time when there was hardly any copyright provision and when, for example, the operatic composer's only benefit was the modest fee paid for his score by the theatre. This explains why an artist at the peak of his fame like Chopin had to eke out a living by giving piano lessons to wealthy ladies, why Schumann had to edit a music magazine, Berlioz had to take a miserably paid job as a critic, Lortzing had to act as a comedian and buffo tenor. It is small wonder that the problem of subsistence looms large in musicians' letters of the period.

Together with Schubert, Carl Maria von Weber *(1786–1826) is one of the leading representatives of the transition period. Unlike Schubert with his gentle, comfortable unpretentiousness, Weber was a fighter all his life. He made himself conspicuous both as pianist and conductor and became one of those distinguished musicians – Spohr, Mendelssohn, Marschner, Liszt, Wagner were others – who did pioneer work in the organization of musical institutions in Germany.*

The most important period of his career started in 1817 with his move to Dresden, where he organized German opera at the Court Theatre, traditionally a stronghold of Italian opera. The last nine years of his life were devoted to this task and the creation of his three masterpieces, 'Der Freischütz' (1821), 'Euryanthe' (1823), and 'Oberon' (1826). The first of these conquered every stage within a year and made the composer popular all over Germany.

WEBER TO HIS FRIEND JOHANN GÄNSBACHER

Dresden, 10 March 1817

Beloved Brother,

I ought to have written long since to tell you of my appointment as *Kapellmeister* to the King of Saxony and Director of the German Opera here, which I received in Berlin on 27th December 1816; but I have really had too much to do. Anyhow, I am at last firmly settled here, and my wonderful travel projects have all melted away. True, I have an annual holiday; but if I get married in the autumn, as please God I shall, it will be more difficult to leave the nest, and thus I shall probably grow into a tolerable Philistine. I had many vexations and intrigues to overcome at the beginning of my residence here, and was several times on the point of moving on again, but this was all to the good in the end, for it showed them they were dealing with a man who would not let himself be trifled with and was too independent to accept snubs or allow his rights to be infringed. Now everything goes on quietly, and those who do not love me at any rate fear me. . . .

I shall soon be setting my hand to a new opera, written for me here by the well-known poet *Friedrich Kind – Die Jägersbraut*, a very romantic, enthralling and beautiful work. On the whole I lead a very solitary and perhaps rather melancholy life, for though I have a host of acquaintances and am generally esteemed, I feel keenly the lack of a real friend; moreover I have no one to talk to about music, and that is really very sad. . . .

My appointment here is only for 1 year; that is the custom, and though it has never been known not to lead to a life engagement, I know my own star so well that I am still apprehensive, if only of circumstances. As God will, I trust in Him and do not tremble, although in future I shall have more than just myself to care for. The business with my Lina's mother [Lina was Weber's fiancée] is now settled too, she is going to her son at Mainz and I am to give her 100 thaler a year, it is worth the sacrifice to have peace and quiet at home. . . .

WEBER TO FRIEDRICH KIND

Berlin, 21 June 1821

Beloved friend and joint father!
We can shoot Victoria. The *Freischütz* has hit the bull's eye. It is to be hoped that our friend Hellwig, as an eyewitness, will have given you a better report than I can, for I have not a moment to myself. Of course, I too shall soon be able to give you a full report by word of mouth. Yesterday's performance, the second, went off just as splendidly as the first, and with just as much enthusiasm; for tomorrow's, the third, all the tickets are sold already. No one can remember *such* a reception for an opera, and after *Olympia* [by Spontini], for which *everything* was done, it is really the most complete triumph imaginable. And you cannot believe how the interest was kept up throughout, and how excellently every part was played and sung. What would I not have given for you to be there!

Several scenes proved much more effective than I would have believed, e.g. the exit of the bridesmaids. The overture and this folksong [the *Bridesmaids' Song*] were greeted with cries of *da capo*, but I would not allow the action to be held up. I expect the newspapers will begin to expatiate on it now. . . .

My dear Kind, I am so grateful to you for your magnificent poem; you gave me the opportunity for so much variety, and I joyfully poured my soul into your magnificent lines, with their depth of feeling. . . .

Weber was a generous friend and colleague. When offered a tempting position at the Court Theatre of Kassel, he warmly recommended Spohr, who actually got the appointment. He tried – unsuccessfully in the end – to pacify his librettist Friedrich Kind, who felt sorely offended by the general enthusiasm for the music and by the lack of appreciation for his, the poet's, contribution to the success. Like other dramatists and composers of the time, Weber suffered from the vagaries of censorship, especially in Vienna, where Samiel, the evil spirit, had to be removed and the action had to be put back into the Middle Ages and cross-bows used, as the Emperor, Francis I, had a nervous aversion to rifle shots. On the other hand it is true that monarchs did not feel particularly safe at that time.

WEBER TO FEIGE, OPERA DIRECTOR AT KASSEL

Dresden, 20 November 1819

. . . We have the celebrated Spohr within our walls. He is thinking of remaining here some years for the sake of his daughter's education, and is thus free and independent. Such a brilliant and renowned artist, whose honoured name cannot but awaken respect in all quarters, would certainly be an ornament to the Elector's Opera, and would justify the confidence His Majesty was graciously pleased to place in me before I had earned it.

Should you think your interests better served by your not negotiating directly with Herr Kapellmeister Spohr, I should be delighted to offer my services as go-between. . . .

WEBER TO FRIEDRICH KIND

Dresden, 28 July 1821

. . . The poet and the composer are so inseparably bound up together that it would be absurd to suppose the latter can do anything worth while without the former. For who gives him the initial impetus? who provides the dramatic situations? who fires his imagination? who makes variety of feeling possible for him? who offers him characters etc.? the *poet*, always the *poet*!

But who makes poets always dissatisfied? Again, always one another. Musicians have said to me a hundred times, 'But then, how fortunate you were to have such a splendid libretto'. Whereas the poets always find something to carp at, and often drive me positively wild, particularly when they try to attribute all the merit to me and *not* the defects they claim to perceive. To this I reply, do you really suppose that a serious composer allows a libretto to be thrust into his hands like an apple into a schoolboy's? that he takes it on without examination and scatters notes over it at random, delighted to release, in no matter what direction, all that has been penned up within him?

No, dear fellow, you may rest assured that no one could be imbued with greater respect for the poet than I am; that I could never for a moment forget that it is to you that my thanks are chiefly due; I keep them faithfully in my heart and shall utter them joyfully whenever and wherever the opportunity occurs. . . .

WEBER TO FRIEDRICH KIND

15 October 1821

. . . I received the enclosed vexatious news from Vienna yesterday. At first I wished to spare you the annoyance I had to stomach; but thinking it over, I see you will have to know. For the last three days I have been indoors, unwell; else I would have come to you myself. What is to be done? – oh, that blessed Viennese censorship! We must talk it over. . . .

Whilst on the subject of censorship, it may be interesting to learn that, sixteen years later, even the most illustrious and respectable of all operatic composers, Meyerbeer, *had to tolerate the mutilation of 'The Huguenots', because St Bartholomew's Night was not an acceptable subject for the Viennese stage. The poet Castelli, to whom this letter is addressed, was the German translator of 'The Huguenots'.*

MEYERBEER TO J. F. CASTELLI IN VIENNA

Paris, 26 June 1837

My dear friend,

I am taking the opportunity by the departure for Vienna of your amiable countrywoman, Fräulein Fanny Elssler, to send you a copy of our joint offspring, *The Huguenots*, as a friendly souvenir. Breitkopf & Härtel have not yet sent a copy of the German vocal score to me in Paris, so I am not yet acquainted with your translation, which I am very curious to see; but Breitkopf and Härtel announce that it will soon reach Paris. They also write that a certain Dr Ott has been commissioned by the Hoftheater in Vienna to write an entirely new plot for the music of *The Huguenots*. I hope this is not so. If anything of the kind should be afoot, do try to prevent it, for love of the work and of your friend. *That* music is especially suited to *that* material, and to it alone. Should it really be so, however, and if it proves impossible to prevent this vandalism, I would like you to take a hand in the adaptation; it would then at least be done with an understanding of the theatre, with taste, and conscientiously. . . .

A successful composer's joys and sorrows are reflected in some letters from Weber to his wife, written whilst he was visiting Prague and Vienna, where he made the necessary arrangements for the forthcoming first performance of 'Euryanthe', and in a letter to the Berlin Court Theatre which is a model of irreproachable courtesy and cutting irony. The cause was the fiftieth performance of 'Freischütz' in Berlin and the munificence shown to the composer on that occasion.

WEBER TO HIS WIFE

Prague, 15 February 1822

. . . Such rejoicings as we had yesterday! When I came into the orchestra, the shouts of jubilation, the clamour and applause went on and on, and it was the same three times over. The house was packed to the doors, regardless of the many balls. Nearly every number was applauded. The Huntsmen's chorus we had to repeat, and at the end they called me in front of the curtain with the appropriate 'turbulence'. The performance went very well. Orchestra very good, full of affection and fire; the same with the choir. Sonntag (Agathe) was very charming, Wohlbrück (Aennchen) disastrous. Max was pleasantly sung. Kainz (Kaspar) did very well. The hermit was abominable. All the rest good. The Wolves' Glen quite different from ours, but excellent. There is imagination. . . .

WEBER TO HIS WIFE

Vienna, 20 February 1822

. . . At last in the evening came my *Freischütz*. What am I to say about it – where should I begin? There were not two passages played at the correct speed. Everything was rushed or dragged. Weigl had rehearsed it without the slightest artistic insight or modulation. I sat there in a fever – the house was very full, the 25th performance and *Shrove Tuesday*. Otherwise all went well. The choruses were excellent. The scenery very pretty, but most of it quite beside the point. The most elementary questions of stagecraft were ignored, the stage was not even darkened at the end of Act I, and so forth. I don't know where to begin or end, in telling you about it all. Overture, taken too fast. Introduction, *good*. Kilian's song, one verse cut. The ensemble number, excellently and stirringly sung by the chorus. Rosner, Max – I am beginning to feel more satisfied with Bergmann [his tenor at Dresden]. Forti, did well – he has a different approach to the role, but a consistent one, and his singing is excellent. Weinmüller, good. Schröder, charming; a lovely voice, she acts in character, her intonation is pure; but of course she is by no means a completely developed singer as yet. Mlle Vio quite spiritless; the duet dragged appallingly. The *Schlanke Bursch* was taken quite fast. The great aria, the prayer, quickly, everything rushed, but not without expression. The trio helter-skelter too. The Wolves' Glen just bundled together, but with all sorts of pretty scenic touches. Agathe's cavatina the only thing that was *quite good*. [Aennchen's] ballad, without the viola and at *Nero, cut*! The finale, all topsy-turvy. I cannot tell you properly till I see you. What is more, for reasons of policy I had to put a good face on it and find everything beautiful. I cannot understand how people can have liked the opera. . . . One must be prudent, and after all, everyone did their best, and the enthusiasm is really boundless. . . .

WEBER TO HIS WIFE

Vienna, 22 February 1822

. . . The throng of people is too great, and I am tossed like a ball from hand to hand. But for all that it is a wonderful thing, and a strange feeling, to see and know that one has given a thrust, or a direction, to one's whole generation which nobody could have anticipated in view of the prevailing taste. You really cannot conceive what respect and affection everyone shows me. . . .

WEBER TO COUNT BRÜHL IN BERLIN

Dresden, 13 January 1823

Hochgeehrtester Herr Graf,
Professor Lichtenstein, of course, described to me the manifestations of my friends' sympathy, by which I was deeply delighted and touched, and he particularly extolled the care and kindness displayed in every way on this occasion by you, whom I so profoundly esteem, and the manner in which you adorned the whole thing by your presence. . . .

But will you not be angry now, and reprove me sternly, if I ask your permission to refuse the sum of 100 thalers? . . . This matter would inevitably come to the public ear, which is now unfortunately bent upon everything that happens in the world. Just imagine an article running as follows: '*The esteemed board of management of our theatre made a public notification of the 50th performance given of 'Der Freischütz' in 18 months. This event, so rare in the annals of the theatre, also merits a special distinction, the more so as the takings at these 50 'House Full' performances are said to have amounted to 30,000 thalers. It was therefore decided to offer the composer a present of 100 thalers.*'

'Such then' – people would say – 'is the reward, the distinction, which a German composer, the *Kapellmeister* of a neighbouring royal house – living in circumstances that raise him above financial anxiety – can look forward to receiving from the foremost German royal art institution and from its Director, that fervent patron of native talent – after achieving such an unprecedented success.'....

The success of 'Euryanthe', Weber's grandest and most ambitious work, did not fufill the composer's hopes, expressed here in a letter to his wife.

WEBER TO HIS WIFE

Vienna, 17 October 1823

... Yesterday and today the rehearsals gave me great happiness. Never was so much weeping in any opera as in this one. To listen to these kind people, one would suppose there had been no great works until now, nor ever would be hereafter. I know, of course, how much allowance I must make for their well-meant enthusiasm, and only hope that some proportion of it will spread to the audience. At such moments I wish I had you here with me, for they are inestimable....

WEBER TO PROFESSOR HEINRICH LICHTENSTEIN IN BERLIN

Dresden, 1 April 1824

My beloved brother,

I have been going through a most agitated period, and perhaps it was as well that my tremendous burden of work (for I am still alone) left me no time for thinking. But I could not prevent myself from feeling great and lasting bitterness. At Prague *Euryanthe* was a failure, at Frankfurt it caused a furore. Everyone was amazed by the really infamous scribblings of the Viennese gossip papers. So I was very curious to see what impression the work would make on our reserved, naturally cold and very peculiar public. The mood was unfriendly rather than favourable to it. So *Euryanthe* was put on yesterday evening – and I had a triumph that beggars all description! I had never seen a Dresden audience so stirred, roused to such enthusiasm. The excitement grew with each successive act. At the end they first called for me, in a real tempest of applause, and then for *everybody*.

I must admit it was a first-rate performance. Particularly Devrient as Euryanthe and Mlle Funk as Eglantine excelled themselves, both in acting and singing. Mayer as Lysiart and Bergmann as Adolar both did very well indeed. The chorus was excellent. The orchestra played with a perfection and subtlety that are to be heard only here. Everyone is now saying with one voice that this opera is far superior to *Der Freischütz*. Tieck, among others, was to have attended a party after the opera, but declared that his mind was too full of it, and said (to other people, of course) that there were things in this opera that Gluck and Mozart would have envied me. I know I can repeat such a thing to you without being misunderstood. I would not venture to do so to anyone else in the world. . . .

Weber's hectic activity had sapped his strength, which had never been robust. Already in an advanced stage of consumption, he was conscious of his impending doom when he accepted the commission for an opera for London, where 'Freischütz' had been enormously successful. The offer of a fee of £1,000 and his anxiety to provide modest security for the needs of his family prevailed over his fear of the fatigue of such a journey. That he was able not only to finish but to produce 'Oberon' at Covent Garden was a phenomenal act of heroism. He conducted the first three performances with tremendous success, was still able to conduct a performance of 'Freischütz', and then was found dead in his bed a couple of days before the date fixed for his return home.

WEBER TO HIS WIFE

London, 12 March 1826

. . . At half past ten I drove to Lord Hertford's. Heavens, what a vast assembly! A magnificent room, 500–600 people there, all of the greatest brilliance. Almost the entire Italian opera company, including Veluti, the celebrated Puzzi, and a double-bass player, the no less celebrated Dragonetti. Some *finales* were sung, etc., but not a soul listened. The shrieking and jabbering of this throng of humanity was atrocious. While I played they tried to get a little quiet, and circa 100 people gathered round, displaying the greatest interest. But what they can have heard, God alone knows, for I myself heard very little of it. Meanwhile I thought hard about my 30 guineas, and so was perfectly patient. At last, about 2 o'clock, they went in to supper, whereupon I took my leave. . . .

WEBER TO HIS WIFE

London, 2 June 1826

... How I envy you all for your good appetites, but unfortunately I am still very much upset and exhausted. Dear God, I cannot wait to be in the coach! My concert turned out even better than I expected, I have nearly £100 sterling left over, a lot for Germany though not for London. If only next Monday's *Freischütz* were behind me. But God will give me strength. Since yesterday I have had a vesicatory as big as one's hand on my chest, they say that will get rid of the terrible breathlessness, etc., etc. Your life seems to be a positive whirl of pleasure, with guests every day! Well, that's quite right, I like it better than if you were in the apothecary's hands. Please God I may be able to play my part when I get home. I shall come with the best will in the world to do so. Since this letter does not expect an answer, it will be very short. A most convenient thing, to have no need to answer! Fürstenau has cancelled his concert, which means that I may get away a few days sooner – Huzza! If only I were with you already!

The post mortem revealed an almost total destruction of the lungs; his endurance and energy during those last weeks were a miracle of will-power.

The perplexing situation of a successful composer in the eighteen-forties, who was unable to make a living, is pathetically demonstrated in the letters of Albert Lortzing *(1801–51), some of whose operas have survived on the German stage to this day. Both his parents were actors. He grew up in the theatre and started his career as an actor and buffo tenor. Later, when his operas had already made him famous, he found temporary employment as a conductor, but had to return to the stage again when his baton was not needed. The type of theatre he served was the German 'Stadttheater' (Municipal Theatre), run by a manager at his own risk, with a repertory of plays and the lighter kind of opera and a miserably paid staff. Neither publishers nor theatres paid the composer more than a pittance for his works, in spite of their popular success.*

LORTZING TO HIS FRIEND FRIEDRICH KRUG IN KARLSRUHE

Leipzig, 19 February 1840

Your letter informing me of the views of your manager caused me the greatest surprise. I know from experience how economical even Court theatres are apt to be, but I have never yet encountered such niggardliness – if you will forgive the expression – even from the smallest commercial theatre. So the poor authors are to make up for what has been squandered by a – probably imprudent – manager? What hope is there for composers, who, God pity us, are in any case so underpaid in Germany and not even protected against theft, if even the Court theatres refuse to pay decent fees? I cannot allow my opera to be performed for the fee your manager declares he paid Marschner – though I almost doubt it, because Ringelhardt used to pay 100 thalers for every opera by Marschner – for I should be really ashamed to tell people about it, when I get 30 thalers from the smallest travelling company. I had to pay out more than 16 Reichsthalers in copyist's fees for *Czar und Zimmermann*. So, simply for your sake, I shall drop 3 Friedrichsd'or and sell the opera for 12 Friedrichsd'or, and be content if your manager finds that price satisfactory; if not, I must deny myself the honour of having my work performed on your stage. The fee I mention is the one paid by a municipal theatre of any importance, and surely no Court theatre will wish to fall below that. Between ourselves, if my opera were to begin its career at Karlsruhe, I would let it go for the lowest price; but by now it has earned its civic rights, so to speak, and has either been given or is now being rehearsed in some 20 theatres – without boasting, there is no end to the requests – so it will not suffer if Karlsruhe does not put it on. . . .

LORTZING TO FRIEDRICH KRUG

Leipzig, 19 September 1842

. . . So far as concerns me personally, I have every cause for satisfaction; my family circumstances are agreeable, so are my circumstances in general, and since fortune has favoured me above many others through the wide circulation of my operas, I should no doubt be content with my lot. Only one thing irks me – acting in plays – and I would gladly seize an opportunity of leaving the stage and appearing before it with a conductor's baton in my hand, if only an acceptable opening would offer. But such things are rare, and I shall no doubt spend some time longer, perhaps my whole life, in cramming parts. I could put up with acting them, but learning them – oh, my dear fellow, when one longs so much to devote the mornings to one's favourite occupation, it is horrible to have to drag oneself off to memorize lines! But that is how things are, for directors are unreasonable enough to demand that in return for one's wages, one shall act as well. . . .

LORTZING TO HIS FRIEND P. J. DÜRINGER IN MANNHEIM

October 1845

My dear brother,

You suppose things must be going badly with me because I do not write; indeed, they are not going well, but not badly as yet, for I and my family are not yet starving, and as long as a German composer – being incidentally a man of renommé – can say that for himself, he can still regard himself as lucky and has reason to hold his fatherland in high esteem. It is true that the occasional small fees come along rarely, and every now and then one must sell a little stock – bought in better days – which is painful; but so it must be, for where else could I take from without stealing! . . .

Our greetings to all your family, and if you get the chance, do strike Lachner [the conductor] dead – by the way, I send him my best wishes. . . .

LORTZING TO HIS FRIEND PHILIP REGER

April 1846

. . . So for about six weeks now my daughter Lina has been a member of the Court theatre company at Bernburg. . . . I am assured by eye-witnesses that she is doing very prettily; what she herself rather dislikes is the amount of crowd work in the operas, of which they put on a great many; I comfort her by pointing out that the greatest artists, prominent among them you and myself, have had to sing in the chorus for years. . . .

LORTZING TO FRIEDRICH KRUG

Vienna, November 1847

. . . I have now been here about 15 months, but still do not feel really at home in 'beautiful Vienna', as it is called. Whether because I had lived for 13 or 14 years in another place and completely settled down there, or because as one grows older one has more difficulty in opening one's heart – at any rate, I do not feel as comfortable as at Leipzig. Musical taste here is the worst that could be found, although Mozart, Haydn, Beethoven, Gluck, etc., lived and worked here. Only Mozart is still sung, the others are never put on, and Spohr and Marschner – to each of whom the Kärntner Tor [the Court Opera] devoted one performance last year, for shame's sake – bore the public fearfully. The Musical Society is about to present *Elijah* in memory of Mendelssohn, and I myself am rehearsing *Antigone* [by Mendelssohn]. But I am firmly convinced that the worthy Viennese would rather listen to a Strauss waltz or an opera by the celebrated Maestro Verdi. . . .

To the discomfort of performing in a ramshackle, unheated theatre was added the trouble of getting his fee from a manager always on the brink of bankruptcy.

LORTZING TO HIS WIFE

Gera, 1 February 1850

. . . If one wanted to give somebody a disgust for the theatre, this would be the place to send him. The flimsily-built playhouse stands quite by itself, outside the town gates, and it cannot be heated, so that the cold is fearful. The scenery, costumes and orchestra are atrocious; and the place is permanently shrouded in lamp-smoke, for as the paraffin threatens to freeze, the lamps are turned up higher and higher. In short, it is all of a piece. . . . Today at noon I shall no doubt collect what is due to me and be able to send it to you, for I am afraid your small store of cash must be running out.

Afternoon

This morning I went to see the management and after much beating about the bush, came out with the request to be given what was owing to me from yesterday's takings. I was told the accounts had not yet been made up, and that they would send it to me later. It is now past four o'clock and I have received nothing yet. I suspect that they used yesterday's takings to pay the salaries, and do not suppose me to be as needy as I unfortunately am. So I shall have to send this letter off empty, much as it grieves me. After tomorrow's performance I shall insist on having both instalments. So my dear, kind wife, send a line to Plenkner and ask him for a few thalers until Monday, for you cannot possibly manage until then with the little you have. . . .

LORTZING TO PHILIP REGER

Gera, 4 February 1850

. . . The German composer Albert Lortzing is obliged to desert his family every 8–10 days! Their small supply of ready cash hardly lasts out until he has earned some more! he himself has barely enough for his train-fare. It is only foolishness, but it hurt me to have to spend New Year's Eve away from home for the first time in my life, and to be away from my dear wife on our 25th wedding anniversary! Added to which, there is the hardship of performing in such cold weather in such small theatres; and most of all, my awful horror of acting! But the remarkable thing is that every theatre is set on it, I have not yet written to any of the important ones but I am convinced I would be welcome there as well, and why? Not because I am Lortzing the actor – no, but because I am Lortzing the composer, and that is the bitterest thing of all. . . .

LORTZING TO PHILIP REGER

Leipzig, 4 March 1850

. . . Next month I am off – you will be surprised! – to London, where I have been invited by Lumley, the manager, to present my 'Zar' [*Czar und Zimmermann*] at the Italian Opera House. Unfortunately I shall get nothing for the opera itself, for in dear, free England, copyright is worthless. Mr Lumley is merely paying my travelling expenses and lodging, and has pointed out the flowery prospect of my selling the vocal score to a London publisher (to which my publisher here has generously agreed). If the opera is a success, as may be expected, since it is to be performed at Her Majesty's Theatre and by the foremost artistes (Lablache – van Bett), I shall have the further advantage of being able to place it in other Italian theatres, for manager Lumley has promised me the free use of the Italian translation. And perhaps some other little bits of business can be arranged, if I once become close friends with Albert and Victoria; in any case the whole enterprise is a good thing for me, provided I don't get drowned or eaten by whales. Once safely back from there, I shall probably accept an engagement in Berlin, at the new Friedrich-Wilhelmstadt Theatre. This is to open on 1 May, and though for the time being it will give only comedy, farce and operetta, it is to present comic opera as well next year, and is already a serious rival to the Königstadt – so they say. The salary they offer me is atrocious; but with a benefit performance and what I can earn by the incidental music I am to write for the farces, I can no doubt count on 1,000 thalers – I hope! The thing is that this man (Director Deichmann) thinks that by engaging me he will add lustre to his enterprise; apart from that, any musician he could lay hands on would serve his purpose equally well for what I am really supposed to do – produce farces and take rehearsals. . . .

LORTZING TO HIS SON-IN-LAW IN VIENNA

Leipzig, 30 April 1850

. . . My London plans fell through. Either some hitch must have occurred, although the opera was already announced, with Lablache-van Bett, Mlle Sonntag-Marie, etc. etc., or else the performance has been postponed for so long that they thought I would not be able to come, for I wrote that the thing must be settled before the end of April. Too bad! too bad! . . .

LORTZING TO HIS FRIEND P. H. DÜRINGER

Berlin, 1 August 1850

. . . So, to return to my shattered finances – yes, dear fellow, I am in the same case as Robert [*le Diable*], who had 'nothing left' – only with the difference that I have not gambled it away, as he did. My little savings are gone, my few bits of silver and valuables were pawned long ago; and incidentally, I still owe several hundred thalers in Leipzig. My small salary (without a benefit) amounts to 600 thalers, which of course is hardly enough to buy food; and I even had to ask for an advance on that, which is being deducted in instalments. I can assure you I am sometimes without the barest necessities – I have nothing left to pawn, and I really cannot go naked before the world, for I should be ashamed – for the world! I am working solely for the publishers, am kicked about by those swine – and have to put up with it. . . .

When Lortzing died at the age of fifty he left nothing but debts and a destitute family, and yet half a dozen of his operas were firmly established in the German theatre.

Felix Mendelssohn-Bartholdy *(1809–47) is a happy exception among musicians. Coming from a wealthy family, he was never beset by the practical problems of how to make a living. Intellectually as well as musically gifted, he was a writer of incomparably lively and spirited letters, and some years of travel, which his father regarded as an essential part of his education, are richly and amusingly illustrated in his letters to his family. His early acquaintance with Goethe, to whom he had been introduced as an infant prodigy by his teacher Karl Friedrich Zelter, a close friend of the great poet, was renewed on one of these journeys.*

MENDELSSOHN TO HIS FAMILY

London, 25 April 1829

. . . It is terrible! It is crazy! I am dazed and my head is spinning! London is the grandest and most complicated monstrosity on the face of the earth. How can I pack into a single letter all I have been through in the last three days? I can scarcely remember the main points myself by now, but I must not keep a diary, for that would cut down my experience further, and I don't want that – I want to absorb everything that comes my way. . . . But just step out of my lodging and turn to the right down Regent Street, look at the splendid wide street lined with porticos (unhappily, today again it is lying under a thick fog), and look at the shops with their inscriptions, in letters as tall as a man, and the stage-coaches piled high with passengers, and see how at one point a string of conveyances is out-distanced by the pedestrians because it has been held up by some elegant carriages, and how at another point a horse is rearing up because its rider has acquaintances in yonder house, and how men are used to carry round posters that promise us graceful and artistic performances by trained cats – and the beggars and the negroes and the fat John Bulls with a slim, pretty daughter on each arm. Oh, those daughters! But never fear, I run no danger in that respect, either in Hyde Park, with its throng of ladies, where I took a fashionable stroll yesterday with Madame Moscheles, or at the concert, or at the Opera (for I have been all over that already); the only danger is at street-corners and crossings, where I often murmur to myself a familiar phrase: 'Take care not to fall under the wheels!' Such confusion! Such a maelstrom! I ask nothing better than to become historical and describe it all calmly, else you will make nothing of it; but if you could only see me, sitting near the heavenly grand piano that Clementi have just sent along for the duration of my stay, beside a cheerful fire, within my own four walls, with my shoes on, and my grey open-work stockings and my olive-green gloves (for I have calls to pay presently), and next door my huge four-poster bed, in which I can 'lie down for a walk' at night, with the bright-coloured curtains and old-fashioned furniture, my breakfast tea and dry toast still in front of me, the *servant-girl*, with her hair in curl-papers, just bringing me my new cravat and asking for my orders – at which I try to nod in the polite English manner, jerking my head backwards – and the fashionable, fog-shrouded street; and if you could only hear the pitiful tones of the beggar who has just struck up a song under my window (but his voice is almost drowned by the cries of the hawkers), and if you but knew that from here to the *City* is a three-quarter-hour drive and that all the way along, and at every glimpse down the side streets and far into the distance one finds uproar, and that even so one has gone through only perhaps a quarter of populated London, you would understand that I am half out of my senses. . . .

London, 15 May 1829

On Monday evening there was a ball at the Duke of Devonshire's; everything that wealth, luxury and taste could devise by way of beautiful touches for a ball, was assembled there. . . . I had heard people coming up the steps behind me, but had not looked round, now I saw with a shock that it had been Wellington and Peel. In the main ballroom instead of the chandelier there was a broad thick wreath of red roses, some fourteen feet in diameter, which seemed to float in the air; hundreds of tiny lights were burning on it. The walls were covered with life-sized portraits and full-length figures by Van Dyck, round the room was a raised platform on which the old ladies, loaded with diamonds, pearls and jewels of every description, took their seats; in the middle danced the beautiful girls, among whom were some heavenly faces; a band with its own conductor played for them; the doors stood open into the neighbouring rooms, which were hung with Titians, Correggios, Leonardos and Dutch masters; to see the lovely forms moving below the lovely pictures, and to glide around, tranquil and completely unknown amid the bustle and general excitement, unseen and unnoticed, seeing and noting many things – it was one of the most delightful evenings I have ever spent. Next to the ballroom was a small conservatory, cool air and fragrance wafting through its open doors! All the fruits of every season were heaped in profusion on the buffets; and there one saw the aristocracy flirting, and waltzing so badly, and how the ladies *perched on* the tables, and the gentlemen sprawled with their feet on the sofas and stretched themselves – during a tender conversation with ladies! . . .

MENDELSSOHN TO HIS FAMILY

Weimar, 25 May 1830

. . . Goethe is so friendly and affable with me that I do not know how to thank him or to deserve it. This morning he made me play the piano to him for about an hour, pieces from all the great composers, in chronological order, and tell him how they had worked at them; while he sat in a dark corner, like *Jupiter tonans*, and his old eyes flashed lightning. He would have none of Beethoven. But I told him I could not help that, and thereupon played him the first movement of the C Minor Symphony. That affected him strangely. At first he said, 'But it does not move one at all; it merely astounds; it is grandiose', and then went on growling to himself, until after a long time he began again: 'That is very great, quite mad, one is almost afraid the house will fall down; and only imagine when they are all playing together!' And at table, in the middle of talking of something else, he began again about it. You know already that I dine with him every day now; he asks me very penetrating questions, and after the meal he is always so gay and communicative that we usually sit on alone in the room for over an hour, while he talks without a pause. It is a real delight, how he brings me etchings, for instance, and explains them, or gives his views on 'Hernani' and Lamartine's Elegies, or about the theatre, or about pretty girls. . . .

As a man of good breeding I sent to enquire yesterday if I were really not coming too often. But he growled at Ottilie [Goethe's daughter-in-law], who carried the message, and said he had hardly begun to talk with me yet, for I was so clear about my subject, and he wanted to *learn a great deal from me*. I waited, however, until Ottilie told me again, and when he even said it to me himself yesterday evening, and declared he still had many things on his mind that I must explain to him, I said 'Oh yes', and thought 'This is an unforgettable honour for me.' It is more often the other way round! . . .

MENDELSSOHN TO HIS FAMILY

Munich, 6 June 1830

. . . After a morning drive I found old Goethe in a genial humour; he began telling stories; from [Auber's] 'La Muette de Portici' he was led on to Walter Scott, thence to the pretty girls at Weimar, from the girls to the students, to 'Die Räuber' and so to Schiller; after that he talked cheerfully and without pause, for over an hour it must have been, about Schiller's life, his writings, and his position at Weimar . . . then he told stories from his period as theatre manager, and when I tried to thank him, he said: 'It is purely accidental, it all comes out at random, called forth by the pleasure of your company.' Words that sounded wonderfully sweet to my ears; in short, it was a conversation to remember all one's life. Next day he sent me a page of his *Faust* manuscript, at the bottom of which he had written: 'To my dear young friend F.M.B., strong and tender master of the piano, in friendly remembrance of happy days in May 1830. J.W. von Goethe', and with this he gave me three letters of recommendation as well. . . .

The German musician, in love with the Italian landscape and art treasures, was critical of Italian music and the easy-going Italian habits of performing. Of the latter, we shall learn more later. Marchese Torlonia, mentioned in the following letter, was a noble amateur, responsible for the financial and artistic enterprise of the operatic season in Rome. Antonio Pacini was one of the most respected operatic composers of the time – and the lover of Countess Samoilov, a lady of enormous wealth and dubious reputation, who is also alluded to in a letter of Bellini's of 28 December 1831. (See p. 250.)

MENDELSSOHN TO HIS FAMILY

Rome, 17 January 1831

. . . There can be no question of a performance here. The orchestras are unbelievably bad; there is a real dearth of musicians, and of the right feeling. Each of the few violinists strikes up in his own way, all beginning or coming in at different times; the wind-instruments are tuned too high or too low and add flourishes to their accompaniments such as we are used to hearing from street musicians, but scarcely as good; the general effect is a real caterwauling – and this with pieces they know. The question is whether someone can and will reform the whole business from the ground up, bring new performers into the orchestra, teach the musicians to keep time, and in fact re-educate them, in which case they would undoubtedly give pleasure to their audiences. But until that happens there can be no improvement, and the general indifference is such that there is no prospect of it. I heard a flautist play a solo with the flute pitched more than a quarter-tone too high; it set my teeth on edge, but no one else noticed it, and after the final trill they applauded mechanically. And if only things were really better in singing! All the great singers have left the country; Lablache, David, Mlle Lalande, Pisaroni, etc., are singing in Paris, and now the little ones are copying their great moments and making an intolerable caricature of them. We may try to carry through something incorrect or impossible – but it is certainly something *different*, and just as a *cicisbeo* will seem to me, to all eternity, to be a low, mean creature, so it is with Italian music. I may be too dull to understand one or the other; but I cannot help that, and the other day at the Filharmonica, when, after all their Pacinis and Bellinis, Cavaliere Ricci asked me to accompany him in *Non più andrai* [Mozart], and the first notes were heard, so profoundly different and divinely remote from all the rest, I saw the thing clearly, and there can be no assimilation, so long as the skies here are blue and the winters as pleasant as this one. . . .

. . . The evening before last a theatre which Torlonia has fitted up and is to manage, opened with a new opera by Pacini. There was a tremendous crush; the boxes all full of the most elegant people; young Torlonia appeared in the stage-box and was much applauded, together with his mother, the old Duchess. People called out 'Bravo Torlonia, grazie, grazie'. Opposite him was Jérôme, in his court dress, with bemedalled chest; in the next box a Countess Samoilov, etc. Above the orchestra is a picture of Time, pointing to a dial which slowly moves round, enough to make one melancholy. Then Pacini took his seat at the piano and received an ovation. He had not written an overture; the opera began with a chorus, during which a tuned anvil was beaten in time to the music. The Corsair appeared, sang his aria and was applauded, at which the Corsair, up on the stage, and the Maestro down in the orchestra, both bowed (by the way, the pirate sings contralto and is called Mme Mariani). Many other pieces followed and the thing grew tedious. The audience thought so too, and when Pacini's great *finale* rang out, the Pit rose to their feet, began talking in loud voices and laughing, and turned their backs on the stage. Mme Samoilov swooned away in her box and had to be carried out. Pacini vanished from the piano, and amid considerable tumult the act-drop was lowered. Next came the great Bluebeard Ballet, and then the last act of the opera. Having once started, they hissed the whole ballet from beginning to end, and accompanied the second act of the opera, likewise, with hisses and laughter. At the end they called for Torlonia, but he did not come. That is a sober account of a first night and theatre-opening in Rome. I had expected it to be great fun, and came away in low spirits. If the music had caused a *furore* I would have been vexed, for it is sorry stuff, quite beneath criticism. But it vexes me, too, that they should suddenly turn their backs on Pacini, their great favourite, whom they wanted to crown on the Capitol, ape his tunes and sing parodies of them; and it shows what a low opinion the public has of such music. On another occasion they carried him home shoulder-high – that is no amends. They would not behave like that with Boieldieu in France – simply from a sense of propriety, apart from any feeling for art. . . .

MENDELSSOHN TO HEINRICH BÄRMANN IN MUNICH

Rome, 14 February 1831

. . . Life here is delicious, of course, richer and more exciting than one could find anywhere else; but after all, fellows like us are musicians and long for music that sounds good, and there is none to be had here. There are indeed other things by way of compensation which have beautiful music in them – the most lovely spring air, a warm blue sky, heavenly pictures everywhere, and nature and antiquity so colourful and rich that it beggars the imagination; but now, while writing to you, I feel the lack of a note of music or a musical companion, and would give a great deal for just half an hour's chat with you. Since I came to Italy I have heard no music except what I play myself, the orchestras and singers here are really too bad. Those I met playing small parts in London are singing the leading roles in Venice and Florence; Mlle Carl, from Berlin, was engaged as *prima donna* for Rome (however, she did not give satisfaction, so her contract has been terminated), and there is no question of having people like Pasta, Malibran or David, they are in London or Paris.

So it is only natural that people here take no real pleasure in it any more, and I would go so far as to say that nowhere in Rome have I felt such an unmusical atmosphere as at the Opera. Imagine an orchestra you might find in the poorest village in Bavaria, words can hardly describe it, among other things there is a first clarinet here at the Teatro di Apollo, – oh, Bärmann, you should hear him! The fellow begins everything with an *appoggiatura*, sticks fast at the third note, and winds up with a little trill, flapping his elbows; and he has such a timbre that I thought for a moment it was a very bad oboe; but then the oboe followed on with a solo, and I saw the whole thing. The bassoons imitate combs to the life, every instrument is off key except the big drum, one or another of them makes a wrong entry every few seconds, the tympani come crashing valiantly into a tender solo, but then the first violin goes 'Sssh!' and holds the thing together. The double bass is a terrible fellow, wears a red cap in the orchestra, has a thick moustache, lies in ambush for notes, watching where he can grab a semibreve now and again – and so it all goes on with fire and precision, as the critics say in Germany.

No symphony has ever yet been played in Rome. But it is their proud boast that Haydn's *Creation* was given here a few years ago and that the orchestra – as they put it – got through the thing quite tolerably; for a good performance of such horribly difficult music can hardly be possible even in Germany, where people understand that learned stuff. At which I pull a face like St John of Nepomuk, remind myself that I am in the native land of music, where they have everything except musicians, and confine myself as far as possible to the young girls, who have little to say about music, and are all the prettier for that. I forgot to mention that the trumpeters usually play those cursed key trumpets, which affect me like a pretty woman with a beard or a man with a bosom. . . . So when I now tell you that in spite of all this I am leading a quite delightful life here, that the winter went by in a flash and that I spend my time in the greatest happiness and contentment, you will think I have deserted the banner of good music. But this is the way of it: I have been composing every morning in my room, and diligently, so that I can show you something new again when I get back, and I have been pleased with it and there has been nothing wrong with me; then, about noon, I go out to visit Rome, to a gallery, or to look at ruins, or into the country, and there of course one feels pleasure again. In the evening I have always been, more than ever, in company, seeing a mass of people from the most different nations and countries enjoying themselves together – and that is not bad either, especially as the mild spring air makes one quite forget the winter and is itself enough to put one in spirits. I have stopped the heating now, and sit at my open window, the almond trees are in flower everywhere, the bushes are bursting into leaf, one already has to seek the shade; for February that's quite tolerable. In addition to which in the last few days there has been the crazy carnival, when everyone spent the whole day out of doors; the place swarmed with the craziest masks, the Italian women are at their most brilliant, people throw confetti at one another like mad, they fling themselves with real passion into the childish game and one cannot keep out of it, nosegays of roses and violets are thrown to the ladies in their carriages and they reward one with a shower of bonbons and sugared almonds, one lies in wait for acquaintances, the men have flour thrown at them till they look like miller's apprentices, and the intrigues and quizzing go on all the time; but unfortunately the last 3 days, when everything is at its maddest, were lost for us. For the day before yesterday, when I arrived on the Corso with my load of confetti, I found the whole street black with men, no ladies, not a mask to be seen, and at last I discovered, posted up at a corner, a papal edict proclaiming that the carnival was over, because of inauspicious circumstances; in other words they claimed to have discovered a revolution, and soldiers with loaded guns had been posted in all the streets; that evening a few shots were actually fired, people were arrested, one man badly wounded. So the fun changed to bitter earnest; and although the fasting does not begin until the day after tomorrow, the streets are already silent and have their everyday aspect. . . .

In Milan Mendelssohn became acquainted with a humble Austrian civil servant whose name was Karl Mozart – which makes one realize the small distance in time which still separated the mortals from the Gods. The Baroness Dorothea von Ertmann, wife of the Austrian governor-general of

Milan, had been a piano pupil of Beethoven's and his Pianoforte Sonata Op. 101 was dedicated to her.

MENDELSSOHN TO HIS FAMILY

Isola Bella, 14 July 1831

. . . Another acquaintance I am delighted to have made there [in Milan] is Herr Mozart, who is a government official there, but in mind and heart is really a musician. He must take after his father very much, especially in character; for one hears from his lips a host of the naïve, unaffected remarks we find so touching in his father's letters, and one cannot help loving him from the first moment. For instance, I think it exceedingly fine that he should be as eager for his father's fame, and to hear him praised, as though he were a young, rising musician; and one evening at the Ertmanns', when a lot of Beethoven's music had been played, the Baroness whispered to me that I should play something by Mozart as well, otherwise his son would not be so merry as usual; and when I played the overture to *Don Giovanni*, he warmed up for the first time and asked, with his Austrian accent, for the overture to his father's' *Magic Flute* as well, and was as delighted as a child with it; one could not help loving him. . . .

Some of Mendelssohn's most outstanding works – the 'Hebrides' Overture, the Scottish Symphony, the Italian Symphony – have their roots in impressions gathered during those three happy years which were largely spent abroad. Received everywhere with the utmost distinction, he made the best of his opportunities, became widely known and acclaimed as a composer, especially in England where he was adored. He had become a mature artist by the time he returned to Germany, ready to pull his weight in the organization of modern musical institutions.

MENDELSSOHN TO GOETHE

Lucerne, 28 August 1831

. . . I came here from the land of cheerful skies and warmth; Switzerland indeed gave me a very different reception, I had rain and storm and fog, and in the mountains quite often met with falling snow, But even that suited me, I do not know why; and when at times a couple of black peaks emerged from the clouds, or the mist parted to reveal a whole landscape bathed in sunshine, that too was magnificent. . . .

. . . I have just come from the theatre, where they are giving Schiller's *William Tell*; I would like, if you will permit, to give you a short account of this performance in Tell's native land. The whole company consists of about ten people; and the stage is as big and as high as a medium-sized closet; but they were set on giving the big crowd scenes. So there were two men with pointed hats to represent Gessler's army, and two with round hats to stand for the Swiss peasants. Some of the actors had only learnt the gist of their lines, and kept rendering it in verse they improvised themselves; Gessler's crier hit his drum so hard at the first stroke that it broke out of his buttonhole and fell to the ground; and he could not contrive to hook it in again – to the great glee of the freedom-loving audience, who laughed without restraint at the slave of tyranny. But even this could not kill the play, it still made its effect. When the curtain rose on the well-known places they had seen the day before they were in their seventh heaven, nudging one another and pointing to the cardboard lake, which they could see far better in real life by going outside. The whole thing was quite arcadian and primitive, like the childhood of acting. And when, sitting there, I thought of an opera by Spontini, where everything is so realistically, anxiously imitated, where four hundred people sing when a great army is to be represented, where anvils are attuned to make the Cyclops' smithy more convincing, where the scenery changes every few minutes and each scene is more brilliant than the last, I ended by feeling that this Lucerne theatre, with its knobbly lake-waves, had really a more natural effect, with greater illusion; for here one's imagination could join in the game, and had much ado to keep pace – whereas there it is hemmed in and its wings are clipped. . . .

MENDELSSOHN TO PROFESSOR ZELTER IN BERLIN

Paris, 15 February 1832

. . . But the most important and remarkable of all that I had not yet heard is the Orchestre du Conservatoire. It is only natural that this should be the most perfect that can be heard in France, for after all it is the Paris Conservatoire that gives the concerts; but more than that, it is the most perfect performance to be heard anywhere. They gathered together, the best in Paris, brought in the young violinists who were studying at the Conservatoire, appointed an able and energetic musician as their conductor, and then rehearsed for two whole years before venturing to appear in public – until they were playing together like one man and a false note was out of the question. In point of fact every orchestra should be like that, false notes and wrong time should be ruled out once and for all; but unfortunately things are not like that, and so this is the best I have ever heard. The school of Baillot, Rode and

Kreutzer has provided the violinists, and it is a pleasure to see the young fellows crowding into the orchestra and setting to work with the same style of bowing, the same manner, the same calm and the same fire. Last Sunday there were fourteen on each side. Habeneck was conducting, and kept time with the bow of his violin. . . .

. . . The general arrangements, too, are very appropriate and sensible; the concerts are not frequent (once a fortnight) and take place at 2 o'clock on Sunday afternoon, so that it is a feast-day in every sense of the word; people do nothing afterwards except go home to dinner, and their impressions remain with them, for there is seldom if ever an opera that evening. Moreover, the hall is a little one, so that for one thing the music makes twice the effect and we hear every detail twice as clearly, and for another thing the audience is small, very select, and yet seems a large gathering. The musicians themselves delight in Beethoven's great symphonies; they have made themselves thoroughly familiar with them, and are happy to have mastered the difficulties. Some of them, including Habeneck himself, undoubtedly have a perfectly genuine love of Beethoven; but as for the others, who are the loudest in their enthusiasm, I do not believe a word they say about it; for they make this an excuse for decrying the other masters – declaring Haydn was merely a fashionable composer, Mozart an ordinary sort of fellow; and such narrow-minded enthusiasm cannot be sincere. If they really felt what Beethoven meant, they would also realize what Haydn was, and feel small; but not a bit of it, they go briskly ahead with their criticism. Beethoven is uncommonly popular with the concert public, as well, because they believe that only the connoisseur can appreciate him; but only a small minority really enjoy him, and I cannot abide the disdainful attitude towards Haydn and Mozart; it infuriates me. . . .

MENDELSSOHN TO HIS FATHER IN BERLIN

Paris, 21 February 1832

. . . But it is now high time I wrote to you about my travel plans, my dear Father, and what I have to say this time will for many reasons be more serious than usual. First let me sum things up and speak of the aims you fixed for me before I went away, telling me to hold firmly to them. I was to take a close look at different countries, so as to find one where I should like to live and work; I was to make my name and abilities known, so that people would welcome me wherever I decided to settle, and sympathize with what I was trying to do; and finally, I was to make use of my good fortune and your kindness to lay the foundations of my future career. It makes me feel very happy to be able to tell you that I believe all this has been done. Apart from possible mistakes which one does not notice until too late, I think I have achieved the aims you set me. People already know I exist and want to do something, and they are sure to welcome anything good I may produce. . . . Before I leave here (if it can be arranged), and certainly in London, if the cholera does not prevent me from going there in April, I intend to give a concert on my own and make a little money, which is something I also wanted to do before coming home to you; so I hope that *this* part of your plan – that I should make a name for myself – may be said to have been fulfilled. But your other intention, that I should find a country for myself, has also been met, at least in a general way. The country is Germany, I have now become quite convinced of that. . . .

London, 11 May 1832

. . . I must tell you about an amusing morning I had last week. Of all the signs of recognition I have so far received, this was the one that pleased and touched me most, and perhaps the only one I shall always look back on with fresh delight. On Saturday morning the Philharmonic Orchestra was rehearsing, but they could not include anything by me because my Overture had not yet been copied out. After Beethoven's 'Pastoral' Symphony, during which I was in a box, I went down into the hall to greet a few old friends. But I was scarcely down before someone in the orchestra called out 'There is Mendelssohn', at which they all began to shout and clap so heartily that for a time I did not know which way to turn; and when that was over, someone else called out 'Welcome to him', and they began to make the same noise again, and I had to go right through the hall and climb up among them on the platform and thank them. You know, I shall never forget that, for it meant more to me than any distinction – it showed that the musicians liked me and were glad I had come, and I cannot tell you how happy it made me. . . .

First in the Rhineland, then in Leipzig, where he was in charge of the 'Gewandhaus' concerts and founded the Conservatoire, still one of the foremost institutions of its kind in Germany, Mendelssohn became the centre of all serious musical efforts. In addition he undertook special duties in Berlin when King Frederick William IV, keenly interested in the promotion of music and literature, appointed him 'Generalmusikdirektor'.

Skimming through Mendelssohn's letters makes one marvel at his incredible burden of responsibilities, resulting from the coincidence of an extraordinary ability both as performer and organizer, an incomparable capacity for systematic work, a keen awareness of and devotion to his duties, and the inevitable claims made on the kindly disposition of a man of his character and efficiency. The question remains – what about the composer? If one feels somehow disappointed by the undeniable fact that Mendelssohn's creative life lacks that impressive climax of concentration of all his faculties towards the highest achievement marking the lives of other great musicians, the cause may be found in the ruthless overtaxing of his forces in the pursuit of innumerable practical affairs, combined with a facility which enabled him to throw off a work with a short, concentrated effort. How much he was aware of the danger, as an artist of impeccable integrity, is shown by cases such as 'Walpurgisnacht', which he published only after years of heart-searching, or the 'Italian Symphony', which remained in his desk and was only published after his death. The activity of the last fifteen years of his life would have exhausted the richest soil, and it obviously hastened his early death.

MENDELSSOHN TO FERDINAND HILLER IN MILAN

Leipzig, 10 December 1837

. . . All this conducting has taken more out of me in two months than two years of composing all day long – I can hardly ever settle down to that here during the winter – and when, after some tremendous rush, I ask what has really happened, it turns out to be scarcely worth mentioning; at least I am not much interested in whether or no all the music that is recognized as good is performed more often, or better – the only thing that interests me nowadays is new music, and there is all too little of that. I often feel like getting out of it, doing no more conducting, only writing music – but on the other hand there is a certain charm about this well-organized musical establishment, and about being at the head of it. . . .

MENDELSSOHN TO FERDINAND DAVID OF THE LEIPZIG GEWANDHAUS ORCHESTRA

Berlin, 30 July 1838

. . . I am planning to begin writing out my symphony in the next few days and to finish it in a short time, probably before leaving here. I would like to write you a violin concerto for next winter as well; I have one in E minor in my head, the opening leaves me no peace. My symphony will certainly be as good as I can make it; but I don't know at all whether it will be popular, whether the barrel-organs will want it. I feel that with every piece I get further towards being able to write what is really in my heart, and in fact that is the only rule of conduct I have. If I am not destined for popularity I do not want to study or struggle to win it; or if you think that is not the way to speak, let us say I *cannot* study to win it. For I really cannot, and I don't want to be able to. Whatever comes from the heart makes me happy, in its outward effects as well, and so I should be very happy if I were able to grant you and my other friends the wish you have expressed – but I don't know how to manage this one way or the other. . . .

MENDELSSOHN TO HIS MOTHER

Leipzig, 18 March 1839

You ask what happened about the Overture to *Ruy Blas* – it was quite amusing. Six or eight weeks ago I was asked to compose an Overture to *Ruy Blas* [by Victor Hugo] and a tune for the ballad sung in the play, for the performance by the Theatrical Pensions Fund (a very worthy and serviceable institution here, which wanted to give *Ruy Blas* for money-raising purposes), because it was thought the receipts would benefit if my name appeared in the programme. I read the play, which is unbelievably bad, in fact beneath all serious criticism, said I had no time for an Overture, but did the ballad for them. The performance was fixed for last Monday (a week ago today). On the previous Tuesday the people came and thanked me profusely for the ballad, and said it was such a pity I had not written an Overture, but they quite realized that a thing like that took time, and next year, if I would permit them, they would give me longer notice. That annoyed me – and I thought the matter over that evening and began my composition. On the Wednesday we had concert rehearsals all morning, and Thursday was the concert. All the same, the Overture went to the copyist on the Friday; it could not be rehearsed until the Monday – three times in the concert hall, once in the theatre. That evening it was performed before the horrible play, and gave me almost as much pleasure as any things of mine have ever done. . . .

MENDELSSOHN TO HIS MOTHER

Leipzig, 25 January 1841

. . . This is the 35th letter I have written in the last two days, it appals me to see how the tide rises if I have to let a few days go by without damming it. Variations from Lausitz and Mainz – Overtures from Hanover, Copenhagen, Braunschweig and Rudolstadt – German patriotic songs from Weimar, Braunschweig and Berlin, the latter of which I am expected to compose, and the former to look over and find a publisher for. And most of the accompanying letters are so kind and friendly that I would be ashamed not to send kind and friendly replies, so far as possible. But how make up for all the valuable time that is lost in this way! Then there are the people who want an audition, and who are waiting to tell their anxious relatives whether or no they should take up music as a career – there are a couple of Rhinelanders here about that at the moment – and one is expected to decide the matter in a few hours; it is really a terrible responsibility, and I often think of La Fontaine's rat, which hid itself in the cheese and made oracular pronouncements from its depths. . . .

MENDELSSOHN TO HIS MOTHER

Leipzig, 11 December 1842

On the 21st or 22nd we are giving a concert here for the King, who has sworn death and destruction to every hare in the district, and in which we are to perform for him the bird hunting and hare hunting scene from *The Seasons* (very touching!). The second part is to be another performance of my *Walpurgisnacht*, but in a somewhat different dress from the previous one, which was much too warmly lined with trombones and rather shabby on the vocal side; but in that respect I had to rewrite the whole score from A to Z and put in two new arias – not to mention other snipping and patching. If it doesn't satisfy me now, I swear I shall never touch it again as long as I live. I am also planning to bring parts of the *Midsummer Night's Dream* and of *Oedipus* [incidental music] to Berlin with me, and, please God, the Music School here will be under way by February. Hauptmann, David, Schumann and his wife, Becker, Pohlenz and I are to teach there at first; it begins with ten free scholarships; anyone else who wishes to study there must pay 75 thalers a year. Now you know as much about it as I do, further developments will be decided by trial and error.

I wish you could have been at the subscription concert the other day; I think I played Beethoven's G major Concerto, my old war-horse, better than ever; especially the first cadenza and a new [improvised] transition to the solo gave me a great deal of pleasure, and even more to the audience, it seemed! . . .

So far as externals are concerned, we artists are now as much pampered as our forerunners were neglected; this is pleasant enough for us, of course, but it does no good to the cause; too much pampering makes art sluggish; so one should be grateful for one's enemies, rather than resentful of them. Among the items I include under 'pampered' is my appointment by the King of Prussia as his Director-General of Music; a new title, a new honour, before I even know if and when I can do enough to justify those I have already....

MENDELSSOHN TO HIS SISTER REBECCA

Frankfurt, 10 January 1847

... Fanny told you in her letter that I had to resign from my Berlin post. It went against my conscience to remain at the head of a public organization which I consider to be bad, and which I could do nothing to improve – that being *solely* a matter for the King, who, it is true, has other things on his mind....

Mendelssohn was a generous colleague. He was the first to perform Schumann's symphonies, he introduced W. Sterndale Bennett, one of the foremost figures in the revival of English music in the nineteenth century, to Germany, and practically discovered the composer Niels W. Gade, who became a leading spirit in the development of music in Denmark.

MENDELSSOHN TO HIS SISTER FANNY HENSEL IN BERLIN

Leipzig, 13 January 1843

... Yesterday we rehearsed a new symphony by a Dane named Gade, which we are to perform some time next month, and it gave me more pleasure than any piece has done for a long time. The man has a really considerable talent, and I wish you could hear his Danish symphony, which is highly original, very serious and agreeable to the ear. I wrote him a few lines today, though I know nothing whatsoever about him except that he lives at Copenhagen and is 26 years old. But I had to thank him for the pleasure he had given me; there can hardly be a greater pleasure than to hear beautiful music and to find one's admiration increasing with every bar, while at the same time one feels more and more at home with the thing. If only it were not so rare!...

MENDELSSOHN TO NIELS W. GADE IN COPENHAGEN

Leipzig, 3 March 1843

... Yesterday, at our 18th subscription concert, your G Minor Symphony was performed for the first time, to the warm and unanimous delight of the whole audience, which broke into loud applause after each of the four movements. After the *Scherzo* there was a positive uproar, it seemed as though the cheers and clapping would never stop – the same after the *Adagio* – the same after the last movement – and after the first, in fact after each one! To find the musicians so unanimous, the audience so enraptured and the performance so successful, gave me as much pleasure as though the work had been my own composition! Or even more; for what one sees most clearly in one's own work are always the mistakes and shortcomings, whereas yours gives me unadulterated pleasure by its many beauties. Yesterday evening you won the lasting friendship of every genuine music-lover in Leipzig; your name and your work will never be mentioned henceforth without the sincerest respect; and whatever you may write in future will be received with open arms, put into rehearsal at once with the greatest attention, and welcomed with delight by all the local amateurs of music. . . .

The following letter contains a lucid formulation of thoughts on music which deserve attention as they touch on a point of basic importance.

MENDELSSOHN TO MARC-ANDRÉ SOUCHAY IN LÜBECK

Berlin, 15 October 1842

There is so much talk about music, and so little is really said. I do not think words are at all adequate for the subject, and if I found they were, I should end by writing no more music. People usually complain that music is so ambiguous, that it leaves them in such doubt as to what they are supposed to think, whereas words can be understood by everyone. But to me it seems exactly the opposite. Not only with whole speeches, but with individual words as well – they too seem to me to be so ambiguous, so vague, so capable of misinterpretation, in comparison with real music, which fills the spirit with a thousand better things than words do. A piece of music that I love does not give me too *vague* ideas for being expressed in words, but too *definite* ones. So in every attempt to express those ideas in words I find something that is right, but always something insufficient as well, and so it is with yours too. This is not your fault, it is the fault of words, which simply cannot do any better. If you ask me what I was thinking about at the time, my answer will be – about the tune, just as it is. And if now and then a particular word or words were in my mind, I cannot repeat them to anyone, because a word does not mean the same thing to one person as to another; only the tune says the same thing, awakens the same feeling, in both – though that feeling may not be expressed in the same words. . . .

As if all his other activities were not enough, Mendelssohn undertook the revision and editing of Handel's oratorios, which had always been near his heart as a conductor, and he was one of the first to insist on the modern principle of faithful adherence to the original. In this respect he was opposed to the habits of his time. 'Moselwasser' (water of the Moselle) is an allusion to I. F. von Mosel of Vienna, whose dreadfully garbled editions of Handel were widely used at that time.

MENDELSSOHN TO THE PUBLISHER N. SIMROCK IN BONN

Berlin, 10 July 1838

. . . Surely it would now be worth some publisher's while to have the *original* scores of a few of Handel's principal oratorios engraved in Germany? It would have to be done by subscription, but I should think a good deal of money could be raised, since not one of those scores so far exists in this country. It had occurred to me that if that were done I might add the organ accompaniment; but in that case it would have to be printed in smaller notes in a different colour, so that (1) anyone who wished would have Handel, complete and pure, (2) my organ accompaniment would be there for anyone who wanted it and had an organ, and (3) there could be an *appendix* giving the organ accompaniment arranged for clarinets, bassoons and other present-day wind instruments, to be used where there is no organ. In that way any orchestra that plays oratorios could use these scores, and we would at last have the real Handel in Germany instead of one who has first been baptized in Moselle water and drenched through and through with it. . . .

MENDELSSOHN TO I. MOSCHELES IN LONDON

Frankfurt, 7 March 1845

. . . I am sorry about the business with the Handel Society, but I cannot change my views in the matter. I am quite ready to give way over inessentials, such as the accidentals (though even there I prefer the old method because of the long bars), but I cannot possibly add indications of tempo or expression markings, etc., if it is to be left uncertain whether they are mine or Handel's own; he himself put in *pianos* and *fortes* and figurings where he thought they were needed, so either I must omit those, or the public would be unable to discover which were his and which mine. Those who wish to have a marked score can easily arrange for the copyist to transfer the signs from the vocal score *if they agree with what I have put*; whereas it would be quite wrong to make no distinction, in the edition, between the editor's opinion and Handel's own. . . .

. . . Above all things I have to know, without the slightest doubt, what is Handel's and what is not. The council held the same view when I discussed it with them, but now they seem to take the opposite attitude. If it is to remain like that, then I (and *many* other people too, I am afraid) would much prefer the old edition, with its false notes, to the new one with its different views and expression marks incorporated in the text. I have written to Macfarren as well, telling him all this. You will not be cross with me for speaking so frankly? My opinion is so closely bound up with everything I have always felt to be right that I cannot abandon it. . . .

Mendelssohn loved to be in England, where he enjoyed tremendous popularity. The first performance of 'Elijah' under his direction (Birmingham, August 1846) was the greatest triumph of his life.

MENDELSSOHN TO HIS MOTHER

London, 21 June 1842

. . . So if this letter sounds rather weary and stiff-jointed, it merely reflects my feelings. They really have been driving me a little too hard; sitting at the organ in Christchurch, Newgate, the other day, I thought for a moment that I should be stifled, there was such a crowd and such a throng round the organ. And a few days after that, when I had to play to an audience of 3,000 people in Exeter Hall, and they cheered me with 'Hurrahs' and waved their handkerchiefs and stamped their feet until the whole place rang with it – I noticed no ill effect at the time, but next morning my head felt dizzy, as though I had not slept. And then there is the sweet, pretty Queen Victoria, who is so girlish and shyly friendly and polite, and speaks German so well, and knows all my things so well – the four books of Songs Without Words, and those with words, and the Symphony, and the Song of Praise. Only yesterday evening I was at the Palace, where the Queen and Prince Albert were almost by themselves, and she sat down beside the piano while I played to her: first of all, seven Songs Without Words, then the Serenade, then two improvisations on *Rule Britannia* and on *Lützow's wilde Jagd* and *Gaudeamus igitur*. The last was a bit difficult to do, but I could hardly protest, and since she gave the themes it was up to me to play them. All this and then the magnificent gallery in Buckingham Palace, where she drank tea and where there is a picture of two pigs by Paul Potter, and several others I found quite pleasant. And then the fact that they had very much liked my A Minor Symphony, that they had all welcomed us with a pleasant friendliness that surpassed anything I ever experienced in the way of hospitality – all this sometimes makes my head positively spin, and I have to take myself firmly in hand so as not to lose my composure. . . .

22 June

. . . Yesterday evening I played my D Minor Concerto and conducted my overture *The Hebrides* at the Philharmonic, where they received me like an old friend and played so devotedly that I was quite overjoyed. This time the audience made such a noise over me that I was quite astounded; I really think they clapped and stamped for a good 10 minutes after the Concerto, and *The Hebrides* had to be repeated. . . .

MENDELSSOHN TO HIS BROTHER PAUL

Birmingham, 26 August 1846

. . . Never before has any of my pieces gone so splendidly at the first performance, or been so enthusiastically received by the musicians and the audience, as this Oratorio. It was clear during the first rehearsals in London, that they liked it and enjoyed singing and playing in it; but I confess that even I had not expected it to go with such a swing straight away when it was performed. If only you had been there! For the whole three and a half hours that it lasted, the big hall, with its 2,000 people, and the big orchestra, were so tensely concentrated on the one point at issue that not the faintest sound came from the audience, and I could sway that tremendous mass of orchestra and chorus and organ just as I wished. I thought of you so often! Especially when the rain-clouds gathered and during the final chorus when everyone played and sang like mad, and after the first part was over and the whole passage was encored. No less than four choruses and four arias had to be repeated, and not one mistake was made in the whole of the first part – there were a few later, in the second part, but even those were trifling. A young English tenor sang the last aria so beautifully that I had to hold myself in so as to control my feelings and keep beating time properly. As I say, if only you had been there! . . .

One year later he died of a heart attack, at the age of thirty-eight.

There is a similar contrast of character between Mendelssohn and Robert Schumann (*1810–56*) *as there was between Weber and Schubert: the one active, with inexhaustible energy, the other retiring and disinclined to any extrovert manifestation. When towards the end of his career Schumann turned to conducting, it was a failure and a disappointment. With a lyrical poet's contemplative nature, he was ill-equipped for the artist's unavoidable struggle for success. His struggles were imposed upon him by circumstances of his private life: his decision to give up studying law and become a musician, against the wishes of a respectable middle-class family of scanty means, and the heroic fight for his beloved Klara against the tenacious opposition of the father, Schumann's teacher Friedrich Wieck.*

SCHUMANN TO HIS MOTHER

Heidelberg, 30 July 1830

... My *whole life* has been a *twenty-year-long battle* between poetry and prose, or if you prefer, between music and law. In practical matters my ideals were just as high as in art. My ideal was, in fact, to have a practical influence, and my hope, that I should have to wrestle with a wide sphere of action. But what prospect can there be of that, particularly in Saxony, for a plebeian with no powerful patron or fortune and no real love of the cadging and money-grubbing that goes with a legal career! At Leipzig I was quite unconcerned about future plans; I went on my way, dreaming and loitering and really doing nothing worthwhile; since I came here I have done more work, but in both places my attachment to art has been growing deeper and deeper. Now I have come to the crossroads, and think with terror, 'Whither now?' If I follow my own instinct it will lead me to art, and I believe that is the right path. But really – do not take this amiss, I say it lovingly and in a whisper – I always felt as though you were barring my way in that direction, for worthy, motherly reasons that I could see as clearly as yourself – the 'uncertain future and unreliable living', as we used to put it. But what is to happen next? A man can have no more tormenting thought than the prospect of an unhappy, lifeless and superficial future for which he would have only himself to blame. But it is not easy, either, to choose a way of life in complete contrast to one's early upbringing and disposition; it requires patience, confidence and rapid training. I am as yet in the youth of my imagination, able to be cultivated and ennobled by art; and I have become convinced that with diligence and patience and a good teacher I shall be a match for any pianist, for the whole business of piano-playing is simply a matter of technique and nimbleness; now and then I have imagination too, and perhaps some creative ability. ...

SCHUMANN TO FRIEDRICH WIECK

Heidelberg, 21 August 1830

. . . I shall keep to art, I wish to do so, I can and I must. I shall shed no tears on taking leave of a study for which I feel no love and very little respect; but it is not without dread that I look forward over the long road leading to the goal I have now set myself. Believe me, I am modest, as I have good reason to be; but I am also courageous, patient, confident and docile. I trust you completely and place myself entirely in your hands; take me as I am, and be patient with me in everything. No blame will depress me, and no praise make me idle. A few buckets of ice-cold theory would do me no harm either, and I shall endure them without a murmur. I have been over your five 'Buts' calmly and attentively, asking myself firmly each time whether I can do all you say. My judgement and my feelings invariably replied, 'But of course'.

Honoured friend! Take my hand and lead me – I shall follow wherever you wish, never tearing the bandage from my eyes, lest I be dazzled by the radiance. I wish you could see into my heart at present; all is quiet there now, and a delicate, luminous dawn enfolds the whole world.

So have confidence in me; I am resolved to earn the right to be called your pupil. . . .

Klara, her father's pride and master pupil, already widely acclaimed as a child, became engaged to Schumann when she was eighteen, but her father firmly refused to give his consent. It took Schumann three years of patient waiting to win his case, which in the end had to be decided in a court of law.

SCHUMANN TO KLARA WIECK

18 September 1837

The interview with your father was terrible. Such coldness, such malice, such distraction, such contradictions – he has a new way of destroying one, he thrusts the knife into your heart up to the hilt. . . .

So what now, dearest Klara? I cannot tell what to do next. *I have no idea.* It baffles my understanding, and it is completely useless to approach your father on a basis of sentiment. So what now? So what now? Above all, arm yourself and *do not let yourself be sold* . . . I trust you, oh *with my whole heart*, indeed that is what sustains me – but you will have to be *very strong*, more than you have any idea. For your father gave me with his own lips the dreadful assurance that 'nothing would shake him'. You must fear everything from him; *he will overcome you by force* if he cannot do so by guile. So fear everything!

Today I feel so dead, so humiliated, that I can scarcely grasp one beautiful, pleasant thought; even your picture eludes me, so that I can scarcely remember your eyes. I have not grown faint-hearted, capable of giving you up; but so embittered, so offended in my most sacred feelings, reduced to the level of all that is most commonplace. If I only had a word from you. You must tell me what to do. Otherwise everything within me will turn to dust and ashes and I shall go away. To be forbidden even to see you! . . . I try in vain to find some excuse for your father, as I have always thought him an honourable, kindly man. I try in vain to discern in his refusal some finer, deeper reason – such as that he may be afraid your art would suffer if you were prematurely betrothed, that you are altogether too young, and so forth. Nothing of the kind – believe me, he will throw you to the first comer who has enough money and position. His highest ambition is giving concerts and travelling; for that he oppresses you and shatters my strength just when I am trying to bring something beautiful into the world; for that he laughs at all your tears. . . .

But keep your eyes firmly on the goal. It is through your sweetness that you must achieve everything now, not through your strength. There is little or nothing I can do but keep silent, any new plea to your father would merely bring me fresh mortification. Brace yourself to decide what must be done. I will follow you like a child. . . . But my head is in such a whirl; I feel like laughing out of desperation. This situation cannot last long, my nature could not endure it. . . . My life has been torn up by the roots.

Afternoon of the same day

. . . I can see that everything now depends on our proceeding calmly and prudently. In the end he is bound to realize that he must give you up. His obstinacy will shatter against our love; *it must be so*, my Klara. . . .

SCHUMANN TO KLARA WIECK

Leipzig, 8 November 1837

. . . Your father has written to me – this is more or less what he says: 'You are a remarkable man, but there are more remarkable ones – I do not really know what my plans for Klara are, but that does not bother me at present. The heart? what do I care about the heart? etc. . . .' But I shall copy two passages for you word for word: 'Rather than see two such artists together, socially and domestically unhappy, their wings clipped, I would sacrifice my beloved daughter in one way or another', and then the magnificent statement: 'And if I have to marry off my daughter in haste to someone else, you and you alone will be to blame.' Those last words, dearest Klara, were clear and to the point. What can I do about such a letter? Only keep silent, or else tell him the truth – in short, all is over between us – for what further dealings can I have with such a man? It is a bad situation, of course, and I do not know what will come of it. . . . Unless you are convinced that you will be the happiest of wives – completely convinced – it would be better for you to break our bond at once. I shall give everything back to you, including the ring. But if you are happy in my love, if it fills your whole heart, if you have weighed everything, my failings, my uncouth behaviour, if you can be satisfied with what little I can offer you, even though it does not include pearls and diamonds – then let things remain as they are, my faithful Klara! . . .

SCHUMANN TO KLARA WIECK

2 January 1838

. . . For let me just whisper it in your ear, I love and respect your father for his many great and admirable qualities, holding him in an esteem I feel for no one else except you; what I feel for him stems from a kind of primitive, constitutional attachment on my part, an allegiance I pay to all vigorous personalities. So it hurts me doubly that he will have nothing more to do with me. . . .

SCHUMANN TO KLARA WIECK

5 January 1838

. . . Do play not quite so well now and then, so that they do not go utterly crazy about you – with every torrent of applause your father pushes me a step further from you, remember that! But no! with all my heart I wish you joy of your laurels – still, even a thousand wreaths of laurel do not amount to one of myrtle, and only I can place that on your beautiful black locks. . . .

. . . The *Davidbündler Dances* and the *Fantasy Pieces* will be ready in a week – I shall send them to you if you like. In the dances there are many wedding thoughts – they were composed in the most wonderful excitement I ever remember feeling. One day I shall explain them to you. . . .

SCHUMANN TO KLARA WIECK ON A CONCERT TOUR IN VIENNA

Leipzig, 6 February 1838

. . . All the papers are full of you – I go specially to the Museum every day and look for the reviews from Vienna. It was only to be expected, of course. You say in your letter that I do not really grasp what you can do as an artist. You are right in one way, but quite wrong in another; perhaps it is all even more perfect, more individual and more fully developed now – but in any case I know my enthusiastic little girl so well from the old days – one can hear you through mountains. Grillparzer's poem is *absolutely the most beautiful* ever written about you; at this again I saw the poet's status as something so god-like, his right hand hits the mark with so few words and they endure for all eternity. . . . The poem made me happy – and if your beloved, or any other lover, were able to sing and write poems, he would do it in the same way.

. . . Have you not received the *Davidbündler Dances* (there is a daguerrotype with them)? I sent them to you a week ago last Saturday. Take care of them, do you hear? they belong to me. . . . But what there is in the dances, my Klara will discover for me, for they are dedicated to her even more than anything else by me – in fact the story is an absolute wedding-eve, and now you can picture the beginning and end for yourself. If ever I have been happy at the piano, it was while composing those dances. . . .

SCHUMANN TO KLARA WIECK

[*Leipzig, 17 March 1838*]

. . . I have discovered that nothing lends wings to the imagination so much as suspense and longing for something, as happened again in the last few days when, waiting for your letter, I composed whole volumes – strange, crazy, even cheerful stuff. It will make you open your eyes if you ever come to play it – indeed, nowadays I am often ready to burst with sheer music. And I must not forget to tell you what I composed. Perhaps it was a kind of echo of one of your letters, where you wrote that 'I sometimes seemed to you to be like a child too' – at any rate I felt just as though I were in short frocks again, and I wrote some 30 little droll things, from which I have chosen about 12 and called them *Scenes from Childhood.* You will enjoy them, but of course you must forget you are a virtuoso – they have titles such as *Fürchtemachen, Haschemann, Am Kamin, Bittendes Kind, Ritter vom Steckenpferd, Von fremden Ländern, Kuriose Geschichte* and so forth. In short, all kinds of things, and easy to play withal. . . .

SCHUMANN TO KLARA WIECK

Leipzig, 14 April [18]38

. . . It is only human that once again, hatred of him often rises up in me, hatred so deep that it contrasts strangely indeed with my love of his daughter. But he has broken his promises so many times already, and he will do it again repeatedly – in short, I shall not wait for him, we *must take action ourselves*. . . . If we fix the time for Easter 1840 (*two* years hence), you will have fulfilled the whole duty of a daughter and will have no need to reproach yourself, even if you have to break with him violently. We shall both be of age, you will have complied with your father's request to wait for another two years – there can be no question of testing our fidelity and endurance, for I shall *never* give you up. . . . So give me your hand: *two years hence* is the watchword.

Schumann's intention of becoming a pianist was upset by a lasting injury to his right hand. An excellent writer, he founded a music magazine, the 'Neue Zeitschrift für Musik', to support serious and productive artistic efforts against philistinism and shallow virtuosity. Having started this periodical in Leipzig, he tried to move with it to Vienna, where he expected more opportunity both for himself as a composer and for the 'Neue Zeitschrift', but soon he became discouraged and returned to Leipzig.

SCHUMANN TO HIS RELATIVES AT ZWICKAU

Vienna, 10 October 1838

For the moment I still have not sufficient peace and quiet to tell you of all that has happened around me and within me since we parted. Only two days after reaching here, I received bad news from Leipzig which so much alarmed me that I had no thought for anything else. The old . . ., made even more furious by our energetic behaviour, had been storming at Klara again; but she held out, calmly and seriously. What has happened since, I do not know, but I fear many things. My plea to Klara to leave her father at once and come to live with you for a time, may have arrived too late. But if she comes, I know you will welcome her like a sister.

As a result, I have not got very far with my own affairs. This town is so big that one needs half as much time again for everything. I have found a friendly welcome everywhere, even from the Minister of the Interior, with whom I had an audience two days ago. He told me there was and could be nothing to prevent my remaining here, provided an Austrian publisher joined in with me at the head of the thing. If I could not find one, there would be difficulties for me as a foreigner, etc. . . . You would hardly believe how many petty groups and coteries, etc., there are here, and to gain a footing needs the cunning of a serpent, of which I think I possess very little. . . .

Klara is positively worshipped here; wherever I go people tell me so, and say the most affectionate things about her. But one could hardly find more encouraging audiences anywhere in the world; they are much too encouraging; at the theatre one hears more clapping than music. It is a funny thing, I sometimes get angry about it. Well, in the next few weeks our affairs will take a decisive turn. . . .

SCHUMANN TO KLARA WIECK

Vienna, 3 December 1838

. . . It often grieves me, especially here in Vienna, that I have a disabled hand. And to you I will admit that it grows worse and worse. I have often complained to heaven about it and asked 'God, why did you do this, of all things, to me?' For here it would be so particularly useful; all kinds of music are so formed and alive within me, and I long to breathe them out lightly; and I can only drag them out when absolutely necessary, stumbling with one finger after the other. It is quite dreadful, and has already caused me much distress.

But after all, I have you as my right hand, and you must take great care of yourself, so that nothing shall happen to you. I think often of the happy hours you will give me one day through your art. Are you really still working very hard? I am sure you are, and that your wonderful skill gives you happiness, and will perhaps give you even more when there is always a listener at hand who understands you and can follow you through the heights and the depths. . . .

SCHUMANN TO KLARA WIECK

Leipzig, 3 June 1839

. . . The most certain thing is still that we continue to love each other with all our hearts, and I feel sure that in your heart there is a rich fund of love, and that you will be able to make your husband happy for a long time. You are a wonderful girl, Klara! There is such a host of beautiful and varied qualities in you that I cannot think how you have managed to bring them together during your short life. And most of all in the environment in which you grew up. One thing I do know is that with my gentle way of expressing myself I made an impression on you at a very early stage, and I believe you would have been a different girl if you had never met me. Leave me this belief, it makes me happy. I taught you to love, and drew you close, to be the ideal bride as I imagined her; you were my most gifted pupil, and as a reward you said to me, 'Well then, take me!' . . .

SCHUMANN TO H. DORN

Leipzig, 5 September 1839

. . . It is indeed probable that my music bears many traces of the battles I have had to fight for Klara, and equally certain that you too will have understood it. She was almost the sole inspiration of the Concerto, the Sonatas, the *Davidbündler Dances*, the *Kreisleriana* and the *Novellettes*. But I have seldom come across anything more clumsy and shortsighted than what Rellstab wrote about my *Scenes of Childhood*. He supposes I took some screaming child as my model and then tried to find the right notes. It was the other way round. Though I do not deny that I saw a few children's faces in my mind's eye while I was composing; but the titles were added later, of course, and are really no more than slight pointers to the way of interpreting and playing the pieces. . . .

The most precious result of Schumann's visit to Vienna was his discovery of Schubert's Symphony in C major ('*The Great*'). *He found it among piles of forgotten manuscripts in the house of Schubert's brother, Ferdinand, and sent it to Mendelssohn, who conducted the first performance in the Leipzig* '*Gewandhaus*'.

SCHUMANN TO KLARA WIECK

Leipzig, 11 December 1839

. . . Klara, today I have been in the seventh heaven. At the rehearsal they played a symphony by Franz Schubert. If only you had been there! For I cannot describe it to you; all the instruments were like human voices, and immensely full of life and wit, and the instrumentation, regardless of Beethoven – and the length, the divine length, like a four-volume novel, longer than the Ninth Symphony. I was utterly happy, with nothing left to wish for except that you were my wife and that I could write such symphonies myself. . . .

Always responsive to any truly artistic impression, Schumann was ready to appreciate Liszt's dazzling and spectacular virtuosity, for which Klara, with her very different style, had but little sympathy.

SCHUMANN TO KLARA WIECK

Leipzig, 20 March 1840

. . . I wish you could have been with me this morning to see Liszt. He is really extraordinary. He played some of the *Novellettes*, and passages from the *Fantasy* and the Sonata, in such a way that I was quite spellbound. A great deal of it not as I had intended, but always showing genius, and with a tenderness and daring display of feeling such as he probably does not reveal every day. Only Becker was there, and I think he had tears in his eyes. The second *Novellette* in D major gave me particular delight; believe me, it made a tremendous effect; indeed, he intends to play it at his third concert here. If I tried to tell you all about the hubbub that is going on here, it would fill volumes. He has not yet given his second concert, he preferred to take to his bed and announce two hours beforehand that he was ill. I can quite believe he is and was out of sorts, but his illness was a matter of policy, I cannot go into it all here for you. For me it was very pleasant, as now he is in bed all day and apart from me he will only admit Mendelssohn, Hiller and Reuss. If only you had been there this morning, my lass! I wager you would have been the same way as Becker. . . .

Would you believe it, at his concert he played one of Härtel's pianofortes, which he had never seen before. I find it charming, to have such confidence in his precious ten fingers. But do not follow his example, my Klara Wieck: you stay just as you are, for no one can touch you. . . .

At an early stage Schumann already had a premonition of the catastrophe that was to end his life at forty-five after two years of suffering and progressive mental decay.

SCHUMANN TO KLARA WIECK

29 November 1837

. . . But as regards the whole of this dark side of my life, I would like some day to reveal to you a deep secret about a *serious emotional disorder* I once went through; but it would take a long time, and covers the years from the summer of 1833 onwards. All the same, you shall hear about it one day, and then you will have the key to all my behaviour, my whole strange character. . . .

SCHUMANN TO KLARA WIECK

Leipzig, 11 February 1838

. . . My life did not really begin until I became clear as to myself and my talent, decided to devote myself to art, and turned all my strength in a definite direction. That is to say, in 1830. In those days you were just a strange, headstrong little girl with a pair of beautiful eyes and a passion for cherries. . . . A few years went by. And already, in 1833, I began to be attacked by a melancholy that I avoided trying to account for; it came from the disappointment every artist feels when things do not go as quickly as he had hoped they would. I found little appreciation, and then came the loss of my right hand for playing. Then, amid all these gloomy thoughts and visions, only yours used to cheer me; indeed, without meaning or knowing it, you alone kept me all the long years from any association with women. As long ago as that I may have had an inkling that you might even become my wife; but it was all still too far away in the future; however that may be, I loved you from the very first as deeply as went with our age. . . . During the night of 17 to 18 October 1833, I was suddenly visited by the most terrible thought that can possibly come to a human creature – the most terrible thought that heaven can send as a punishment – that of 'losing my reason' – it overpowered me so violently that all comfort, all recourse to prayer, was silenced and turned to derision. But the anguish drove me from place to place – my breath failed me at the thought, 'suppose you lost the power to think' – Klara, anyone who was once reduced to that need fear no suffering, no sickness, no despair. . . .

A melancholy epilogue to the Schumann tragedy is found in a letter of Joseph Joachim, *the great violinist, one of his closest friends. Its subject is a violin concerto, Schumann's last work, which was found in manuscript among Joachim's music and rather irresponsibly published in the nineteen-thirties, duly performed a few times, and put to rest again. Klara Schumann knew better, when, on Brahms's and Joachim's advice, she decided to leave the concerto unpublished.*

JOSEPH JOACHIM TO ANDREAS MOSER

Berlin, 5 August 1898

. . . You ask me for information about the manuscript of a violin concerto by Rob. Schumann which is in my possession.

I cannot speak of it without emotion, for it dates from the last six months before the mental illness of my dear master and friend. . . .

The fact that it has never been published will be enough to lead you to the conclusion that it is not worthy to rank with his many magnificent creations. A new violin concerto by Schumann – with what delight would all our colleagues greet it! And yet no conscientious friend, concerned for the fame of the beloved composer, could ever mention the word publication, however eagerly the publishers might call for it.

For it must be regretfully admitted that there are unmistakable signs of a certain weariness, though his intellectual energy still strives to master it. Some passages, indeed (how could it be otherwise!) give evidence of the profound spirit of its creator; but this makes the contrast with the work as a whole all the more depressing.

The first movement has something wayward about its rhythm, sometimes starting off impetuously, sometimes stopping short in obstinacy; in the first *tutti* this is effective, as a rapid introduction to a second, gentle theme with a beautiful soft melody – genuine Schumann! But this is not developed into anything really refreshing. . . . The second movement begins with a characteristic passage of deep feeling, leading up to an expressive melody for the violin. Glorious Master – the blissful dream is captured, as warm and intimate as ever! But though my heart bleeds to say so, this blossoming fantasy gives way to sickly brooding, the stream stagnates, though the theme meanders on; and then, as though the composer himself were yearning to escape from this drab introspection, he rallies himself, hastening the tempo, for a transition to the final movement. . . . The main theme is introduced with great energy, but as it develops it becomes monotonous, again taking on a certain ominous rigidity of rhythm. Even in this movement, however, there are interesting points of detail. . . . But here again there is no sense of spontaneous enjoyment. One can see that the thing is being carried forward by habit rather than soaring in happiness. . . .

Now that I have satisfied your wish to be told something about the concerto, my dear Moser, you will understand why you had to press me so often. One is always reluctant to turn the light of reason in a direction where one has been accustomed to love and adore with all one's heart. . . .

If we consider the early deaths of Weber, Schubert, Mendelssohn, Chopin, and Bellini, the dark fate of Schumann and Donizetti stricken by insanity in their prime, it seems as if the whole generation was subject to a tragic destiny. Romantic music has remained an 'Unfinished Symphony', just as romantic poetry, as the work of Byron and Shelley, of Novalis, Hölderlin, Kleist, Büchner, and Raimund.

THE CAPITAL OF EUROPE

From Chopin to Bizet

In the complicated pattern of cultural life in Europe during the period of the 'Holy Alliance' that followed the cataclysm of the Napoleonic wars, Paris emerges as the focal point of events, the centre from which the most fertile political, literary, and artistic stimuli radiated.

Frédéric Chopin (*1810–49*), *the son of a French father and a Polish mother, remained a fervent Polish patriot all his life, but he submitted to the charm of Paris, where he settled when he was twenty-one and which remained his domicile to the end of his life. His first impressions of the city and his own situation as a budding artist of uncanny gifts and precociousness are reflected with the utmost liveliness in his letters. The enthusiastic German whom he mentions in the first of them is Robert Schumann; in the music magazine he published in Leipzig ('Neue Zeitschrift für Musik') he had introduced a review of the first work of Chopin that came into his hands, Variations on Mozart's 'Là ci darem la mano', with the words: 'Hats off, gentlemen, a genius'! In these letters we shall also learn something of musical customs and eccentricities of the period, of long forgotten celebrities, and of the most sensational operatic event of the time, Meyerbeer's 'Robert le Diable'.*

FRÉDÉRIC CHOPIN TO HIS FRIEND TITUS WOYCIECHOWSKI IN POTURZYN

Paris, 12 December 1831

. . . Paris is whatever one chooses to make of it. In Paris you can divert yourself, or be bored, laugh or cry, do whatever you like; nobody so much as looks at you, for there are thousands doing the same, each in his own way. I do not know if any place has more pianists; and I cannot say if there are as many fools and virtuosi elsewhere. I arrived in Paris with some very modest introductions. A letter from Malfatti to Paër, a letter from Vienna to the publishers. . . . Thanks to Paër, who is Conductor to the Court, I met Rossini, Cherubini, etc., Baillot, etc. It was through him, too, that I was introduced to Kalkbrenner. You cannot imagine how curious I was to meet Herz, Liszt, Hiller, etc. They are all ciphers compared to Kalkbrenner. Between you and me, I have played like Herz, and I should be glad to play like Kalkbrenner. If Paganini is absolute perfection, Kalkbrenner is his equal, but in an entirely different way. It is very hard to describe his *calm*, his bewitching touch, the incomparable regularity of his playing, and the mastery evidenced in every note. He is a giant, towering above men like Herz and Czerny, and so above me. . . .

. . . After listening to me attentively, he advised me to take lessons with him for three years, declaring he would make me into someone very, very. . . . I know my shortcomings, I replied, adding that I did not wish to imitate him and that three years was too long. . . .

I shall give a concert on 25 December. Baillot, that celebrated rival of Paganini, and the famous oboeist Brodt will take part, and I shall play my Concerto in F minor and my Variations in B flat major.

About the latter, only imagine, I received from Kassel a few days ago a ten-page review by an enthusiastic German. After lengthy preliminaries, he analyses them phrase by phrase, declaring that they are no ordinary variations, but a kind of fantastic panorama. Speaking of the second variation, he says it shows Don Juan and Leporello running. In the third, Don Juan is clasping Zerlina in his arms, while at his left hand Masetto stands in a fit of rage. Finally, he declares that in the fifth bar of the *Adagio* Don Juan kisses Zerlina in D flat major. 'Whereabouts is that D flat major on Zerlina?' Plater asked me yesterday. The imagination of that German is very droll. . . .

But to return to my concert. Another thing I shall play there, with Kalkbrenner, is a *Marche suivie d'une Polonaise* for two pianos, with accompaniment by four more. It's something quite mad. Kalkbrenner will play on an immense pantaléon [an obsolete keyboard instrument]. I shall have a small monochord piano, but the sound carries like giraffes' bells. As for the other instruments, they are all large and will make an orchestral effect. . . .

I doubt whether anything so magnificent as *Robert le Diable* – the new five-act opera by Meyerbeer, who wrote *Il Crociato* – has ever before been done in the theatre. It is the masterpiece of the modern school. There are devils, immense choruses singing through tubes, and souls rising from the tomb. . . . The stage is a diorama, with the interior of a church right at the back, all lit up as though it were Christmas or Easter. There are rows of benches with a host of monks and worshippers holding censers, and the most extraordinary thing of all is the organ, the sound of which, coming from the stage, delights and astonishes one and almost drowns the orchestra. Meyerbeer has won eternal fame. But after all he lived three years in Paris before he could get his opera staged. They say he has spent twenty thousand francs on the company. . . .

CHOPIN TO HIS TEACHER, JOSEPH ELSNER, IN WARSAW

Paris, 14 December 1831

. . . I have to make my way in the world as a pianist and must reserve until later the loftier artistic prospects that you so rightly hold out in your letter. To be a great composer requires immense experience. As you have taught me, one acquires this by listening not only to other men's work, but above all to one's own! More than a dozen talented young men, pupils of the Paris Conservatoire, are marking time while they wait for the performance of their symphonies, cantatas or operas, which have only been seen on paper by Cherubini and Lesueur. . . .

Meyerbeer, highly esteemed for ten years as a composer of operas, had to work for three years and maintain himself in Paris before he could achieve a performance of *Robert le Diable*, which is now all the rage. . . . I am now known as a pianist here and there in Germany. . . . At present I have a unique opportunity of fulfilling the promise that my inherent abilities seem to hold out. Why not seize it? . . . I feel so convinced that I shall never be a copy of Kalkbrenner that nothing could deprive me of the idea and the wish – too bold, perhaps, but noble – to create a new world, and I am working so as to stand more firmly on my own feet. . . . Spohr was regarded as merely a violinist for a long time, until he produced *Jessonda*, *Faust*, etc. I hope, Sir, that you will not refuse me your blessing when you learn by what principles I am guided, and hear what my plans are. As my parents will certainly have told you, my concert has been put off until the 25th. I have had great difficulty in arranging it, and without Paër, Kalkbrenner, and most of all Norblin (who sends you his compliments), I should not be able to give it at such short notice. They think two months is very little for Paris. Baillot, very pleasant and civil, will play a Beethoven Quintet; Kalkbrenner and I, a duet accompanied by four pianos. I know Reicha only by sight. You are aware how much I wished to be introduced to him. I am on friendly terms with several of his pupils. They have given me a very different idea of him. Reicha has no love of music. He does not even go to the concerts at the Conservatoire, and will not discuss music with anybody. While giving a lesson he is always looking at his watch, etc. As for Cherubini, he merely babbles about the revolution and the cholera epidemic. These gentlemen are like dried-up puppets who have to be considered with respect and whose works must be used for teaching. . . . There are three orchestras: at the Académie, the Théâtre Italien and the Théâtre Feydeau. They are excellent. Rossini is the director of his opera house, where the staging is the best in Europe. Lablache, Rubini, Pasta (who has only just left), Malibran, Devrient-Schröder, Santini, etc., delight the fashionable world three times a week. Nourrit, Levasseur, Derivis, Mme Cinti-Damoreau and Mlle Dorus are adding lustre to the Grand Opéra, Cholet, Mlle Casimir and Prévost are winning general admiration at the Opéra Comique. In short, to discover what singing really is, one must come to Paris. Today, without question, the finest *cantatrice* in Europe is not Pasta, but Malibran (Garcia) – she is wonderful! . . . The King does not throw his money about, and generally speaking these are lean years for artistes. Only the English pay. . . .

CHOPIN TO JOSEPH NOWAKOWSKI IN WARSAW

Paris, 15 April 1832

. . . At the moment I would willingly hand you my ticket for the concert at the Conservatoire; it would certainly exceed your hopes. The orchestra is unsurpassed. Today they are playing Beethoven's Choral Symphony and one of his quartets. The quartet will be performed by all the violins, all the altos and all the cellos. There will be at least fifty violins. This quartet was played at an earlier concert and it is in response to public demand that it is to be repeated today. It is as though one were listening to four gigantic instruments: the violins like a palace, the violas like a bank and the cellos like the evangelical church. . . .

Chopin had gone to Paris with the aim of establishing himself as an artist, just as Paganini or Liszt had done before. His physical constitution, however, was not made for the strenuous life of a travelling virtuoso and he seems to have realized this very soon. Already at that time the fascination of the composer outshone the charm of the pianist, much though the latter was admired and cherished wherever he went. All the same, the composer could never provide more than pocket-money, and to the end of his life Chopin found himself compelled to earn his living by giving piano lessons to noble ladies who could afford such a distinguished teacher.

CHOPIN TO DOMINIQUE DZIEWANOWSKI IN BERLIN

Paris, mid-January 1833

I am now received in high society, among ambassadors, princes and ministers; by what miracle I know not, for I have done nothing to push myself forward. But I am told it is essential for me to make an appearance, for it is there, they say, that good taste originates. You are immediately credited with great talent if you have played at the

English or Austrian Embassy. You play better if you are under the protection of the Princesse de Vaudamont, last of the Montmorency family. I cannot say 'you are' literally, for the old lady died a week ago. In this city she was the equivalent of the late Madame Zielonkowa, or of Madame Polaniecka in her château. The Court frequently visited her. She did a great deal of good. During the first Revolution she provided a refuge for many aristocrats, and after the July Revolution she was the first great lady to appear at Louis-Philippe's court. She had a whole host of little black and white dogs, canaries, parrots, and the drollest monkey in this great world. At receptions he was so bold as to bite the . . . of the visiting *comtesses.*

I enjoy the friendship and esteem of the artists. I would not say this if it were not that only a year after making my acquaintance, highly reputed composers have dedicated works to me without my even having dedicated anything of mine to them. . . . In short, if I were still more stupid than I am, I might believe myself to have reached the apex of my career. But I know how far I fall short of perfection; I am all the more aware of it because I am constantly in the company of the greatest artists, and know their failings. . . . I am to give five lessons today; I suppose you think I am on the road to fortune? Let me undeceive you; my cabriolet and my white gloves cost more than I earn, but without them I should not be *de bon ton. . . .*

At this time Chopin's position in Paris was already firmly founded. It is interesting to read what one of the most outstanding publicists of the time, the German poet Heinrich Heine, wrote in a report on musical events in Paris in 1837. One has to remember that he was an incorrigible scoffer who could never resist the temptation of poking fun even at the powerful Meyerbeer, or at Berlioz or Mendelssohn. When he speaks about Chopin, who was still in his twenties, he lays down his critical arms:

'. . . *It would be unjust not to mention a pianist in that context who can claim to be the most celebrated beside Liszt. He is* Chopin, *who is not only a dazzling virtuoso but a composer of the highest order. That's indeed a man of supreme quality! Chopin is the favourite of a certain* élite *of connoisseurs who are out for the choicest spiritual satisfaction in music. His glamour is of an aristocratic kind, scented with the glorification of the highest circle of society, noble as his person. Chopin was born in Poland of French parents [his mother was Polish, as mentioned before] and partly educated in the German tradition. The influence of three nations is noticeable in his personality – he has absorbed the best these three nations were able to give him. Poland gave him her chivalrous mind and her historical sadness, France her lightness and grace, and Germany her romantic depth of feeling. Nature gave him a slim, graceful frame, the noblest of all hearts and – genius. Yes, with respect to Chopin one must speak of genius in the fullest meaning of that term. He is not merely a virtuoso, he is a poet. And he is able to project to his listeners the poetry of his feeling. He is a tone-poet and nothing equals the delight he gives us when he sits at the piano and improvises. Then, he is neither a Pole nor a Frenchman nor a German; one has a feeling of a far higher parentage; one becomes aware of an origin in the country of Mozart, of Raphael, of Goethe: his real fatherland is the dreamland of poetry.'*

An incomparably impressive and gripping sketch of Chopin as a personality and a suffering, lonely, pathetic human being is to be found in the memoirs of George Sand (Mme Aurore Dudevant), the celebrated French novelist of the thirties and forties, with whom he was living at the time of the first acute outbreak of the mortal illness to which he eventually succumbed.

'He was a man of the world in the truest sense; not of the official big world, to wit, but of an intimate type of company, a drawing-room of twenty persons, at the time when the crowd has dispersed and only those of the closest circle have stayed, grouped round the great artist, set upon drawing from him the purest of his inspiration by gentle persuasion. There only would he pour out all his talent, all his genius. On such an occasion he was able to plunge his audience into profound bliss or into an abyss of sadness, as his music gripped one's soul with a sharp pang of hopeless despair, especially when he improvised. And then, to remove that impression and that memory of suffering from the others as well as from himself, he would turn surreptitiously to a mirror, arrange his hair and his cravat and instantly become a phlegmatic Englishman, or a sentimental, ridiculous lady, an impertinent old beggar, a sordid Jew. They were always sorry types, however comic; yet perfectly realized and so delicately reproduced that one could not help admiring them over and over again.

'All those sublime, charming or eccentric features made him the life and soul of a chosen circle, and one would literally fight for his company. The nobility of his character, his indifference to mercenary rewards, his pride and justifiable self-esteem as a sworn enemy of everything pertaining to vanity, bad taste or insolent advertisement, the charm of his conversation, the exquisite delicacy of his manner made him an interesting and delightful companion.

'To snatch him away from such flattery, to convert him to a simple, regular, studious way of living – him who had been brought up, as it were, on the knees of princesses – meant to deprive him of all that constituted his life; a fictitious kind of life, to be sure. Because, back home at night, like a woman who takes off her make-up, he would put off all his animation and seductive power and submit to a night of fever and insomnia. . . .

'Chopin, this extreme type of artist, was not made for a long life in this world. He was consumed by a dream of an ideal that was never tempered by

any philosophical tolerance or by any charity with respect to the practical limitations of the world of everyday. Never willing to compromise with human nature, he did not acknowledge reality. Intolerant of the smallest blemish, he had an unlimited enthusiasm for any semblance of light, which his imagination would try to see as a sun. . . . He was a compound of magnificent inconsistencies such as only God can create and which have their own particular logic. He was modest on principle and gentle by habit, but imperious by instinct and full of a legitimate pride of which he was hardly conscious. From this came sufferings for which he was unable to account, as they had no concrete source.'

Another valuable reflection on Chopin can be found in a letter of Mendelssohn, a fastidious critic indeed who was not easily impressed:

FELIX MENDELSSOHN TO HIS FAMILY

Leipzig, 6 October 1835

. . . The day after I accompanied the Hensels to Delitzsch, Chopin arrived here; he would not stay more than a day, and so we spent it together entirely, and played music. I must confess, my dear Fanny [Mendelssohn's sister], that I found that your judgement of him was inadequate; perhaps, too, he may not have been in the mood for playing when you heard him, which is probably often the case; but I was again enchanted by his playing, and I am convinced that if you, and Father too, had heard some of his best things in the way he played them to me, you would say the same. His manner of playing the piano has something so basically individual about it, and at the same time so masterly, that he may really be described as the perfect virtuoso; and as I love and am delighted by perfection in any form, I found the day an extremely pleasant one. . . . I enjoyed being again for once with a true musician – not one of those half-virtuoso, half-classic composers who try to combine *les honneurs de la vertu et les plasirs du vice* in music, but a man who has chosen a quite definite direction. Even if it is a direction entirely different from my own, I can perfectly well adapt myself to it – only not to those half-and-half people. It was really curious on Sunday evening; he wanted me to play him my St Paul Oratorio, while the inquisitive Leipzigers crept in so as to say they had seen Chopin; and between the first and second parts he played his new *Etudes* and a new concerto to the astonished Leipzigers in a torrent, and then I went on with my 'St Paul' – like an Iroquois and a Kaffir meeting and conversing together. . . .

Towards the end of his twenties Chopin's pulmonary disease was already acutely noticeable. George Sand took her suffering friend to the island of Majorca in order to spend the winter in a milder climate. It was an ill-fated journey and his condition became increasingly alarming.

CHOPIN TO HIS FRIEND JULIEN FONTANA IN PARIS

Palma, 3 December 1838

My Julien,
I have been as sick as a dog for the last fortnight. I had caught cold in spite of the eighteen degrees centigrade, the roses, the orange-trees, the palms and the fig-trees. Three doctors – the most celebrated on this island – examined me. One of them sniffed at my spittle, another tapped to find out where I spat it from, the third felt me, listening how I spat. The first said I was going to die, the second that I was actually dying, the third that I was dead already. . . . I had great difficulty in escaping from their bleedings, vesicatories and pack-sheets, but thanks be to providence, I am myself again. But my illness was unfavourable to the *Preludes*, which will reach you God knows when. In a few days' time I am moving to the most beautiful place in the world; I shall have the sea, the mountains, everything you can imagine. I am to live in an old monastery, huge and deserted, from which Mend[izabal] seems to have expelled the Carthusians for my benefit. It is near Palma and nothing could be more beautiful. There are arcades, the most poetic cemetery, in short I shall be comfortable there. . . .

CHOPIN TO JULIEN FONTANA IN PARIS

Palma, 28 December 1838
or rather a few leagues from there,
at Valdemosa

Imagine me, between rocks and sea, in a cell in an immense, deserted Carthusian monastery, its doors bigger than the coach entrance to any Paris mansion. Here I am with hair uncurled, no white gloves, and as pale as usual. My cell, shaped like a big coffin, has a vast, dusty, arched ceiling, and a little window looking on to the garden with its orange-trees, palms and cypresses. Opposite the window, below a rosace in the lacy Moorish style, is a camp-bed.

Beside the bed is an old *untouchable*, a kind of square desk, very awkward for writing, on which stands a lead candlestick with (great luxury here) a wax candle. . . . On the same desk, Bach, my scribbles, and other papers, not mine. . . .

Silence. . . . If you shout . . . silence again. In short, I am writing from a very strange place. . . .

What George Sand has to tell us about the time they spent in an ancient convent near Palma has the precious quality of acute and anxious observation, based on a passionate personal relationship:

'. . . The poor great man was an abominable patient. What I had feared – not sufficiently, alas! – happened indeed: he became totally demoralized. Bearing his suffering with remarkable courage, he was unable to counteract the morbid anxiety created by his own imagination. The cloister became for him a place of terrors and phantoms, even on days when he felt better. He never spoke of it; I had to guess. One evening, back from an exploration of some ruins with my children, I found him at his piano, pale and haggard, his eyes wild, his hair bristling with fear. It took him some moments before he even recognized us. He tried to laugh it off and played for us sublime things he had just written – or, to put it more exactly, fearful, heart-rending ideas that had got hold of him, as if unconsciously, during an hour of loneliness, sadness and terror.'

The 'sublime things' which Chopin finished during those months of anguish were his 24 Preludes, the most precious miniatures ever written.

There was some improvement after his return to France in the following spring, but he never fully recovered. Moreover, he had to pay off the debts incurred by his escapade in Majorca, which meant even more drudgery, more piano teaching.

GEORGE SAND TO HIPPOLYTE CHATIRON IN MONTGIVRAY

Paris, 1841

. . . Several fine ladies declared that the Rue Pigalle [where Chopin lodged] was too far from their fashionable districts. His reply was: 'Ladies, I give much better lessons in my own room and on my own piano for twenty francs than I give outside for thirty, and then you have to send a carriage for me as well. Do as you wish.' Several of them chose to come to his rooms, several others give him thirty francs a lesson and send their carriages to fetch him and take him home. The dear child is not sufficiently interested in money to have thought of this for himself. I suggested it, and with great difficulty persuaded him to agree. But I am pleased with myself, for with his poor health he needs to earn a great deal of money for little work. . . .

In these circumstances, the obstinacy with which he maintained his creative work with his own critical fastidiousness appears like a martyr's achievement. This fastidiousness is strikingly illustrated in his manuscripts: what he corrects – and he corrects frequently and painstakingly – is crossed out with such furious energy that it is hard to guess a note of the original version – as if he could not bear to see again something not yet perfect.

What he always maintained besides was a lively correspondence with his relatives and his friends; there he unbuttons, and even indulges in small-talk.

CHOPIN TO HIS FAMILY IN WARSAW

Nohant, 11 October 1846

. . . Monsieur Faber, of London, a very skilful mechanic and a teacher of mathematics, has exhibited an automaton of his own manufacture. He calls it Euphonia. This automaton utters, in distinct sounds, not merely one or two words, but long sentences. It also sings an aria by Haydn and *God save the Queen*. If opera managers had a number of these androids at their disposal they could dispense with chorus-singers, who are expensive and troublesome. . . .

There is to be great rivalry between Italian operas in London next year. Mr Salamanca, a Spanish banker and Member of the *Cortes*, has taken a lease of Covent Garden Theatre. This is one of the largest in London, but owing to its position it has never been fashionable; it is too far from the districts where the fine people live. Mr Lumley, manager of Her Majesty's Theatre – which has been adopted by London society and is therefore the most fashionable – was in no hurry to engage his usual singers for next season. He relied too much on the attractions of his theatre, with its silk hangings. Mr Salamanca outstripped him, and has engaged la Grisi, Mario, Persiani, in short all except Lablache, at higher salaries. So there will be two theatres. As well as Lablache, Mr Lumley, they say, has engaged Mlle Lind and Mr Pischek, whom Berlioz considers to be the best Don Juan. And as in London elegant tradition is more powerful than the greatest artistic miracle, the next season will be extremely curious. People say the old opera (Mr Lumley's) will hold its own, for there is every prospect that the Queen will continue to go there as usual. . . . The Italians [in Paris] have reopened. The new star, the baritone Coletti, has made his début there in *Semiramis*. He is very well spoken of. He is young and handsome and has long been celebrated for his talent and his amorous adventures. His father wished to make a priest of him. He became an actor at Naples after running away from Rome. They say he turned all the women's heads at Lisbon for several years, and two ladies are declared to have fought a duel for him. If with all this he sings very well, he can be sure of success. I very much doubt whether duels will be fought for him in Paris, but he will certainly be better paid than at Lisbon. . . . I am playing a little, and writing a little too. Sometimes I am pleased with my cello sonata and sometimes dissatisfied. I throw it into a corner and then I take it up again. While one is composing, the thing seems to be good, otherwise one would never write anything. Reflection comes later, and then one rejects or accepts what one has done. Time is the best of critics; and patience the best of teachers. . . .

CHOPIN TO GEORGE SAND AT NOHANT

Paris, 25 November 1846

. . . I called on Mme Marliani yesterday evening. She was going out with Mme Scheppard, M. Aubertin (who has had the audacity to read your *Mare au Diable* to the whole college as an example of style) and M. d'Arpentigny. They were going to listen to a new prophet whom the Captain is patronizing (he is not an apostle). His new religion is that of the *Fusionistes*, revealed to the prophet in the Bois de Meudon, where he saw God. He promises, as the highest happiness, that at a certain point in eternity sex will disappear. This idea does not appeal greatly to Mme de M. [Marliani], but the Captain is in favour, and calls the baronne tipsy whenever she laughs at his *fusionisme*. . . .

CHOPIN TO HIS FAMILY IN WARSAW

Paris, April 1847

. . . [Racine's] *Athalie* is being performed with choruses by Gossec. The French composer Gossec was well thought of and well known at the end of the last century. In course of time it became the custom to add at the end of the choruses he had composed for *Athalie*, which are tedious, the magnificent choruses from Haydn's *Creation*. Hearing these one day, Gossec said in all simplicity (this was thirty-five years ago, so he was already very old): 'I have no recollection of writing that.' Which surprised nobody. . . . I must go now. I have to give a lesson to the little Rothschild girl and then to a young lady from Marseilles. After that comes an Englishwoman, then a Swede, and finally a family from New Orleans, recommended to me by Pleyel. . . .

In Spring 1848 Chopin set out on another tour, the last of his life. He went to London, where he had often been urged to go, his main aim being to improve his financial situation by the rich reward which so many of his colleagues had found there before. An unfortunate venture again, it took the last force of resistance out of his ailing body. And although he was given the most flattering reception, the net result remained far below his expectations, as he was physically unable to satisfy more than a modest number of the demands and offers that came his way.

In comparing letters written from London by Haydn, Weber, Mendelssohn, Chopin, Bellini, Verdi, as one finds them in this anthology, one will see that they add up to a colourful backcloth of the London scene during a period of fabulous wealth of the ruling classes, a craze for celebrities, and a genuine, though sometimes rather indiscriminate, love of music.

CHOPIN TO ALBERT GRZYMALA IN PARIS

London, 11 May 1848

. . . I am just back from the Italian theatre. Jenny Lind sang for the first time this year, and the Queen made her first public appearance since the Chartist riots. Both of them caused a great sensation. Old Wellington impressed me; he sat below the Queen's box, like an old royalist dog in his kennel. I made the acquaintance of J. Lind, who had very politely sent me an excellent stall, with her card. I was well placed, so I heard well. She is a matchless Swedish woman, lit not by the usual radiance but by a kind of aurora borealis. She produces a tremendous effect in *La Sonnambula*. She sings confidently, with a pure tone; her *piano* is as continuous and even as a hair.

A stall costs two guineas. . . .

CHOPIN TO ALBERT GRZYMALA

London, 13 May 1848

. . . If the 'season' lasted 6 months, I might be able to make a little money. So far, I do not know. It is not until the day after tomorrow that the Duchess of Sutherland is to present me to the Queen, who is coming to her house *in gratiam* of a christening. If it pleases the Queen and Prince Albert, who have heard about me, all will be well and I shall thus have begun to make myself known in high places. The Philharmonic Society has asked me to give a concert, but I am not eager, for it would be with orchestra. I went there and looked into the question. Prudent gave his Concerto to the Philharmonic Society, and it was a fiasco. They have to have Mozart, Beethoven or Mendelssohn. All the same, the conductors and others tell me my Concertos have been played there. But I prefer to refrain, for I cannot expect any good result. Their orchestra resembles their roast beef and their turtle soup; it is strong, it is famous . . . but that is all. Yet none of this would prevent the fulfilment of that plan if there were not a further circumstance, impossible to accept: time is so valuable to the English that their orchestra holds only one rehearsal, and that in public. . . .

CHOPIN TO ALBERT GRZYMALA

London, 2 June 1848

. . . The old Rothschild woman asked me how much I cost, because a lady who had heard about me had enquired of her. As I had asked 20 guineas from the Duchess of Sutherland (it is Broadwood, whose pianos I play, who fixed the price for me) I told her 20 guineas. The good lady, visibly very kind-hearted, then told me that I did indeed play very well but that she advised me to charge less, because this season more '*modérécheune*' is needed. . . . As for the fashionable world which travels, it is haughty but civil, and has very good judgement when it chooses to exercise it; but it is so much distracted by a thousand matters, so closely hemmed in by tedious conventions and etiquette, that it no longer cares whether music is good or bad – hearing it from morning to night. There is not a flower-show without music, not a dinner without music, not a charity bazaar without music. There are as many Savoyards and Czechs and colleagues of my own as there are dogs, and they are all mingled pell-mell. . . .

CHOPIN TO ALBERT GRZYMALA

London, 8–17 July 1848

. . . The season is over now. How shall I follow up my plans? I have no idea. I have not much money in hand, and do not know what I shall do. Go to Scotland, perhaps. My Scots women are kind and affectionate, but they bore me to death at times. . . .

The intended journey to Scotland, mentioned in the last letter, was carried through. The fatigue of travelling and the inclement weather had a disastrous influence on his failing strength and the proceeds hardly justified the enterprise. In Chopin's letters one can feel his growing exasperation, his difficulties in defending himself against advantage being taken of his gentle helplessness, the gradual ebbing of his will to live. His last letter from England, announcing his impending return, is heart-rending, with a last flicker of his ineradicable fastidiousness.

CHOPIN TO HIS FAMILY IN WARSAW

Calder House, 19 August 1848

. . . Although in good society everyone can speak French, particularly the ladies, the conversation is usually conducted in English, and I then regret my ignorance of that language; however, I have neither the time nor the wish to learn. Besides, I understand the ordinary words; I shall not let myself be swindled or starve to death; but that is not enough. . . . I am expected at Manchester on 28 August. I am to play at a concert in which the Italian singers from London are also taking part; Alboni, etc. They offer me 60 guineas, which is not to be despised, so I accepted and I shall leave in a week. Nearly 250 English miles and 8 hours in the train! After the concert I shall return to Glasgow to visit my lord's sister-in-law. From there I shall go to Lady Murray's, then to Stirling and finally to Edinburgh, where they want me to play at the beginning of October. If it can bring me in something and if I have the strength, I shall do it, for I do not know how I shall manage this winter. I still have my Paris lodging, but I do not know how things will go on. Many people want me to remain in London, in spite of the climate. As for me, I would like something different, but what? . . . I myself do not know. In October I shall see and act according to my state of health and my purse; which is precisely why another 100 guineas in my pocket would do no harm. If London were not so black, if the people were not so stolid, if it were not for the fog and the coal-dust, I would even set myself to learn English. But the English are so unlike the French, to whom I have grown as much attached as though they were my own people. They reckon everything in pounds sterling and respect art only because it is a luxury. They are excellent people, but such unusual, exceptional beings that I realize one would end here by ossifying and turning into a machine. If I were younger I might perhaps opt for the machine; I would give concerts everywhere, and play the most tasteless lucubrations provided they brought me a lot of money; but now I would have difficulty in turning myself into a machine. . . .

CHOPIN TO ALBERT GRZYMALA

Keir, Perthshire, 1 October 1848

. . . I shall soon forget all my Polish, I shall be speaking French with an English accent and learn to speak English with a Scots one; in the end I shall be like old Jaworski, who spoke five languages all at the same time. If I do not deluge you with lamentations it is not because you would not try to comfort me; you are the only person who knows everything about me, but if I once began I should never stop and it would always be the same thing; for as regards my future, matters are going from bad to worse. I grow weaker and weaker, and cannot compose anything at all, not because I do not want to, but owing to practical difficulties; each week I drag myself to some new perch. What can I do? At least in this way I am saving a few *grosz* for the winter. I have received a multitude of invitations, but I cannot even go where I would like, e.g. to the Duchess of Argyll's or Lady Belhaven's, because it is already too late in the year for my health. All morning, and until two o'clock, I am good for nothing; later, when I am dressed, everything oppresses me and I gasp until dinner, after which I have to sit on at table with the men, watching what they say and listening as they drink. Sitting there, my thoughts are far away from them, in spite of all their kindness and their snatches of French; and soon, in the clutches of a mortal tedium, I go to the drawing-toom, where I have to summon all my moral courage to rouse myself a little, for they are anxious to hear me. Then my good Daniel carries me up to my bedroom (which is on the floor above, that being the habit here, as you know), undresses me, puts me to bed, leaves me a candle, and I am at liberty to gasp and dream until the same thing begins again. No sooner do I grow a little accustomed to a place than I have to move on, for my Scotswomen cannot leave me in peace, either they come to fetch me or else they take me on a round of their families (N.B. where they always get themselves invited too). In the end they will smother me with their amiability and I, also out of amiability, shall let them do it. . . .

CHOPIN TO ALBERT GRZYMALA

Hamilton Palace, 21 October 1848

. . . Art, here, means painting, wood-carving and architecture. Music is not considered to be an art. An Englishman hearing the word 'artist' takes it for granted that a painter or wood-carver is meant. Music, for him, is a profession, not an art. . . . Lady . . . is one of London's greatest ladies, and is said to be very musical. I went to spend a few days in her country house and one evening when I had played and this great Scottish lady had afterwards sung a great many airs, they brought her a kind of accordion and she began, with the utmost gravity, to play horrible tunes on this species of instrument. What can one do? All these creatures seem slightly mad. . . . Their praises invariably end with 'leik water', meaning 'your music flows smoothly'. I have never yet played for an Englishwoman without hearing her say 'leik water'. They all look at their hands and play wrong notes with sentiment. What strange creatures! God preserve them. . . .

CHOPIN TO ALBERT GRZYMALA

London, 21 November 1848

. . . I shall spend Thursday night at Boulogne; on Friday I shall be back in the Place d'Orléans and go to bed. . . . Have a bunch of violets bought on Friday, so that the drawing-room will smell sweet. Let me at least find a little poetry at home when I arrive, if only as I cross the drawing-room to my own room, where I shall take to my bed, for a long time no doubt. So, as I said, I shall reach Paris about midday. Another day here and I shall go mad without dying of it. My Scotswomen bore me so much that God save me from them. They have got such a hold on me that I cannot tear them off. . . . Have a good fire lit, the place well warmed and well dusted; perhaps I may yet be myself again. . . .

He was slowly dying already, much though his interest in people and events remained alive. A letter to his sister (25 June) is like a desperate cry for help.

PAULINE VIARDOT TO GEORGE SAND AT NOHANT

Paris, 15 February 1849

You ask me for news of Chopin, here it is. His health grows slowly worse, with tolerable days when he can take a drive and others when he spits blood and fits of coughing threaten to choke him. He no longer goes out at night. But he still manages to give a few lessons, and on his good days he can be cheerful. . . .

CHOPIN TO SOLANGE CLÉSINGER [DAUGHTER OF GEORGE SAND] AT GUILLERY

Paris, 13 April 1849

. . . I hope the spring sun will be my best doctor. One has to specify the *spring* sun, for at the Opera they are preparing a sun for *Le Prophète* [by Meyerbeer] which it seems is more wonderful than anything seen in the tropics. It only rises, and stays a very short time, but it is so strong that it casts a shadow over everything except the music. It is made of clusters of electric lights. I was too ill to go to the rehearsal the day before yesterday – but I am counting on the first night, next Monday.

There are great rumours of a *skate dance* and of skaters (on roller-skates) – one hears of a marvellous fire, of a fine production, and of Mme Viardot, who will draw tears from everyone, in the role of the mother. . . .

CHOPIN TO HIS SISTER LOUISE JENRZEJEWICZ IN WARSAW

[*Chaillot*] *Monday 25 June 1849*

Mon Âme,

Come, if you can. I feel weak, and no doctor will do me as much good as you. If you are short of money, borrow some. When I get better I can easily earn some and pay back whoever lends it to you, but at the moment I am too short to be able to send you any. My lodgings at Chaillot have room for you, even with two children. . . . I am sitting in the drawing-room, from where I have a view all over Paris: the towers, the Tuileries, the Chambre des Députés, St Germain-l'Auxerrois, Saint-Étienne-du-Mont, Notre-Dame, the Panthéon, Saint-Sulpice, the Val-de-Grâce, the Invalides, through my five windows; nothing but gardens between us. You will see when you come. Now attend to the money and the passport, and be quick. Write me a line at once. . . . God will perhaps let everything go well; if not, behave as though he were doing so. . . .

He was still able to finish the 'Cello Sonata mentioned in a letter of his (of 11 October 1846). It was his last major work.

Hector Berlioz (*1803–69*), *the most picturesque character of the romantic period, shows in his prose the same fascinating flashes of originality, the same epigrammatic neatness of formulation, the same unexpected turns of fancy, that one finds so stimulating in his music. A characteristic anecdote vividly illustrated in a letter of Berlioz refers to his friendship with Mendelssohn, whom he had met in Italy in 1830, having won the 'Prix de Rome' of the Paris Conservatoire – a friendship based on mutual respect, undisturbed by a total incomprehension of one another. A number of years later they met again in Leipzig, Mendelssohn's centre of activity, where Berlioz performed some of his works. At that time, Fenimore Cooper's Red Indian stories were popular. As a token of sympathy, Berlioz suggested an exchange of batons, whereupon Mendelssohn sent him his slim, simple white stick. Berlioz returned the compliment by sending him an enormous wooden cudgel with the following note:*

HECTOR BERLIOZ TO MENDELSSOHN

Leipzig, February 1843

To Chief Mendelssohn,
Big Chief! We promised to exchange tomahawks. Here is mine, it is roughly made, yours is simple. Only squaws and pale-faces like ornate weapons. Be my brother, and when the Great Spirit sends us to the happy hunting-grounds, may our braves hang up our tomahawks side by side by the door where they meet to palaver.

Hector Berlioz

All the same, Berlioz's opinions regarding music in Italy were hardly different from his German colleague's. His general attitude, however, was of another kind, and akin to that of a typical Byronic character, of Childe Harold, who inspired one of Berlioz's most remarkable works.

BERLIOZ TO FRANÇOIS-HIPPOLYTE RÉTY

Rome, 14 September 1831

. . . To tell you a word of myself by the way, I have nothing to talk about except the unspeakable boredom that is killing me, sapping my strength, eating me away, stifling me, choking me. . . . This town has no music, no theatre, no books, and when I am minded to escape from my habitual occupations, I do not know what to do with myself.

In fact the 'spleen' to which, as you know, I am so liable, has never before shown itself in such hideous guise; I can feel myself becoming as savage and violent as a madman. . . .

BERLIOZ TO GASPARO SPONTINI

Rome, 29 March 1832

. . . You are too skilled at distinguishing between truth and falsehood to entertain a moment's doubt regarding my feelings towards the great man whose very name brings the flush of enthusiasm to my cheeks. The perpetual agitation in which I have been living, the heart-break, the storms of every kind that have thundered over me for the past year, must serve as my excuse. I have hardly ever been in Rome for two months at a time, constantly hurrying off to Florence, Genoa, Nice or Naples, on foot across the mountains, with no other aim than to tire myself, distract my mind and more easily resist the 'spleen' that was tormenting me. It would be tedious for you to learn the causes of the moral sickness from which I am by no means cured as yet. My existence up to now has been a strange, romantic tissue of adventures and distressing emotions, in which the latest episode is not the least. You may perhaps remember trying to dissuade me from a marriage I was about to contract while you were in Paris. Your advice, the soundness of which I now recognize, would have been useless and powerless against love; that was destroyed, a month after my departure, by the unfaithfulness of her who had inspired it. I now perceive the full extent of the danger I escaped, and congratulate myself upon my freedom with transports of delight. . . .

Heinrich Heine gives a precious thumb-nail sketch of Berlioz and the impression he made in Paris, where he remained an odd outsider all his life and where the autobiographical character of his first work of genius, the 'Symphonie Phantastique', was a matter of notoriety. Heine reports (May 1837) on a performance of that work at the Conservatoire and on the composer:

'. . . It is a pity he has cut his gigantic mop of hair that stood above his forehead like a forest on the top of a steep cliff. So I saw him for the first time six years ago, and so he will remain in my memory for ever. It was in the Conservatoire at a performance of a big symphony of his, a bizarre nocturnal landscape, only occasionally lit by a sentimental white female skirt, fluttering to and fro, or by a sulphurous flash of irony. My neighbour at that performance, a garrulous young man, pointed to the composer who sat at the back of the orchestra, beating the timpani, because that's his instrument. "Look at the front box," said my neighbour, "do you see the fat Englishwoman? That's Miss Smithson; Mr Berlioz has been desperately in love with her for three years, and we are indebted to that passion for the wild symphony we are going to hear just now." And there indeed, in the front box, sat the famous Covent Garden actress. Berlioz stared at her all the time, and whenever their eyes met, he hit his drum like a madman. Miss Smithson has become his wife meanwhile and her husband has had a haircut. When I heard his symphony again in the Conservatoire last winter, he sat again at the back of the orchestra, handling the timpani, the fat Englishwoman sat in the front box, and their eyes met again – but he did not hit his drums half as furiously. . . .'

The poet's impression was correct. Owing to the intellectual incompatibility of the partners, Berlioz's marriage could not last. His feelings for his wife, however, are movingly expressed in a letter written after her death. One will admire his penetrating distinction between instinct and knowledge; one should also remember that a number of important works of his – the Overture 'King Lear', the symphonies 'Lélio' and 'Romeo and Juliet', the opera 'Beatrice and Benedict' – were inspired by Shakespeare.

BERLIOZ TO HIS UNCLE FELIX MARMION[1]

Brunswick, 4 April 1854

. . . Though not unexpected, the separation was terrible. We had remained friends and besides, after all, our artistic sympathies had always united us. Poor Harriet had such a deep understanding of the world of poetry! She had an intuition of things she had never learnt. Besides, she revealed Shakespeare to me, and God knows what an influence that revelation has had, and will continue to have, upon my career. It is incalculable . . . it is infinity. Hence the impossibility, cruel yet at the same time sweet, of my ever forgetting her. . . .

During his lifetime Berlioz never achieved real, decisive success in his native country, with his operas or with his symphonic works. He found his main artistic satisfactions abroad, especially in Germany, where Franz Liszt became a generous promoter of his music. Berlioz's opinions were as unorthodox as his art and he was usually at loggerheads with the pundits in Paris.

LISZT TO FERDINAND DENIS

September 1838

. . . I heard this evening that Berlioz' opera [*Benvenuto Cellini*] was not a success. Our poor friend! Fate treats him very harshly! I fear this failure will sadden him a great deal. Have you heard his score? There must certainly have been very beautiful things in it. What a victory for all the malicious mediocrities who lounge about on your boulevards! That is the most intolerable aspect of failure – the insolence of all those whipper-snappers who had predicted it six months beforehand. Be that as it may, Berlioz is and remains the most vigorous musical brain in France. . . .

BERLIOZ TO VICTOR SCHOELCHER

1 February 1839

. . . I am writing a third symphony, which absorbs me completely; it will take at least four months' steady work. Mlle Pauline Garcia I disliked extremely, it was not worth while to make such a stir about her alleged talent. She is half-way to a diva. I loathe *Divas*, they are the curse of true music and true musicians. How she wrecked that sublime duet in *Orphée*, with Dupré! There's a back number for you! Gluck

[1] This letter, hitherto unpublished, is owned by the National Library of Scotland, Edinburgh.

is a colossus who towers above everything, everything, everything; and whatever people say, Mozart comes far behind him in stage music, prodigiously far. But Gluck needs singers with voices, souls, and – genius. . . .

BERLIOZ TO CHARLES LEWIS GRUNEISEN

Paris, 8 February 1853

. . . As for Paris, everything is in the same condition as before; in other words, nothing is possible for me. Everything is closed to me, the theatres, the Conservatoire, even the Church. The business of my *Te Deum*, which should have been given at the Emperor's marriage and was not, would take too long to tell you . . . they preferred to perform fragments of an oratorio by Lesueur, a Mass by Cherubini, a Sanctus by Adam, a March from an old opera ballet (*Les filets de Vulcain*) and a plain-song scored by Auber. . . .

The manager of the Opéra has given Gounod my libretto, *La Nonne Sanglante*, of which I had already written two acts; the Opéra Comique does not much attract me, and as for the third theatre, the so-called *Lyrique*, it is no better than a musical gutter where every donkey in Paris comes to piss. The Conservatoire is a club, unfriendly to me, and the committee of the Société des Concerts would never dream of asking me for so much as an overture; so you see I have considerable leisure, where music is concerned. I can no longer get my work performed except abroad. My visit to Weimar was festive beyond words, so much was I moved and delighted by the warm-heartedness of all the company and of Liszt, and the graciousness of the ducal family. . . .

BERLIOZ TO ROQUEMONT

Hanover, 1 April 1854

. . . On learning of my arrival, the King of Hanover gave orders for the artistes, singers and others who were to appear in the last concert given by the Société Philharmonique to be countermanded; he wished the programme to be changed and to include nothing but music by me. The Queen sent to ask me to put in at least two pieces from *Roméo*, the Adagio and *Queen Mab*. She came to the rehearsal yesterday, and after the Adagio from *Roméo*, of which she is so fond, she sent for me to congratulate me; and she added: 'Now I know it by heart, that admirable piece, and I shall never forget it'. . . . Tomorrow I leave for Brunswick, to take part in a concert to be given there on Tuesday. . . .

His admiration for Liszt, and gratitude to his great friend, did not blind him to his limitations. Liszt was indeed an indifferent conductor, judging from many contemporary accounts; he was obviously defeated by the problem of applying his capriciously free and rhapsodic style of a virtuoso pianist to conducting, without having the necessary technique.

BERLIOZ TO HIS SISTER NANCI, AFTER A BEETHOVEN FESTIVAL AT BONN[1]

Frankfurt, 26 August 1845

. . . Whatever may have been said, the occasion was a fine one, both in its purpose and in the feelings that animated those present. Liszt was a paragon of devotion and generosity, imbued with a sense of his mission; he played Beethoven's sublime concerto like all the gods in Olympus; now *that* was an occasion when I would have allowed you a touch of hysterics – that was indeed music, inspired, grandiose, poetic! . . . Unfortunately he had to conduct the orchestra at one of the concerts, and that is something utterly alien to him; he conducts like *Musard* [a dance band leader in Paris] !!! That is to say, he not only fails to lead the orchestra, but at times even prevents it from playing properly. Hence an opposition which is quite formidable in a way, because it is based on genuine and justifiable causes. . . .

For some years Berlioz appeared as a conductor in London, where he was in charge of the New Philharmonic Society and where, in 1855, he met Richard Wagner, who was conducting the season of a rival institution, the London Philharmonic Society. Berlioz was impressed by the terrific vitality and pugnacious eloquence of his German colleague, who quarrelled with everybody and had violently attacked Meyerbeer in some theoretical publications. In general the relationship of the two artists was a curious one and never free from mutual distrust.

WAGNER TO LISZT

Zürich, 5 July 1855

. . . One real profit I brought back with me from England: a warm, close friendship I have formed with Berlioz and which unites the two of us. I heard a concert by the New Philharmonic Society which he conducted, was not, it is true, greatly pleased by his rendering of Mozart's G minor Symphony and felt sorry for him over the performance of his *Romeo and Juliet* Symphony, which was very inadequate.

[1] This letter, hitherto unpublished, is owned by the National Library of Scotland, Edinburgh.

However, a few days later we dined alone together at Sainton's house; he was very lively, and thanks to the progress I had made in the French language in London I was able to discuss all aspects of art, philosophy and life with him in rapid review during the five hours we spent together. In so doing I formed a deep sympathy for my new friend; I found him quite other than I had previously supposed him; we suddenly saw ourselves as companions in affliction, and it seemed to me that I was more fortunate than Berlioz. After my last concert he visited me with my few other London friends; his wife was there too; we were together until 3 in the morning and on that occasion we embraced warmly at parting. . . .

BERLIOZ TO THÉODORE RITTER

London, 3 July 1855

. . . Yesterday a frightful rehearsal at Exeter Hall, Glover's cantata, in a piquant style, but difficult, which made me sweat enough to swell the gutters in the Strand, and the Finale of *Harold* [by Berlioz] and a ferocious concerto by Henselt played by Mr Klindworth in a free style, which kept me dancing on the slack rope for an hour, and Cooper, our First Violin, who could bear it no longer, cried out: 'Sempre tempo rubato!', and the cornet-players who could not come because of the *banque*[1] *militaire* in the *Etoile du Nord* [opera by Meyerbeer] which delayed them at Covent Garden . . . always the *Etoile du Nord*: Glover gave a soirée to which Meyerbeer was to have come, the great man sent to excuse himself, pleading a terrible colic . . . then, finally, Meyerbeer arriving when everyone had finished regretting his absence, congratulations on the end of his colic, wandering through the London streets by moonlight, I go to Ernst's house to join my wife; Mme Ernst asks if I like Molière, yes indeed, and hop! I'll recite or declaim something by him for you: a scene from the *Misanthrope*, after which they bring the chess-board and Ernst sits down with Mr Louis Blanc and they wear themselves out over those stupid moves until three in the morning. . . . Wagner has gone, after the worthy Mr Hogarth had introduced him, in his turn, to Meyerbeer, asking the two celebrities *whether they were acquainted*, Wagner's delight at leaving London, a fresh outburst of fury against him among the critics after the last concert in Hanover Square, it is true he conducts *in free style*, like Klindworth playing the piano, but his ideas and conversation are very winning, we went to drink punch with him after the concert, he assured me again of his friendship, embraced me furiously, saying he had had

[1] A pun on *bande*: Meyerbeer's wealth was notorious.

a host of prejudicies about me; he wept, he pranced; hardly had he gone away, when the *Musical World* printed the passage from his book where he cuts me up in the drollest and most witty fashion; Davison [a London critic] was delirious with joy as he translated it to me. . . .

BERLIOZ TO CHARLES HALLÉ

Paris, 4 April 1860

My dear Hallé,
I would like to congratulate you on the brilliant success of your attempt to reveal Gluck to the English. So it is really true that sooner or later the flame shines forth, no matter how thick the layer of filth under which it was thought to be safely buried. The success is prodigious when one considers how little *Iphigénie* lends itself to the concert platform and how Gluck's work in general is theatrical in its essence. All lovers of eternal beauty must be warmly grateful to you and Chorley. . . . I have not been attacked by Wagner, so far as I know; he simply replied to my article in *Débats* by a letter he alleged to be explanatory, of which nobody understood a word. It was rambling and pompous and did him more harm than good. I did not answer a single word. . . .

BERLIOZ TO WAGNER

23 May 1860

I am delighted that you liked my articles on *Fidelio*. I had thought them out carefully, but without the least hope that they would do any good. I have practically lost my belief that the critics can educate the public; or at least I think it takes a very long time for criticism to bear fruit. . . . Why, when you write to me, do you put 'cher maître', in that formal way? It's not the thing with us. So yesterday was your birthday! You Germans always pay great attention when such days come round. . . . Farewell, *bonjour*, courage, and do not say 'cher maître' to me any more. It makes me cross. *Mille amitiés*.
Yours sincerely,

Hector Berlioz

In 1856 a seat in the 'Académie Française' became vacant and Berlioz was very desirous to be elected. He succeeded in the end, but it was a close shave, as his friends found it difficult to get a majority for him.

BERLIOZ TO TOUSSAINT BENNET AND THÉODORE RITTER

End of May 1856

. . . I am going to spend the day on a round of the Academy circles. Just imagine, Mr Ingres himself is weakening and has promised me his vote . . . in the second ballot, if Gounod, his Benjamin, is not elected in the first.

The musicians in the sector are very warm, including Halévy, in spite of my last article on his *Valentine*. Auber is still very calm and determined to be on the side of the big battalions, like God and other rascals. As for Carafa . . . a dullard, impossible to move. . . .

BERLIOZ TO THE PRINCESS CAROLYNE SAYN-WITTGENSTEIN

Paris, 24 June 1856

. . . The Academy has elected me, as you know already. . . . I still have to see twenty-two fellow-members in order to thank them all; I saw fifteen this morning, and was obliged to be embraced by a quantity of people who had voted *against me*.

So now I have become a respectable fellow, no longer a vagrant or a bohemian, past the *cour des miracles*! What a farce! I don't despair of one day becoming Pope. . .

Ready to be enthusiastic about things near to his heart, easily nettled and inclined to be rude, more and more bitter in his feelings about his situation in Paris, Berlioz at sixty was a sad, disappointed, sick man, when his most ambitious work, 'Les Troyens', gained no more than an ephemeral success and soon disappeared from the repertory. Liszt remained his only trusted friend among the famous musicians of his time.

BERLIOZ TO RICHARD POHL

April 1858

. . . I am now arranging the vocal score of my *Troyens* which (as you no doubt know) has been completely finished for the last month. This occupation has brought to my notice a great number of small defects which even the most thorough reading would not have shown me, and I am correcting them as best I can. If, later on, by God's will I am able to let you hear it, I hope you will like it. In any case it is the best I can do, and I am devoting all my attention and all my efforts to removing the blots I discover in it. One thing I can guarantee is that it contains a wealth of true expression and that it is *musical*. If a Cassandra, a Dido and an order from the Emperor should come along, I shall be able to produce the thing.

But there is a personage who may well arrive before any of these; I mean Death. . . .

BERLIOZ TO THE PRINCESS CAROLYNE SAYN-WITTGENSTEIN

Paris, 13 December 1859

. . . Besides, if you only knew how I waste my time. . . . I give hardly one hour in forty to art. What plans can I make, with such habits, with such a shattered life? Of the forty hours a good twenty are spent in pain of one kind or another, at least twelve in sleep, and seven in chasing the devil's tail in order to scrape a living. . . .

LISZT TO DR FRANZ BRENDEL, EDITOR OF THE 'NEUE ZEITSCHRIFT FÜR MUSIK', IN LEIPZIG

Rome, 10 August 1862

. . . Berlioz has been kind enough to send me the printed vocal score of his opera, *Les Troyens*. Although with Berlioz a piano arrangement is sheer treachery, a cursory reading of *Les Troyens* has nevertheless made a strangely powerful impression on me. Impossible to deny that it has colossal force, and tenderness – I would almost say *subtlety* of feeling – is certainly not lacking either.

Pohl will report to you on the performance of Berlioz's comic opera, *Beatrice and Benedict*, at Baden, and I imagine that this work, which requires little in the way of scenery and is based on a well-known Shakespearean subject, will be favourably received. Berlin or some other big German theatre would really not demean itself by adding a Berlioz opera to its repertory. It is no excuse, or valid objection, that Paris has been equally negligent – for when others fall short we ought not to imitate them. Besides, for many years Paris has shown a theatrical activity and initiative that leaves Germany far behind – and if exceptional, regrettable personal circumstances prevent Berlioz from presenting his works in Paris, that is no concern of the Germans. . . .

BERLIOZ TO JEROME HOPKINS IN NEW YORK

Paris, 6 February 1863

Monsieur et cher Confrère,
I was greatly touched by the letter you did me the honour of writing. You say you are suffering for the sake of art, unfortunately I am not the man to offer you consolation. You probably have a very mistaken idea of the life led by artists (those worthy of the name) in Paris. If New York, for you, is the musicians' purgatory, Paris, for me who know it, is their hell. So do not be too much disheartened. For one thing you are young, that is a great happiness, a great advantage, a great strength, a supreme quality. I should be delighted to see you and to make your acquaintance. Well, if you were to come to Paris (to this hell), perhaps, for all my wish to give you pleasure, you might find my welcome unsatisfactory, cold, not cordial. You might see me absent-minded, preoccupied, in the throes of some storm, some violent grief, such as I so often feel. At such times my behaviour, my very appearance, belie my deepest feelings, and I inevitably make a bad impression. I should certainly regret this very keenly. Let us hope it will not occur. I only fear you may come too late; for I rise every day with the hope that it will be my last. My physical and moral sufferings leave me scarcely any respite; I have bidden farewell to the illusions of music, I no longer work. I have so arranged matters that I can say to death at all times: When you wish!

If I speak so much about myself, my dear sir, it is in order to contrast our respective situations and thus make yours more tolerable to you.

Music is the greatest of the arts; but it is the one which in the present state of civilization must cause the greatest unhappiness to those who regard it as great, who respect and honour it. Yet one must always honour it, always respect it, always love it. Yes, love it, with that great *love* which is the quintessence of the noblest passions of the human heart. One must therefore scorn the mob and its prejudices, set no store by success if it is purchased by cowardly concessions, and keep carefully out of reach of fools and madmen, and of the sophists who are able to make folly look like reason. . . .

BERLIOZ TO RICHARD POHL

Paris, 7 November 1863

My dear Pohl,
The 2nd performance of *Les Troyens* was given yesterday and far surpassed even the brilliance of the first; it aroused feelings I shall not

attempt to describe to you on the one hand, and rendered a few individuals inconceivably furious, I am told. Two of these maniacs heap me with insults this morning in the *Figaro* and the *Nain jaune*. Mme Charton is superb as Dido; you would probably not believe her capable of such lofty tragedy. The Septet was encored with tremendous applause, the love duet drew tears from a great part of the audience. It was an evening of embraces: a steady stream of musicians, men of letters, artists and critics came behind the scenes during the intervals to congratulate me. I had heard there would be a cabal, but it did not venture to declare itself. Apart from the two small newspapers I mentioned, all the rest express very warm approval. On Monday and on Sunday we shall see some more important papers. . . .

BERLIOZ TO THE PRINCESS CAROLYNE SAYN-WITTGENSTEIN

Paris, 13 July 1866

. . . As for famous men who were not artists, I am beginning to be tired of them. Those poor little scoundrels who are called great men fill me with nothing but overwhelming horror. Caesar, Augustus, Antony, Alexander, Philip and Peter and so many others, were no better than bandits. . . . And the war! Oh yes, this is the right moment to speak of that. To speak of the hundreds of thousands of idiots who are cutting one another's throats, slitting one another's bellies, shooting one another at close range and dying furiously in mud and blood, in obedience to three or four rascals who take care to do no fighting themselves, and with no clear understanding of the pretexts invoked to lead them to this butchery !!! . . .

The war to which Berlioz refers is the Austro-Prussian War of 1866.

Franz von Liszt (*1811–87*) *was a genuine cosmopolitan. Born in Hungary of German parents, French in his upbringing, and always inclined to write French rather than German, a Hungarian patriot who never mastered the Hungarian language, he probably felt most at home in Paris, where he came as a child, where he started his career as a great virtuoso, and which, in a certain sense, remained the centre of his spiritual world. All his life Liszt, the composer, stood in the shadow of the dazzling pianist, the greatest perhaps whom the world has ever known.*

Compared with the eccentric Berlioz, Liszt was a man of the world, used to moving in aristocratic circles and enjoying it. The generosity with which he appreciated the great musicians who were his contemporaries – Schumann, Chopin, Berlioz, Wagner – is expressed in many of his letters, and he did not restrict his appreciation to kind words: he was indefatigable as a performer of music he regarded as valuable, and he became the leading spirit of the progressive movement in the music of his time.

LISZT TO SCHUMANN

5 May 1838

... The *Carnival* and the *Fantasy Pieces* I found extraordinarily interesting. I play them with real delight, and God knows there are not many things of which I can say as much. To be absolutely frank and precise, only Chopin's compositions and yours interest me strongly. The rest do not deserve the honour of being mentioned by name....

LISZT TO SCHUMANN

Albano, 5 June 1839

My dear Monsieur Schumann,
At the risk of seeming very monotonous I must tell you once again that the last pieces you were so kind as to send to me in Rome seem to me admirable in their inspiration and in their workmanship. The *Fantasie* you have dedicated to me is a work of the loftiest description – I am indeed proud of the honour you do me in placing my name on a composition so majestic. My intention is to work at it and come to know it thoroughly in order to render it with full effect.

As for the *Scenes of Childhood*, I owe them one of the keenest joys of my life. As you may or may not know, I have a little daughter, 3 years old, who everyone agrees is *angelic* (you see the platitude!). Her name is Blandine-Rachel and her nickname *moucheron* [midge]. It goes without saying that her complexion is milk and roses and that her golden hair falls to her feet, like a savage's. For the rest, she is the most silent, the most gently grave, the most philosophically merry child in the world. I also have every reason to hope that she will not be a musician, may God preserve her from it!

Well, my dear Monsieur Schumann, two or three times a week (on the fine good days!) I play your *Scenes of Childhood* to her in the evening; this enchants her, and me still more, as you can imagine; so much so that often I simply play the first repetition to her 20 times over without going further. Really I think you would be pleased with this success, if you could witness it!

I think I have already told you in one of my previous letters how much I wish you would write some pieces for an ensemble – trios, quintets or septets. Will you forgive me if I urge this again? It seems to me that you could do it better than any other living composer. And I feel sure they would not lack success, even *commercial success.*

If you could complete such a piece by next winter, it would give me real pleasure to make it known in Paris, where compositions of this kind, when well performed, have more chance of success than you may think. I would even gladly undertake to place your manuscript, should you wish it, and that would in no way prevent you from disposing of the German rights yourself.

Meanwhile I expect to give a public performance of your *Carnival*, some of the *Davidbündler Dances* and some of the *Scenes of Childhood*. The *Kreisleriana* and the *Fantasie* that is dedicated to me are more difficult for the public to digest – I shall reserve them until later. . . .

MENDELSSOHN TO HIS MOTHER

Leipzig, 30 March 1840

There has been a tremendous coming and going in the last few weeks. Liszt was here for a fortnight and caused a hullabaloo, in the good and bad sense. I think he is basically a good, warm-hearted man and a splendid artist. . . . In short, I have never seen a musician whose feeling for music filled him to the very finger-tips and flowed directly out from them, as it does with Liszt; and with this directness and his immense technique and practice he would leave all others far behind, were it not that, for all that, original ideas are still the most important thing; and these nature appears – so far at least – to have denied him, so that in this respect most of the other great virtuosi equal or even surpass him. . . .

LISZT TO SIMON LÖWY IN VIENNA

London, 20 May 1841

. . . My two *solo* recitals, and above all the 3rd, for the Beethoven Monument at the Conservatoire, are unrivalled concerts, such as I *alone* can give in Europe at the present moment.

The newspaper accounts can have conveyed only a very imperfect idea. Without vanity or self-deception, I think I may say that an effect so striking, so complete, so irresistible had never before been produced by an instrumentalist in Paris. . . .

I have just discovered a new vein of Fantasies, and am working it energetically. *Norma, Don Juan, Sonnambula, Maometto* and *Moisé* heaped one upon another, *Freischütz* and *Robert le Diable* are 96-pounders or even 200-pounders, like the old cannon of the Genoese

Republic, I think. When I have really finished my tour of Europe I shall come and play them to you in Vienna; and however weary people may be there after applauding me so much, I still feel strong enough to stir a public so intelligent and so outstandingly appreciative, which I have always regarded as the born judge of a pianist. . . .

The time of Liszt's most important and productive work started when, in his late thirties, he gave up his activity as a virtuoso and took charge of music and opera at a small German residence, Weimar. Here he became tremendously active as a conductor, performing works of uncommon difficulty and interest such as Berlioz's 'Benvenuto Cellini' and Wagner's operas, and he was always ready to help deserving young talents such as Peter Cornelius, Bülow, Tausig, Smetana, to the limit of his capability. He certainly acted according to his own device 'génie oblige', and he was equally generous as an artist and with his money.

No wonder gifted young musicians were attracted by Liszt and his artistic idealism. His residence, the 'Altenburg' near Weimar, became a centre of a brilliant circle of ambitious artists. One of his protégés was Joseph Joachim, the young leader of his orchestra. What Joachim writes to him from London, where he later became a frequent guest as a soloist and quartettist, is interesting because it coincides with the impressions of other artists who, drawn to London by financial reward, often missed a deeper, more genuine kind of appreciation, just as we have learnt from some letters of Chopin.

JOSEPH JOACHIM TO LISZT

London, 27 May 1852

. . . I was playing here for the first time, and it was Schubert's Quartet, which was still unknown here. It made no impression; people consider that, as Schubert was a novice in instrumental composition, they can dispose of the subject by expressing polite doubt as to his talent for that branch. It is extraordinary how reluctant these people are to surrender to a spontaneous impression; they are so corrupted by the screaming of the speculators (and here all music is in the hands of those creatures) that they respond to a composer's name in exactly the same way as to that of a firm of merchants which they protest or accept a bill from, as the case may be, simply according to whether they have heard the name seldom or frequently. Beethoven has long been established here, so that Op. 1 and the Ninth Symphony both produce an equally great effect! I feel so helpless here, having the desire but not the means to fight against such preposterous conditions! . . .

LISZT TO LOUIS KÖHLER

Weimar, 16 March 1855

Dear and honoured friend!
Hans von Bülow is bringing you these few lines. You will have the pleasure of meeting *the* artist who is closer to me than any other virtuoso now working or on the decline – one who might be called the child of my musical heart. When Hummel heard me play in Paris 25 years ago, he said: 'This fellow is a fire-eater.' That title, with which I was very gratified, belongs to Hans von Bülow by right, and I admit that I have never seen another musical being so extraordinarily gifted, complete and full-blooded. . . .

LISZT TO J. W. VON WASIELEWSKI IN DRESDEN

Weimar, 9 January 1857

. . . The repeated failure of my performances of Schumann, both in restricted circles and in public, discouraged me from including and retaining them in my rapid succession of concert programmes (which, partly from lack of time and partly from indolence and weariness of my pianistic 'golden age', I very seldom drew up myself, just leaving the choice of pieces to one person or another). This was a mistake I recognized and sincerely regretted later on, when I had come to perceive that for any artist who wishes to be worthy of the name, the danger of displeasing the public is of far less significance than that of allowing himself to be swayed by their whims – and this latter danger is particularly likely to overtake the practising artist unless he has the courage to make a firm principle of standing up seriously and consistently for his own convictions and performing what he recognizes to be the best things, whether people like it or not.

Moreover, although my hesitation with regard to Schumann's piano compositions may have been to some extent justified in view of the dominant taste of the day, I unintentionally set a *bad example*, which I am now scarcely in a position to efface. The force of habit and the slavish condition of the artist, who depends upon the encouragement and applause of the masses for the maintenance and improvement of his existence and reputation, are so binding that even the better-intentioned and most courageous, of whom I am proud to account myself one, find it extremely hard to protect their better selves from the cheerful, muddle-headed and – despite their number – unaccountable mob.

In matters of art there is one pernicious sin of which most of us are guilty, owing to our negligence and fickleness; I will call it 'the sin of Pilate'. In *following the classics* and *playing the classics*, which has been the fashion for some years now and may be regarded in general as an improvement of our musical condition, many of us conceal this sin without compensating for it – much could be said on this subject, but it would lead me too far. . . .

LISZT TO DIONYS PRUCKNER IN VIENNA

Weimar, 11 February 1857

. . . *In private*, throughout our lives, we must study, reflect, bring our work to maturity and come as near as we can to the ideal in art. But when we enter the concert hall we must never lose the feeling that this conscientious, serious striving has raised us a little above the audience and that we have to represent our share of *human dignity*, as Schiller puts it. Do not let us be led astray by *false* modesty, but let us hold fast to the *genuine* kind, which is far more difficult to preserve and more rarely found. The artist, in our sense, should be neither the servant of the audience nor its master. He is and remains the representative of *beauty*, in all the inexhaustible multiplicity of which man's thought and feeling are capable – and his unfaltering conviction of this is sufficient warrant for him. . . .

Liszt's disciples, who professed the ideals of 'The Music of the Future', took that term from a famous publication by Wagner, in which he had formulated his artistic creed, and Wagner's works remained objects of Liszt's boundless enthusiasm.

LISZT TO DR GILLE IN JENA

Zürich, 14 November 1856

. . . I shall have much to tell you about Wagner when we meet. We are seeing each other daily of course, and spending the livelong day together. His *Nibelungen* is a completely new and magnificent world, for which I have been yearning for a long time; even the most sober-minded people will be enthusiastic about it some day, despite the fact that it cannot be measured by average standards! . . .

LISZT TO ALEXANDER RITTER, DIRECTOR OF MUSIC AT STETTIN

Zürich, 4 December 1856

. . . I have spent some delightful days with Wagner, and *Rheingold* and *The Valkyrie* are incredibly *perfect miracles*.

LOUIS SPOHR TO MORITZ HAUPTMANN

Kassel, 27 May 1857

... A few days ago Liszt came through on his way to the music festival at Aachen and sent me an invitation to spend the evening with him. He told me many wonderful things about Wagner's latest works, two of which – operas entitled *Das Rheingold* and *Die Walküre* – he had with him; but the composer had asked him not to present them until the last two parts of the Nibelungen cycle are ready as well. I asked him whether it was true that in the *Rheingold* the singers would have to be suspended from wires, because the scene alternated between the bottom of the river bed and the surface of the water. Fischer had told me that at Dresden. Liszt laughed heartily and said that was a good joke invented by Wagner's enemies; but he went on to say that the production of these operas would raise plenty of difficulties, as Wagner demanded all kinds of changes in the orchestra, among other things that it should be quite invisible to the audience! I asked whether he would comply with that demand. 'So far as possible, certainly!' was his reply. . . .

To the end of his life Liszt maintained his lofty idealism, his hatred of mediocrity, and his unswerving support of everything he found remarkable and deserving.

LISZT TO RICHARD POHL AT BADEN-BADEN

Rome, 7 November 1868

... Courage is the mainspring of our best qualities; where it is lacking they wither, and without courage one is not even sufficiently prudent. One must, of course, consider, reflect, calculate, weigh the pros and cons. But after that one must make up one's mind and act, without paying undue attention to the direction of the wind or to any passing clouds. . . .

LISZT TO PROFESSOR S. LEBERT

Villa d'Este, 2 December 1868

... Our pianists have scarcely an inkling of the wonderful treasures to be discovered among Schubert's piano compositions. For the most part they run through them *en passant*, noticing that here and there there are repetitions, tedious passages or signs of what appears to be carelessness ... and they put them aside. Schubert himself is partly to blame, of course, for the very inadequate attention paid to his excellent piano compositions. He was too overwhelmingly productive, he wrote without pause, mingling the insignificant and the important, the noble and the mediocre, ignoring criticism and going wherever his wings carried him. He lived in music like a bird in the air, singing like an angel all the time.

Oh, ever-flowing, ever-loving genius! Beloved hero of the paradise of youth! Harmony, freshness, strength, sweetness, reverie, passion, tranquillity, tears and flames pour from the depths and heights of your heart; and we almost overlook your supreme mastery, so much are we bewitched by your natural charm! . . .

LISZT TO HIS COUSIN EDUARD VON LISZT

Budapest, 2 January 1877

. . . Unhappily there are far too many concerts and concert performers. As Dingelstedt so rightly remarked, 'the theatre is a necessary evil, concerts are a superfluous one'. I am doing my best to impress these words upon my disciples at the Hungarian Academy of Music. . . .

LISZT TO OTTO LESSMANN

Meiningen, December 1883

. . . Under Bülow's leadership the Meiningen orchestra is doing wonders; nowhere else can one find such an understanding of so wide a range of works, which are performed with the most exact and subtle rhythmic and dynamic shading. The fact that the Duke closed down the Meiningen Opera some twenty years ago is very advantageous to the concert system. It means that having no demands from the Opera, the orchestra has time to hold a good number of partial and general rehearsals without undue fatigue. Bülow is almost as lavish with rehearsals as Berlioz would have been if he could. The result is admirable and in some respects incomparable, not excepting the Paris Conservatoire and other celebrated concert societies. Thanks to its present director, the little Meiningen phalanx is ahead of the biggest battalions. . . .

LISZT TO COUNTESS MERCY-ARGENTEAU

Rome, 20 January 1885

. . . I shall certainly not desist from my propaganda for the remarkable compositions of the new Russian school, which I esteem and appreciate with keen sympathy. For the last 6 or 7 years, orchestral works by Rimsky-Korsakoff and Borodin have been played at the big annual concerts of the Music Association (Allgemeiner Deutscher Musikverein), of which I have the honour to be president. Their success is rising *crescendo*, despite the kind of stubborn prejudice against Russian music. It is not eccentricity that determines me to make them known, but a sense of fair play based on my belief that these works, bred of a fine tradition, have real value. I do not know which of them were chosen by Hans von Bülow, that Achilles of propagandists, for the Russian concert he gave recently with the Meiningen orchestra, with its unparalleled discipline and perfection. . . .

Georges Bizet *(1838–75) was, like Berlioz a generation before him, a graduate of the Paris Conservatoire. In Italy with the 'Prix de Rome', he was as much a severe critic of Italian music as Berlioz had been, but enjoyed his years in Italy all the same.*

If one feels inclined to take exception to some of his judgements, one has to consider his youth – he was hardly twenty at the time – and the climate in which he had grown up in Paris, when Meyerbeer was towering over the musical scene.

BIZET TO HIS MOTHER

Rome, 26 February 1858

. . . I have already seen Rome a little. There is much to admire, but there are many disappointments. Bad taste is poisoning Italy. It is a country completely lost to art. Rossini, Mozart, Weber, Paër, Cimarosa, are unknown, despised or forgotten here. Sad! . . .

BIZET TO HIS MOTHER

Rome, 25 June 1858

. . . So I looked about, and I have found an Italian farce in the *Don Pasquale* style. It is very amusing to do and I hope to come out of it creditably. Comic music is decidedly in my line, and I throw myself into it heart and soul. You would never believe what trouble I had finding the poem. I went round all the bookshops in Rome and read two hundred plays. No libretti are written nowadays in Italy except for Verdi, Mercadante and Pacini. The others do the best they can with translations of French operas; for here, where there is no protection for author's rights, a man will take a play by M. Scribe, translate it, and sign it without altering a word. At most they may change the title. For instance, *Il Domino nero* (*Le Domino noir*): not a mention of Scribe, Auber's music is used; *Roberto di Picardia* (*Robert le Diable*) is made into a Picard instead of a Norman, and that does the trick; but they keep Meyerbeer's music. . . .

BIZET TO HECTOR GRUYER

Rome, 31 December 1858

. . . Until now I wavered between Mozart, Rossini and Meyerbeer. Now I know what one has to worship. There are two kinds of genius – natural genius and rational genius. Though I admire the latter immensely, I must confess that my whole feeling responds to the former. Yes, my dear fellow, I make bold to prefer Raphael to Michelangelo, Mozart to Beethoven, and Rossini to Meyerbeer. . . .

BIZET TO HIS MOTHER

Rome, 19 March 1859

. . . You attribute the succession of failures our best composers have suffered for the last few years to the weakness of their *libretti*; you are right, but there is another reason – the fact that not one of them has an all-round talent. Some – Massé, for example – lack style, breadth of vision. Others – David, I imagine – fall short in musical groundwork and in intelligence. Even the best of them lack the only thing that enables a composer to make himself understood by the present-day public: the *motif*, which is usually and quite wrongly called the 'idea'. One may be a great artist without having the *motif*, in which case one must give up hope of money and popular acclaim; but one may be a man of great talent and have that precious gift as well – look at Rossini. Rossini is the greatest of them all, because, like Mozart, he has every quality – elevation of views, style, and – the *motif*. I am convinced and persuaded of what I am saying, and it gives me hope. I know my job very well, I am very good at orchestration, I am never commonplace, and at last I have discovered this *open sesame* for which I have been seeking. In my opera I have a dozen *motifs*, but real ones, rhythmic and easy to remember, and yet I have made no sacrifice as to taste. I wish you could hear it all; you would see that I have already found something of what I so entirely lacked. Next year I shall try to find the *motif* in grand opera, that is much more difficult; but it is already something to have found it in comic opera. . . .

BIZET TO HIS MOTHER

Rome, 26 November 1859

. . . A new opera by Verdi was given here just lately. It was horrible. And the singers, the orchestra and scenery were pitiful!!!!!!!!

[Gluck's] *Orfeo* is being given at the Théatre Lyrique. That is the only place where such good music can be heard. I was looking over the score again the other day; it is marvellous! And some people declare it lacks melody; it's enough to make one die laughing. . . .

BIZET TO HIS MOTHER

Rome, 23 June 1860

. . . They say Verdi will write nothing more, and even if he did I doubt whether he would often recover such flashes of genius as he revealed in *Il Trovatore*, *Traviata* and the fourth act of *Rigoletto*. He is an example of a fine artist ruined by negligence and the wrong kind of success. . . .

. . . On sirocco days I cannot touch *Don Giovanni*, the *Nozze* or *Così fan tutte*; Mozart's music affects me too directly, and it really makes me very ill. Some things by Rossini have the same effect on me. The strange thing is that it never goes so far with Beethoven and Meyerbeer. As for Haydn, he has been sending me to sleep for a long time. . . .

The 'new opera' Bizet had heard in Rome was one of Verdi's most outstanding masterpieces, 'Un Ballo in Maschera'. The young musician's judgement of Verdi reveals the unbridgeable abyss – we shall learn more about it in Verdi's letters – between the emotional directness of Italian melodrama and the fastidious French taste in which Bizet had been brought up. The performance, however, must have been atrocious, judging from Verdi's own account of it. As so often, slothful routine and managerial stinginess were the culprits, and Verdi was an implacable opponent of avaricious impresarios.

VERDI TO VINCENZO JACOVACCI

Busseto, 5 June 1859

You were wrong to defend *Un Ballo in Maschera* against the newspaper attacks. You should behave as I invariably do – don't read them, or rather let them sing whatever tune they choose, as I have always done! For the point is that the opera is either *bad* or *good*. If it is bad, the journalists are right to speak ill of it; if it is good, and they refuse to admit the fact owing to their own or other people's prejudices or for some other reason, one should let them talk and pay no attention. Besides, you must admit that if anyone or anything in the carnival season had need of being defended, it was the worthless Company you saddled me with. Put your hand on your heart and acknowledge that I showed myself to be a model of rare unselfishness in not picking up the score and going away to look for dogs less given to howling than those you offered me. . . .

Forgive me, but I cannot write to Ricordi to ask him to reduce his rates, for I am not in the habit of entering into such matters. Besides, the prices you offer for *Aroldo*, *Boccanegra* and the *Ballo in Maschera* seem to me (little as these works may be worth) to be too low. I don't know whether Ricordi will take the same view; if so he will say, as I do and as you say yourself, that you must *get your supplies some other way*. . . . You need three operas? Well, here they are: *Nina Pazza*, by Paisiello, *Armide*, by Gluck, and *Alceste*, by Lully. Apart from the economy, you can be sure that with these you will not have to fight the journalists or anyone else. The music is beautiful, the composers are dead, everybody has been speaking well of them for a century, for two centuries, and will continue to speak well of them, if only as an excuse for speaking ill of those who have not yet been so foolish as to die.

Good-bye, my dear Jacovacci. Don't let us think of new operas. . . .

Not long after this, Bizet found himself confronted by a far more dangerous contemporary. How well he stood that test is born out by the fact that the German philosopher Friedrich Nietzsche, who was Wagner's most ardent admirer at first, and later his most devastating critic, could single out Bizet's 'Carmen' as a shining example of a diametrically opposed artistic tendency. Bizet did not live to see the triumphant progress of his masterpiece. He died three months after the first, rather indifferent production of 'Carmen' in Paris.

BIZET TO HIS MOTHER-IN-LAW MME HALÉVY

29 May 1871

. . . I will not talk to you about Wagner today. How unjust you are! . . . But it is the fate of these great geniuses to be unappreciated by their contemporaries. Wagner is not a friend of mine and I have no great opinion of him; but I cannot forget what tremendous pleasure I owe to his original genius. His music has an indescribable, inexpressible charm. It is all voluptuousness, tenderness, love!

If I could play it to you for a week, you would dote upon it! . . . The Germans, who, alas, are at least our equals in music, have realized that Wagner is one of their cornerstones. He is the very incarnation of the German spirit of the nineteenth century.

You well know how a great artist can be wounded by contempt. Happily for Wagner, he is so insolently proud that criticism cannot touch his heart – assuming he has one, which I doubt.

I will not go so far as you, I will not couple Beethoven's name with Wagner's. Beethoven is not a man, but a god! – like Shakespeare, or Homer or Michelangelo! Well, take the most intelligent audience, and play them the finest page that exists in our art, the Ninth Symphony; they will understand nothing, absolutely nothing. The experiment has been made and is repeated every year, with the same result. But Beethoven has been dead for fifty years, and it is the fashion to find his work beautiful.

Judge *for yourself*, forgetting everything you have heard from other people, forgetting the silly or malicious articles and the worst book he has published,[1] and you will see. It is not *the music of the future* – that means nothing – but, as you so rightly say, it is the music of all time, because it is admirable. . . .

Naturally, if I thought I were imitating Wagner, despite my admiration, I should never write another note. Only a fool *imitates*. It is better to do bad stuff of one's own than by copying other people. Besides, the finer the model the more ridiculous imitation becomes. Michelangelo, Shakespeare and Beethoven have been imitated! God knows what horrors the rage for imitation has brought upon us! . . .

TCHAIKOVSKY TO MME NADEZHDA VON MECK

Simaki, 18 July, 1880

Yesterday evening – to take a rest from my own work – I played through Bizet's *Carmen* from cover to cover. I consider it a *chef d'œuvre* in the fullest sense of the word: one of those rare compositions which seem to reflect most strongly the musical tendencies of a whole generation. It seems to me that our own period differs from earlier ones in this one characteristic: that contemporary composers *are engaged in the pursuit of charming and piquant effects*, unlike Mozart, Beethoven, Schubert, or Schumann. What is the so-called New Russian School but the cult of varied and pungent harmonies, of original orchestral combinations and every kind of purely external effect? Musical ideas give place to this or that union of sounds. Formerly there was composition, creation; now (with few exceptions) there is only research and contrivance. This development of musical thought is purely

[1] A satire on the French defeat in 1870.

intellectual, consequently contemporary music is clever, piquant and eccentric, but cold and lacking the glow of true emotion. And behold, a Frenchman comes on the scene, in whom these qualities of piquancy and pungency are not the outcome of effort and reflection, but flow from his pen as in a free stream, flattering the ear, but touching us also . . . I cannot play the last scene without tears in my eyes; the gross rejoicing of the crowd who look on at the bull-fight and, side by side with this, the poignant tragedy and death of the two principal characters, pursued by an evil fate, who come to their inevitable end through a long series of sufferings.

I am convinced that ten years hence *Carmen* will be the most popular opera in the world.

He was a good prophet indeed.

PART TWO

Nineteenth to Twentieth Century

BEL CANTO

From Rossini to Verdi

Throughout the nineteenth century Paris remained the most distinguished centre of opera in Europe. For an Italian as well as for a French composer a performance in Paris was the hallmark of success, just as London was the yardstick of an artist's financial standing. Italian style, however, was too strongly rooted in a national tradition of three centuries ever to submit to foreign influence, and Italian opera, established in Paris, remained as Italian as ever.

In Italy, one positive factor dominated the situation: a general enthusiasm for opera and a hereditary gift for singing which supplied the necessary stimulus and material for the maintenance of operatic enterprise everywhere. The love of 'bel canto' was rooted in the Italian mind, a cult of beauty in which the whole population took part and in which the nobles found themselves united with the 'lazzaroni', the ragged beggars of the Neapolitan streets.

There is a contemporary witness of the customs of operatic life in Italy in the earlier part of the nineteenth century, who combines enthusiasm and liveliness of impressions with a great writer's art of presentation: the French novelist Stendhal, who lived in Italy at the time when Rossini's star was rising to its zenith. The following description of how operas were created and produced in Italy is taken from his biography of Gioacchino Rossini *(1792–1868), who was still in his early thirties at the time of its publication in 1824:*

'From Bologna, one of the headquarters of music in Italy, there came commissions to Rossini to write operas for every place where a theatre was to be found. Everywhere the impresario was put under pressure to secure an opera from him. On an average, he received a fee of 1,000 Fr. [about £50] for an opera, and he would write four or five a year. [This is an exaggeration.]

'Here is a description of how opera is run in Italy. A financier – usually some rich patrician, as that function yields pleasure and prestige, but is often ruinous – makes himself responsible for the theatre of the town where he is a bigwig. He forms an ensemble consisting, say, of a "prima donna", a "tenore", a "basso cantante", a "basso buffo", a second lady and another buffo. He engages a "maestro" (composer), who will write for him a new opera and direct the performance, taking into consideration the available voices in distributing the parts. The impresario buys a libretto: that's an expense of 60 or 80 Fr. The author is some unfortunate clergyman, a parasite of one of the rich houses of

the county. The comic character of the parasite, so well depicted by Terence, is still in its flower in Lombardy, where even in the smallest town there are five or six families with a yearly revenue of 100,000 Fr. The impresario, the head of one of these families, leaves the financial technicalities of the enterprise to a manager, usually the most rascally lawyer of the region. Our rich man, the impresario, duly falls in love with the primadonna. The main object of curiosity in the little town is whether he will appear with her publicly arm in arm.

'The operatic ensemble, organized this way, gives its first performance after a month of burlesque intrigues that provide abundant material for gossip. The "prima recita" (first performance) is the main public event of the year, of a kind to which I can compare nothing that happens in Paris. Eight or ten thousand people discuss the virtues and shortcomings of the new opera for three weeks, with all the emotional intensity given to them by heaven, and with all the power of their lungs. If not interrupted by riotous opposition [the reader will find an example of this in Mendelssohn's letter, pp. 158–9], this performance is followed by another twenty or thirty. Thereupon the ensemble disperses. The event is called a season (una stagione); the best season is at carnival. Singers who have remained unengaged are usually to be found in Milan or in Bologna, the headquarters of the agents whose job it is to place and to exploit them.

'From this description of the theatrical customs the reader will glean some idea of the peculiar kind of life, without any parallel in France, Rossini was leading between 1810 and 1816. He went successively to most towns in Italy, spending two or three months in every place. On his arrival he was received and fêted by the "dilettanti" of the county; he would spend the first fifteen or twenty days at dinner parties, shrugging his shoulders at the stupidity of the libretto presented to him. "You have given me verses but no action", I have heard him tell a dingy poetaster, who apologized profusely and, two hours later, came back with a sonnet, "umiliato dalla gloria del più grande maestro d'Italia e del mondo" [Confounded by the glory of the greatest maestro of Italy and the whole world].

'After fifteen or twenty days of such dissolute life, Rossini would decline invitations to dinners and musical parties and pretend to busy himself seriously with studying the voices and characters of his singers. They would sing for him at the piano, and he would find himself compelled to mutilate his best melodic inventions because the tenor would not get that high note, or the primadonna would always botch a certain passage. It may happen that only the bass can sing tolerably.

'At last, twenty days before the first performance, the composer, well acquainted with his ensemble by now, starts writing assiduously. He gets up late in the morning and composes his music during the conversation of his new

friends, who, whatever he does, will not leave him alone for a moment. He has dinner with them at the "osteria", and even supper. He gets home very late and his friends bring him right to his door, singing at the top of their voices music he has just improvised, sometimes a "miserere", scandalizing the pious neighbourhood. At home at last, it is at this time, towards three in the morning, that he invents his most inspired tunes, writing them down on scraps of paper, all in a hurry, without a piano; on the next day he puts them properly into shape and orchestrates his music while talking to his friends who have duly appeared again.

' "Composing, that's nothing", says Rossini. But rehearsals are a despair. At that stage the poor maestro has to endure the sufferings inflicted upon him by having to hear his most beautiful inventions most cruelly disfigured. He leaves the rehearsal sadly out of spirits, disgusted by what he was so much satisfied with only yesterday.

'But these sittings, painful for the young composer, are, to my mind, a triumph of Italian sensibility. There, assembled round a paltry, ramshackle piano in a hole called the "ridotto" of the theatre of some small town such as Reggio or Belletri, I have seen eight or ten poor devils of actors rehearse to the accompaniment of the noises of an adjacent kitchen; and I have heard them improving and in the end performing admirably the most subtle and fragrant music.

'During this period, the work of the ensemble is being discussed everywhere in the town, in expectation of the pleasure or the annoyance to come during the most brilliant month of the year, the success or downfall of the new opera. A small town, at this stage of intoxication, forgets the existence of the rest of the world. It is during this period of uncertainty that the impresario has really the time of his life, being indeed the king of the castle. I have seen stingy bankers who did not regret having bought that flattering position with the loss of fifteen hundred louis. . . .

'The decisive night has arrived at last. The maestro sits at the piano in the orchestra. The theatre is as full as can be. People have come from a distance of twenty miles around; curious visitors are camping in their carriages on the road; all the inns have been crowded out since the day before; all work has stopped. When the performance starts, the town has become a desert. All the passion, all the uncertainty, all the life of the population is concentrated in the theatre.

'The performance begins. One could hear a pin drop. The overture being over, a terrific hubbub starts. One extols it to the clouds, or one hisses it and howls it down without mercy. And after every piece of the new opera, after hushed silence, the same noise starts all over again. The roar of the stormy sea would offer an imperfect comparison. One can hear the singers as well as the composer being judged. One shouts "bravo Davide, brava Pisaroni!". Or the

whole theatre rings with shouts of "bravo maestro!". Rossini rises from his place at the piano, his handsome face takes on an expression of gravity, a rare occurrence with him; he bows three times, is covered with applause, deafened by shouting; then one proceeds to the next number.

'The maestro appears at the piano during the first three performances of his new opera. After this, he receives his fee of seventy sequins (eight hundred francs), takes part in a banquet given to him by his new friends, which means the whole town, and leaves by mail coach, carrying his portmanteau with more manuscript paper than belongings, only to begin the same cycle of activities forty miles further on in another little town.'

So far Stendhal. One has to add, however, that the delightful provincial idyll described by him did not survive into the second half of the century. Shrewd, unscrupulous businessmen found out in due course that there was not only pleasure in the promotion of opera, but also money and power, and the amateur impresario was gradually squeezed out of the business. Already when Stendhal wrote his 'Life of Rossini', Domenico Barbaja, an adventurer of fabulous energy, controlled the two most distinguished opera-houses in Italy, La Scala in Milan and San Carlo in Naples, and he was followed by Bartolomeo Merelli, an equally energetic professional manager. Besides, both in turn were in charge of the Imperial Court Opera in Vienna, where in 1842 Donizetti was appointed 'Court Composer and Master of the Imperial Chapel'.

The following letters illustrate the situation, and also the close links between the Italian theatre and opera in Paris, especially from the time when Rossini, at the peak of his fame, established himself in that metropolis of Europe and, in 1824, became the head of the 'Théâtre Italien'. London, with infinite wealth and a keen demand for music, had become another centre of gravity in the west of Europe, irresistibly attractive to successful artists.

The conditions under which operas were written and the resulting desperate pressure of time have certainly contributed to a profusion of indifferent music; but they also produced masterpieces such as Rossini's 'The Barber of Seville' and 'Cenerentola', or Donizetti's 'L'Elisire d'Amore' and 'Don Pasquale'. The positive elements of this system were an enormous stimulation to the composer's productivity by incessant demand and a live current linking him with his performers and his audience – that live current, the progressive weakening of which has become the foremost problem of music in our century.

A composer who leads the kind of life described by Stendhal would hardly find time for writing letters. Later, when Rossini had settled in Paris, he could take things more easily. He was a European celebrity of the first order and even his German colleagues, who were liable to turn up their noses at the Italian lack of profundity, would admit Rossini's scintillating spirit and graceful inventiveness.

MENDELSSOHN TO HIS MOTHER AND REBECCA, HIS SISTER

Frankfurt, 14 July 1836

And then Hiller is here, someone I have always been delighted to see, and we have always had a multitude of interesting things to discuss together. . . .

I called on him yesterday morning, and who should be sitting there but Rossini, as large as life, in the very best of humour. I really know of nobody who can be so diverting and witty when he is in the mood; he kept us in fits of laughter the whole time. I promised to arrange for the St Cecilia Society to sing Sebastian Bach's Mass in B Minor and several other things by the same composer, for him; it would be too wonderful to make Rossini admire Sebastian Bach! But he believes that when in Rome one should do as the Romans do, and he wants to conform. He declares he is in raptures over Germany, and says that when, in the evening by the Rhine, he has had a good look at the wine-list, the waiter has to show him to his room or he would never find his way to it. He has the drollest, most amusing things to say about Paris and all the musicians there, and about himself and his compositions; and he speaks of all contemporaries with such tremendous respect that one might take him quite literally if one had no eyes to see the sly expression on his face. But all his looks and words are full of wit and liveliness and intelligence, and anyone who denies his genius would certainly recant on hearing him holding forth like this. . . .

At this period, however, Rossini had already retired from opera. 'William Tell' (1829), his most ambitiously designed work, was also his last. He lived, for all one could see, a contented, easy-going, lazy life, was a gastronomic expert of the first order and a generous, helpful friend to his younger Italian colleagues, who could always count upon his advice and support, especially during the years when, as the head of the 'Théâtre Italien', his influence in Paris was decisive. As to his own work, it would be difficult to find a more modest, detached attitude than his. Like all his Italian compatriots at the time of the 'risorgimento' he was an ardent patriot, passionately devoted to the ideals of Italian music. He took a hand in the reorganization of the 'Liceo' at Bologna, where he had received his own scanty training. His creed, expressed in some of his letters, is an unfaltering adherence to the Italian heritage of melody and vocality.

ROSSINI TO HIS FRIEND ANTONIO ZOBOLI IN BOLOGNA

Milan, 26 December 1837

My musical evenings are making quite a sensation here at Milan. Amateurs, artists, composers, all sing in the chorus; about 40 voices, not counting the soloists. Madame Pasta [one of the most celebrated singers of her time] is to sing next Friday. As you can imagine, this news is received with amazement as she refuses to sing at any other house. I have all the singers from the theatres, who vie with one another to sing here, and I have to fight all day against the admission of more satellites. Persons of the greatest distinction are guests at my parties; Olimpia [Mme Rossini] does the honours very successfully, and we all enjoy ourselves. . . .

ROSSINI TO THE IMPRESARIO SIGNOR BANDINI IN FLORENCE

Bologna, 18 August 1838

. . . I can give you no instructions regarding *Elisabetta* [one of his earlier operas, 1815] because I can remember nothing whatsoever about the costumes, scenery, etc. *These works should be left in peace.* Give modern music to the public which loves novelty, and do not forget that ancient composer, your friend

G. Rossini

ROSSINI TO DONIZETTI

Bologna, 12 April 1842

My best-beloved Donizetti,

I send you some corrections made on the sheet left with me by Marchese Bevilacqua, which I would like you to take into consideration, though without regarding them as an ultimatum. You having said you were to give lessons in harmony [at the *Liceo* in Bologna], the above-mentioned Marchese supposes that you are also ready to give lessons in counterpoint, advanced dramatic and sacred composition, etc. But I remember quite clearly that you did not wish to have the drudgery of the school subjects, wishing to concern yourself with only the more interesting part, and there we are in entire agreement. If the Municipality is to meet the cost of a teacher of harmony and counterpoint, you would have to content yourself with 50 z. [zecchini] a month. But let me point out that during the holidays your salary, although small, would not stop or even be reduced, which means that for 8 months' service you would receive about 77 z. a month. True, that is a trifle, but we are in Bologna!!!

. . . Do not forsake me, Donizetti: the gratitude and affection in which I hold you deserve some sacrifice on your part. . . .

ROSSINI TO DONIZETTI IN VIENNA

Bologna, 15 June 1844

Is it true that you may make a short visit to Bologna next September? True that you may stage your 'Maria' [Donizetti's opera, *Maria di Rohan*] at our Teatro Communale? The Society would make every possible effort, to show you its gratitude, and I should be the happiest of all, because we could eat four *tagliatelle alla Bolognese* together again; write a line about it, make us all happy, it costs you so little!! . . .

ROSSINI TO FERNANDO GUIDIGINI IN BOLOGNA

12 February 1851

To fulfil his part properly, the good singer needs only to be a capable *interpreter* of the ideas of the Maestro, the composer, trying to express them to full effect and bring them out in the clearest light. And the musicians need only be accurate *performers* of what they find written for them. In short, the composer and the poet are the only serious *creators*. Some skilful singers occasionally try to show off with additional embellishments; and if this is to be called creative, well and good; but it is a form of creative work which is quite often unsuccessful and frequently spoils the composer's ideas, robbing them of the simplicity of expression they were intended to have.

The French use the phrase *créer un rôle*, a vainglorious French expression used only by singers who give the first performance of some leading part in a new opera; their intention being to suggest that they are more or less an example to be imitated later by other singers when called upon to perform the part in question. Here again, however, the word *create* seems hardly appropriate; for 'to create' is to *produce from nothing*, whereas in such cases the singer undoubtedly has something to work on – that is to say the poem and the music, which are not his creations. This is all I can find to say to you; and it seems to me to answer your question. . . .

ROSSINI TO HIS FRIEND DOMENICO DONZELLI

Florence, 30 October 1852

In your last letter you asked me for a piece of music for your daughter and for the *Barber of Seville*. But have you, my dear friend, forgotten in what a state of mental debility I now live, and that it is constantly increasing? I can assure you I should not have hung my lyre on the wall so early if feelings of delicacy rather than of vanity had not required me to withdraw from fame and profit. Music needs fresh ideas; I can bring to it only languor and spleen. Be assured that I should be delighted to give you proof of my affection by doing as you ask; but believe me, I cannot. . . .

ROSSINI TO GIUSEPPE BELLENTANI, PORK BUTCHER AT MODENA

Florence, 28 December 1853

The Swan of Pesaro [Rossini's birthplace – a title bestowed upon him by his contemporaries] to the Eagle of Salted Provisions of the Este.

You have undertaken a lofty flight for me by treating me to specially-prepared *zamponi* and *cappelletti* [Italian delicacies]; and it is only right that, as though from the depths of the marshy lands of ancient Padusa, I should utter a harsh cry of particular gratitude to you. I found your collected works complete in every respect; and their inner mastery will be appreciated by all who, like me, have the good fortune to delight in the subtlety of your celebrated handiwork.

I am not setting your praises to music, because as I told you in my last letter, I have withdrawn from the uproar of the musical world and am now an *ex-composer*. All to the good for me and all the better for you! You know how to touch certain chords that satisfy the palate, a sounder judge than the ear because it relies on the sense of touch at its most extreme point, which is the very principle of life; to give you pleasure I touch only one of those chords, that of my warm gratitude for the many attentions you have shown me. I hope this may stimulate you to still loftier flights so that you may deserve the laurel wreath with which I should be delighted to crown you.

Your most obliged servant. . . .

ROSSINI TO HIS FRIEND ANGELO CATELANI AT MODENA

1854

Now let us turn to the pork-butcher question, since you are willing to convey my message to your celebrated Bellentani. This is what I would like to have sent to me at whatever time the Este Eagle may deem appropriate: 8 *cappelli da prete*; 6 *zamponi* [pig's trotters]; 10 *cotechini* [sausages] of various size; in all, 24 jewels of porcine origin. Please accept my thanks in anticipation. . . .

ROSSINI TO THE POET FELICE ROMANI

Paris, 15 December 1857

The bearer of this letter is Monsieur Bizet, winner of the first prize in composition at the Imperial School of Music in Paris. He is travelling in order to complete the practical side of his musical education; he has studied with the greatest success and won considerable acclaim with an operetta performed here. He is a good pianist and an excellent young man, who deserves your solicitude together with mine. . . .

ROSSINI TO THE DIRECTOR OF THE 'THÉÂTRE ITALIEN' IN PARIS

11 November 1859

Monsieur,

I am told that your theatre is announcing on its posters a new opera by me, entitled *Un curioso Accidente*. I do not know whether I have the right to prevent the performance of a medley in two acts (more or less) of old pieces of mine; I have never concerned myself with such questions in respect of my works (of which none, be it said in passing, bears this title of *Un curioso Accidente*). In any case I have not opposed the performance of this *curioso Accidente* and do not intend to do so. But I cannot allow the audiences who will visit your theatre, or your subscribers, to believe, firstly, that this is a new opera by me, and secondly, that I have any hand in whatever arrangement is to be made. I am therefore writing to request you to remove from your poster the word *new* and my name as composer, and to replace them by the following: *Opera put together by M. Berrettoni from pieces by M. Rossini*. I must insist that this alteration appears on tomorrow's poster; otherwise I shall be obliged to appeal to the law instead of, as at present, to your sense of justice. . . .

ROSSINI TO MAESTRO GIOVANNI PACINI

Paris, 8 April 1864

Dearest friend,

Giorgione, Titian, Van Dyck and Velasquez could not paint a portrait of me like that which you put at the beginning of your most welcome letter of the 2nd inst.; I refer to the smile with which you assumed I should greet the request you were kind enough to make, for a small instrumental composition by me for the celebrated *Società del Quartetto* in Florence. I did not smile, on the contrary I shed a little tear at the thought of being obliged to refuse your flattering request . . . I gave up my musical career in 1829; long silence has deprived me of the power to compose and of my knowledge of the different instruments. Now I am merely a fourth-rate pianist. . . .

ROSSINI TO DR FILIPPO FILIPPI, COMPOSER AND CRITIC IN MILAN

Passy, Paris, 26 August 1868

I was informed not long ago that several of your musical compositions had been performed at Milan in various *academie* with brilliant success; as you can suppose, my dear Dr Filippi, this gives me the most heartfelt satisfaction.

I am happy to tell you as well that the little air in A with the hearing of which you favoured me in my house in Paris, sung in a slightly veiled voice by its author, that eminent pianist and composer, *me trotte toujours dans la tête* [still runs in my head]. That little air in the Venetian dialect is a real gem; and by heaven, I will not have it said that it belongs to what is called 'the music of the Future'!!! Apropos of this subject, so much in fashion and so often discussed without rhyme or reason, I am obliged to admit that when I read big, ugly words such as *Progress, Decadence, Future, Past, Present, Convention*, etc., my stomach heaves with a motion I find extremely difficult to repress. If I had the resources of your *savante plume*, many and vigorous would be the lessons I should try to give to those phrase-spitters (believed to be musical Demosthenes all) who talk about everything with never a sensible word. . . . Do not imagine, my good Dr Filippi, that I am systematically hostile to the drama – far from it; and although I was an accomplished singer of Italian *bel canto* before becoming a composer of music, I agree with the philosophy of the great poet who declares that:

Tous les genres sont bons
Hors le genre ennuyeux.

[All styles are good/Except the tedious style]

But as for the present behaviour of our dear colleagues, it must be admitted that the social upheavals produced by hope, fear, revolution and so forth have had the inevitable consequence of forcing our poor composers (most of whom are spurred on to work by *hunger and ambition*) to rack their brains for new forms and diverse means of delighting their young coevals, many of whom have a past history of rapine, the barricades, and other little things of the kind!! It now behoves you, as a distinguished critic, to do your utmost in preaching to young composers that there is no such thing as progress or decadence in the latest novelties, and to make them realize at the same time that these are sterile inventions, born solely of perseverance and not of inspiration. Let them at last find the courage to shake off convention and embrace, with light hearts and in full confidence, those elements of Italian music that are divine and truly charming – *Simple melody, and variety of rhythm.* If our young colleagues obey these precepts they will win the fame they aspire to, and their compositions will have the long life enjoyed by those of our revered forebears, Marcello, Palestrina and Pergolese, and undoubtedly in store for those of the present-day celebrities, Mercadante, Bellini, Donizetti and Verdi. You will have noticed, shrewd as you are, my dear Doctor Filippi, that I have deliberately omitted the word *imitative* from my recommendations to you on the subject of Italian music for the benefit of young composers, inasmuch as I have referred *solely* to melody and rhythm. I shall remain forever *inébranlable* [unshakable] in my conviction that Italian music (and especially vocal music) is entirely *ideal and expressive*, never *imitative*, as certain materialist philosophizers make out. Allow me to say that the feelings of the heart may be expressed, but not imitated.

However, in support of my statements about the art of music and its compass, I would add that the word *expressive* by no means excludes *declamation*, still less what is known as *dramatic* music, indeed I would assert that at times it requires such music. . . . Let us therefore say once and for all that imitation is the prerogative, the inseparable companion and often the chief assistant of those who cultivate the fine arts of painting and sculpture. But if imitation is accompanied as well by lofty artistic feeling and a touch of genius (of which nature is not lavish), then this last, genius, though sometimes it rebels against the rules, will be as it has always been, at one stroke, the creator of beauty!

Lastly, in order not to leave those two little words *Progress* and *Decadence* without employment, I will say that I recognize *progress* only in the manufacture of the countless new instruments that have been produced (that progress which delights the self-styled lovers of imitative music, and they may be wrong.) But I cannot deny a certain decadence in vocal art, for its new adepts incline towards the feverish style rather than the *italo dolce cantare che nell' anima si sente* [the sweet Italian song that speaks to the soul]. May God forgive those who were the first cause of this. . . .

'Music of the Future' was the slogan of the progressive movement led by Liszt and Wagner. Rossini's lack of sympathy with their tendencies was shared by his successor, Verdi, as one will find expressed in some of his letters.

ROSSINI TO AN UNKNOWN CORRESPONDENT

(*Undated*)

Wait until the evening before the day fixed for the performance. Nothing stimulates one's ardour as much as necessity, the presence of a copyist waiting for your work and the urgings of an impresario who is at his wits' end, tearing out his hair by handfuls. In my time in Italy all impresarios were bald by the age of thirty. I composed the overture to *Othello* in a little room in the Palazzo Barbaja where the baldest and most ferocious of the directors had shut me up by force with nothing except a plateful of macaroni, threatening not to let me out as long as I lived, until I had written the last note. I wrote the overture to the *Gazza Ladra* on the very day of the first performance, under the roof of La Scala, where I had been imprisoned by the director under the guard of four stage carpenters who had orders to throw my manuscript out of the window, page by page, to the copyists, who were down below waiting to copy it out. If the pages of music failed to arrive, their orders were to throw me out myself. For the *Barber* I managed better: I composed no overture at all, I just took one I had been intending for a semi-serious opera entitled *Elisabetta*. The public was more than satisfied. I composed the overture of *Le Comte Ory* while I stood with my feet in the water, fishing, in the company of Signor Aguado who was talking about Spanish finance. The overture of *William Tell* was written in much the same circumstances. For *Mosé* I did not write one at all. . . .

ROSSINI TO THE PUBLISHER GIOVANNI RICORDI IN MILAN

(*Undated*)

The edition you are bringing out will give rise to much (justified) criticism, because the same pieces of music will be found in several different operas; the time and money allowed me for my compositions were so paltry that I scarcely had leisure to read the so-called poem I was to set to music: the only thing I had at heart was to support my beloved parents and poor relations. . . .

Ricordi had planned a complete edition of Rossini's operas.

ROSSINI TO THE PUBLISHER TITO RICORDI IN MILAN

Paris, 21 April 1868

I know *Don Carlos* is all the rage in Milan; I am delighted, for your sake and Verdi's. Tell the latter that if he comes to Paris again he must ask a lot of money, for he is the only man capable of composing a *Grand Opéra* (may our other colleagues forgive me for saying so).

I would like to be remembered to Boito [Arrigo Boito (1842–1918), operatic composer and poet, librettist of Verdi's *Otello* and *Falstaff*], for whose fine talent I have an infinite appreciation. He sent me his *Mefistofele* libretto, from which I perceive that he is in too great a hurry to make innovations. Do not imagine that I am hostile to innovators! But I wish they would not try to do in one day what can only be achieved in several years. If dear Giulio will read *in a kindly spirit* my first work, *Il Demetrio e il Polibio*, and my *William Tell*, he will see I was no laggard either!!!

When in 1829 Rossini retired from the operatic field, two of his younger compatriots had already come to the fore, Gaetano Donizetti *(1797–1848) and* Vincenzo Bellini *(1801–35), both immensely productive, working to the limits of their capacity, providing a rich supply of new operas for an insatiable demand. Both, in due course, won European fame when they made their mark in Paris and London. Like Rossini, Donizetti was a generous colleague, as he later proved by his active support of young Verdi, whose works he, as head of the Court Opera, introduced in Vienna. His life of hectic activity – he left more than sixty operas – ended as tragically as Schumann's: he died insane.*

DONIZETTI TO HIS TEACHER MAESTRO SIMONE MAYR IN BERGAMO

Naples, 30 May 1826

This evening our Bellini's *Bianca e Fernando* is to be performed for the first time at the San Carlo; it is his first production, beautiful, beautiful, beautiful, particularly as it is the first thing he has written. Alas, so beautiful compared with mine that I shall be aware of it for the next fortnight. Yesterday I began the rehearsals of my favourite *Don Gregorio* at the Teatro Nuovo, with the addition of a few new little pieces. On Thursday it will open at S. Carlo, to be followed on 6 July by the other in one act [Donizetti's opera *Elvida*]. Little cash and much toil, but patience; if I win great honour I shall be well rewarded. . . .

DONIZETTI TO THE LIBRETTIST JACOPO FERRETTI

Rome, 6 March 1836

Dear friend,
I have seen, with infinite pleasure, the pieces composed by our mutual friend Ottone Nicolai; he is so well versed in the art of music that in my opinion he lacks nothing but an opportunity for the public to echo my approval, and you may be certain that if you find any occasion to propose him to any theatre whatsoever, the fact of having supported him can only redound to your credit. . . .

Nicolai was a young German composer who later became famous through his opera, 'The Merry Wives of Windsor'.

DONIZETTI TO TEODORO GHEZZI IN NAPLES

Milan, 27 December 1831

Norma [by Bellini], which had its first performance yesterday evening at the Scala, was not understood, and was judged over-hastily by the Milanese audience. For my part I should be most delighted to have composed it, and would willingly put my name to that music. The introduction and the last *finale* of the second Act are enough in themselves to establish the greatest musical reputation; and the Milanese will soon realize how foolish they were to pass premature judgement on the merits of this work. . . .

DONIZETTI TO SIGNORA GIUSEPPINA APPIANI IN MILAN

Vienna, 9 March 1844

As I write to you I am still ignorant of the artistic fate of our Verdi, which I hope at all events will be most auspicious; indeed I have no doubts as to that. You know me, so I need hardly assure you that my good wishes are sincere; but just by way of proof I may add that wherever I go I speak in the highest praise of the man and his talents – quite apart from my bonds of friendship with him. . . .

On the same date, 9 March, the first performance of Verdi's 'Ernani' took place in Milan. Donizetti's kindly interest in his young colleague was sincere, as can be seen from the following letters.

GIUSEPPE VERDI TO DONIZETTI IN VIENNA

Milan, 18 May 1844

Most esteemed Maestro,
It was a welcome surprise to me to read your letter to Pedroni, in which you kindly offer to attend the rehearsals of my *Ernani*.

I have no hesitation in accepting your kind suggestion with the utmost gratitude, for I am certain that my music cannot but profit greatly when *Donizetti* deigns to give it a thought. I can thus hope that the musical spirit of the composition will be appreciated.

I would ask you to be good enough to concern yourself both with the general direction and with the passages which may need some adaptations in Feretti's part.

To you, *Cavaliere*, I will pay no empty compliments. You are one of the small number of men who possess sovereign talents and stand in no need of individual praise. The favour you are showing me is too outstanding for you to doubt my gratitude. . . .

VERDI TO GIACOMO PEDRONI IN MILAN

May 1844

You can imagine my pleasure on hearing that Donizetti is to take charge of my *Ernani*. I can thus feel certain that the spirit of the music will be fully interpreted. Please pay him my respects and assure him of my gratitude for this tremendous favour. . . .

DONIZETTI TO THE PUBLISHER GUGLIELMO COTTRAU

Vienna, 26 February 1845

You see how right I was to say that Verdi had talent! Even if *I Due Foscari* [opera by Verdi, first performed in Rome, 3 November 1844] only allows it to reveal itself in flashes, you will feel the rest. Setting aside all envy – which is a feeling unknown to me – he is a man with a brilliant future, as you will see.

Yesterday evening I went to the house of H.H. Prince Metternich [the Austrian Chancellor] to play the same music we gave on three evenings at Count Taaffe's. Apart from the three leading singers, my company consisted entirely of amateurs – three men and about a dozen girls of the aristocracy, Baronesses, Countesses, Duchesses, Princesses, not one of them more than 17 years old. They sang well, I assure you. They had to encore Rossini's chorus, *La Carità*. . . .

One can learn from some of Donizetti's letters how much even a famous composer had still to be on his guard against the unpredictable tricks of impresarios and to stipulate his rights carefully, and how a powerful manager such as Merelli, who ruled opera in Milan and Vienna, could be sublimely negligent of the artistic standards of his institutes. Duponchel, to whom the next letter is addressed, was the Director of the Académie Royale de Musique in Paris.

DONIZETTI TO MONSIEUR DUPONCHEL

Naples, 25 May 1838

Monsieur le Directeur,
A success on the stage of the Académie Royale de Musique is a title to fame that every composer must aspire to win, and I am delighted to receive and accept your kind offer to admit two of my works to a theatre made illustrious by so many great names.

But despite my very natural desire to embark on a course so attractive, I cannot close my eyes to the gravity of the undertaking. My *début* in France must be worthy of what I have done already in Italy, and I cannot make a worthy entry into the Paris Opera except with a work equal in importance to what is customarily seen there. So I will ask you to give me a libretto in 5 Acts and to put *all your leading performers* at my disposal, giving me the option of using M. de Candia, as you seem to wish me to do in this first work, if his *début* proves as successful as his fine talent and abilities already suggest it will be. The great masters in whose footsteps I shall be following have been aided in their success by all the resources your Theatre has to offer, and you will think it only just, Monsieur, that I should claim the same assistance for myself; otherwise the contest would be too unequal and I should be rash to undertake it.

The contract bearing your signature, which you will be good enough to send me in duplicate for me to sign, should specify the *exact dates* when my two works are to be presented – especially the first one (for which I ask three months' rehearsals for three hours a day) – as I shall have to arrange my visit to France to suit my present engagements and my position. At the same time you should send me the libretto, for I will set about the work as soon as the poem for it comes to hand. . . .

DONIZETTI TO ANTONIO VASSELLI

Vienna, 21 February 1845

My visit to France, which is expected to take place in July, depends on the libretto and on Meyerbeer, whether or no he is to give his *Prophète*. There the composers come and go; if he gives up – that is, if he cannot find the singers he wants – I am to go there; if the company is suited to the eternal *Prophète*, he will go. If he goes there, I shall go to Italy (with more cursing from Michele [Michele Accursi, Donizetti's agent in Paris] who wants to drag me to Paris for comic operas). If not, I shall hurry to get down to the grindstone. We shall know this month. . . .

DONIZETTI TO SIGNOR TOMMASO PERSICO, MERCHANT AT LARGO DI CASTELLO

Vienna, 20 May 1845

. . . At Berlin, however, the newspaper said, 'Mr Donizetti is coming here to occupy the most brilliant position in the musical world and will present his *Don Sebastiano*, etc. I replied by announcing in the newspapers here that no one had written to me, and that as for the post of greatest honour, I held it here in any case. That as for the *Don Sebastiano* which is to be given, I knew nothing about it; and that a city where such men as *Spontini*, *Meyerbeer* and *Mendelssohn* are living is already so rich in composers that it has no time to wish for more. . . .

I am still undecided whether to go to Paris or to Naples – You call me from one side, others call me from another! And I? I toy with both ideas, for as for business I have that everywhere. My own Naples would carry the day, but I have suffered too much. Do not let us think about it!

The Italians are not lucky this year! They are losing . . . *per Bacco*, how much! How can they bring out singers who have no voice, beginners entirely ignorant of music and who have never set foot on a stage: who jump 10 or 12 bars and are convinced they have sung like gods or goddesses? And those who have put up with them, what do they deserve? . . .

The first attack of his illness – paralysis of the brain – ended Donizetti's artistic activity, but he lingered on for three more years of progressive decay.

DONIZETTI TO SIGNORA APPIANI IN MILAN

Vienna, 18 June 1845

I had a dreadful winter. This climate sets my nerves on edge so badly that to stay here a whole year would be the death of me. I expect to leave for Paris about 10 July. . . .

The Italian company here was received with some contempt . . . one really cannot offer the Viennese mere beginners in the leading roles! The privy purse will pay, and for that reason one of the managers is at Milan already. Is that a way to put on operas? No costumes, hardly any new scenery – the actors not in contemporary dress. . . . Merelli received a lesson he will long remember! . . .

Elssler [prima ballerina at Vienna] was fêted, but not as much as in other years. . . . It is disgusting to see and hear an opera rehearsed twice with piano and once on the stage. . . .

DONIZETTI TO GUGLIELMO COTTRAU

Paris, 9 September 1845

What can I say to you? That I nearly died? Well, there, it is said – that I fell out of bed during the night . . . that I was found next morning on the floor in my shirt . . . that it was 12 hours before I came to myself. . . . You would never believe how thin I have become!

I am allowed no excitement. I had four operas to write, I have had to set them all aside. I said I wanted to die in Italy! I wanted our mineral waters for my lungs. . . .

VERDI TO SIGNORA APPIANI IN MILAN

Paris, 22 August 1847

You ask me about Donizetti and I can give you news that is true, though not cheerful. . . . Outwardly he looks well, except that he always hangs his head and keeps his eyes shut; he eats and sleeps well and hardly ever utters a word; when he does, it is very indistinct. If anyone is introduced to him he opens his eyes for a moment, if someone says to him *give me your hand*, he holds it out, etc.; this it seems is an indication that his understanding is not completely extinguished; for all that a doctor who is a devoted friend of his told me that these symptoms are more in the nature of mechanical reactions and that it would be better if he were animated, even *raving mad*. Then there would be some hope, but as things are only a miracle could help. For the rest he is now as he was six months or a year ago, there has been no improvement and no deterioration! That is the true state of Donizetti at the present moment! It is distressing, too distressing. If things take a more cheerful turn I will write to you at once. . . .

Four years younger than Donizetti, Bellini *had preceded him in an early death, caused by an acute attack of dysentery which carried him away in his thirty-fifth year, at the height of his fame and mourned by the whole of Europe. A totally different character, with a desperate craving for success and a burning ambition, Bellini gives in his letters the impression of an aggressive inferiority complex, possibly due to the consciousness of a poor training and a deficient technique which, however, he was able to improve gradually by arduous discipline. In love with every note he has put on paper, he is inclined to attribute every failure to intrigues of his competitiors such as Pacini or Donizetti – how wrongly with respect to the latter, we have learnt already. He is mortally afraid of Rossini, whose superiority he cannot but admit, whom he regards as all-powerful and whom he desperately strives to impress, in the end with success. When Bellini writes about his work, one can feel the fervent love with which he shaped a vocal phrase, inspired by a beautiful voice, and one can understand how irresistibly he appealed to his contemporaries. One of these letters, addressed to the librettist of his last and finest opera, 'I Puritani', contains a splendid proclamation of his tendencies, which puts the principles of Italian melodrama in a nutshell.*

From Bellini's habit of indicating a number in his opera with reference not to the character, but to the actual singer for whom it is written ('Mme Tosi's cavatina', 'Tamburini's scene'), one can gather the enormous importance of the direct relation between the composer and his interpreters under these conditions of operatic creation. The success of the composer and of his singers was one and indivisible, the end and aim of the whole enterprise. With the great 'maestri' of the twenties and thirties, with Rossini, Donizetti, Bellini, a generation of great singers rose to fame – Pasta, Grisi, Malibran, Tosi, Rubini, Tamburini, David, Nourrit – who were the craze of Europe and extravagantly rewarded.

VINCENZO BELLINI TO HIS FRIEND FRANCESCO FLORIMO IN NAPLES

Milan, 5 March 1828

To tell you something of the music I am arranging [revision and partly new composition of *Bianca*], you must know I have already done the *largo* and the *cabaletta* for Mme Tosi's new *cavatina* and arranged the instrumentation while waiting for Romani [his librettist] to write me some good lines I can substitute for certain feeble ones I was obliged to use. I like the piece, particularly the *largo*; I took that from Ruggi's solo, which I shall cut out of Act 2. . . . I am in good health, in spite of the fatigue of the last few days – to give you an idea of this I once sat writing for ten hours at a stretch, from six in the morning till four in the afternoon. . . .

BELLINI TO FRANCESCO FLORIMO

Genoa, 2 April 1828

This is my first opportunity of giving you some account of the rehearsals of the opera, which is already quite finished. The pieces for Mme Tosi which were rehearsed yesterday evening, the *cavatina* and the scene, both of which are absolutely new, produce a great effect and in general they please; the two *cavatinas*, one for David in which there is a new *cabaletta* and one for Tamburini in which I have made further changes – that is, only in the *allegro* – give great pleasure and particularly the *largo*, which he sings like an angel. . . . In Act 2, Tamburini's scene is not of his usual kind so I do not know what he will do; but at the rehearsal it pleased; then David's scene and Mme Tosi's gave great, great pleasure, I think they are quite certain to be successful: anyhow, we must await the result before we can be really satisfied. In any case the word has spread round Genoa that I have written some heavenly music, that it shall cause a *furore* like *Il Pirata*, and David believes even more so. . . . After the son's release he sings a *cabaletta* of such delight, I have thought of a tune that is so beautiful, my dear Florimo, that yesterday evening everybody was enchanted. So cheer up, I tell you again, your dear Bellini will perhaps score another triumph over his jealous enemies. . . .

BELLINI TO FRANCESCO FLORIMO

Genoa, 9 April 1828

The opera made the desired effect. On the first evening the new theatre was brilliantly lit, the whole Court sat in the big box, flanked by other members of the royal family in the four boxes to either side, with all the Genoese and foreign beauties in full fig; the music and the singers made what effect they could on such an occasion. . . . The King sent his Chamberlain to thank the conductor and singers and to say that since this was a formal public appearance he regretted that he could not applaud. Indeed, yesterday evening he was as good as his word, reserving his applause for the only occasion when Court etiquette permits it in the Turin theatre, after the duet in Act 2, which they sang indescribably well. He listened to the rest of the music without ever taking his eyes off the singers, all of whom without distinction gave infinite pleasure. Yesterday evening Mme Tosi sang a hundred times better than at the first performance, so did David and Tamburini. My enemies had already begun to speak ill of the opera after the first performance, but when the King applauded they ate their words. . . . If the King had not applauded, all our enemies would have said the opera had been a fiasco; whereas yesterday evening they listened with pleasure to the three *entrées* in the first act, and still more to the whole of the second act; the silence of the audience as they listened to the music even impressed the singers themselves. I had terrible palpitations for fear the singers and the orchestra might make a mistake; they had made a good many on the first night. The orchestra, in particular, is a horror. . . .

BELLINI TO FRANCESCO FLORIMO

Milan, 4 August 1828

I have heard about all the intrigues planned and carried out against *Bianca*, and what can I say to you? Be patient: our enemies must inevitably rejoice to see the downfall of an opera that had been applauded and appreciated to the point of being preferred to the work of so many other composers in the repertory at Milan. . . . Remember Coriolanus, Themistocles, Socrates, Tasso, even Rossini himself, and see whether their mother country was not the bitterest enemy of those great men; and what can you expect for a miserable worm like myself, other than afflictions the moment I make my appearance?

BELLINI TO HIS UNCLE VINCENZO FERLITO AT CATANIA

Milan, 16 February 1829

My *Straniera* had its first performance on Saturday, the 14th of this month, and I can find no words to describe its reception, which cannot be called a *furore*, *raising the roof*, *frenzy* – no, none of these terms is sufficient to express the pleasure aroused by the entire music, which made the whole audience shout as though they had gone mad. Everybody was stunned, for they had thought I could never repeat my *Pirata*, and now they found this was far superior. . . . Let it suffice for me to tell you that I have nothing left to wish for; but nevertheless I shall continue my studies so as not to slip back; and with God's help

I hope to set my name on a generation. For it seems to me to have become well established in a career in which, by the goodness of God, the public esteems me as an original genius, not a plagiarist of the presiding genius, Rossini. . . .

BELLINI TO VINCENZO FERLITO AT CATANIA

Milan, 28 December 1831

In spite of a formidable cabal against it, worked up by one powerful and one very rich person, my *Norma* astounded the public even more last night, at the second performance, than at the first. Yesterday's official gazette at Milan had announced a complete fiasco, because at the first performance the opposing party had sat in silence while the well-intentioned applauded; and because the powerful person is in command and can order the newspaper to write whatever she likes.

The powerful person acts thus because she is an enemy of Mme Pasta and the wealthy one because she is Pacini's mistress and therefore my enemy; yet the opera was even more appreciated last night, and the theatre was crammed full, a real sign of an opera's success. . . .

Mme Pasta is an angel, the word is enough to suggest how she played her part, both singing and acting. Donzelli is very good and sings well, but hardly knows his part as yet; Giulietta Grisi, in the role of Adalgisa, does nicely although she has a rather cold temperament; the chorus was excellent. The public is cursing the journalist; my friends are jumping for joy; and I am most satisfied, doubly pleased because I have discomfited so many of my mean and powerful enemies. . . .

BELLINI TO HIS FRIEND AUGUSTO LAMPERI IN TURIN

London, 16 May 1833

It would be superfluous to talk to you about this city; you need only know it is the first in the world, peerless except for wealthy Tyre of ancient times. My *Sonnambula* has been given here in English, the title-role being taken by Maria Malibran, who performed it with great taste: the opera was all the rage, and attracts the public more and more. . . . Today at 3 in the afternoon my *Pirata* is to be presented, sung by Mme Pasta, Rubini and Tamburini for Rubini's benefit performance; *Norma* will be given early in June for Mme Pasta's benefit.

I must say I am enjoying myself extremely here, among continual festivities – balls, theatres, dinners, concerts, country houses, etc. I know everyone in London and they all invite me, until I am almost smothered under so many entertainments. . . .

So you see I am naturally placed amidst a world of beauties, really divine beauties; but one finds nothing here but sentiment, and for one who is to leave the country in two months this is not much; yet I would rather lay the stress on friendship than love, so as not to run the risk of landing myself with a wife. . . .

BELLINI TO COUNT CARLO PEPOLI, LIBRETTIST

Puteaux, Monday morning [June 1834]

Do not forget to bring with you the *pièce* already sketched out, so that we can settle the matter of the first act – which, if you will arm yourself with a good supply of moral patience, will emerge as an interesting, magnificent and worthy poem to music, in spite of you and all your ridiculous rules, which are good for nothing except as a subject of endless chatter that can never convince a soul who has once been introduced to the difficult art of *drawing tears by means of song*.

If my music turns out to be beautiful and the opera pleases, you can write a million letters protesting against the misuse of poetry by composers, etc., without proving anything at all. . . . Carve in your head in letters of brass: *An opera must draw tears, cause horror, bring death, by means of song*. . . . Poetry and music, to make their effect, must be true to nature, and that is all: anyone who forgets this is lost and will end by producing a dull, heavy work which can please only the pedants. It will never appeal to the heart, that poet which is the first to be penetrated by the passions; whereas if the heart is moved one will always be in the right, despite a flood of words that can prove nothing whatosever. Will you or will you not grasp this in the end? I beg you to do so before beginning the libretto: and do you know why I tell you that good drama has nothing to do with good sense? It is because I know only too well what intractable animals the *literati* are, and how ridiculous, with their general rules of good sense: what I say has been proved by the facts in the world of art, for almost the majority of your famous men have gone astray in this respect. . . .

BELLINI TO COUNT PEPOLI IN PARIS

Puteaux, Friday morning [8 September 1834]

The trio does very well as you have arranged it. When I came to the chorus that opens the second part, I realized it was far too short; so try to extend it to eight lines and to make a chorus worthy of the lines

Giorgio has to sing; think it over carefully, my dear good fellow!

Another little thing. In the chorus: *Qual novella?* Giorgio: *Or prende posa.* Chorus: *Miserella! è insana ognor?* [What news? . . . Poor girl! is she still mad?] . . . here, instead of launching into '*Cinta di rose*' [Crowned with roses], etc., I would like Giorgio to be able to reply '*Ah! si, ognor*' (for instance). Then the chorus: '*Senza tregua?*' [Without respite?]. To which Giorgio answers: '*Accostatevi, ascoltate*' [Come closer, listen] (for instance), or something like that, etc. That makes a preparation for the scene, and the audience will listen more eagerly to the beginning of the story. When you have something ready, come here: even if you run into difficulties of some kind, come just the same to see your tormentor, who loves you in spite of your pig-headedness. . . .

BELLINI TO FRANCESCO FLORIMO

Puteaux, 4 October 1834

If I am to have Rossini's protection I shall be in an excellent position; so far he has always spoken against me, the worst he could, declaring that the greatest genius in Italy is Pacini, and Donizetti for popular hits; and the fools of journalists listen to Rossini, and always have done, as though he were an oracle, and he has always abused whoever displeased him and praised his clumsy plagiarists to the skies in a positively shameful way. . . .

BELLINI TO FRANCESCO FLORIMO

Paris, 18 November 1834

And now to talk of Paris and the news. The finest piece of news is that Rossini (do not tell anybody this) loves me very, very, very much. Two days ago he began to look at the score of my introduction and found it magnificent (and there are wonderful things in it). So much so that he has given orders that I am to have an organ on the stage to accompany the prayer quartet in a particular passage, etc. He said I had orchestrated as he would never have believed me capable of doing. He found Tamburini's *cavatina* graceful, the duet between Lablache and Mme Grisi most beautiful, and the chorus just before Rubini's entrance orchestrated with great taste and most beautifully. So Rossini is enchanted: he is singing my praises to everybody, for several people have told me so; and besides, he has talked to me in such a way that I see this time he is not deceiving me. He told me the day before yesterday, after looking at the introduction, that he would make sure I remained in Paris; that if this opera were a success the directors of all the theatres would make me handsome offers; that I ought to stay on in Paris and think no more about Italy. . . .

BELLINI TO FRANCESCO FLORIMO

Paris, 30 November 1834

I am working like Hercules, but I am happy, delighted, because everything I do turns out well and pleases me; the libretto is full of feeling, as you guessed, it is not tragic, not high-flown, but tender and passionate, and I think I have hit on the right music; there is not a single piece that does not please me, that I do not feel glad to have composed. In short I need only tell you that I have been and am still working with a diligence that no one will ever equal. For if my tunes suit the taste of the French public the opera will cause an unprecedented furore, because of its *soignée* with the most delicate and original accompaniments, with harmonies that are tasteful and limpid like some of those in *Norma* and *La Sonnambula*, which lend interest to a piece without disturbing the melody; anyhow, I hope my labours will be crowned with success. . . .

BELLINI TO VINCENZO FERLITO IN CATANIA

Paris, 13 March 1835

Donizetti's new opera, *Marino Falieri*, had its first performance last night and was a semi-fiasco. The newspapers will perhaps not speak ill of it, but the audience was not really pleased; as will be proved by the fact that *I Puritani* is to be presented very soon. . . .

BELLINI TO VINCENZO FERLITO

Paris, 1 April 1835

The management of the *Théâtre Italien* made me offers it suited me to accept, in the first place because they paid better than I had so far been accustomed to in Italy, though not much more; then for the sake of the company; and finally so that I could remain in Paris at other people's expense.

But at that time Rossini was my most ferocious enemy, simply on professional grounds, etc., etc. As it was not usual to commission composers to write for the *Théâtre Italien*, Rossini, who really has a tremendous influence in Paris, especially with all the newspapers, had the idea of commissioning an opera from Donizetti, so that, thus brought into competition with me, he should crush me, wipe me out, with the help of Rossini's colossal influence. And indeed, the news that Donizetti had been commissioned threw me into a fever for three days, for I realized what a plot was being laid for me; and someone of my acquaintance told me I could not hope for much success in Paris, that if anyone had success it would be Donizetti because of Rossini's support.

However, once recovered from the first impression, I plucked up courage and began to consider how to put an end to these devilish intrigues, which were threatening to damage me in the eyes of all Europe, and would have done so if I had fallen victim to them!

I told myself firmly that the first thing to be done was to study my new situation more closely than usual and then to pay court to Rossini and approach him to tell him how much I admired his immense talent, etc. . . . All of this was no effort to me, for I have always adored Rossini; and I succeeded, while in the meantime I went on working as hard as I could. . . .

Having won Rossini's friendship, I said to myself that now Donizetti was very welcome. This was the third time I had found myself writing for the same theatre as he: in '31, I think, he wrote *Anna Bolena* for the Carcano at Milan and I replied with *La Sonnambula*; the following year he wrote *Ugo* for the Scala (it was a fiasco) and I gave them *Norma*; and now here I was with him again. Having overcome Rossini's dislike of me I had no more fears, and with redoubled courage I finished the work that was to bring me so much honour—as Rossini foretold three months before the first performance. . . .

In short, last night *I Puritani* gave such pleasure that Donizetti's party was fully persuaded to send *Marino* [Donizetti's opera] to the cemetery, it having died between Sunday, 12 March and the 31st. *Marino* had five performances and *I Puritani* 14, plus Tamburini's benefit and the last two nights of the theatre season, making 17 performances in all, between 25 January and 31 [March]. This is unheard of in Paris, where the public, volatile by nature, will not usually submit to seeing the same opera more than about six times in the season, which lasts six months. . . .

In short, last night was a real *festa*, an evening that will stand out in the annals of the *Théâtre Italien*.

The *Puritani* has now put me in the position that was my due – that is, the first after Rossini. I say this because Rossini had convinced everyone that Donizetti had more talent (because he had nothing to fear from him) than Bellini; but now Italy, Germany and France grant me the position I have worked so hard to earn, and which I hope ever to enhance. . . .

ROSSINI TO BELLINI'S FRIEND FILIPPO SANTOCANALE AT PALERMO

Paris, 27 September 1835

My dear Sir,

I have the grief of informing you that we have lost our mutual friend Bellini; the unfortunate young man expired on Wednesday a little before 4 in the afternoon. A dysentery, which increased over a period of 15 days to the point of inflammation, had defeated all the resources of the medical profession. I am inconsolable at the loss of such a friend, and at the thought of the distress you will feel on receiving this letter, and of the grief caused to his parents. All Paris is mourning him; and if there could be some consolation in misfortunes of this kind (which are irreparable), our sorrow should indeed be greatly lightened by such a demonstration on the part of a cultivated, civilized population like that of Paris. I loved him and helped him while he was alive, and I must now tell you what I have done since his death, so that you may inform his family of it without loss of time. . . . I at once set up a committee composed of the leading artists of the three royal theatres in Paris, of which I am President, in order to have a mass celebrated at the Invalides with all appropriate ceremony in honour of our friend. . . . I have already ordered prospectuses to open a subscription for erecting a monument to Bellini. . . .

I do not know whether I have been able to write clearly in my present state of emotion; make allowances for me, and tell Bellini's relatives and friends that the only consolation left to me is to devote all my care to honouring him as friend, fellow-countryman and artist. . . .

There are obvious dangers in the indiscriminate publication of letters, especially in a case such as Bellini with his naïve vanity and uncontrolled outbursts against real or supposed enemies. His greatest successor, Giuseppe Verdi (*1813–1901*), *found it necessary, when Bellini's letters were published, to defend him against such indiscretion.*

VERDI TO COUNT OPPRANDINO ARRIVABENE

[*1882*]

But what need is there to go dragging letters out of a composer of music? Letters that are always written in haste, carelessly, as something of no importance, because a composer does not realize he is expected to uphold his reputation as a literary man. Isn't it enough that they hiss him for his notes? Not a bit of it! Letters as well! Ah, fame is a great nuisance! Poor little famous great men, they pay a high price for popularity! Never an hour's peace, alive or dead. . . .

Verdi himself, however, is unique in his total lack of vanity, his inflexible strength of purpose, his unconditional honesty as a man and an artist. He never asks for a favour, never pretends to like something he doesn't, goes his own way without looking right or left. He appears in his letters in his full stature without any effort. With a genuine urge for communication and the gift of formulating his thought vividly and exactly, he is a letter-writer of unmatched interest. He rarely writes about his private affairs; when he does so, it is with a superb pride and an impetuous urge for independence. The main subjects of his correspondence are connected with three matters that seem ever present in his mind: his work, its difficulties and progress; the problems of music in Italy, its tradition, practice, and future; and the great events concerning the liberation and unification of his country, from the unsuccessful revolution of 1848 to the proclamation of the united kingdom of Italy in 1861 and the accession of Venice after the defeat of Austria in 1866.

Verdi found himself almost actively involved in these events which he followed with passionate interest. He was an enthusiastic supporter of Count Cavour, who united Italy under the crown of Vittorio Emanuele, the King of Piedmont and Sardinia. As the 'Risorgimento', the Italian liberation movement, started and developed almost exactly contemporaneously with Verdi's growing fame and popularity, his music, sung and played in every tavern, became a symbol of Italian national feelings and his name, written on every wall, stood for the slogan of the liberation and unification: V*ittorio* E*manuele* R*e* D*'* I*talia. As a spontaneous act of gratitude, Verdi was elected a deputy to the first Italian parliament. He was no politician, however, and neither desirous of nor suited for public activity.*

In 1847 he made his first visit to London, where he wrote his opera 'I Masnadieri' for Covent Garden. It was only a moderate success, but it marked the beginning of Verdi's lasting relation with operatic life in London. Impressed by the magnificence of the town, appalled by the English climate, he kept aloof of the hubbub of social life in London, by which Bellini's vanity had been flattered so much. Verdi never felt comfortable under the northern sky, nor did his growing affluence alter his simple habits of living. Money was necessary to him only because it meant freedom and independence.

GIUSEPPE VERDI TO CLARINA MAFFEI

9 June 1847

I have been barely two days in London. . . .

In Paris I went to the Opera. I have never heard worse singers or a more indifferent chorus. Even the orchestra (with apologies to all our *Lions*) is little more than mediocre. What I saw of Paris pleased me very much, and in particular I liked the freedom of life in that country. I cannot tell you anything about London because yesterday was Sunday and I have not yet seen a soul. But the smoke and the smell of coal annoy me a great deal: it is like continually being in a steam-boat. Soon I am going to the Theatre to find out how my business stands. . . .

My health is excellent. The journey did not really tire me, because I made it in all possible comfort. True, I arrived late and the impresario may grumble about that; but if he says a word that rubs me up the wrong way I shall give him back ten and then leave again at once for Paris, come what may.

VERDI TO CLARINA MAFFEI

London, 27 June 1847

Long live our sunshine, which I always loved so much and which I positively worship since I have been plunged into this fog and smoke, which suffocates me and drains my spirits! On the other hand, what a magnificent city! There are things here that would bring admiration from a stone . . . but this climate takes the life out of all beauty. Oh, if only the sky of Naples lay overhead I think there would be no need to dream of paradise. . . .

The theatres are packed and the English enjoy performances that. . . . And they pay so well!! If only I could stay here for a couple of years, I should be able to carry away bags of *those holy lire*! But there is no point in cherishing all these fine ideas, because I could never stand the climate. I am dying to leave for Paris, which has no particular attraction for me, but which is bound to please me very well because there I shall be able to live as I choose. It is such a pleasure to do just as one likes!! When I think that I shall be in Paris for several weeks without becoming involved in musical affairs, without hearing any talk about music (because I shall show the door to all music publishers and impresarios) it cheers me beyond all measure.

In London my health is really quite good, but I am always afraid of falling ill. I stay at home a great deal, writing (or at any rate with the intention of writing), I move very little in society and seldom go to the theatre, so as to avoid annoyances. . . .

VERDI TO CLARINA MAFFEI

17 July 1847

You will be astonished to hear that I am still in London and that my opera has not yet been put on! But it is all due to the smoke and fog and the infernal climate here, which robs me of all desire to work. Now, at last, everything or almost everything is ready, and I shall have my first performance on Thursday the 22nd without fail. I have rehearsed twice with the orchestra, and if this were Italy I could give you a cool-headed opinion of the opera, but here I understand nothing. All the fault of the climate – the climate! . . .

It is true they offered me 40 thousand francs for an opera and that I refused. But do not be surprised, because that is not an exorbitant fee, and if I come here again I shall ask much more. . . .

VERDI TO CLARINA MAFFEI

Paris, 24 August 1848

You want to know what the French think about Italy? Heavens, what will you be asking me next!! Those who are not hostile are indifferent: and I may add that the idea of a united Italy terrifies the petty ciphers who are in power here at present. France will certainly not make any armed intervention, unless some unforeseen event compels her to do so. The Franco-English diplomatic intervention can only be lamentable, shameful for France and ruinous for us. They say its aim is to persuade Austria to give up Lombardy and be satisfied with the Veneto. Even supposing Austria could be induced to leave Lombardy (at present she is hanging back; and before leaving the Austrians might sack and burn everything), we should be left with one more insult, the devastation of Lombardy, and yet another ruler in Italy. No, no, no: we want nothing from France or from England; as for me, if I place my hopes in any quarter . . . do you know where I place them? In Austria – in the disturbances there. Something serious should emerge from all that, and if we seize the right moment and fight the war we ought to fight, a war of insurrection, Italy may yet be free. But may God protect us from placing trust in our own kings and in foreign countries. . . .

That is my opinion; but please attach no importance to it, because as you know, I do not understand politics. For that matter, France herself is in the doldrums and I do not know how she is to recover. The investigation that is being made of the events of May and June is the meanest and most revolting ever seen. What a wretched age of pigmies! Nothing great about it, not even its crimes! I think another revolution is imminent; there is the *smell* of it everywhere. Another revolution would deal the death-blow to this poor Republic. Let us hope it may not come, but there are serious reasons to fear that it will. . . .

Verdi refers in the following letter to the recasting of 'Rigoletto' after objections from the censor. In the first draft of the libretto Rigoletto appeared under the name Triboletto.

VERDI TO PRESIDENT MARZARI IN VENICE

Busseto, 14 December 1850

I have had very little time to look through the new libretto: but I have seen enough to show me that cut down in this way it lacks character and weight, and that the chief passages of the action have lost all their vigour. If the names have to be changed then the place should be changed as well and there should be a Duke or Prince of some other country – Pier Luigi Farnese, for instance, or someone like that – or the action should be carried back to the time before Louis XI when France was not a united kingdom, the Duke be made Duke of Burgundy or Normandy, etc., etc., in any case an absolute ruler. In Act 1, Scene 5 the courtiers' anger against Triboletto has become completely meaningless. The old man's curse, so terrible and sublime in the original, now becomes ridiculous because his reason for cursing has lost its importance and because this is no longer a subject speaking so fierily to his king. Without that curse, what purpose or dramatic force remains? The Duke becomes an insipid creature: it is essential for the Duke to be a libertine, otherwise Triboletto has no grounds for fearing to let his daughter out of her hiding-place, and all the drama is lost. Why on earth, in the last Act, should the Duke go alone to an outlying tavern, with no guests and no appointment to meet anyone? And I cannot understand why the sack has been cut out! What did the sack matter to the police? They were afraid it would miss the effect? But may I ask why they suppose they know better than I do about this? Who can take charge? Who can say this will make an effect and that will not? . . . If the sack is not there, Triboletto is unlikely to talk to a corpse for half an hour before a flash of lightning reveals it as his daughter's body. Finally I notice that Triboletto is no longer to be ugly and hunchbacked!! A singing hunchback? Why not! . . . Will it make a good effect? I don't know; but once again, if I do not know nobody knows, not even whoever has suggested this alteration. I personally think the whole beauty lies in showing Triboletto as completely deformed and absurd in appearance, but inwardly passionate and full of love. I chose the subject precisely because of these qualities and these original features, and if they are to be removed I can write no more music for you. If I am told that my notes can remain as they are even with this libretto, my answer is that I do not understand such arguments, and I say frankly that my music, whether it be beautiful or ugly, is never written at random, I always take care to give it character.

In short, an original, powerful drama has been made into something completely banal and cold. It distresses me greatly that the Presidency has not answered my last letter. I can only repeat what I said there and beg that it will be done, for my conscience as an artist does not permit me to write music for this libretto. . . .

Always up in arms against slothful or rapacious managers, sceptical with respect to the opinions of critics and the favour or disfavour of the public, Verdi was ready, all the same, to accept the latter as a judge against whom there was no appeal. One experience he could never forget: the worst fiasco of his career, when 'Un Giorno di Regno' (1840), written with heroic stoicism during the darkest period of his life, after the death of his wife and two children, was hooted from the stage in Milan.

VERDI TO ANTONIO BAREZZI, FATHER OF HIS FIRST WIFE

Paris, 21 January 1852

Dearest Father-in-law,
After waiting so long I did not expect such a cold letter from you, and one which, unless I am mistaken, contains some very sharp phrases. If that letter were not signed *Antonio Barezzi*, which means my benefactor, I should have answered it very heatedly, or not at all; but since it bears a name I must always feel in duty bound to respect, I shall do my best to convince you that I do not deserve a rebuke of this kind. . . .

I have nothing to hide. There is a lady living in my house, she is free and independent, like me she is fond of a solitary life, she has a fortune amply sufficient for her needs. We are neither of us accountable for our actions to anyone whatsoever; but on the other hand who knows what are the relations between us? How we stand together? What links we have? What rights I have over her and she over me? Who knows whether she is or is not my wife? And in the latter case, who knows what private reasons there may be, what grounds we may have for keeping it to ourselves? Who knows whether it is a good thing or a bad one? Why should it not be a good thing? And even if a bad one, who has the right to call down anathema upon us? I maintain that in my house she is to be shown as much respect as myself, or even more, and that no one is allowed to fail in that respect for any reason whatsoever; in short she has every right to it, by her attitude, by her spirit, and by the special attention she never fails to show to others.

All this long discourse is only meant to tell you that I claim my freedom of action because all men have the right to that, and because my nature rebels against doing things in other people's way; and that you, who are at bottom so kind, so just and warm-hearted, should not allow yourself to be influenced or accept the views of a place which only some time ago – the fact must be faced! – would not deign to have me as its organist, and is now gossiping about me and my affairs, of which it knows nothing. This cannot go on; but if it does, I shall act accordingly. The world is a big place, and the loss of 20 or 30 thousand francs would never prevent me from finding myself a country elsewhere. There is nothing in this letter to offend you; but if by chance something does displease you, consider it as not having been written, for I swear on my honour that it is not my intention to displease you in any way. I have always regarded you as my benefactor and still do so, I take it as an honour and am proud of it. . . .

VERDI TO THE MARCHESE CARACCIOLO S. TEODORO

1855

For my part I shall always try to do the best I can and leave the journalists to say whatever they choose, without ever complaining or distressing myself overmuch. So much the worse for me if the music is bad. So much the worse for them if it is good and they criticize it. Such criticism must inevitably reflect against either their talent or their conscience. . . .

VERDI TO CALZADO, MANAGER OF THE PARIS OPERA

Paris, 12 December 1855

Yesterday I received your letter, for which I thank you. I entirely approve the decision not to give *Rigoletto* or *Traviata* this year. I ask nothing better than to lend you *my assistance* (as you put it), on condition that my own interests permit of it, and *above all* that you succeed in engaging artists suitable for performing these works; for a clever manager must either choose operas for the artists he has engaged, or engage artists for the operas he has chosen – which is much more difficult than people imagine. Believe me, I am speaking from long experience.

I cannot prevent the performance of *Ernani*; if I could prevent it, I tell you frankly I would do so. Those who tell you it will be well done, to full effect, are deceiving you, deceiving themselves, or know nothing about music. I think *Ernani*, as a whole, will be badly done. Please note that I say as a whole! In any case the receipts will prove me right or wrong; and in this instance I ask nothing better than to be wrong. My pride as a composer and your box-office would both gain by it. But I advise you once again, indeed I beg of you, to give up the idea! . . .

VERDI TO CLARINA MAFFEI

Busseto, 12 May 1858

I got back from Naples ten or twelve days ago, and would have written to you at once, but I was obliged to make several visits to Parma and Piacenza. . . . I shall perhaps return to Naples in the autumn and to Rome for the carnival, if the Censor there will give permission for the opera that was written for Naples; if not, so much the better, for it means I shall write nothing, even for the coming carnival. Ever since *Nabucco* [1842] I have had scarcely an hour's peace. Sixteen years' hard labour!

VERDI TO TITO RICORDI

1 February 1859

Boccanegra at Milan was bound to be a fiasco, and so it was. A *Boccanegra* without *Boccanegra*!! Cut a man's head off, and then recognize him if you can. The *unseemly behaviour of the audience* astonishes you? It does not surprise me in the least. The public always jumps at an opportunity of making a scandal! When I was 25 years old I too had my illusions and believed in the courtesy of audiences; a year later the scales fell from my eyes and I saw whom I had to deal with. It makes me laugh when people hint, with a kind of disapproving air, that I owe a great deal to this or that public! True, on other occasions *Nabucco* and *I Lombardi* were applauded at the Scala; but those were performances where the music, the singers, the orchestra, the chorus and the *mise en scène* combined to make up something that did not discredit those who applauded. Yet little more than a year before, that same public had given the worst reception to an opera by a poor, sick young man who had been pressed for time and whose heart was broken by a terrible misfortune! All this was common knowledge, but it did not restrain their bad manners. I have never seen *Il Giorno di Regno* again since, and I am sure it was a bad opera; but who knows how many others which were no better have been tolerated or even applauded? Or if, without applauding, the spectators had suffered that opera in silence, I would be unable to find words enough to thank them! But since they have shown favour to operas that have been round the world, honours are equal. I do not mean to blame the public; I accept its severity and submit to its hissing, on condition that it asks me nothing in return for its applause. We poor bohemians, mountebanks or what you will, are obliged to sell our labours, our ideas, our ravings, for gold – the public pays three *lire* for the right to hiss or applaud us. Resignation is our fate – that is all!

VERDI TO CLARINA MAFFEI

Busseto, 14 July 1859

Instead of singing a hymn of triumph, it seems to me we should be chanting a lament for the eternal misfortunes of our country.

At the same time as your letter I received a Bulletin dated the 12th which said . . . *The Emperor* [Napoleon III] *to the Empress . . . peace is concluded . . . Austria keeps Venice!!*

So where is the longed-for and promised independence of Italy? What is the meaning of the proclamation of Milan? Or is Venice not Italy? So many victories, for what result! So much blood, shed for nothing! So many poor lads deluded! Garibaldi even sacrificed his firm, long-standing [republican] views in favour of a King, without achieving his aim. It is enough to drive one mad! I write under the influence of the greatest indignation, and I do not know what you will say to me. So it is perfectly true that we can never hope for anything from foreigners, of whatever nation! What do you say about it? Perhaps I am wrong again? I would like to think so. . . .

VERDI TO THE MAYOR OF BUSSETO

S. Agata, 5 September 1859

The honour my fellow-citizens propose to bestow upon me by appointing me to represent them in the Assembly of the Provinces of Parma flatters me and I am deeply grateful for it. If my few talents, my studies and the art I profess do little to fit me for an office of this kind, I can at least plead the great love I have always felt for our noble and unfortunate Italy.

Needless to say, I shall proclaim on behalf of my fellow-citizens and myself:

The fall of the Bourbon dynasty [the former rulers of Parma]
Our union with Piedmont
The Dictatorship of that illustrious Italian, Luigi Carlo Forini [The leader of the national rising in the State of Parma]

Union with Piedmont is the key to the future greatness and regeneration of our common motherland. All who are conscious that Italian blood flows in their veins must strive for it vigorously and unremittingly; thus we, too, shall see the day when we can declare ourselves to be members of a great and noble Nation.

Count Camillo Benso di Cavour, to whom Verdi refers in the following letter, devoted his life to the unification of the numerous Italian states and kingdoms under the crown of Piedmont.

VERDI TO FRANCESCO MARIA PIAVE,
LIBRETTIST OF 'RIGOLETTO' 'ERNANI', 'LA TRAVIATA', ETC.

8 February 1865

You ask me for news of my public life? I have no such thing as a public life. True, I am a Deputy, but that happened by mistake. However, I will tell you how it came about. In September 1860 I was at Turin. I had never seen Count Cavour and I was very eager to make his acquaintance. I asked the then English Minister to present me. Since the Treaty of Villafranca [the peace treaty with Austria] the Count had withdrawn from public life and was living in retirement in his estate, which I think was on the Vercellese; and one fine morning we went to visit him. After that I had occasion to write to him and to receive from him several letters, in one of which he urged me to accept the nomination to parliament that my fellow-citizens were offering me and which I had refused. His letter was extremely amiable, and I did not feel I could answer no. I decided to go to Turin; I arrived in his presence one December day at 6 in the morning, when the thermometer stood at 12 or 14 degrees [centigrade] below freezing-point. I had prepared my speech, which I considered a masterpiece, and I poured it out at full length. He listened attentively, and when I described how unsuited I was to be a Deputy, and how impatient I would become with the long speeches one would sometimes have to swallow in the Chamber, I spoke so quaintly that he burst out laughing. Good, I said to myself, I have made my point. But then he began to demolish all my arguments, one after another, and he advanced some of his own that I found quite sensible. 'Well, *Signor Conte*,' I said at last, 'I accept; but on condition that I am allowed to resign after a few months.' 'Very well,' he replied, 'but let me know beforehand.' I became a Deputy, and at first I used to go often to the Chamber. Then came the ceremonial sitting when Rome was proclaimed the capital of Italy. After giving my vote, I went up to Cavour and said: 'I think the time has come for me to bid farewell to this assembly.' 'No,' said he, 'wait until we go to Rome.' 'Are we going?' 'Yes.' 'When?' 'Oh, that's to be seen!! Meanwhile I'm off to the country. Good-bye, take care of yourself, good-bye!' Those were the last words I heard him speak. A few weeks later he died! . . . After several months I left for Russia, then I went to London, from there to Paris, back to Russia again, then to Madrid, travelled round Andalusia and finally returned to Paris, where I stayed several months for professional reasons. So I was away from parliament for over two years, and I have hardly ever set foot there since. Several times I have tried to hand in my resignation; but either because that was not the moment for a by-election, or for one reason or another, I am still a Deputy against all my wishes and tastes, without any political position, any gift for the work, and completely lacking in the patience which is such a necessity in that gathering. So there you are. If ever you want or are obliged to write my biography as a Member of Parliament, you need only print in the middle of a blank page: 'The 450 are in reality only 449, because Verdi as a Deputy does not exist.' . . .

Verdi's curious feelings towards Paris, where in spite of the enormous success of several of his operas he never found himself at ease as an artist, are expressed in this magnificent letter to the Director of the Opéra Comique in Paris.

VERDI TO CAMILLE DU LOCLE,
MANAGER OF THE PARIS OPÉRA-COMIQUE

Genoa, 7 December 1869

What holds me back is not the labour of writing an opera, nor the judgement of the Paris audience, but the conviction that I cannot get my music performed in Paris in the way I wish. It is a very strange thing that an author invariably meets with opposition to his ideas and finds his conceptions misrepresented. In your musical theatres (I say this with no intention of being witty) you are all too learned! Everyone wants to judge in the light of his own knowledge and taste and, what is worse, according to a *system*, with no allowance for the character and personality of the author. Everyone wishes to give an opinion, to express a doubt, and the author who lives for long in this atmosphere of doubt is bound sooner or later to be slightly shaken in his convictions and to end by correcting, adjusting or, to be more precise, ruining his work. So in the end, instead of an opera that is all of a piece, you have a *mosaic*; and however beautiful it may be it remains a *mosaic*. I shall be told that the Opera has a whole series of masterpieces created in this fashion. Masterpieces they may be; but if I may say so, they would be much more perfect if signs of *piecing together* and *adjusting* were not evident from time to time. Nobody would think of denying Rossini's genius: but genius as he was, his *William Tell* breathes out that fatal atmosphere of the *Opéra*, and every now and then, though less frequently than with other composers, one can feel that something has been added or taken away, and that the development is not so firm and confident as in the *Barber*. I do not mean this as a criticism of what is done in your theatres, only to tell you that I myself cannot possibly pass again under their Caudinian Yoke, since I realize that I can have no real success except by writing in my own way, with no outside influence and without considering whether I am writing for Paris or for the Moon. And then the artists must sing not in their way, but in mine; the crowds, who have great ability, must show an equal amount of good will; in fact, everything has to depend on me and only one man's wishes – mine – must prevail. You may find this a bit tyrannical . . . and that is perhaps true; but if the opera is all of a piece it has one idea throughout, and everything must contribute to this *One* idea. You will say, perhaps, that nothing prevents me from obtaining all this in Paris. No. In Italy it is possible, in fact I can always do so, but not in France. If I arrive with a new opera in the green-room of an Italian theatre, for example, no one will venture to express an opinion, a judgement, before he has thoroughly understood the thing; and no one will ever dare to ask irrelevant questions. They respect the opera and the composer, and they leave the public to decide. Whereas in the *Foyer* of the *Opéra* no sooner have four notes been played than the whisper begins to go round '*Olà ce n'est pas bon . . . c'est commun, ce n'est pas de bon goût . . . ça n'ira pas à Paris!*' What on earth is the meaning of those pitiful words, *common . . . good taste . . . Paris . . .* when confronted with a real work of art that is to appeal to the whole world!

All this points to the conclusion that I am not a composer for Paris. I do not know whether I have the talent for it, but I do know that my ideas about art are entirely different from yours.

I believe in *inspiration*; you people believe in workmanship; I accept your criterion as a basis of discussion; but I need the enthusiasm you lack in order to feel and judge. I look for Art in all its manifestations, not the *amusing*, the *ingenious* and the *systematic*, which are what you prefer. Am I wrong? Am I right? However that may be, I am right in saying that my ideas are quite different from yours, and I may add that my back is not supple enough to bow before you and deny my own convictions, which are deep-seated and firmly-rooted. . . .

VERDI TO FRANCESCO FLORIMO IN NAPLES

Genoa, 4 January 1871

My dear Florimo,

If anything could give me particular gratification, it is the invitation to become Director of the Naples Conservatory which I have received through you from the Professors themselves together with so many musicians in your city. I very much regret my inability to reply as I should like to this mark of confidence; but with my work, my habits and my love of independence it would be impossible for me to take on such a serious task. You will say 'What about art?' Well and good; but I have done my best, and if I am to do anything more now and again I must be free from any other concerns. If this were not so, you can imagine how proud I should be to occupy a post that was held by founders of a school, *A. Scarlatti*, and later *Durante* and *Leo*. I should have been honoured to guide the students in their studies of those early Masters of our art, grave and stern, yet so brilliant. I should have tried to keep one foot in the past, as it were, and the other in the present and future (for I personally am not afraid of the *music of the future*); I would have said to the young students: 'Practise the *Fugue* constantly, tenaciously, to satiety, until your hands have become sure and firm in bending the notes to your will. In that way you will learn to compose confidently, to arrange the parts well and to modulate without affectation. Study Palestrina and a few of his contemporaries. Then jump forward to Marcello, go to *a few performances* of modern opera, without allowing yourselves to be hypnotized either by its many harmonic and instrumental beauties or by the *diminished seventh* which is the rock and refuge of those of us who cannot compose four bars without half a dozen of these *sevenths*.' After they had completed these studies and acquired a wide knowledge of literature, I would say to them: 'Now put your hand on your heart; begin to write, and (assuming that you have an artistic organization) you will be a composer. In any case you will not swell the mob of present-day plagiarists and decadents who search and search and (though sometimes they do good work) never find.' In teaching singing, too, I would have promoted the study of the old ways, combined with modern declamation.

In order to apply these few maxims, which look easy enough, one would have to supervise the teaching so zealously that twelve months in the year would hardly be sufficient, so to speak. And I ask you yourself, how could I do it – I, who have my house, my interests, my fortune – all, all, here?

And so, my dear Florimo, please be good enough to inform your colleagues, and the many other musicians in your beautiful Naples, that to my very great regret I cannot accept their invitation, which does me so much honour. I hope you will find an exceptionally learned man, and a strict supervisor. Freedom and mistakes in counterpoint can be permitted in the theatre, and sometimes have a fine effect; but not in a school of music. Let us turn back to the old Masters: that will be progress. . . .

VERDI TO GIULIO RICORDI

Genoa, 11 April 1871

I have read your article on the orchestra, which I return herewith, and I think it is open to criticism:

1. On the subject of the intentions of those of our composers to whom you refer, and their skill in instrumentation.

2. On the perceptivity of conductors . . . and on the idea that *every performance is a fresh creation*. . . . This is a principle that leads to exaggeration and artificiality. It was the path that led the art of music into exaggeration and artificiality at the end of the last century and the beginning of this, when singers took it upon themselves to *create* their roles (as they still say in France) and consequently served up all kinds of muddle and nonsense. [See Rossini's letter on the same subject, p. 235.] No: I want to have one single creator, and all I ask is that what is written down shall be performed simply and accurately; the trouble is that this is never done. I often read in the newspapers about *effects undreamt of by the composer*; but I myself have never come across them. I appreciate everything you say about Mariani. We are all agreed as to his merits; but the question here is not one individual, however great, but art itself. I do not admit that either singers or conductors have the power to *create*; that, as I said before, is a principle that leads to disaster. . . . Shall I give you an example? You once spoke to me in praise of an effect drawn by Mariani from the overture to *La Forza del Destino*, when he brought in the *brass* in G with a *fortissimo*. Well, I do not approve of that effect. My idea was that the brass, coming in *mezzo forte*, was to express the religious chanting of the Friars and only that. Mariani's *fortissimo* altered the whole character and turned the passage

into something by a military band: something which has nothing to do with the plot, where the warlike part is quite secondary. And so we are led into the exaggerated and the artificial. . . .

VERDI TO TITO RICORDI

2 January 1873

As for Glory and for the *justice of history*, to which you refer at the end of your letter, for heaven's sake let us say nothing about them. You see how I was handled by the Press right through the year, when I had taken so much trouble and expended so much money and effort! . . . Stupid criticisms and even more stupid praises: not a single fine, artistic idea; not one critic attempting to discover what I was trying to do . . . nothing but foolishness, comments that went wide of the mark, and underneath it all a kind of indefinable spite against me, as though in writing *Aida* and getting it well performed I had committed a crime. Last but not least, not one of them even bothered to point out the plain fact that the performance and *mise en scène* had unusual aspects! Not one of them said to me so much as *Good dog, thank you*! And you remember how I had to battle with the theatre inspector and the management.

So let us hear no more about *Aida*; it has brought me a lot of money, but it has also brought me an infinity of annoyances and tremendous artistic disillusionment. If I had known I would never have written it, or at least never have made it public! If after the first performance I had put it away and only allowed it to be presented under my own direction when and where I chose, I should not have become the butt of ill-natured curiosity and had to submit to discussion by the mob of critics and inept would-be composers who know only the ABC of music, and even that imperfectly. Speculation might have been the loser, but to the infinite benefit of art. . . .

VERDI TO CLARINA MAFFEI

Naples, 9 April 1873

For your information, the success of *Aida* was frank and decided, not poisoned by ifs and buts and dreadful talk about *Wagnerism*, the *Future*, the *Art of Melody*, etc., etc. The audience surrendered to its impressions and applauded. That's all! . . . It even indulged in transports of applause and emotion of which I disapprove; but at any rate it showed its feelings unreservedly and without *arrière-pensée*! And do you know why? Because here there are no critics who set up as prophets; no mob of bunglers who know nothing of music except what they have learnt by slavishly copying *Mendelssohn, Schumann, Wagner*, etc.; no aristocratic amateurs who follow the fashion of going into raptures over what they do not understand, etc., etc. And do you know what all this leads to? The young are led astray and bewildered. Let me explain what I mean. Imagine, for example, that a young man like Bellini should come along today – diffident, ill-assured through lack of study; with only his instinct to guide him: tormented by men like Filippi [a critic in Milan], by the Wagnerians and so forth, he would end by losing all faith in himself, and would perhaps be lost to music. . . . Amen, amen. . . .

VERDI TO COUNT OPPRANDINO ARRIVABENE

S. Agata, 14 July 1875

I cannot tell you how we shall escape from this musical maelstrom. One man wants to equal Bellini in melody, another to rival Meyerbeer in harmony. I would not wish one or the other; and I wish that every young man when he begins to write music would not concern himself with being a melodist, a harmonist, a realist, an idealist or a futurist or any other such devilish pedantic things. Melody and harmony should be simply tools in the hands of the artist, with which he creates music; and if a day comes when people stop talking about the German school, the Italian school, the past, the future, etc., etc., then art will perhaps come into its own. Another present-day trouble is that all the operas produced by these young men are the fruit of *fear*. No one lets himself go in writing; when these young fellows begin to compose, they do it with the overriding idea that they must not offend the public and that they must win the good graces of the critics.

You will tell me I owe my success to my amalgamation of the two schools. *I never gave it a thought*. Anyhow, that is an old story, which others have repeated for some time past!

But don't worry, my dear Arrivabene; art will survive, and you may be sure that the moderns too have done something worth while. . . .

VERDI TO AN UNKNOWN ADDRESSEE

[*April 1878*]

Everybody is contributing, unintentionally, to the ruin of our theatre. Perhaps I myself, you, etc., may be among them. And suppose I tell you that the first cause of this in Italy was the Quartet groups and that the more recent cause has been the success achieved in Paris from the standpoint of performance (not of composition) by the Scala orchestra?

There, I have said it; don't throw stones at me. . . . It would take too long to give you the reasons. But in the devil's name, since this is Italy, why do we go in for German art? 12 or 15 years ago I was nominated for the chairmanship of a Quartet Society, I forget whether it was at Milan or somewhere else. I refused, and said, 'Why do you not set up a Society for vocal Quartets? That is part of Italian life. The other is German art.' That may have been blasphemy even then, as it is now; but a vocal Quartet singing Palestrina, the best of his contemporaries, Marcello, etc., etc., would have kept alive our love of singing, and consequently our capacity for expression and for opera. At present they are all struggling to instrumentalize and harmonize. The *alpha* and *omega* is Beethoven's Ninth Symphony (sublime in its first three movements; shockingly written in the last movement.) We shall never reach the heights of the first three movements; we shall easily imitate the bad arrangement of the singing in the last, and on Beethoven's authority there will be cries of 'that is the right way to do it. . . .'

Very well; let them! It may be better so; but that betterment will undoubtedly be the ruin of opera. Art is universal, no one is more convinced of that than I; but it is created by individuals; and as the Germans have other means than ours, they must somehow be different inside as well. We cannot, I would even say we should not, write like the Germans, or the Germans like us. If the Germans sometimes borrow certain of our qualities, as Haydn and Mozart did in their day, while still remaining faithful to the quartet; if Rossini even took over certain forms from Mozart, while still remaining a melodist – all well and good; but to give up our own qualities to suit the fashion, out of a mania for novelty or an affectation of learning – to renounce our art, our instinct, our sure, spontaneous, natural, sensitive way of doing things, our bright sparkle, is absurd and foolish. . . .

Verdi was indefatigable in readapting and rewriting operas which he found unsatisfactory on the stage in one or another respect. There are different versions of 'Macbeth', 'La Forza del Destino', 'Don Carlos', 'Simon Boccanegra'. The last mentioned, a favourite of his that caused him endless trouble, is the subject of the following letter.

VERDI TO GIULIO RICORDI

20 November 1880

The score as it stands is impossible. Too gloomy, too depressing! There is no need to touch anything in the first Act or in the last. . . . But Act II will have to be entirely rewritten, to give it more vigour and variety, put more life into it. Musically speaking, one might keep the *cavatina* of the soprano, the duet with the tenor and the other duet between the father and daughter, although they are *cabalettas*!! (Let the earth swallow me!) *Cabalettas* don't shock me so much as all that, and if a young man should come along tomorrow who could write one as good – for instance – as *Meco tu vieni o misera* or *Ah perchè non posso odiarti*, I should listen to it with all my heart and be glad to forget all the sophistical quibbles and affectations of our clever orchestrations. Ah, progress, learning, realism . . . ! Ah, ah! Be as realistic as you like, but. . . . Shakespeare was a realist, but he didn't know it. His realism was inspired; ours is planned, calculated. So what difference does it make; if we must have a system I prefer the *cabalettas*. The worst of it is that in its rage for progress, art is going backwards. Art without spontaneity, naturalness and simplicity is no longer art. . . .

VERDI TO COUNT OPPRANDINO ARRIVABENE

12 February 1884

Good music has always been a rarity, at all periods, and now it is almost an impossibility. Why? you may ask. . . . Because too much music is composed; because people think too hard; because they stare into the darkness and ignore the sunshine! Because we have exaggerated the minor details! Because what we do is *big*, not great! The *big* leads to the petty and the baroque! That's where we stand. . . .

VERDI TO THE CONDUCTOR FRANCO FACCIO

Montecatini, 14 July 1889

You speak of a *triumph of Italian art*, but you are mistaken! Our young Italian composers are not patriotic. The Germans started with Bach and have arrived at Wagner, they work like good Germans, and that's all right. But when we, the descendants of Palestrina, take to imitating Wagner, we are committing a musical crime and our work is useless, even harmful. . . .

VERDI TO THE MARCHESE GINO MONALDI

Genoa, 13 December 1890

For forty years I have been wanting to write a comic opera, and for fifty years I have known *The Merry Wives of Windsor*; and yet . . . the usual *buts*, which crop up in all directions, continually prevented me from carrying out my wish. And now Boito has got rid of all the *buts* and written me a comedy for music such as was never seen before.

I am enjoying myself composing the music for it; with no plans for its performance, and I don't even know whether I shall finish. . . . But as I say, I am enjoying myself. . . .

Falstaff is a deplorable fellow who does all kinds of wicked things . . . but in an amusing way. He is a *type*! And *types* are so varied! The opera is out-and-out comic!

Amen. . . .

VERDI TO GIULIO RICORDI

10 January 1891

And this brings us to *Falstaff*; I really think all planning on the subject is madness, sheer madness! What I mean is this. I began to write *Falstaff* simply to while away the time, with no preconceived ideas, no plans; as I say, *to while away the time*! And nothing else! Now all the talk that is going on about it and the proposals that are being made, though vaguely, the things you are being induced to say, all end by creating obligations and commitments that I absolutely refuse to accept. As I keep telling you, *I am writing to while away the time*; I told you the music was about half done . . . but let us get this clear, it is only *half sketched out*; and in that half the bulk of the work still lies ahead – fitting the parts together, revising and adapting, quite apart from the orchestration, which will be a tremendous undertaking. In short, the whole of 1891 will not be enough to see it through. So why make plans and give undertakings, even in vague terms? Besides, if I feel that I am tied up in any way, however slightly, I shall be no longer *à mon aise* and then I cannot do good work. In my young days, sickly as I was, I could spend 10 or even 12 hours at my desk!! working all the time; and more than once I worked from 4 in the morning till 4 in the afternoon with no more than a cup of coffee . . . and working without pausing for breath. But now I can't do it. In those days I was in control of my own physique and of time itself . . . but now, alas, I can't do it. . . . So to conclude: The best thing will be to tell everybody, from now on, that I cannot and will not make the very slightest promise about *Falstaff*. If it comes off, well and good; and we shall see how it turns out! . . .

VERDI TO GIULIO RICORDI

S. Agata, 18 September [1892]

As for *Falstaff*, I do not want to commit myself to anyone, but *I promise the publishing house of Ricordi* that I shall give *Falstaff* at the Scala for the Carnival season of 1892–93, when the company for that theatre has been made up, reserving the right to have any performer changed who does not come up to scratch at rehearsals. *Falstaff* can have its first performance right at the beginning of February, if the Theatre can be at my entire disposal as from 2 January 1893.

As for the rehearsals, they will be the same as usual. Only the dress rehearsal will have to be different. I have never been able to get a dress rehearsal at the Scala that was worthy of such a theatre. This time I shall be inexorable. I shall make no complaints, but if there are shortcomings I shall walk out of the theatre, and then you will have to take the opera away from them. . . .

VERDI TO THE DIRECTOR OF THE DEUTSCHE VERLAGSANSTALT, STUTTGART

S. Agata, 21 June 1895

Never, never will I write my memoirs!

It is quite enough for the musical world to have put up with my music for such a long time! . . . I will never condemn it to read my prose. . . .

VERDI TO THE CRITIC CAMILLE BELLAIGUE

I have delayed replying because I wished to read your book, *Les Musiciens*, very carefully; it is a fine book, well thought out and excellently expressed. . . .

Of Rossini and Bellini you say much that may well be true, but I confess I cannot help thinking that for its wealth of original musical ideas, its comic verve and natural style of singing, the *Barber of Seville* is the finest *opera buffa* ever written. Like you, I admire *Tell*, but what a number of noble, sublime passages are to be found in many of his other operas as well! – True, Bellini was poor in orchestration and harmony! . . . but rich in feeling and in an individual melancholy that was all his own! Even in his less familiar operas, such as *La Straniera* or *Il Pirata*, there are long, long, long melodies such as no one ever wrote before his day. And what truth and power of expression, for instance in the duet between *Pollione* and *Norma*! And what loftiness of thought in the opening phrase of the Overture to *Norma* . . . badly orchestrated, but nobody ever wrote a lovelier or more celestial passage of the kind. . . .

VERDI TO THE CHAIRMAN OF THE COMMITTEE FOR THE CELEBRATION OF THE DONIZETTI CENTENARY AT BERGAMO

[*1897*]

Dear Sir,
Donizetti succeeded in creating such a monument to himself with his own hands that we later composers could never set up a greater one to his memory!

A musical 'thought' or a *Cantata d'occasione* would be a very paltry way of honouring him. I may add that I was never able to write such things even in my young days, and at my present advanced age it would be quite impossible. . . .

It is one of the rarest events when a critic offers his apology. Here is one; it is true that the critic happened to be an artist of the highest order.

HANS VON BÜLOW TO VERDI

Hamburg, 7 April 1892

Illustre Maestro,
Please deign to listen to the confession of a contrite sinner! It is now eighteen years since the undersigned was guilty of a great . . . great journalistic *bestiality* . . . towards the last of the five Kings of modern Italian music. He has repented in bitter shame – how many times! When the sin in question was committed (in your generosity you may have quite forgotten it) he was really not in control of his own mind – forgive me if I remind you of what may be called an attenuating circumstance. His mind was clouded by an ultra-Wagnerian fanaticism. Seven years later, the light gradually dawned on him. His fanaticism was purified into enthusiasm. Fanaticism is an oil lamp, enthusiasm an electric light. In the intellectual and moral world, light means justice. Nothing is more destructive than injustice, nothing more intolerable than intolerance, as the most noble Leopardi once said. . . .

I have begun to study your latest works, *Aida*, *Otello*, and the *Requiem*, a rather feeble performance of which was recently enough to move me to tears: I have been studying them not only in the letter which kills, but in the spirit which gives life! Well, *illustre Maestro*, now I admire you, love you! . . .

VERDI TO HANS VON BÜLOW

Genoa, 14 April 1892

Illustre Maestro Bülow,
There is no taint of sin in you! – and no need to talk of repentance and absolution!

If your former views were different from what they are today, you were perfectly right to express them, and I would never have ventured to complain of that. Besides, who knows . . . perhaps you were right then.

Be that as it may, such an unexpected letter from a musician of your quality and importance in the world of art has given me great pleasure! Not out of personal vanity, but because it shows me that really fine artists form their opinions unprejudiced by schools, by nationality or by period.

If artists in the North and those in the South have different tendencies, then let them be *different*! They should all preserve the *characteristics proper to their respective nations*, as Wagner so well expressed it.

Happy you, to be still the sons of Bach! And we? We too, the sons of Palestrina, once had a great school – of our own! Now it has become bastardized and is in danger of collapsing!

If only we could turn back again?! . . .

Verdi closed his glorious career with a comic opera. It is only fitting to conclude this selection from his letters with a little comedy. Here, the composer of 'Falstaff' appears with a twinkle in his eye, when he answers a presumption of almost sublime impudence.

PROSPERO BERTANI TO VERDI

Reggio (Emilia), 7 May 1872

Much honoured Signor Verdi,
The 2nd of this month I went to Parma, drawn there by the sensation made by your opera *Aida*. So great was my curiosity, that half an hour before the commencement of the piece I was already in my place, No. 120. I admired the *mise en scène*, I heard with pleasure the excellent singers, and I did all in my power to let nothing escape me. At the end of the opera, I asked myself whether I was satisfied, and the answer was 'No'. I started back to Reggio and listened in the railway carriage to the opinions given upon *Aida*. Nearly all agreed in considering it a work of the first order.

I was then seized with the idea of hearing it again, and on the 4th I returned to Parma; I made unheard-of efforts to get a reserved seat; as the crowd was enormous, I was obliged to throw away five lire to witness the performance in any comfort.

I arrived at this decision about it: it is an opera in which there is absolutely nothing which causes any enthusiasm or excitement, and without the pomp of the spectacle, the public would not stand it to the end. When it has filled the house two or three times, it will be banished to the dust of the archives.

You can now, dear Signor Verdi, picture to yourself my regret at having spent on two occasions thirty-two lire; add to this the aggravating circumstance that I depend on my family, and that this money troubles my rest like a frightful spectre. I therefore frankly address myself to you, in order that you may send me the amount. The account is as follows:

	Lire
Railroad – going	2.60
„ – returning	3.30
Theatre	8
Detestable supper at the station	2
	15.90
Twice	31.80

Hoping that you will deliver me from this embarrassment, I salute you from my heart.

Bertani

My address: Bertani Prospero, Via San Domenico, No. 5.

VERDI TO HIS PUBLISHERS, MESSRS RICORDI, MILAN, ENCLOSING THE PRECEDING LETTER

[*May 1872*]

You may well imagine that to protect the son of a family from the spectres which pursue him, I will willingly pay the little bill which he sends me. I therefore beg you to forward by one of your correspondents to this M. Prospero Bertani at Reggio, Via San Domenico No. 5, the sum of 27 lire 80 centimes. It is not the amount he demands; but that in addition I should be expected to pay for his supper, certainly not! He might very well take his meals at home.

It is understood that he will give you an acknowledgement, and further a short letter in reply, undertaking to hear my new operas no more, exposing himself no more to the menace of spectres, and sparing me further travelling expenses. . . .

RECEIPT

Reggio, 15 May 1827

I the undersigned acknowledge to have received from the maestro G. Verdi the sum of 27 liri 80 centesimi, by way of repayment of my travelling expenses to Parma to hear *Aida*, the master having considered it fair that this sum should be returned to me, as I did not find his opera to my taste. It is at the same time agreed that in future I shall not make any journey to hear new operas of the maestro unless I undertake the entire expense, whatever may be my opinion of his works.

In faith of which I have signed,

Bertani Prospero.

CONFLICTING IDEALS

From Wagner to Wolf

A period of disintegrating religious, moral, philosophical, and political creeds and values is necessarily reflected in the arts, and perhaps more directly and truthfully in music than in all the others because, conveyed in a pure medium of its own, its expression is more directed by the instinct than by conscious reflection. Changing values, moreover, produce violent clashes of opinions, and the musician of the last hundred years was of necessity dragged into a perennial war of opposed creeds and factions, the ends and aims of which are sometimes difficult to disentangle, as their reality is obscured by their dynamic emotional content. The resulting impetuosity of feelings and impulses is almost clinically demonstrated in the writings of Richard Wagner *(1813–83), and even more directly and spontaneously in his letters than in the cooler, more maturely considered statements of his numerous books and essays.*

Wagner was fantastically argumentative. As a musician, dramatist, politician, philosopher, and philanthropist, he held his own strong views and was indefatigable in formulating and communicating them. He won his battles as much by the drumfire that came from his pen as by his artistic achievements. One may often find his methods demagogic, his reasons spurious, his propaganda crude, but one cannot help admiring a man of such burning conviction and tremendous vitality.

Wagner's letters are a fount of information on every aspect of the man and the artist. His correspondence fills many volumes, a unique document of an intellect of unmatched versatility and almost explosive energy. The following selection is restricted to one main aspect: to the creative artist and his struggles, from the period when, involved in an armed insurrection in Dresden in 1849 and indicted for high treason, he took refuge in Zürich. Without any regular income, prevented from doing anything for the promotion of his works in Germany, he found in Franz Liszt a generous friend who supported him financially to the limit of his resources, and an inspired prophet, who incessantly worked for him both as a performer and a propagandist. His first performance of 'Lohengrin' in Weimar (1850) was the starting-point of Wagner's fame and an ever-growing demand for his works, most of all 'Tannhäuser' and 'Lohengrin', which within the following decade conquered all the German operatic stages.

Even Liszt, with his admirable generosity, was not exempt from occasional attacks of ill feeling on the part of Wagner. One will also appreciate that at a time when a composer's work was still ruthlessly exploited by others, Wagner's claim to a comfortable living solely for the purpose of his creative activity seemed as extravagant as his determination to refuse any additional practical work such as almost all his predecessors had had to do, and as he had done himself as a conductor at the Court Opera in Dresden. In point of fact, the responsibility for his ever-growing needs devolved on devoted friends and admirers and he contracted debts that grew like an avalanche, being rescued in the end by an exalted patron, King Ludwig II of Bavaria, who enabled him to realize his most extravagant artistic dream, Bayreuth.

The opening letter, written before the composition of 'Lohengrin', throws an interesting light on Wagner's manner of creation. His attitude to the revolutionary movement of the mid-nineteenth century can only be understood in the context of that time. Just as the early Christians fervently believed in the Millennium, the coming of the Kingdom of God on Earth, the revolutionaries of Wagner's generation such as Karl Marx and Alexander Herzen, or Wagner's friends Michael Bakunin and Georg Herwegh, were unshakable in their belief that the world revolution was just round the corner. What democrats, socialists, anarchists expected from the inevitable cataclysm was widely divergent. For Wagner, with the obsessive fascination of his artistic ideas, the main result was to be a total reconstruction of the theatre and of the function of dramatic art in society, as he explained in his pamphlet 'Art and Revolution' (1849).

WAGNER TO KARL GAILLARD IN BERLIN

Dresden, 5 June 1845

I have made up my mind to be idle for a whole year – I mean, to exhaust the resources of my library, without doing any productive work. Unfortunately I already have a strong impulse towards the latter again, being captivated by a new subject; but I intend to restrain myself by force. For one thing because there is a great deal I still wish to learn, and for another thing because I have come to the conclusion that if a dramatic work is to have concentrated meaning and importance, it must be the result of a kind of step upward in life, the outcome of an important period in the composer's artistic development. And such steps, or periods, do not come every six months; maturity and concentration take several years to acquire. Whereas to produce just one insignificant composition can only be satisfactory to *money-makers*, and I shall *never* make any money – I have resigned myself to that. . . .

WAGNER TO HIS WIFE MINNA ON HIS FLIGHT AFTER THE COLLAPSE OF THE REVOLUTION IN DRESDEN

Weimar, 14 May 1849

Just think, dear wife, how for years my situation at Dresden had been the source of the deepest dissatisfaction to me; the new path I had begun to follow in my art had proved a thorny one indeed, I was wounded wherever I turned. At last, full of inward fury, I turned my back on my art, which had been bringing me little but suffering, . . . and thus, in the deepest dissatisfaction with my position and almost with my art, groaning under a burden that you unfortunately refused to understand in full, deeply in debt, so that it would have taken me many years of ignominious penury to have paid off my creditors out of what I normally earned, I grew disgusted with the world, ceased to be an artist, threw my creative powers to the winds and became, in intention if not in actual fact, simply a revolutionary, holding the view that only in a completely transformed society could I find the foundation for new creative work. The Dresden revolution and its results have now shown me that I am not a real revolutionary: I have seen from the disastrous outcome of that uprising that a genuine, victorious revolutionary must be remorseless – he must not think of his wife and children, his house and home, his whole effort must be given to the work of destruction. . . . But men like myself are not intended for such terrible tasks; we are revolutionaries only in order to build later on new foundations; it is not *destruction* that attracts us, but *reconstruction*. So we are not the men required by destiny; they will come from the dregs of the nation; we and our hearts can have nothing in common with them. You see? *So I am parting company with the revolution*. . . .

WAGNER TO HIS FRIEND FERDINAND HEINE IN DRESDEN

Zürich, 19 November 1849

As for Liszt, it has also become evident that he himself is unable to maintain me; he is in continual money difficulties, which are aggravated by the fact that he has to keep his mistress, Princess Wittgenstein, entirely. He is a most excellent fellow, with a lively partiality for me; but it is in the nature of things that he should have no understanding of the real essence of my character, which will always be a closed book to him. In short, I have been living for more than three months on a few hundred florins advanced to me by a local friend, and which represent the utmost he could manage. After the end of this month I simply do not know how I am to live at all. . . .

I have poured out my heart to the world, that is to my friends, with my latest piece of writing, *Das Kunstwerk der Zukunft* [*The Art of the Future*]. From now on I shall be a writer no longer, but increasingly an artist. If I can avoid outside disturbances I shall create work after work – for I am overflowing with material and artistic projects. . . . My *Lohengrin* was completed long ago and I am longing heart and soul to write at last the music for my *Siegfried*. . . . So that the only thing that matters to me is to *gain time*, i.e. to *gain life*. Unfortunately for me I have no trade by which to earn my daily bread: as things are, it *must* be given to me, so that I can remain an artist. Who will do this?

Only those who love me – who love me, my work and my artistic aims and efforts so much that they set store by preserving my art and enabling me to continue my artistic efforts. . . .

'Siegfried', which Wagner here yearns to write, is the opera from which, eventually, 'Der Ring des Nibelungen' evolved.

WAGNER TO HIS FRIEND THEODOR UHLIG IN DRESDEN

Zürich, 27 December 1849

My art has always met with a warm response from the hearts of women, probably owing to the fact that although vulgarity is the order of the day, women still find great difficulty in toughening their souls as completely as our politically-minded male society has done to its entire satisfaction. Women, indeed, are the music of life; they absorb everything more openly and unconditionally, in order to embellish it by means of their sympathy. . . .

WAGNER TO LISZT IN WEIMAR

Thun, 2 July 1850

But now I want to make you a very important request!

Give the Opera [*Lohengrin*] *just as it is, make no cuts!*

This time I have been at pains to set the music in such a firm, graphic relationship to the poem and the action, that I feel I can be entirely confident of success. Trust me, and do not think I am infatuated with my own work. If at any point you feel obliged to make cuts because the thing is too difficult, I would like you to consider whether it would not be better to cancel the whole performance on the plea that the material resources are inadequate. I assume, however, that all possible resources will be made available to you, and that you yourself – if you bring your full determination to bear on the subject – will undoubtedly succeed in overcoming any difficulties that may arise. If you make up your mind that it has to be done, I know that it will be done – or else that you will prefer to give up the whole thing. As to that, I think, we are of one mind! . . .

LISZT TO WAGNER

[*Weimar, July 1850*]

Your *Lohengrin* will be performed in the most exceptional conditions, with every possible prospect of success. The management is spending nearly 2,000 Thalers on the production, a thing that has never before happened at Weimar in living memory. The Press is not being forgotten, and serious, well-informed articles are to appear one after another in various newspapers. Everyone in the theatre will be aflame with enthusiasm. . . . I shall take charge of all rehearsals, piano, chorus and orchestra; Genast will follow your instructions for the staging with warmth and vigour. It goes without saying that we shall not cut a single note, a single iota, from your work, and that to the best of our ability we shall present it in all its beauty. . . .

I now come to a matter that distresses me, but which I feel it my duty not to conceal from you. It is quite impossible for you to return to Germany or to come to Weimar for the performance of *Lohengrin*. Next time we meet I shall be able to give you the details; to do so in writing would take too long and serve no useful purpose. . . .

WAGNER TO LISZT

[*Zürich, July 1850*]

I must say *you are a true friend*! There is no need for me to say more than that! for I have always looked upon friendship between men as the finest and most honourable of all human relationships, and you give me the most complete illustration of that idea; for in your case I do not merely think what friendship means, I feel and grasp it. . . . To have found you not only lessens the pain of my banishment from Germany but almost makes it seem a happiness, for I could never have done so much for myself there as you are managing to do for me. . . .

I have certain convictions which you cannot share, perhaps, but which you will see no need to challenge when you realize that they do not in the least impede my artistic activities. I have felt the pulse of our modern art, and I know its death is approaching. However, this does not depress me; on the contrary it delights me, for I also know that it is not art itself but only *our* art – which bears no relation to real life – that is to perish so that the true, imperishable, ever-new art may at last come to birth. . . . As matters now stand with me I am no longer spurred to creative effort by ambition, but by the urge to communicate with my friends and the wish to give them pleasure: whenever I know that this urge and wish have been satisfied, I am happy and entirely content. The fact that you are presenting my *Lohengrin* at little Weimar happily and lovingly, joyfully and successfully – if only for the two performances about which you write to me – makes me so delighted, meets my views so completely, that I feel no more concern for that work and can turn all my attention to fresh efforts to prepare something new for you. . . .

WAGNER TO THEODOR UHLIG

Zürich, 20 September 1850

I think I need hardly assure you that I really *gave up Lohengrin* when I allowed it to be put on at Weimar. True, I received a letter yesterday from Zigesar in which he describes the second performance – which thanks to my vigorous admonitions was given only after very detailed further rehearsal and without cuts – as a marvellous success which made a tremendous impression on the audience, and expresses the definite conviction that the opera is destined to become and remain a box-office success; but I need hardly enter into the details of my reasons for saying that I would like to send *Siegfried* out into the world in a manner that would not be possible for the good people at Weimar. In this connection I have recently been full of wishes and plans which may at first glance seem very chimerical; but these alone enable me to think with any pleasure of finishing *Siegfried*. What is needed to achieve the best, most decisive and most significant project that I can undertake in the existing circumstances, and to carry out what I regard as my task in life, is a sum of perhaps 10,000 Thalers. If I had such a sum at my disposal I would proceed as follows. Here, where I am placed and where in many respects things are not at all bad, I would have a makeshift theatre of planks and beams set up according to my own plans, in a beautiful meadow just outside the town, and equipped with the bare minimum of scenery and machines required for a performance of *Siegfried*. I would then select the most suitable singers wherever they might be, and invite them to Zürich for 6 weeks. As for the chorus, I would try to assemble that locally, among amateurs (there are magnificent voices and strong, healthy people here). I would get the orchestra together by invitation, in the same way. In the New Year I would put advertisements in all the German newspapers, with invitations to all lovers of musical drama to attend the proposed festival of music: all those who announced their intention of coming to Zürich for this purpose would be guaranteed a seat – free, of course, as all seats would be. Then I should invite the local young people, the University, the Choral Societies, etc., to come and listen too. When everything was in good order, I would give three performances of *Siegfried* in the course of a week; after the third the theatre would be pulled down and my score burnt. To those who had enjoyed the thing, I should then say 'Now go and do the same!' But if they wanted to hear some other new thing by me, I would say 'Now *you* get the money together!' Do you think I am completely crazy? That may be; but I assure you that to achieve this is the great hope of my life, the only prospect that can stimulate me to take up any creative work. So find me 10,000 Thalers – that's all I ask!

WAGNER TO LISZT

Zürich, 2 October 1850

In your letter you emphasize particularly that the enemy we have to fight resides not only in the singers' throats, but in the sluggish philistinism of our public and the asinine minds of our critics. My dear friend, I agree with you about this so completely that I have never even mentioned it to you! Only I refuse to admit the senseless demands that are made on the public; I refuse to reproach the public for their lack of artistic appreciation and to expect the salvation of art from cramming the public with artistic appreciation from above: ever since connoisseurs of art came into existence, art has been going to the devil. In trying to stuff the public with artistic appreciation, we shall only end by making them completely stupid. I said I ask nothing from the public except *common sense and human hearts*. . . . Nothing more – but that is everything, when we realize how utterly the sense of this so-called public has become perverted and their hearts hardened into cowardice and wickedness. You must admit it would take a second Flood to correct these little defects! I fear that even our fieriest efforts can do nothing to heal such infirmities. The most we can do, since after all here we are, compelled to live in *this* period and in no other, however much we might wish it, is to take care that we ourselves preserve our dignity and independence, as artists and as human beings; let us show by our own example at least, that human beings have a certain value! . . .

WAGNER TO THEODOR UHLIG

Albisbrunn, 12 November 1851

With this new concept [*The Ring*] I sever all connection with our present-day theatre and its audience: I make a definite and permanent break with present-day forms. Would you like to know what my intentions are regarding my plan? In the first place, to *carry it out*, so far as lies in my power as poet and composer. This will take me at least three full years.

I cannot look for a performance until *after the revolution*; only revolution can bring the artists and audiences to me; the next revolution must necessarily put an end to our whole system of theatre management; it must and will collapse, that is inevitable. And out of its ruins I can call forth what I require; *then* I shall find what I need. I shall then build a theatre on the Rhine and send out invitations to a great dramatic festival; after a year's preparation I shall give a performance of my entire work, spread over four days. In this way I shall reveal to the men of the revolution the significance of their revolution in its noblest sense. *That audience* will understand me, as the present-day public is incapable of doing.

However extravagant this plan may be, it is the one to which I am now devoting my whole life, my writing and my endeavours. If I live to see it carried out, I shall have had a splendid life; if not, I shall have died for something beautiful. But only this can give me any pleasure now!

Wagner was an optimist. It took him twenty-two years to finish his great work, the Tetralogy.

WAGNER TO THEODOR UHLIG

Zürich, 20 March 1852

The performance of the Overture to *Tannhäuser* has now taken place [at Zürich]: it exceeded all my expectations, for it really went splendidly. You can most readily realize this from the effect it produced, which was positively *shattering*. I am not even referring to the storm of applause it called forth on the spot, but in particular to the signs of its effect of which I only gradually became aware. Among the women in particular there was an absolute upheaval; they were so overcome with emotion that they sought relief in sobs and tears. . . . Much as I was again gripped on this occasion by my own work, I was astonished at first by the uncommonly violent effect it produced. As it happens, it was a woman who solved the riddle for me: people took the view that

I had delivered a crushing penitential homily against the sin of *hypocrisy*. In view of what I have achieved with it here, I have suddenly begun to feel rather proud of this piece of music: I really cannot think of any other poetical composition capable of producing such an effect on sensuous and sensitive minds. . . .

WAGNER TO THEODOR UHLIG

Zürich, 26 February 1852

A few new acquaintances have thrust themselves upon me; the men among them leave me completely indifferent, but the women less so. A wealthy young merchant named Wesendonck – brother of the Member of Parliament – settled here recently, and lives in great luxury; his wife is very pretty and seems to have developed a crush on me, on the strength of the forewords to my three operatic poems. It is the same with some local Swiss aristocratic families (I only mean the women, the men are horrible). It astonishes me to discover so much liveliness, even charm, among them. . . . True, I can no longer enjoy the company of men, or even that of women; but the latter are the last element that still now and *then* creates some slight illusion for me. . . .

The most passionate episode of Wagner's life, his love for Mathilde Wesendonck and its transfiguration in 'Tristan and Isolde', is foreshadowed in the last two letters. Against the haunted restlessness of his life as an exile, a period punctuated by crises of all kinds, his capacity for quiet, patient devotion to his artistic work seems miraculous. The love and care he bestowed on every page of music he wrote is reflected in the shapely finish of his handwriting. The outside world had no access to his workshop. He may have been the despair of his wife, an unscrupulous sponger on his friends, a pest to all law-abiding philistines, but the artist's idealism was as unshakable as the reality of his vision.

Hans von Bülow (1830–94), to whom the next letter is addressed, was Wagner's most distinguished disciple. He became the greatest conductor of his time, but soon gave up his ambition as a composer. His wife Cosima, Liszt's daughter, left him and after the death of Minna became Wagner's second wife.

WAGNER TO HANS VON BÜLOW

Zürich, 26 October 1854

I was struck at once by your inventiveness: you undoubtedly have a great gift in that respect, and it reveals itself particularly in the most recent composition, the orchestral fantasy. . . . In general you show much greater self-reliance in that composition. . . . But in both works I admire your technique; in what seem to me to be rather intractable forms, both in detail and in general development, you will not easily be surpassed. So that I can only recognize that you have mastered your art and in my opinion can accomplish whatever you choose to undertake. In the matter of style, however, I am inclined to make one fundamental objection – regarding your attitude towards harmony: here I must confess that so far my only impression is that of very notable compositions for instruments out of tune. This is precisely why I would like to be able to gain a definite impression by hearing a first-class performance, which might relieve me of this uneasiness. I know well enough from experience that there are musical subjects which can only be expressed by harmonic forms which are bound to offend the ear of the musical Philistine. But whenever I have found this in my own work I have always felt a definite impulse to cover up these harsh passages as far as possible and finally to arrange them in such a way that (in my opinion) they can pass entirely unperceived. Whereas I cannot help feeling that with you it is exactly the opposite – that you make a point of presenting the asperities for their own sake; and I feel this most unpleasantly in places where the whole idea seems to be expressed with this asperity from beginning to end. . . . You know, Hans, I really did go through this kind of thing myself, in my earliest period as a composer, when I subordinated all other aspects to the search for some such clever harmonic device. But in those days I was not yet capable of good work, I could never have written a piece of music that held together like your Fantasy and revealed such mastery as that. So in you it surprises me: you are certainly mistaken about yourself, you have far too much inventiveness to indulge in tricks of that kind. . . .

The wisdom of Wagner's criticism is so striking that it hardly demands comment.

WAGNER TO LISZT

Zürich, 1 January 1855

For the sake of the most cherished of my dreams, concerning the young Siegfried, I have still to complete the Nibelungen dramas: The *Valkyrie* has agitated me so terribly, that I cannot possibly deny myself that exhilaration; I have now reached the second half of the last Act. So I shall not have finished the whole thing until 1856; and in 1858, the tenth year of my Hegira, I can present it on the stage – if that is to be. But as I have never really experienced the full happiness of love in my own life, I want to erect one more memorial to this most beautiful of all dreams, one in which love shall find its full satisfaction from beginning to end. I have worked out in my mind a *Tristan and Isolde*, the simplest yet the most full-blooded musical conception; and at the end, when the 'black flag' is hoisted, I shall cover myself with it – and die. . . .

WAGNER TO LISZT

London, 5 April 1855

My position here is completely anomalous; I am right out of my element and in an absolutely false situation. At Zürich I occasionally conduct a concert, but there I do it to pass the time and to please a few friends. To take it as my official occupation and the basis on which I am to be judged as an artist by a public and critics whom I find utterly antipathetic, is a piece of great foolishness. I am heartily sorry to have come here, and never intend to set foot in the place again. There is no prospect of financial success, and even if they offered me a higher salary for the next year I think I should let it go; for the unpleasantness involved is too great. . . .

Really beautiful performances, which would be my only possible compensation, are something I cannot manage; there are not enough rehearsals, and the whole attitude here is much too business-like. The pieces from *Lohengrin* were applauded, but I am sorry I gave them, so great is the mortification of being restricted to excerpts from that opera and obliged to leave my entire essence to be judged by them. It goes utterly against the grain as well, to take the slightest step to win over the pack of blackguards who write for the newspapers. They keep on abusing me in the most comical fashion, and the only thing that surprises me is that so far the public has not been really led astray by them. . . .

Blackguardliness, obstinacy and divinely protected stupidity are sheltered by walls of brass in this place; only a blackguardly Jew can succeed here. . . .

WAGNER TO LISZT

Zürich, 13 April 1856

Will you take it upon yourself to ask the King of Saxony for an audience, on the strength of a letter of introduction from the Grand Duke of Weimar? There is no need for me to prompt you to what you should say to the King; but we certainly agree that in asking for a pardon for me, the whole emphasis should be placed on the fact that I am an *artist*, since this fact in general, and my individual character as *artist* in particular, account for and excuse my flagrant political excesses and provide justification for an amnesty. With regard to those excesses – the results of which, it may be remarked, have made themselves felt for several years already – I am prepared to admit that it now seems even to me that in those days I was in error and carried away by passion; though as I am conscious of not having actually committed any actionable crime, I should find it hard to confess to such a thing. As for my future conduct, however, I am prepared to give any pledge required of me, since I should only be expressing my inner, clarified and amended views, which now show me the things of this world in a light in which I did not see them before, and lead me to devote myself entirely to my art, henceforth ignoring political speculation of any kind. . . . As an artist I have fortunately arrived at a stage where I have a mind only for my work and its successful completion, not at all for the applause of the multitude. I should therefore, in full accord with my inmost wishes, be prepared to give the most definite undertaking to abstain completely from any public demonstration of sympathy, even if offered to me as artist. . . . I have no desire even to conduct one of my own operas, should the occasion arise; all I should wish would be to attend rehearsals so as to make sure that the performers and directors were giving a correct interpretation. Were it necessary in order to avoid the risk of a demonstration, I would undertake to leave the town at the end of the rehearsals, before the performance; which clearly shows what is my only real concern. I also pledge myself to avoid in my writings, even those on art, any words likely to be misconstrued or to give offence, such as may have escaped me in moments of irritation in the past. . . .

WAGNER TO HIS FRIEND DR ANTON PUSINELLI IN DRESDEN

Zürich, 28 April 1856

. . . After cruel birth pangs the *Valkyrie* is now completed, it is more beautiful than anything I ever wrote before – but it has taken a terrible lot out of me. If I can now secure some air, light and peace, I shall hope to compose *Young Siegfried* [this was the original title] this summer. But peace, peace I must have, or I shall not be able to keep going. . . .

WAGNER TO FRAU JULIE RITTER IN DRESDEN

Zürich, 6 May 1857

If you would like to hear another piece of good news about me, it is that this last winter (though much delayed first by Liszt's visit and later by the great strain put on me) I finished the first Act of *Siegfried* – true, only the first Act, but that has exceeded all my expectations. I was breaking entirely new ground, and after the terribly tragic atmosphere of the *Valkyrie* I moved on to it with an unprecedented feeling of freshness: the way this one act has turned out convinces me that *Young Siegfried* will be my most popular work, winning favour rapidly on a large scale, and will draw all other pieces in its wake, so that it may well become the forerunner of a whole Nibelungen dynasty. The first performance of the whole thing is not likely to be given before 1860, however, because when I have quite finished the music I shall need a full year for the preparations, though these will be facilitated from the start by the fact that I have already come across several talented performers who are suitable. . . . For the rest, I shall allow nothing to disturb me in my work from now on; in the first place I shall not leave my beautiful retreat this summer until *Siegfried* is quite finished. Then may providence grant me good progress next year with the last piece: and once that is finished I have so many more ideas in mind that for the time being I would rather not think at all about staging it!

WAGNER TO LISZT

Zürich, 28 June 1857

I am planning to write *Tristan and Isolde* as a work of limited dimensions and modest technical demands, for the sake of easier production, and to present it at Strasbourg in a year's time with Niemann and Mme Meyer. There is a fine theatre there, and an orchestra, and I can get the other (unimportant) members of the cast from some nearby German Court Theatre – Karlsruhe, perhaps – and I hope it will thus be possible, with God's help, to put on something again in my own way and thus refresh myself and increase my self-confidence. Another consideration is that this represents my only possible chance of keeping my head above water. . . . For I hope I can take it for granted that a work like *Tristan*, which is to be perfectly straightforward, will soon bring me in a good financial return and keep me going for some time. Whether I shall go back to the Nibelungen after that, I cannot of course say in advance; it depends upon my frame of mind, and I cannot command that. This time I have done violence to myself; when I was in the best possible frame of mind I tore Siegfried out of my heart and put him under lock and key as though buried alive. I shall keep him like that, and no one shall have a glimpse of him, for I must conceal him even from myself. Sleep may of course prove good for him; but I have made no decision about waking him up. I had a hard, bitter struggle to bring myself to this! So let us take that as settled too!

Again Wagner was an optimist: eight years had to pass before Tristan was performed for the first time; nor did he guess how far this work would carry him into a new world of experience and sound.

WAGNER TO MATHILDE WESENDONCK

Venice, 12 October 1858

I am now going back to *Tristan*, so that the profound art of sonorous silence can speak for me to you through him. For the time being I am invigorated by the great solitude and retirement in which I am living and which is helping me to gather together my painfully shattered energies. . . . I shall relish this until my marvellous work reaches a successful conclusion. Not until then will I look round me to discover how the world is disposed to treat me. The Grand Duke of Baden has managed to obtain permission for me to visit Germany for a time in order to superintend the staging of a new work. I may use this opportunity for *Tristan*. Until then I shall remain alone with him in the living world of dreams that now surrounds me here. . . .

WAGNER TO LISZT

Venice, 19 October 1858

In external matters I look upon my destiny with unruffled patience as a prospect of bright, serene years filled with peaceful activity. My work has grown dearer to me than ever: I took it up again a short time ago and ideas are flowing from my mind in a gentle stream. . . . And now I have my Erard. It stands in a big, echoing room I use for my work, where I intend to finish *Tristan* this winter. The first Act is now quite finished, my dear man. . . . I was interrupted by visitors while working on Act Two, when I had only outlined it. Now I have taken it up again; it will be very beautiful, and I mean to finish it and have it printed by the end of this year at the latest. The last Act will follow between then and March, and if all goes as I hope I shall see the first performance by about Easter. . . .

WAGNER TO LISZT

Venice, 2 January 1859

You must believe me unreservedly when I tell you that my only real reason for wishing to live any longer is the irresistible urge to complete a number of works of art that are still striving to come to birth in me. I have come to realize most clearly that this work of creation and perfection is the only thing that satisfies me and gives me a (frequently unaccountable) disposition to cling to life; whereas I really set no store whatsoever by the idea of the operas being actually performed. It has thus become clear to me that a pardon granted to me before I have quite finished *Tristan* could only be an embarrassment. Until I have finished that work, not even the prospect of staging *Lohengrin* myself could induce me to leave this place. From which you can draw your own further conclusions!

In other words, any prospect that might be held out for securing me a more becoming style of living would be of no value to me if it were dependent upon a pardon and upon any services this would make necessary for me to render. I cannot and will not accept an official post, or anything of that kind. What I do ask for is to be granted an honourable and generous pension, solely to enable me to go on with my creative work undisturbed and completely independent of material success. . . .

WAGNER TO MATHILDE WESENDONCK

Venice, 22 February 1859

Posterity will certainly find it astonishing that I should have been obliged to hawk my works about; for only posterity understands such things – and then forgets, with childish self-deception, that it too is a 'present generation' and in that capacity invariably dull-witted and insensitive. But that is the way of the world, and we cannot change it. You tell me the same thing about people in general. And nothing much can be done to change me, either; I still have my little foibles; I like to live comfortably, love carpets and fine furniture, and at home and when at work I am fond of dressing in silk and satin. . . . Well, all that matters is for *Tristan* to turn out well: and so it will, better than anything before!

WAGNER TO MATHILDE WESENDONCK

Venice, 2 March 1859

Parsifal has been much in my mind, for a strange character in it, a wondrous demoniac woman (the Grail's messenger) is becoming more and more vivid and fascinating. If I ever complete this poem to my satisfaction it will be something very original. Only I cannot imagine how long I shall still have to live in order to carry out all my plans. . . . Humboldt relates that Kant still had a host of ideas he was intending to work out in detail when his death at a very advanced age put a natural end to his projects.

I am already aware of a fatalistic reluctance to finish *Tristan* this time; but I cannot induce myself to work more hastily at it. On the contrary, I am composing as though I meant to do nothing else for the rest of my life. As a result, however, it is becoming more beautiful than anything I ever did; I work out even the briefest phrase so carefully that it means as much to me as a whole Act. . . .

The following two letters tell us how, unaccountably, the composer's inspiration, the source of his invention, may dry up temporarily and how he suffers from such spells of unproductiveness which may disappear as suddenly as they have come.

WAGNER TO LISZT

Lucerne, 8 May 1859

Children, children! I am afraid I shall be left in the lurch for too long, and that the words 'too late' will sooner or later come into your minds in connection with me as well. For now I am told: 'Finish *Tristan* and then we shall see!' But suppose I do not finish *Tristan*, because I cannot? I feel as though I were gradually going to fade away within sight of the – goal (?). At any rate I turn to my paper every day, full of good intentions, only to find that my mind is a blank, my heart empty; and I stare out into the mist and rain-clouds. . . . People say: just get down to work and everything will be all right again! Excellent; but poor devil that I am, I have no organized routine, and if things do not go of their own accord there is nothing I can do to make them. . . . I cannot tell you strongly enough how pitiful I feel myself to be as a musician; from the bottom of my heart I look upon myself as an absolute bungler. You should just see me sitting there as I do so often, telling myself 'something is bound to come of it', and then going to the piano and turning out some wretched stuff, only to give up the attempt like an idiot. Imagine my feelings! My deep-rooted conviction of being a poor wretch as a musician! . . .

WAGNER TO MATHILDE WESENDONCK

Lucerne, 9 May 1859

Child, child! The biscuits did help; they suddenly jerked me out of a bad patch where I had been stuck for a week, unable to go further. Yesterday my attempts to work were miserably unsuccessful. I was in a shocking humour, and gave it vent in a long letter to Liszt in which I informed him that I had come to the end of my composing days. . . . Today I was staring up at the grey sky, utterly disconsolate, simply wondering to whom I could now write something acrimonious. For a whole week had gone by since I had made any progress in the actual composition; I was stuck at the transition from '*vor Sehnsucht nicht zu sterben*' to Tristan's voyage [Act 3]. So I had put that aside and turned back to work further on the beginning, the part I played to you. But today even that was making no progress, because I feel I did it much better before and cannot remember now how it was.

When the biscuits arrived, I realized what had been lacking; the biscuits I had here were much too salty, so they could not give me any sensible ideas; but when I took the sweet ones I had always been accustomed to, and dipped them in milk, everything suddenly fell into place. And so I threw aside the revision and went back to composing, on the story of the woman physician from far away. And now I am delighted; the transition is unbelievably successful, with a quite wonderful combination of two themes. Heavens, how much can be achieved by the right sort of biscuits! – Biscuits! that is the proper remedy for composers when they get stuck – but they must be the right kind. Now I have a good reserve of them; when you notice it getting low, be sure you send for more: I can see it is important. . . .

WAGNER TO MATHILDE WESENDONCK

Paris, 23 September 1859

My friend, only in these last years have I really matured into a man. I feel in complete harmony with myself, and whenever it is a question of the truth I am always confident and know my own mind. In real life I allow myself to be guided serenely by instinct; I am the instrument of something greater than the value of my own personality. I know this so profoundly that I smile and often hardly ask myself whether I want a thing or not. The miraculous genius I am to serve for what life remains to me takes care of that, and wills me to complete what no one but I can do. . . .

WAGNER TO HANS VON BÜLOW

Paris, 7 October 1859

But in confidence I must tell you sorrowfully that I am now quite unable to find the right tone in which to write to Liszt. For weeks I have been tormenting myself about what to say in a letter. I probably need not worry so much, for I never really get a letter from Liszt – at most only replies to those I send him, and his are never more than half or a quarter the length of mine. So he does not feel drawn to me at all. If I address him, he is the most splendid friend imaginable; but he never takes the initiative. So what makes me go on approaching him? How matters stand between Liszt and me – or rather *what* stands between us – you must explain to yourself by his behaviour . . . I know that Liszt's generous nature always has the last word. . . . So for me, Liszt will always continue to be a noble, profoundly congenial, much-admired and much-loved figure; but there is little prospect of extracting any more comfort from the cultivation of our friendship. It was obviously he who first ceased to cultivate it and now I can only follow his example; I should henceforth have *too much to conceal* from him, and in those circumstances no friendship can be cultivated. I can find nothing to say to him any more, and I do not want to write him mere empty phrases; I am too fond of him for that. . . .

WAGNER TO MATHILDE WESENDONCK

Paris, 29 October 1859

It is a fundamental characteristic of my nature to swing rapidly and violently from one extreme to another: opposed states of extreme tension are almost bound to border closely upon one another; indeed that is often a life-saving factor. At bottom, too, the *motive* for all true art is to bring these exalted moods together at their point of climax, for only the extreme contrasts can yield the one thing that matters, the vital decision. In practice, however, the employment of these extremes in art is apt to foster disastrous mannerism which may degenerate into a striving for superficial effects. That is what I saw happening to the modern French school, led by Victor Hugo. . . . I now realize that the special texture of my music (always, of course, inseparably bound up with the poetic conception), which my friends now find so novel and important, is due to my extraordinary sensitivity to the connection and integration of all elements in the transition of these extreme moods. I might say that today what is finest and deepest in my art consists in transition: I have come to dislike the abrupt, the sudden; it is often unavoidable and necessary, but even so it should never occur until the mood is so definitely prepared for the sudden transition as to evoke it spontaneously. My greatest masterpiece in the art of extremely subtle and gradual transition is surely the great scene in Act II of *Tristan and Isolde*. It opens with life pulsating at the highest emotional pitch, and closes with the most solemn, the most profound yearning for death. Those are the two pillars: now, my child, see how I have connected those pillars, how I manage the transition from one to the other! For that, too, is the secret of my musical style, which I make bold to say has never yet been even remotely approached for harmony of form and clarity in every detail. If you only knew how this dominating feeling has stimulated my musical inventiveness in the matter of rhythm, harmony and melodic development, you would realize that even in the most specialized branches of music there can be no true invention unless it derives from those main sources. . . .

Amnestied and permitted to return to the countries of the German Confederation, Wagner now heard his work in Vienna for the first time, after an exile of twelve years.

WAGNER TO MATHILDE WESENDONCK

Vienna, 11 May 1861

I have just been to a rehearsal of *Lohengrin*! I cannot keep to myself the unbelievably moving effect it produced on me, heard thus for the first time in the most wonderful atmosphere of devotion, both artistic and human: I must tell you about it at once. I lived through twelve years of my life – and what years!! You were right to say so often that you wished I could have that joy. But nowhere could it have been offered to me with such perfection as here. Oh, if only you could be here tomorrow!!

WAGNER TO KARL KLINDWORTH

Starnberg in Bayern, 16 May 1864

As for me, my dear man, a fortnight ago I was in the most desperate position of my whole life. But the unexpected death of King Max of Bavaria suddenly gave an angel, sent into the world by Destiny for my special benefit, full power to be to me all that in ideal circumstances a man, a King, could be. He sent for me: now I am at his side for ever, relieved of all my anxieties, to work and to present the work I have completed, for which he will provide everything that is needed.

I have now promised to finish the *Nibelungen* as well: he will make a gift of it to the German nation with a performance where all my ideas will be realized. . . .

The miraculous turn of Wagner's fortunes came as suddenly and dramatically as a climactic turn in one of his operas. But even then, when through a King's favour he could enjoy a freedom and independence as hardly any artist before, he remained as quarrelsome and intractable as ever, a supreme artist and a most problematic character.

WAGNER TO LUDWIG SCHNORR VON CAROLSFELD

Starnberg bei München, 29 August 1864

My young King is always trying to bolster up my courage; his own determination is enthusiastic and unassailable. He is making every possible economy, has stopped work on some buildings ordered by his father, and so forth, so as to have ample means with which to put my artistic ideas into practice. Faced with his warm-hearted urging, all I have to do now is to keep asking myself where I am to find the artistic means. I cannot decide whether it is better to concentrate on something out of the ordinary and seldom repeated, or to aim at some permanent, educational form of organization. The extraordinary, confident and enthusiastic idealism of this gracious King, who stands beside me like the embodiment of my good genius, makes me quite bewildered when I try to estimate possibilities. . . .

WAGNER TO MALWIDA VON MEYSENBUG

Triebschen [Lucerne], 1 July 1867

I could not go too far from Munich if I wanted to prevent the young King from abdicating. At the beginning of April 1866 I took a lease of this house in the country near Lucerne, where I have now settled for six working years. I went through a period of terrible anxiety last summer, but all the same I pushed on with the music of the *Meistersinger*. At last I have completed another work! I go to Munich only for visits. The *Meistersinger* is to appear at the beginning of next winter. You are to come to the performance, do you hear? It is my masterpiece, nothing else comes up to it. . . .

WAGNER TO HIS FRIEND PETER CORNELIUS

Triebschen, 8 September 1869

As soon as I revisited Munich for the first time, at the end of 1867, I realized that the confidence we had all felt, on the strength of the conditions existing there $2\frac{1}{2}$ years before, was completely unfounded. I resolved firmly that once the *Meistersinger* had been put on I would never set foot in Munich again. . . . Frau von Bülow's honour was again attacked before His Majesty; taking this as a portent, her only course was to sever her connection with Munich once and for all and arrange for her divorce from the man whose name and honour she did not wish to be stained any longer by the hatred with which she herself was regarded. He was hesitant, but a few months ago she rightly pointed out to him that to divorce her would also be of advantage to his future in his post at Munich, since he could then no longer be accused of obtaining it by being a complaisant husband. For this consideration she was even ready to take upon herself all the hardships of a divorce. Bülow thanked her and agreed that she was right; but he declared that he found his position extremely disagreeable, simply because of the worthlessness of everything in Munich and the permanent irritation this caused him, and that in any case he meant to resign from his post. . . .

Intrigues and conflicts of all kinds, culminating in a public scandal aroused by his liaison with Bülow's wife Cosima, drove Wagner from Munich, just as his affair with Mathilde Wesendonck, ten years before, had driven him from his sanctuary at Zürich. In his resentment against Munich he tried to obstruct the performance of the finished parts of the tetralogy, 'Rheingold' and 'The Valkyrie', which, in spite of his resistance, were performed in his absence on the King's command at his Court Theatre. After this, Wagner sulked and his relations with Ludwig were strained; the latter, however, maintained his generous support of the artist whom he adored.

WAGNER TO PETER CORNELIUS

Lucerne, 2 October 1869

So far as I am concerned I can only say that I gave up as long as two years ago all hope of being able to influence future developments in Munich, I only assumed that, thanks to the talents of those I had already recommended, who were established there by that time, it would be possible – quite without reference to my personal tendencies and higher plans – to achieve some kind of respectable standard in art.

Even this proved impossible, for a variety of reasons, chief among them the fact that things in Munich and Bavaria utterly defy change. And so farewell! What remains is a purely personal relationship between myself and the King, who loves my music and does not care in the least how it is played to him. . . .

WAGNER TO KARL KLINDWORTH

Lucerne, 4 February 1870

Here at home (where you should really visit us sometime soon) all goes well, except that my young King at Munich is again causing me great, great trouble. As you will soon discover, the nastiness that went on over the *Rheingold* is now likely to be repeated with the *Valkyrie*. This is the price I have to pay for as much bourgeois tranquillity as will at least enable me to finish the composition of my works. . . .

WAGNER TO KING LUDWIG II OF BAVARIA

Siena, 28 September 1880

I have now been compelled to hand over all my works, which were conceived with such idealism, to commerce with our theatre and public, which I recognize to be utterly immoral; and I had to ask myself seriously whether I ought not to protect this, the last and holiest of my compositions, from the same fate, a vulgar career as an opera. A decisive reason for doing so, and one to which I can no longer close my eyes, is to be found in the very nature of the thing, in the actual subject of my *Parsifal*. For is it possible and permissible for a work in which the loftiest mysteries of the Christian faith are represented on the stage, to be produced in theatres such as ours, as part of the operatic repertory, before audiences like ours? I really could not blame our ecclesiastical authorities if they objected, as they would be fully justified in doing, against the presentation of the holiest mysteries on the same boards where frivolity had freely expressed itself the previous night and would do so again the night after, before an audience to which frivolity alone makes any appeal. I had entirely the right feeling about this when I sub-titled *Parsifal* 'A Sacred Festival for the Theatre' [*Bühnenweihfestspiel*]. So I must now try to find a stage to consecrate to it, and that can only be my remote Festival Theatre at Bayreuth. *Parsifal* shall be given there and only there, to the end of time; it shall never be offered as an amusement to the audience of any other theatre. To make certain of this is now my only concern, and I have to think of ways and means of thus ensuring the future of my work. . . .

There is a basic antithesis between Wagner and his younger contemporary, Johannes Brahms *(1833–97). To the former, his own achievement, his unique realization of dramatic and musical unity in the 'universal work of art', represented an ideal for which all that had happened before in history was only a gradual preparation. With an unshakable conviction of his own unsurpassable greatness, he could not but regard all his predecessors, including even Beethoven, whom he worshipped, as mere forerunners who only dimly and imperfectly realized the ultimate truth. Brahms stood, as on a rock, on his consciousness of classical tradition, of the music of Bach, Mozart, Haydn, Beethoven and Schubert, as the Revelation, the transcendental reality. Deep communion with their spirit, and devoted study of their form and technique was for him the only legitimate progress to mastery.*

There is no bridge between Wagner's pride and Brahms's humility. As to the latter, a life of hard work and bitter experience made him a realist and sceptic, but his basic attitude never changed. 'The fact that the public fails to understand the very best', he wrote to Klara Schumann (1878), when she hesitated in putting one of Mozart's pianoforte concertos on a programme, 'is the mainstay of people such as me and makes us famous. If they only knew that they get from us only in driblets what they could drink there to their heart's content!'

Brahms had a fortunate start: he had come into the lime light at the age of twenty, when he had been introduced to the world of music by a famous prophetic article by Schumann. All the same, he had a hard uphill struggle as a composer: but in his forties he had already arrived at a position of unquestioned distinction, in which he could not help being pitted against Wagner as the most prominent stronghold of classical tradition. As a letter-writer he is of absorbing interest. An introvert, with a severe emotional restraint, he is honest to the extent of bluntness, often sarcastic and epigrammatic with a peculiar manner of putting things in a nutshell. A reflection of that honesty is already to be found in the young composer's rigorous critical self-control. Conscious of the textural and formal problems of a large-scale work, he incessantly asks his more experienced friends such as Klara Schumann or Joseph Joachim for criticism and advice, and in the end is more critical than they, just as he discarded some of his early works which Schumann, his generous patron, who soon after became incurably ill, had found worth publishing. One will admire equally his favourite critic's thoroughness, enthusiasm, and competence – Joachim was not only a great performer, but also a composer of considerable talent – and the earnest single-minded devotion of the young composer.

Gisela von Arnim, the writer of the next letter, was the daughter of Bettina von Arnim, a close friend of Goethe.

GISELA VON ARNIM TO HER SISTER MAXIMILIANE

Hanover, November 1853

Yesterday evening at Joachim's we heard a musical genius he has discovered, a Mr Brahms – a charming little man, fair-haired, rosy-cheeked and with quite lovely eyes – owing his education to books, which he obtains in the most ingenious ways – a lively young man who has known what it is to go hungry, and yet is always graceful – in short, like a green Christmas tree shining with gold candles. . . .

JOSEPH JOACHIM TO GISELA VON ARNIM

Hanover, 27 November 1853

Brahms got back on Friday evening, when I came home from a late walk to find that little green-and-gold tiger cub lurking in wait for me, twice as green as before from laurels, and freshly gilded by the publishers who are printing all his things. . . . You really saw into him very deeply – he is an egoist and always on the watch – but at least he is frank about his own nature, with none of the false sentimentality with which others of his kind are fond of fooling themselves. Besides, everything he pounces on serves only one purpose, his ambition to become a great artist; in comparison with other people that is a fine thing in itself, and I like him for it – you have no idea what revolting vanity I often meet with among my own colleagues. . . .

BRAHMS TO JOSEPH JOACHIM

Düsseldorf, 19 June 1854

I should like to publish the enclosed pieces, and beg you with all the urgency of which I am capable, to look them through and write me your *most sincere* opinion of them. I have such doubts as to whether they are worth anything or not, that I cannot take any decision without hearing your conclusive judgement.

Above all, I beg you to give me a decisive *yes* or *no* on each of the pieces and variations, or to send me *your objections*! . . . Don't you think the Variations are much too short and insignificant? There is no real place for such childish stuff nowadays. I should like to be able to put my D-minor Sonata aside for a long time. I have often played the first three movements with Frau Schumann (improving them). To tell the truth, even two pianos are not enough for me. I would have liked to put aside the Trio as well, for I should certainly have made changes in it later.

I feel so bewildered and undecided that I cannot ask you too strongly to send me a really definite answer. Don't shrink from making strictures, they can only do me good. . . .

The compositions referred to in the letter to Joachim are the Variations on a theme by Schumann, Op. 9; the first version, for two pianos, of the most monumental work of Brahms's early period, his Pianoforte Concerto in D minor, which took him seven years to finish; and the Pianoforte Trio in B major, Op. 8, published in 1854, but revised and totally reshaped by Brahms thirty-seven years later, when he was at the summit of his mastery and wisdom.

JOSEPH JOACHIM TO BRAHMS

Berlin, 27 June 1854

My dearest Johannes, every note in your Variations warmed me, I revelled in their wealth of feeling and intelligence! In your charming modesty you ask me for criticism, whereas it is I who could learn from you. I find the Variations equal to the most beautiful and profound of their kind, not even excepting those of my favourite [Beethoven]; I avoided mentioning his name for fear of alarming you with such praise; but he lived in the early years of this century. Each variation is like a little temple for the worship of the spirit that lies concealed in the theme; the architecture of the temples is very varied, but the spirit moves lovingly through them all. You are a wonderful builder, but you conceal your art with such modesty, hiding its gems with such bashfulness. . . . But I must stop emptying the cornucopia of my enthusiasm over your head for fear of making you black and blue, my dear Johannes! If I could I would turn every one of the Variations into a triumphal arch and the theme into a laurel wreath for you to wear as I led you through them, you young Emperor of Music!

BRAHMS TO JOSEPH JOACHIM

[Düsseldorf, June 1856]

I sometimes ponder on variation form and it seems to me it ought to be more restrained, purer.

Composers in the old days used to keep strictly to the base of the theme, as their real subject.

Beethoven varies the melody, harmony and rhythm so beautifully.

But it seems to me that a great many moderns (including both of us) are more inclined – I don't know how to put it – to fuss about with the theme. We cling nervously to the melody, but we don't handle it freely, we don't really make *anything new* out of it, we merely overload it. And so the melody becomes quite unrecognizable.

JOSEPH JOACHIM TO GISELA VON ARNIM

Heidelberg, 20 June 1856

You ask for news of Brahms; all is very well with him, I am certain, for he must be feeling aware of his inner riches. Just lately he sent me some work, among which was a Fugue for Organ that combines depth and tenderness of feeling with a wealth of musical art so nobly that even Bach and Beethoven have scarcely excelled it. I was able to send him my heartiest congratulations, and I think myself fortunate in doing him more and more justice in my own mind. So poor Schumann with his enthusiasm was braver than any of those who laughed at his prophetic airs. . . .

KLARA SCHUMANN TO JOSEPH JOACHIM

Bonn, 28 July 1856

Only a few words! I have been here since yesterday with Johannes. . . . I saw him yesterday – you will not ask me to speak of my misery, but I did receive a few tender looks and I shall carry them with me to the end of my life! Once he even put his arms round me, he recognized me! Pray God for an easy end for him – it cannot be long now. . . .

Brahms adds:

Frau Schumann writes you this in case you might wish to see him again for the last time. But I want to add that you should think it over first, for it is a terribly moving and pitiful experience. Schumann has grown very thin and is quite unable to speak or show consciousness. Still, he did recognize his wife, he embraced her and smiled. . . .

BRAHMS TO JOSEPH JOACHIM

Hamburg, 12 December 1856

So I am sending you the Finale [of the Pianoforte Concerto in D minor] so as to be rid of it at last. Will it satisfy you? I doubt it very much. The end ought really to be good, but I don't find it so at present.

Thank you a thousand times for looking through the first movement with such care and kindness. I have learnt a great deal already from your excellent comments. All I can possibly wish myself as an artist is more talent, so that I could learn more from such a friend as you. . . .

BRAHMS TO JOSEPH JOACHIM

[*Early January 1857*]

I hope you are not hesitating to make big and bigger cuts in the Rondo? I know very well they are needed. . . . Dear Joseph, I am so happy to know that I can send you my things, it makes me feel twice as confident. . . .

I would very much like to know whether the variations are really worth printing. . . .

JOSEPH JOACHIM TO BRAHMS

Hanover, 12 January 1857

Your piece – as a whole I find it very remarkable: the bold pithy spirit of the first theme, the gentle, intimate B flat major, and particularly the solemn upward flight after the cadenza which brings it to a majestic conclusion – all this is rich enough to leave an edifying impression when one thoroughly absorbs its different aspects; yes, I think it could make a satisfying conclusion after the passionate breadth of the first movement and the lofty, devotional atmosphere of the second – were it not that much now comes in between which detracts from the beauty of the Finale and positively destroys the general impression by a kind of inconsistency, weakening it here and there by a rigid formalism as well. It seems as though when you first thought of the theme you had felt the glow of the creative artist, but that afterwards you had not allowed time for it to ferment until it really crystallized. Much of the development is forced – in fact, instead of advancing smoothly the harmony sometimes takes a step backwards, which I find doubly upsetting in your case. . . . After talking it over with Frau Schumann, I ended by wishing you would rewrite the last movement altogether, since alterations often give more trouble than an entirely new creation. *But it would be a pity to lose the many remarkable things in the Rondo, and you may still find yourself able to go back to work on it with the same vigour as at first and simply rewrite individual passages; that is what I should like best. . . .*

JOSEPH JOACHIM TO BRAHMS

Hanover, 7 May 1857

My dear Johannes, your Concerto gives me perpetual joy now that I have it by me with all its beauties, the last movement fully equal to the rest in substance. Once you have heard it I think there will be details you will want to touch up; but I won't bother you about points of detail when you have every reason to be delighted at having brought it to so happy a conclusion. I will add that in certain places I have already made changes in the instrumentation, and would like to do so, with all due respect, in a good many; in particular I feel tempted to alter some *Forte-Tutti* passages. But to do that I should have *to keep it by me for a time*. (I should like to wait on inspiration, and for that one must not be under pressure; for instrumentation too calls for invention.) May I do so? You don't need it just now. In the autumn you must come *here* and *listen to it* being played through first by Frau Schumann; the best way of bringing a piece to maturity is to hear it performed in its entirety, taking shape outside oneself. You can only be your own teacher. But I look forward like a child to my share in it. . . .

Brahms is never effusive. Some rare touches of tenderness in his letters are therefore incomparably warming and appealing.

BRAHMS TO JOSEPH JOACHIM

Hamburg, 13 December 1860

I shall whisper the question once more – would you perhaps like to spend Christmas here with us?

I can't make you any special invitation, of course, for what have I to offer? But the Christmas tree and our faces would be twice as bright this time as in other years. . . .

BRAHMS TO JOSEPH JOACHIM WITH THE PUBLISHED SCORE OF A NEW WORK, HIS SERENADE IN A MAJOR, OP. 16

Hamburg, December 1860

. . . And keep the piece by you with feelings of affection, dearest friend, for it belongs very much to you and its notes are for your ear. After all, from where does music draw such a friendly sound, if not from the few people one loves as much as I do you. . . .

BRAHMS TO JOSEPH JOACHIM

Hamburg, 3 October 1861

You will probably have sighed a little at seeing my Sextet already in print. It is true that if I had waited I might have been able to improve it, but waiting has its drawbacks as well.

So now I am to send my *Marienlieder* to Rieter, and though I used to enjoy hearing them they mean no more to me now than a blank sheet of paper; I do not like to send them out, I cannot alter them, in short I wish I were rid of them. . . .

The Sextet to which Brahms refers is the String Sextet in B flat major, Op. 18. Rieter was the publisher of the Marienlieder, Op. 22, for unaccompanied voices.

KLARA SCHUMANN TO JOSEPH JOACHIM

Leipzig, 15 December 1861

Yesterday Johannes' Variations [the Handel Variations] came out very well, and I had enthusiastic applause, curtain-calls, etc. The people I talked to afterwards did at least admit that they were 'interesting', though I found, as usual, that professional musicians are the hardest to impress – they cannot just accept a thing naturally and feel pleased that somebody has again written something intelligent; they can hardly bring themselves to admit that there is anything in it! . . . But at least they have all come to respect these Variations, and the rest will follow later; meanwhile I am delighted we have got so far. . . .

JOSEPH JOACHIM TO KLARA SCHUMANN

Basel, 4 November 1866

On the whole the journey gave me a lot of pleasure, if only because I really find that Johannes plays better and more freely every time, so that his genius is beginning to break through in his playing as well. He seems to enjoy his concerts, too, which encourages me to hope that he will gradually bring even the German audiences round to listening with pleasure instead of carping at him.

Both his [Pianoforte] Quartets gladdened me very much, at Zürich and at Aarau; for many passages in the A major are so tender and radiant that one need only call them to mind and one will forget an occasional inconsiderate action on the part of our friend. A man who writes like that must be noble and good!

With an uncanny insight into the most elusive secrets of great music and a resulting consciousness of the almost insoluble problems of creating a truly great work, Brahms's tendency to an almost hypochondriac mistrust in his own music became more and more accentuated and he was unable to speak of his work without deliberate understatement, even contempt. With a less elementary, exuberant creative gift, such an attitude would have been a grave danger to his productivity. What he incessantly demanded from his expert friends was a critical response, and his greatest happiness was a confirmation that, once more, he had succeeded. Even at the peak of his career, world-famous and saturated with success, he was disconsolate when the opinions of his friends proved negative, as happened at the first appearance of his Double Concerto for Violin and Violoncello. A gloomy despondency resulted, which may have been the reason why he wrote no more orchestral music.

Brahms was not merely fortunate in the choice of his friends; he deserved them. His unconditional adherence to the most sacred ideals necessarily attracted the very best and most congenial individuals; and they were devoted to him and to his art and every new work of his became a precious addition to their most cherished possessions. This can be gleaned from the letters of Joachim, and equally from Brahms's correspondence with Theodor Billroth, one of the pillars of the Vienna medical school, who was also a competent musician, or with his former pupil Elisabeth von Herzogenberg and her husband Heinrich, both distinguished musicians. There is a striking contrast between the ever-growing laconism of his communications – in his late years he rarely wrote more than postcards – and the enthusiastic effusiveness of such correspondents, in which so much of the emotional appeal of his music can be felt. Brahms would rarely utter his innermost thought; he would rather hedge himself behind a non-committal 'etcetera'. Nor could he easily make up his mind with respect to practical activities such as his conductorship with the Vienna 'Singakademie' in the sixties or the Vienna 'Gesellschaft der Musikfreunde' in the seventies, which he soon gave up again, feeling that he needed his freedom and independence more than the stimulus of this kind of work.

BRAHMS TO JOSEPH JOACHIM

Hamburg, November 1868

Now I am going to Vienna, and in January to Switzerland, continuing my amphibian life, half virtuoso, half composer. Just now the virtuoso is winning praise, which does not say much for the composer. . . .

BRAHMS TO JOSEPH JOACHIM

[*Vienna, March 1870*]

I have been receiving fairly strong hints about becoming Director of the *Gesellschaft* [the Society of Friends of Music in Vienna]. But I almost dread an official invitation, which would force me to consider the pros and cons. For much as I used to wish for some work of that kind, this post would bring too many drawbacks with it, and it is probably more sensible not to make the attempt. . . .

THEODOR BILLROTH TO BRAHMS

Vienna, 2 July 1876

In the last few days, being surfeited with thoughts and hungry for sentiments, I have plunged once again into your songs. It seems very boastful, but I really believe there are not so many people who can become immersed in these compositions as I do. Where can I find singers who can render them for me with the perfection they have in my imagination? . . . Even Hanslick probably responds to only a few of them with the perfect sympathy of my own response, which is as though the notes were sounding from the depths of my soul. . . .

THEODOR BILLROTH TO BRAHMS

Vienna, 8 November 1877

After studying your Symphony [No. 1, arranged for piano duet] with Dr Mikulicz the same evening that I had received it, I played it on Sunday with Hanslick, and admired the sureness with which he read and played the really difficult passages as he came to them. The general spirit of the composition, with its overtones of Faust, Bach, Beethoven, makes no appeal to him; there is nothing of Faust about him – on the contrary, it is the modesty of his demands on life that makes him so lovable. He has the enviable quality of enjoying everything beautiful that comes his way warmly and to the full, without allowing his pleasure to be clouded by a nagging desire for the unattainable. Happy man!

BRAHMS TO THEODOR BILLROTH

Vienna, 9 November 1877

I am arranging the new Symphony [No. 2] as a piano duet. This I usually do at the very last moment, when the fee is already in my pocket. This time entirely for your sake!

I hope the new piece will not, for a change, please *only* our gentle friend [Hanslick]!

Brahms's habitual doubts with respect to his new works became almost obsessive in cases such as his Violin Concerto, where he mistrusted his capacity for coping with the technical problems of an instrument he was not master of. A first performance was always an ordeal for him, with no end of hesitation and pangs of conscience.

JOSEPH JOACHIM TO BRAHMS

Berlin, 5 November 1878

Just a line to tell you I mean to be firm about Leipzig for 1 January because I cannot resist the prospect of perhaps being able to play your Concerto there with you. . . .

BRAHMS TO JOSEPH JOACHIM

Vienna, November 1878

Two things have been bothering me a great deal for some time, a No and a Yes.

I wanted to offer you my fingers for your concert here, but on the other hand I would like to keep my Violin Concerto by me for a while longer. I have not managed to make up my mind on the first point, though I am ashamed and angry with myself about it.

I have allowed my dislike for all concert-playing to grow far too strong, and have become far too much accustomed to playing only for myself. But now I am thoroughly depressed by the thought of you wandering about this country while I stand by in complete silence. The one thing that might serve the purpose would be my Concerto, which we could play here, at Budapest or at Prague. Except for your tour, however, I would have left that Concerto alone for a time, I consider it – but never mind. I have had a fair copy made of the solo part, and would like to send you the score soon, in the hope that you can tell me frankly whether this amounts to real hospitality! The middle movements have been cut out – naturally they were the best! But I am adding a wretched Adagio.

We had probably better let the Leipzigers go without that treat; after all we can still go over it here at the piano. . . .

BRAHMS TO JOSEPH JOACHIM

Vienna, 21 January 1879

I should be very grateful if you could have the solo part of the Concerto copied for me before your visit to England, and I would be particularly glad of any *ossia* [suggestions for changes]. I wish I could go through it with a violinist less good than you, for I am afraid you are not sufficiently blunt and severe! To impress me, you would have to make a great many suggestions and alterations!

BRAHMS TO JOSEPH JOACHIM

[Vienna, March 1879]

If you keep the Concerto by you longer, so much the better for it and for the world.

But I am very curious to know how frequently and energetically your writing will appear in the score and the part; whether I shall be 'convinced' or have to ask a second opinion, which I should not like to do. In short, is the thing at all good, and practical enough to be printed? . . .

THEODOR BILLROTH TO BRAHMS

Vienna, 20 June 1880

I have enjoyed much beauty in my life, for which I can consider myself fortunate; a man who plans his life on a large scale must not be surprised if his gradually widening circle finally begins to narrow again. To hold firm to you and your glorious art is a necessary part of life for me, it is rest and refreshment. So forgive me if I bore you occasionally!

BRAHMS TO THEODOR BILLROTH

Ischl, 28 August 1880

The *Akademische* [Academic Festival Overture] has lured me on to a second Overture; the only title I can think of for this is *Dramatische* [its final title was *Tragic Overture*] – which does not please me either. In the old days it was only my music I disliked, now it's the titles as well – is all this due to vanity?

Brahms's friendship with Joachim was clouded by the latter's divorce from his wife Amalie, whose part Brahms took at that occasion with some vehemence and probably in an offensive way. His Double Concerto, written in 1887, offered him a welcome opportunity for a reconciliation, after seven years of rather strained relations between the two old friends.

BRAHMS TO JOSEPH JOACHIM

Ischl, 27 July 1880

. . . But I had hoped your letter would strike a more comforting and optimistic note. It made me really unhappy, and I cannot get its depressing effect out of my mind. There was so much about you both to justify one's hopes that you would have a long, happy life together. And now! It is hard to imagine that there is any really serious cause for what could it be. Unfortunately it is difficult for me to see at all clearly into the matter, except to realize that it is certainly easier for two people to separate than to come together again, just as it is probably easier to lose one's wits than to recover them. So I will not say much or ask many questions, but just hope from the bottom of my heart that something unexpected – though not a misfortune – may occur to mend matters.

And then there is the discord of a friendship torn apart as well! I don't suppose you are in any mood for my work now, or for your own. . . . If any new development occurs, don't fail to let me know. The thought of you both is constantly thrusting itself upon me, and any better news would come as a relief. . . .

BRAHMS TO JOSEPH JOACHIM

Vienna, 20 October 1880

I am writing to make you a request that I am most anxious for you to think over and gratify. It concerns one of your singing students [at the Academy], Frl. Agnes Dönninghoff. I owe a great debt of affection and friendship to this girl's family (her grandparents!), and remember her grandfather with the warmest esteem it is possible to feel.

I learn that the D.s are finding it difficult to do as well for their children as they have done up to now.

So I would like first to ask, with regard to her studies at the Academy, whether it would be possible to obtain a scholarship for her, and whether she is promising enough to justify this? If not, then I would like to pay her fees – without her knowing it, of course.

In that case you could say (which will be true, in fact) that in addition to the free places officially awarded you have certain special funds to draw upon, or something of that kind. In short, now you know of my warm and eager wish to show my grateful affection to that family, I am sure you will send me a line at once to say it can be arranged like this. . . .

Have you no good news for me otherwise? I so much long to hear some! . . .

JOSEPH JOACHIM TO BRAHMS

Berlin, early November 1880

Fräulein Dönninghoff had made no application for a scholarship, so you can have the pleasure of carrying out your work of love in complete secrecy; we will do as you suggest, telling her a fund has been discovered out of which provision can be made for her. I wish we really had the money, but funds are completely exhausted until the Easter term; the Finance Minister is terribly parsimonious! Skinflint Prussian budgeting. Incidentally, Fräulein D. is said to be working hard and coming along nicely. . . .

BRAHMS TO JOSEPH JOACHIM

Thun, 24 June 1887

Brace yourself for a slight shock! Just lately I could not resist the sudden idea I had of a Concerto for *Violin and Violoncello*, hard as I kept trying to argue myself out of it.

Now I am completely indifferent to the whole thing, except as to what you might like to do about it.

Above all, I beg you, sincerely and affectionately, to be absolutely frank. If you send me a postcard to say 'Thank you for nothing', I shall know what else to say to myself, and in good measure.

Otherwise, here come my questions: would you like to see a sample of it? I am just writing out the solo parts; would it be too much trouble for you and Hausmann [the cellist of the Joachim Quartet] to see whether they are playable? Could you envisage the idea of trying out the composition somewhere or other with Hausmann, and myself at the piano, and ultimately playing it with us and an orchestra in whatever town you would prefer?

Please send me a line, and as I said before, I—Well, you may perhaps send that postcard after seeing the samples, too.

I won't say aloud and in detail what I am secretly hoping and what I would like. . . .

JOSEPH JOACHIM TO BRAHMS

Berlin, 27 July 1887

The solo parts have arrived, and so far as I can tell at a quick glance, the piece seems lively and delightful! I think that at the most there will be not more than four or five trifling alterations to be made in the violin passages; I took the score at once to Hausmann, who is excited and happy, and the next thing is for us to meet tomorrow to try fingerings or any necessary changes in the music. . . .

Meanwhile, a thousand thanks for the suggestion; before I go away I shall send you back the parts, with my pencil markings. . . .

ELISABETH VON HERZOGENBERG TO BRAHMS

Leipzig, 4 February 1880

You gave me real joy by sending me these splendid pieces [Two Rhapsodies, Op. 79, still in manuscript]. . . . They seem to me to be indescribably beautiful, and this impression grows stronger and stronger as I note their lovely curves and windings and their wonderful ebb and flow, which I find so moving in them both, and particularly in the G minor piece. . . . But although the G minor is my favourite, I fully appreciate the strong, pungent beauty of the B minor, with its very sweet Trio. And there is something absolutely unique about your way of hinting at the Trio theme beforehand; this whole passage, with the triplets for the right hand and the wonderful, fluent bass notes, is so perfect, again, that it leaves one speechless – only so glad that it concludes the piece, leaving one with this great final impression!

BRAHMS TO ELISABETH VON HERZOGENBERG

Vienna, May 1880

It is really not kind of you to go so far away without even giving me your address! That can bring the most flourishing business to a standstill, and I have a business question to put to you today. . . .

The thing is that I would like to publish the two piano pieces you know.

Can you think of a better title than *Two Rhapsodies for Pianoforte*? And you do not know of a better dedication; but will you allow me to put your beloved and honoured name to such rubbish?

And how should one write the name? Elsa, or Elisabeth? *Freifrau* or *Baronin*? *Née*, or not? . . .

ELISABETH VON HERZOGENBERG TO BRAHMS

Florence, May 1880

What a delightful surprise you have given me – for although now and then you had murmured something about your kind intention of 'dedicating something' to me, I had never taken it seriously, especially since that manuscript was so ignominiously torn away from me by Herr Allgeyer – and now, to my shame, I discover that it is precisely these magnificent pieces you think of dedicating to me, dear friend. There is no need for me to expatiate on the happiness it gives me; you know how fond I am of the pieces, and how glad I must necessarily be to see my name flaunting itself on something you have created. So I will only say thank you, but heartily and with great feeling! As for your question, you know I always prefer the non-commital term, 'Pieces for the Piano', for the very reason that it is non-commital; but I suppose that will not do, and *Rhapsodies* is probably the best title, though both pieces are so compact that they almost seem the contrary of rhapsodical. But of course it is more or less characteristic of these names that in the process of being used they have lost all character, and can thus be employed however one chooses, with no particular scruples, and a name is mere 'sound and vapour, a mist-wrapped glow from the firmament' [Goethe's *Faust*]. So welcome to my heart, these nameless ones in the misty robes of Rhapsodies!

Brahms had a nice collection of musical absurdities which, with his whole library, he left to the 'Gesellschaft der Musikfreunde' in Vienna. To him, the absurd offered a valuable negative confirmation of the facts of truth and common sense. His reaction to an absurd event on one of his frequent travels to Italy for recreation is rather amusing as a burlesque interlude.

BRAHMS TO THEODOR BILLROTH

Florence, 3 May 1881

This evening I am supposed to be going to a performance of the *Barber of Seville*, but – I really cannot trust my knowledge of Italian – said to be newly composed! This must really be a mistake, a misunderstanding on my part. . . .

BRAHMS TO BILLROTH

Pisa, 4 May 1881

Believe it or not, I did hear a new musical setting of the *Barber* last night! The man's name is Achille Graffigna, and the poster said: *Studio musicale informato allo spirito, al carattere, al colorito dell' immortal lavoro Rossiniano* [Musical study imbued with the spirit, the character and the colour of the immortal work by Rossini].

He conducted it himself, a man of 50. The music was just the kind of bloodless, prosaic stuff one would expect from a fellow capable of conceiving such an idea. Wherever possible, of course – key, time and so forth – he imitated his model. I thought I should be obliged to leave before long, out of sheer human sympathy, for at first he had a reception that forced him to keep mopping the sweat of anguish from his brow. Later – incredibly enough – things improved. Good singers, a good production – in short, the audience grew kinder. The idea in itself had not really outraged the Italians. As I left, posters announcing the second performance were being put up outside. But I had witnessed a piece of quite exceptional stupidity (to say the least of it). . . .

As already mentioned, Brahms was a master of understatement, which in his later years became almost a kind of mannerism. There is plenty of it in his letters.

BRAHMS TO THEODOR BILLROTH

Pressbaum, 11 July 1881

I am sending you enclosed a couple of little pieces for the piano [his Second Pianoforte Concerto, B flat major]; please don't show them to anyone else, and send them back to me as soon as possible to Pressbaum (Westbahn). If they interest you and you can gain any impression from the hasty, badly-written lines, perhaps you will let me know. Otherwise you will have to be patient until they are submitted to you once again in better writing by

Your
J. Br.

BILLROTH TO BRAHMS

Vienna, 11 July 1881

It is always a red-letter day for me when I receive one of your manuscripts, but today it gave me quite special pleasure. So now we have it at last, the long-awaited second Pianoforte Concerto! What a splendid composition, how effortlessly it flows along, with what splendid sound, noble and full of charm! . . . I cannot perceive its full wealth of detail as yet, of course, but the general effect, and the various individual passages, lie clearly before me; its relation to the first Concerto is that of the grown man to the youth; unmistakably the same, yet in every way sturdier, more mature. . . . I anticipate a specially poetical effect from the rapturous *adagio*, to which the instrumentation will contribute its share. Here a comparison with the *adagio* of the first Concerto at once springs to mind, and so far as I am concerned it operates decidedly in favour of the second; in the former one occasionally feels as though groping blindfold, whereas here the way is clear at once; and in this I find the melodic effects particularly superb. . . . Hanslick will have another attack of nerves if he has to play quavers with one hand and triplets with the other; but in my opinion it is just this that confers infinite fanciful charm. . . . If I have been chattering too much to you about your work, you have yourself to thank, for you invited it. . . . I would like to return the manuscript to you myself, so I shall come to Pressbaum the day after tomorrow (Wednesday), arriving at half past 6 and leaving again at 9 o'clock; and there are a few points I would like you to clear up for me on the piano. . . .

His Fourth Symphony is a typical example of the composer's pretended or genuine lack of self-confidence. It is true that it failed dismally when he played it to some friends of his in Vienna in an arrangement for two pianos. The Herzogenbergs proved considerably more responsive, although not quite without hesitation at first sight, which seems to have seriously disturbed him. However, the symphony conquered the public right from its first performance by the Meiningen Orchestra under von Bülow.

BRAHMS TO ELISABETH VON HERZOGENBERG WITH THE MANUSCRIPT OF THE FIRST MOVEMENT OF HIS FOURTH SYMPHONY

Mürzzuschlag, 29 August 1885

Will you allow me to send you a piece of a piece of mine, and would you have time to glance at it and send me a word about it? Generally speaking, my pieces are, unfortunately, pleasanter than I am, and people find less in them that needs putting right! The cherries in this part of the world never grow sweet and are uneatable – so if the thing is not to your taste don't hesitate to say so. I am not at all eager to write a bad No. 4. . . .

ELISABETH VON HERZOGENBERG TO BRAHMS

6 September 1885

The movement from the Symphony has already been heaving many sighs and groans under my unskilled hands. It is a really unique piece of misfortune that we have already announced our visit to Frau Schumann for tomorrow and cannot put it off; and we go away on the 10th and our hands are quite full with preparations. . . . So I shall make a poor showing tomorrow with dear Frau Schumann, and really don't know if I should venture to play her what little I can fumble out so far. If only I had had a little more time I should have been so happy and proud to play her the piece, but there are a lot of passages where I still get quite lost. . . .

BRAHMS TO HEINRICH VON HERZOGENBERG

Mürzzuschlag, 30 September 1885

It seems that my latest attack resulted in a complete defeat (and a Symphony at that). So I beg your dear wife not to misuse her charming gift for charming-letter-writing – not to tell me any fibs after the event. . . .

ELISABETH VON HERZOGENBERG TO BRAHMS

Berlin, 31 September 1885

Now I already know it much better, that precious E minor movement; I have so often played it over either in my mind or on the piano – really in every minute I could rescue from the work of settling in [the Herzogenbergs had just moved to Berlin] – that we have become quite intimate friends already. . . . I now have such a definite sense of the hills and valleys in this movement that I have lost the impression that it is complicated; or rather I have changed my mind about the complications being a defect, as I was inclined to think at first. . . . Just while I was struggling to write this very bad letter, your strange postcard of yesterday arrived (incredibly quickly). What can you possibly mean about a defeat? The memory of that excited Sunday afternoon spent with your composition, the sleepless night that followed, how I strolled up Frau Schumann's hill in bright sunshine on the Monday morning, with the music in my raincoat pocket (and scraps of it in my heart as well), Frau Schumann's kind little rosy cheeks glowing as she listened, and my excitement over the mission I could only carry out so imperfectly – that memory is one of the very fondest I possess, and now you talk so horridly about it. . . . Heinrich asks me to say that if his wife were less of a chatterbox he would not have lost the opportunity of thanking you himself for sending us the movement, and that he *implores* you to send some more. . . .

BRAHMS TO ELISABETH VON HERZOGENBERG

Vienna, 10 October 1885

You deserve to be given evidence that gratitude has not vanished from the face of the earth. And for the moment at least I can find no better way of demonstrating the fact than by sending you this Arrangement [for two pianofortes]. Now you can contemplate the landscape at your ease – through a rather dark glass. Of course this gives you the opportunity for drastic second thoughts.

In the Scherzo three timpani, triangle and piccolo naturally make a bit of a hubbub.

Can you really bear the Finale right to the end? . . .

But do let me hear something about it soon! Please, please!

I am still doubtful whether I should bother the public with it. Bülow, however, wants to lead off with it, preferably on 3 November, at Frankfurt! And here [in Vienna] they have already put it on, at their own risk.

And now thank you very much indeed for your dear letter – I needed it badly! For I am much more diffident about my work than you think. . . .

ELISABETH VON HERZOGENBERG TO BRAHMS

Berlin, 30 October 1885

Many, many thanks from the bottom of our hearts for your generous kindness in sending us the piano arrangement at once. True, we still see in a glass darkly, but heaven be praised we know the music of Brahms well enough for our imagination to help us with the notes, and we often felt we already knew as well how the other movements should really sound as we did with the first, which we know intimately already.

Dear friend, we are delighted with this new evidence of your power, and only wish we could *tell you* properly what a favourite it is certain to become.

The Andante is new and original as only you could make it, but it flows from an inner source you have not opened up before. . . . And how beautifully the second theme is introduced and briefly prepared for, and how all the cellists will revel in that magnificent, long-drawn-out, summer-bright melody! And you compare all this to the cherries at Mürzzuschlag, which never ripen and grow sweet? . . . This is a feast from which one rises satisfied and happy and tranquil, after which one really longs for a pause in which to attune oneself . . . for the wild, elemental humour of the Scherzo. But before long one is head over heels in that, gripped by its joyous, multi-coloured movement. When played in full array it must of course produce a very different effect from that necessary, sparse-sounding evil, the piano. . . . But now to the last movement – yes, will you let me love that the best, or at least let me think so for the time being? The theme sweeps me off my feet at once, and the way it changes from the bass to the treble and then hides, only to reveal its strength. . . . You asked the other day whether I could bear the last movement right to the end, and my answer is that I would not mind if it were three times as long; and in my opinion the public will surely appreciate it too, even if they cannot understand or follow this kind of *passacaglia*. For a thing so full of life, so continually novel, with no laborious spinning-out of threads, is bound to have its effect, to grip people and carry them along; thank heaven, one need not be a musician for that. . . . When passion lends such wings to ingenuity, people must needs respond to it. So don't ask if we can get through the last movement, because that is just fishing for compliments. . . .

JOSEPH JOACHIM TO BRAHMS

Frankfurt, 21 November 1890

A new composition from you is always a most joyful event for me, and I am waiting impatiently for it to come from the press. May we perform the Quintet [String Quintet in G major, Op. 111] in public on 10 December? At our last Quartet Concert we gave No. 1 [String Quintet in F major, Op. 88], and I should be delighted to provide a sequel. . . .

BRAHMS TO JOSEPH JOACHIM

Vienna, 27 November 1890

Naturally it is at your disposal for the 10th or any other date; but the mere performance of a new work doesn't count as a *Bravo* for me; that needs to be said separately!

However, I should set much greater store by any comments you might make on it, of whatever nature. . . .

I hope with all my heart that the piece may please you a little; but don't hesitate to tell me if it does not. In that case I shall console myself with my first one [Op. 88], and for both of them with Mozart's! . . .

JOSEPH JOACHIM TO BRAHMS

Berlin, 11 December 1890

The reception was enthusiastic, the packed house applauded every movement rapturously and I was compelled, willy-nilly, to let my rigid principles be disarmed by the sweetness of your delicious Intermezzo [the Third Movement] and allow it to be encored. Charm cannot be gainsaid! The Adagio received the least appreciation – to my surprise, for it is perhaps my favourite movement. . . .

The custom of not applauding single movements dates only from the nineteen-twenties.

BRAHMS TO JOSEPH JOACHIM

Ischl, 26 June 1891

And now I must thank you warmly for repeating your kind praise of my Quintet. Your pleasure in the thing is the greatest pleasure I could have myself. But I must not carry on like this, otherwise I shall again start thinking of nothing but myself and my own music. I can only be delighted if other people think more of it than I do – and feel astonished that with so little encouragement *from myself* I keep returning to the fray. . . .

BRAHMS TO HEINRICH VON HERZOGENBERG, ON THE DEATH OF ELISABETH

Vienna, January 1892

Dear friend,

Near as I am to you in my thoughts, I cannot write to you. I try in vain to express the feelings that are filling my heart to its very depths. And you will be sitting in your silent grief, with no word coming to you and indeed not wishing for one. . . . You know what an inexpressible loss the death of your cherished wife has been to me, and so you can imagine the feelings with which I think of you, who were as closely united with her as it is possible for two human creatures to be. . . .

It would help me so much if only I could sit quietly beside you, press your hand and join with you in thinking of that beloved, glorious woman. . . .

HEINRICH VON HERZOGENBERG TO JOSEPH JOACHIM

Berlin, 18 February 1893

Another great pleasure we had was the sudden arrival of Brahms; he was kinder and more affectionate to me than I have ever known him; at each visit he sat for a long time looking at the bas-relief of Liesl [Herzogenberg's deceased wife], and for once let me see quite calmly into the depths of his heart. At such times there is no one to compare with him! . . .

JOSEPH JOACHIM TO BRAHMS

[*Berlin, beginning of April 1896*]

Thank God, better news has come from Frankfurt today about Frau Schumann [Klara, seventy-six years old, lay on her deathbed]. My head swims at the thought of losing her, but we have to get used to the idea. . . .

BRAHMS TO JOSEPH JOACHIM

Vienna, 10 April 1896

But – I cannot agree that the subject of your letter is a sad thing. It has often occurred to me that Frau Schumann might survive all her children and me as well, but I never wished it for her. We can no longer be horrified at the thought of losing her – not even I, lonely as I am, with all too few ties to bind me to the world.

And after she has left us, will not our faces light up with joy whenever we think of her? The wonderful woman in whom we have delighted throughout a long life, with ever-increasing love and admiration.

That is the only way we should mourn her. . . .

Brahms was already seriously ill at this time. He survived Klara, his most beloved friend, by less than a year.

In the eighties and nineties, there lived two great musicians in Vienna, Anton Bruckner *(1824–96) and* Hugo Wolf *(1860–1903), who had the worst of the chronic strife between the 'Brahmins' and the 'Wagnerians'. This was not so much due to any action of Brahms himself – Wagner was dead by that time – but to Brahms's zealous partisans, such as the most influential critics in Vienna, Eduard Hanslick and Max Kalbeck, who would savagely attack those who stood in the opposite camp. This, however, and a glowing enthusiasm for the master of Bayreuth, were the only things Bruckner and Wolf had in common.*

It was a marvel of obstinate determination that Bruckner ever became a musician. He was thirty, a village schoolmaster in the Upper Austrian countryside, when he secured an appointment as cathedral organist in the provincial town of Linz. For seven years he sacrificed every penny he could spare to travel periodically to Vienna to have lessons with the renowned theoretician, Simon Sechter, whose successor at the Vienna Conservatoire he became in 1867.

One overwhelming experience, the impression of Wagner's music and personality, decided his loyalties and basically influenced his style which, however, remained as strikingly personal as his vision of a monumental symphony, spacious and vast like a Gothic cathedral. He had his first resounding success as a composer when he was in his sixties. He remained in Vienna a rustic outsider, had hardly any contact with intellectual circles and lived for nothing but his duties as a teacher and organist and his symphonies which, slowly but steadily, grew one after another and some of which he never even heard. Apart from a small group of friends and disciples, who enthusiastically supported him, he was hardly taken seriously by the majority of musicians in Vienna during his lifetime.

Bruckner's helplessness regarding all problems of practical life is pathetically reflected in his letters. He found the fair sex alluring, but was too shy and awkward for a successful courtship; the girls of his choice obviously found him unattractive. Desperately anxious to improve his situation, he passed examinations, submissively approached possible protectors, wrote applications and petitions, all in the florid, quaint style of a village schoolmaster of which he could never rid himself.

ANTON BRUCKNER TO IGNAZ ASSMAYR, CONDUCTOR IN VIENNA

St Florian, 30 July 1852

There is not a soul here to whom I can open my heart, and in many ways, indeed, I am misunderstood, which often gives me secret pain. Our Abbey is completely indifferent to music, and consequently to musicians – oh, if only I could meet and talk with you again soon! I know how warm-hearted you are, and it would be such a comfort! I can never give way to cheerfulness here, and never give any hint of my plans. In conclusion, I beg you again, *Herr Hofkapellmeister*, to remember me and not to deny me your kind favour if you see any opportunity to promote my fortunes; for which I shall be grateful all my life.

Your most devoted

Anton Bruckner, Abbey organist.

BRUCKNER TO HIS FRIEND RUDOLF WEINWURM IN VIENNA

Linz, 29 January 1865

I have a bitter week behind me. Having long ago given up my old love (partly on your advice), I turned my attentions to the adopted daughter of a respectable local family, which also has a daughter of its own; but the girl is to have perhaps 6,000 florins, so I was certainly not a fortune-hunter. People encouraged me, her adopted father himself advised me to join the social club and even said he had a bride for me. . . .

Yet when I sent the girl the Schubert Serenade she wished to have, my present was returned to me – so you see even my modest plans miscarry in this place. I am sick of the whole world – all I have left is art, and a few valued friends, of whom you are always the foremost. . . .

BRUCKNER TO JOSEFINE LANG

[*1866*]

Most honoured, gracious Lady,
Convinced that you have long been aware of the silent but unremitting hopes I have set on you, I now take up my pen to importune you. My greatest and most fervent request, which I now venture to put to you, Fräulein Josefine, is that you will be so kind as to give me a frank, final and quite decisive answer in writing, for the sake of my future peace of mind, to the question of whether I may hope for your hand, and ask your dear parents to grant it to me? Or do you feel unable, for lack of inclination towards my person, to contemplate marriage with me? You see, the question is quite decisive, and I ask you to write to me, as quickly as possible, telling me just as decisively, but *definitely as decisively*, either that *I may ask for your hand*, or that *I must give up the idea for ever* (do not try to hedge or to put me off with an ambiguous reply, for it is high time I knew where I stand), besides your feelings are not likely to change, for you are a very reasonable being. I beg you to tell me the strict truth without scruple, for *in either case* it will contribute to my peace of mind. . . .

BRUCKNER TO FÜRST KONSTANTIN HOHENLOHE, IMPERIAL CHAMBERLAIN, APPLYING FOR THE POST OF COURT ORGANIST MADE VACANT BY THE DEATH OF HIS TEACHER SIMON SECHTER

Linz, 14 October 1867

The respectful applicant was born in the year 1824 at Ansfelden in Upper Austria; until 1855 he was teacher and Abbey organist at St Florian, and has since then been organist of Linz Cathedral. . . . He now feels justified in begging on his knees that you may be graciously pleased to recommend that His Imperial Majesty shall deign to admit him to the Imperial Court Chapel as Imperial Court Organist, or as a supernumerary, unpaid Imperial Deputy Court *Kapellmeister*. In the latter case the title and its future prospects would be sufficient to ensure him the necessary income. Furthermore, he could be of use on the chancery staff or as a schoolteacher for the senior classes, having also followed a teaching career for 14 years. . . .

BRUCKNER TO RUDOLF WEINWURM IN VIENNA

Linz, 27 May 1868

Soon after your kind letter, Court *Kapellmeister* Herbeck came to tell me that I could be Sechter's successor at the Conservatory, with a yearly salary of 600 florins. Nine hours' teaching per week – 6 hours' counterpoint and 3 hours' organ class. He said the offer would be sent to me in writing and I could make up my mind then. Although I can never, by lawful means, become a salaried organist in the Court Chapel, which is very sad, this is a very honourable offer. What do you think about it? Write to me quickly! I am not entitled to a pension at Linz, either. Can I manage, at a pinch, on 600 florins? . . .

With a nervous lack of resolution and self-confidence, Bruckner was often in doubt with respect to his work and he would revise and rewrite his scores over and over again. Owing to this there are different versions of all his symphonies, and it is not always easy to decide between the merits of one version or another. The first of his symphonies to appear in print, the Third, was dedicated to Wagner whom Bruckner visited in Bayreuth and who was kind and appreciative to him.

BRUCKNER TO THE DRAUGHTSMAN JOSEF MARIA KAISER WHO WAS TO DESIGN THE TITLE-PAGE FOR HIS THIRD SYMPHONY

[*Vienna, 1872*]

I would like everything relating to me or my work to be kept very simple, only the references to Wagner, and in particular his name, to be given the greatest prominence.

Symphony in D Minor
Dedicated
to that incomparable, world-famous, sublime
Master of Poetry and Musical Composition,
Mr Richard Wagner
with the most profound respect,
by
Anton Bruckner

I would like you, at the very most, to decorate the title, 'Symphony in D minor', with a few pen-drawn arabesques. The name left quite plain. This has a definite significance. But if you think it would be better to reserve all decoration for Wagner's inscription, I am perfectly willing. But on the name 'Richard Wagner' I would like you to use some simple but dignified gold illumination, if you will be so kind.

But my own name should be quite plain (with no marked character) and unadorned. This has the advantage that I shall have the thing more quickly; I am longing for it already. . . .

So let everything be dignified and simple, with the greatest brilliance and pomp for Richard Wagner alone (without detracting from the dignified simplicity). I think we have everything straight now, and please be assured that I shall not be alarmed by your bill, particularly as everything else is simple. The fact that his name is to stand out brilliantly has a definite significance as well. So I hope, for particular reasons, that you will not keep me waiting, and I am greatly looking forward to the thing. . . .

BRUCKNER TO MORITZ VON MAYFELD IN LINZ

Vienna, 12 January 1875

My 4th Symphony is completed. I have made some more considerable improvements in the Wagner Symphony (D minor). Hans Richter, Wagner's conductor, has been in Vienna, and mentioned in several circles how highly Wagner praised it. But it doesn't get performed. . . . Herbeck once told me I should try to ask Wagner to help me in some way. All I have is my Conservatory salary, and it is quite impossible to live on that. As long ago as September, and again later, I was obliged to borrow money so as not to starve (700) [a year's salary]. Nobody gives me any help. . . . By good luck a few foreigners have turned up and are taking lessons with me, otherwise I should have to go out begging. . . . Wild horses would not have dragged me to Vienna if I had foreseen all this. My enemies would have no difficulty in hounding me out of the Conservatory. I'm surprised it hasn't happened already. . . .

BRUCKNER TO WILHELM TAPPERT IN BERLIN

Vienna, 12 October 1877

I have come to the firm conclusion that my 4th Romantic Symphony is in urgent need of radical revision. For instance, in the Adagio there are some violin passages which are so florid and difficult as to be unplayable, and here and there the instrumentation is over-elaborate and restless. Even Herbeck, who likes the composition extremely, made the same remarks and confirmed me in my determination to *rewrite* parts of the Symphony. . . .

BRUCKNER TO ANTON VERGEINER IN FREISTADT

Vienna, 9 May 1884

Sechter was my teacher from 1855 until the end of November 1861, when I took my final examinations at the Vienna Conservatory and, as a result, got my appointment in Vienna in due course. (I used to work for 7 hours a day at Linz, and gave many piano lessons; and every year I paid one or two visits to Vienna, staying 6 or 7 weeks, and spending the whole of every day with my teacher. . . .)

Apart from Herbeck, Mr Hanslick was my greatest and finest source of encouragement. Until 1874 (when I was appointed to a lecturer's post at the University) he kept writing about me in terms I seldom hear nowadays. He even singled me out for praise as composer and conductor. By the way, please do not scold Hanslick about me, for *his rage is terrible*, it takes him to the verge of murder. One cannot fight him, only approach him as a suppliant. *And I cannot even do that*, for he always refuses to see me. . . .

Bruckner's humility towards conductors, even towards his own pupils and disciples such as Nikisch or Mottl, is pathetic, as is his dread of the ferocious critics in Vienna, when he humbly applies to the committee of the Philharmonic Orchestra not *to perform his Seventh Symphony, in order not to endanger the current success of this work in Germany by a fiasco in Vienna.*

BRUCKNER TO ARTHUR NIKISCH IN LEIPZIG

Vienna, 11 June 1884

May I ask again, is the concert to take place? On the 21st? And if so, when are the last two rehearsals, which I should so much like to attend? Otherwise I may perhaps hear the work only *once*, for I can do no good in Vienna; that is why I am so eager to hear it, unless you think I ought *not* to come. If you would like me to be there, I shall have to ask for leave of absence from my various superiors, so do please let me hear soon! It would give me boundless pleasure to know that my youngest child was being brought into the world by the foremost German conductor! I am very much excited already. . . .

BRUCKNER TO FELIX MOTTL IN KARLSRUHE

Vienna, 17 April 1885

Dearest old young friend!
Noble Court *Kapellmeister*!
This must be that fellow Bruckner, you'll say, and sure enough it is. Now listen: Prof. Riedel of Leipzig has asked me to have the Adagio from my Seventh Symphony performed at the All-German Music Festival at Karlsruhe on 30 May. Liszt and Dr Standhartner advise me to agree. But now you are the leading figure in the question.

1. Isn't the orchestra too hostile to me?

2. Have you the new tubas, as used in the Nibelungen? Or can you get them?

3. Would you be willing, like Mr Levi and Mr Nikisch, to fling yourself body and soul into the fray for your old ex-teacher, who has always been so fond of you, and to study and conduct this Adagio with the tubas and the funeral music for our most blessed Master [Wagner] as though it were your own composition? If you can work up an enthusiasm for this, you, being such a famous conductor, are the right man for it!

If my dear Mottl will promise me this on his word of honour as a German, then Hip, Hip, Hurrah! . . .

BRUCKNER TO THE COMMITTEE OF THE VIENNA PHILHARMONIC CONCERTS

Vienna, 13 October 1885

Esteemed Committee!
I beg to request with all submission that the esteemed Committee will cancel for this year the plan – by which I am honoured and delighted – to perform my E major Symphony [the Seventh]. This request is prompted solely by the melancholy local situation with respect to the leading representatives of the press which could only be detrimental to the success I am now beginning to enjoy in Germany. . . .

Reading the following letter, one will learn to appreciate not only the problems of an artist of Bruckner's lofty loneliness, but also the honesty and goodwill of a famous, over-worked conductor, who studied a new score with earnest devotion, but, in spite of the utmost sympathy with the composer, failed in his approach to it.

HERMANN LEVI TO JOSEF SCHALK IN VIENNA

Munich, 30 September 1887

I am at my wits' end and I must appeal to you for advice and help. To put it briefly, I am completely at sea in Bruckner's Eighth Symphony, and haven't the courage to present it.

I am quite sure it would meet with intense opposition among the orchestra and the public. That would not matter to me, if I myself were fascinated by it as I was by the Seventh – if I could say to the orchestra, as I did then, 'By the fifth rehearsal you will have come to like it'. But I am terribly disappointed! I have studied the work for days on end, but I cannot grasp it. Far be it from me to criticize – it is quite possible that I am wrong, that I am too stupid or too old – but I find the instrumentation impossible, and what particularly shocks me is the great resemblance to the Seventh Symphony, almost amounting to mechanical copying. The opening passage of the first movement is grand, but I am nonplussed by the development.

As for the last movement, it is Greek to me.

What is to be done? It makes me shudder to think of the effect of this news on our friend! I cannot write to him. Should I suggest that he come here to listen to a rehearsal? In my despair I showed the score to a musician friend of mine, and he agreed that it could not possibly be performed. Do please write at once to tell me how I should approach Bruckner. If it were merely a question of his thinking me an ass, or worse still, a faithless friend, I would make the best of it. But I am afraid of something worse, I am afraid the disappointment may quite dash his courage. Do you happen to know the Symphony well? And can you make anything of it? Help me, I really do not know what to do!

The addressee, one of Bruckner's most faithful disciples, seems to have shared the conductor's doubts. The result was that Bruckner, deeply disturbed but undaunted, recast his work, as he had done so often with others. Only five years later his Eighth Symphony, in its final version, was performed for the first time. A performance planned by Weingartner in Mannheim in 1891 did not materialize.

JOSEPH SCHALK TO HERMANN LEVI

Vienna, 18 October 1887

Your news naturally came as a great blow to Professor Bruckner. He is still unhappy about it and not to be comforted. It was only to be expected, and yet it was the gentlest way of sparing him a bitter disappointment. I hope he will soon calm down and begin revising the composition in the light of your advice; in fact he has already started on the first movement. For the time being it would be better for him not to work, as he is agitated and in despair about himself, with no self-confidence at all. But with his colossal reserves of physical and moral energy he will soon get over this. . . .

BRUCKNER TO HERMANN LEVI

Vienna, 27 February 1888

I certainly ought to be ashamed of myself – at least on this occasion – about the Eighth. What an ass! It is already beginning to look quite different. . . .

BRUCKNER TO HANS VON WOLZOGEN IN BAYREUTH

Vienna, 1 January 1889

I have quite recovered my health and have been working since last June on the Third Symphony, in D minor (the Wagner Symphony), which I have improved tremendously. If only that noble, immortal genius could see it himself! What indescribable bliss for me!

BRUCKNER TO FELIX WEINGARTNER IN MANNHEIM

Vienna, 27 January 1891

On Sunday the D minor Symphony, No. 3, had its second performance. Conductor: Hans Richter – ideal. Performers: the Philharmonic Orchestra – perfection. And with this, the most sensitive audience, an enthusiasm and applause that could not have been greater. Couldn't you get this into the papers? It would be an excellent thing! How is the Eighth getting along? Have you started rehearsals yet? What does it sound like? Please *cut the Finale firmly, as indicated*; otherwise it would be far too long, and it is only suitable for posterity, and for a circle of friends and connoisseurs. And please alter the tempi to your heart's content (as you find necessary for the sake of clarity). . . .

There is no parallel among composers to Bruckner's fond belief in a conductor's infallibility; nor is there any of such an odd combination of a visionary genius and a simple mind.

Hugo Wolf *was his exact opposite. Whereas Bruckner never felt anything but an alien in the big city, Wolf was a town-dweller born and bred. Bruckner's pious, strict Catholicism and Wolf's modern intellectual scepticism, Bruckner anxiously trying to secure a regular job, however poorly paid, and Wolf never able to submit to the discipline of practical activities – they represented totally different attitudes. With his modest demands Bruckner could find his peace and comfort in safe seclusion; Wolf, a tragic case without comparison, never arrived at a state of tolerable material and mental balance.*

As an artist he grew, with a negligible technical training, on his own assiduous work, led by a true poet's feeling for lyrical expression and an instinctive refinement and fastidiousness. His life stood under the strain of an ever recurring change from blissful creative periods to the despair of temporary sterility. When his inspiration was roused, he would work from morning to night in a frenzy of enthusiasm. The 'Mörike-Songs', the 'Italian Songbook', the opera 'The Corregidor' were written like this, in creative bursts of violent intensity, followed by weeks and months of depressed apathy. Apart from this, a permanent nervous irritability put a strain on his social relations. His earnings were rare windfalls. In general he lived, a true Bohemian, on the help of wealthy friends and admirers, who also took the financial responsibility for the printing of his works, for which no publisher could be found. When in the early years of this century his fame began to rise, his mind was no longer alive: insanity had put an end to his creative work in 1897, but he lingered on for another five years of gradual mental and physical disintegration.

HUGO WOLF TO HIS FRIEND OSKAR GROHE IN MANNHEIM

Unterach am Attersee, 6 June 1890

You are absolutely right, and I am ashamed, now, of having been so mistrustful. Yes, I am very mistrustful; but anyone who has experienced so many bitter disappointments, met with such flagrant treachery, ingratitude and meanness, is bound to grow mistrustful in the end. I may as well confess that I sensed a kind of conspiracy against me, and looked on everybody at Mannheim (except you) as my deadly enemies. I saw myself as once again scorned there, pitied, or at best, buried. It's that cursed passion that keeps driving me back into the arms of the devil of distrust. And then, of course, I can rage like a bad-mannered child, can't I? I am furious with myself! I may count myself lucky to have a considerate, understanding friend like you. I am as childish and irritable as Tasso [in Goethe's tragedy], while you are as wise and shrewd as Antonio, but without his undercurrent of cynicism; you can look upon the world coolly, see it for what it is, and yet carry a warm heart in your breast. Lucky fellow! how much pleasanter life would be for me if I had a little of your balanced character. Now, unfortunately, you've seen the disagreeable side of my nature; in future I shall try to show myself to you only in the most favourable light. . . .

WOLF TO OSKAR GROHE

Ober-Döbling [*Vienna*], *8 May 1891*

Unfortunately I feel completely exhausted, both physically and mentally. As for composing, the whole idea seems to have left me. God knows how it will end! Pray for my poor soul. If only the Allegro for the Overture were written, at least! The thought of it lies like a dead weight on my heart. But to write music without inspiration – horrible! This dreamy, idle, loitering existence is driving me to despair. If there were even a war or some other excitement! This idyllic, vegetable life will be the death of me, it's becoming unbearable!

Wolf had accepted a commission for incidental music to Ibsen's 'Fest auf Solhaug'.

WOLF TO FRAU GROHE

Unterach am Attersee, 6 June 1891

Creative work makes me happy, but the subsequent pauses for rest are all the more painful, for then one begins to think things over, reflection sets to work to shatter the picture built up by imagination, and cold common sense resumes its pettifogging rights. In fact happiness is not for me, so let us leave it at that. . . .

WOLF TO OSKAR GROHE

Bayreuth, 21 July 1891
[*From the Festival*]

The state of my nerves is taking all the pleasure out of my stay here. I get hardly any sleep at night, and unfortunately it comes on in the daytime, during the performances at the theatre. For instance, I literally slept through a great deal of the 1st and 3rd Acts of *Parsifal*. Luckily things went better with *Tristan*, which enchanted me nearly all the way through. . . .

WOLF TO FRAU GROHE

Traunkirchen, 20 September 1891

I gave up all thought of Berlin long ago. That is a place that needs energetic, pushful, industrious, excitable men, pursuing their aim relentlessly, always on the look-out for an advantage and able to exploit it cleverly. Whereas I have become an absolute nightcap, as lazy as an Eskimo and as fatalistic as a Moslem. In short, I am utterly unsuited for Berlin, and indeed for life in general, which disgusts me more with every passing day. . . .

WOLF TO OSKAR GROHE

Vienna, 19 December 1891

Do you know, in the first twelve days of December I composed thirteen songs! And such beauties! Unfortunately, this productive mood didn't last as long as I hoped. I was planning to write another thirty-three *Italienische Lieder* in December. This inordinate ambition may be excused and justified, considering how triumphantly I started out. But man proposes and influenza disposes! In the full tide of work I fell victim to that most idiotic of all illnesses, which reduced me to a wreck for a few days; and now I have recovered my physical powers, the intellectual ones have gone to the devil. I haven't had an idea since then – not one. Isn't it enough to drive one mad?

WOLF TO FRAU GROHE

Berlin, 2 March 1892

I am just home from Professor ——'s house. There's a real German boor for you! And his wife, what an affected goose! M. had invited me to an 'informal' dinner at 5 o'clock. There was a large company, consisting of some not bad-looking women and some baboon-like men. Nobody had a word to say to me, least of all the host and hostess. They were high priests of the Brahms cult and may have been offended by my heretical views on his music; at any rate, they simply ignored me. I did the same, didn't eat a mouthful, drank no wine, and took myself off as soon as the meal was over. It was the most lousy company I was ever in, and they won't catch me again in a hurry. . . .

WOLF TO FRAU GROHE

Berlin, 6 March 1892

I am delighted to be able to tell you that my concert was a most decided success. It is true that only two pieces were encored, but if I had been more ready to give way to the audience I could have repeated at least 6 of the *Lieder*. The applause was warm and unrestrained. . . . It was an unmistakable success, and I am beginning to consider seriously whether I ought not to move to Berlin for a time. I like the people here more and more, with the exception of a few fools and knaves such as ——.

WOLF TO OSKAR GROHE AND HIS WIFE

Döbling, nr. Vienna, 19 March 1892

Were you really so much upset by my references to the 'lousy company' – *sit venia verbo*? Well, I readily admit it isn't exactly the choicest *epitheton ornans* with which to sum up a certain category of people. For your sakes I shall try to express myself with more restraint about Herr Professor M. and his lady, though I cannot think more favourably of them. M., who at once gave me the impression of being a Malvolio, with a kind of smug vanity that could brook no contradiction, reacted to a difference of opinion between us – when I ventured on a slight criticism of Brahms – by assuming an air of studied defiance. His charming wife followed his example. As a result, while the other guests gradually assembled, I was left entirely by myself. . . .

WOLF TO OSKAR GROHE

Vienna, 8 February 1893

My dear fellow, you let fall a little word - between ourselves, a thoughtless little word - about composing 'industriously'.

Leave me in peace once and for all with damned 'industrious' composition. The artist is not a day labourer, my friend. The periods of inspiration are red-letter days, and, as I presume you realize, every day is not Sunday. I cannot say yet, 'The time has come'. But if it does come, it will always be time to say something worthwhile. Chatter can be left to those who have no time to wait for ideas. And so God bless!

WOLF TO HIS FRIEND HUGO FAISST IN STUTTGART

Perchtoldsdorf [near Vienna], 18 April 1895

Today I am taking advantage of a short pause in my creative impulse to send you just a few words. The chief news is that I have been at Perchtoldsdorf since 1 April and since the first day I have been working furiously on my opera [*The Corregidor*]. The fair copy of quite a number of scenes has been made already. I work every day almost without interruption from 7.30 in the morning until 7 at night, and think of nothing except getting the opera finished as quickly as possible. . . .

WOLF TO HUGO FAISST

Schloss Matzen, 26 May 1895

By way of latest news, be it known to you on the 24th inst. I began work on Act II. I expect to finish composing the whole opera in July. You can imagine how the work delights me, and I am throwing myself into it heart and soul. . . .

WOLF TO HUGO FAISST

Matzen, 9 July 1895

I finished the opera today. But I can't send you the manuscript until tomorrow, for I have friends coming and need to keep it by me for them. . . .

WOLF TO HUGO FAISST

Vienna, 10 March 1896

Yesterday, or it may have been the day before, our mutual friend Mrs K. handed me a heavy registered letter from Stuttgart. It was from a Stuttgart Bank, sending me the sum of a thousand marks on the instructions of a 'customer' together with a banker's draft for the equivalent in Austrian money. Of course I was not for a moment in any doubt as to the identity of the mysterious 'customer', for all his discreet attempt to hide behind that term. Our friend Grohe had already prepared me for the unavoidable, and since all protests were in vain I laid down my weapons and surrendered. But the gods were gracious, and the unprecedented, the unhoped-for, has now happened – from one day to the next I have become a capitalist, thanks to the loyal help and unselfish devotion of true-hearted friends to me and my work. . . .

WOLF TO OSKAR GROHE

Vienna, 24 March 1897

Just lately, with the help of a few really sublime ideas, I turned out some settings for poems by Michelangelo. . . . To give you some idea of what a terrific fellow Michelangelo was as a poet too, I'm sending you the first of the songs I composed:

> Much do I dwell upon my former state,
> And on life's course before my love for thee;
> Then was I lonely and disconsolate,
> Each dismal day a wasted day for me . . .

It will delight you. But I think the second poem is even more important, and it seems to me to be the best thing I have strummed out so far:

> All things living have their ending,
> All with all things fused and blending.

If that doesn't send you right out of your mind with emotion, then you've never had a mind. It really is enough to drive one crazy, and at the same time it has a staggering, an absolutely classical simplicity. I tell you, you'll open your eyes! I am really scared by this composition, it makes me fear for my reason. I'm turning out such anti-social and mortally dangerous things just now. . . .

WOLF TO HUGO FAISST, AFTER THE FIRST ATTACK OF HIS MENTAL ILLNESS

Cilli, 2 February 1898

You need not worry about the risk of my over-working. On the contrary, I have developed a real distaste for work and feel as though I should never write another note. I am not in the least tempted by the idea of continuing to work at my unfinished second opera [*Manuel Venegas*], in fact everything to do with music is repugnant to me. That is where my anxious friends have landed me. How I shall get along in my retirement remains to be seen; but I have already been through so many trials that I hope to get over this hurdle too, one way or another. To be sure we are all decadents, and that is some comfort, though a slight one. . . .

WOLF TO HUGO FAISST

Vienna, 21 April 1898

My appetite is excellent, and as for my depression, it is really nothing but a quiet, placid humour, which many people find strange and ascribe to depression. The majority of people are offended because I do not welcome visitors, refuse invitations almost systematically, and hardly ever repay a call. But I feel I now have the right to live as I choose and not as it suits other people – all the more since I keep myself entirely to myself and make no approaches to anybody. One can scarcely ask less of one's fellow-men than that they shall leave one in peace. . . .

Some months later, hopelessly deranged, Wolf had to go to an asylum where he stayed until his death.

THE SLAVONIC SPRING TIDE

From Smetana to Tchaikovsky

In the second half of the nineteenth century the Russian and Czech nations contributed in the most conspicuous way to the great heritage of music. The Russian contribution coincided more or less with the most momentous achievements of Russian literature; both were symptoms of the cultural maturity of a people which had entered the community of European nations only since the reign of Peter the Great, in the eighteenth century, but to which the Czech people had belonged since the Middle Ages. Bohemia, their land, was part of the Austrian monarchy and its administration was unconditionally German, till the widespread revolutionary unrest of 1848 reached it. From that time Czech nationalism came gradually into its own as a political movement, and the founder of that movement in the field of music was Bedřich Smetana *(1824–84).*

The Czech evolution towards national sovereignty, reached in the end as a result of the First World War, was actually led by the cultural representatives of the nation, chiefly by the musicians, whose European fame and authority preceded and certainly facilitated the progress to political independence. In this respect, Smetana and Dvořák have played an incalculable part in projecting their nation's picture to the world.

There has never been a national movement without dissensions and party strife, and this is as true of artistic as of political issues. Smetana was a Lisztian and Wagnerian, Dvořák a Brahmsian, and to radical Russian nationalists such as Balakirev or Mussorgsky, Anton Rubinstein was a 'Westerner', feared and hated, and his pupil, Tchaikovsky, a semi-Westerner.

When Smetana came to the fore, the public performance of music in Bohemia was practically restricted to Prague, the capital, and it was mainly German, maintained by the culturally predominant German minority. All he could do was to make himself known as a pianist and to make a living as a piano teacher. In 1856 a conductorship in Göteborg in Sweden offered him wider opportunities. Some years later a kind of national autonomy, granted by the Austrian government, brought the first possibility of an independent Czech cultural development, and Smetana returned to Prague in 1861 to take a leading part in the creation of Czech opera and in the organization of a national opera-house. It was an uphill struggle, with scanty means and a public which only gradually developed into a culturally minded community. Smetana's conscious approach to this problem resulted in a truly popular operatic style, of which 'The Bartered Bride' has remained an unsurpassed model.

BEDŘICH SMETANA TO HIS PARENTS

Göteborg, 23 December 1856

You know that I am now in the town of Göteborg in Sweden and probably also that I shall make my future domicile here. Why this is so and what moved me to undertake this journey you will probably have guessed. Prague did not wish to recognize me, so I have left it. It is a daily occurrence that the homeland will not recognize her sons, and that the artist has to seek a name and a better existence for himself abroad. This is also my fate. . . .

I have given two concerts and earned great praise but not what you would call much money. I immediately got more lessons than I can possibly cope with, and I have also started a school – although I have still to learn the language – and the Society for the Promotion of Music has chosen me as its director. It is this last which most tempts me to stay here. To all appearance my standing here is better than at home in Prague. But it will nevertheless not be possible to save anything out of my earnings for the first few years because my expenditure is greater than it ever was at home. I have to keep my family and myself, to pay for two apartments and I shall have to pay all my debts in Prague this year. I therefore ask you to allow me to pay you monthly the equivalent of 10 *gulden* in silver of the 400 *gulden* that I owe you until next year when I shall be able to pay you the remainder. . . .

SMETANA TO FRANZ LISZT AT WEIMAR

Göteborg, 10 April 1857

What moved me most to stay here is the wide field of activity open to my art. Out of the sad remains of the old Mozart Society, a new Society for Classical Music, old and modern, has grown up. This society has elected me its director with a fee of 100 Swedish *thalers* a month. We come together once a week on an appointed day and great works are then studied. This gives me the best possible opportunity of doing something to further the progress and form the taste of these people. I chose Mendelssohn's *Elijah* for our first object of study, so that it should be possible *gradually* to arouse pleasure in and understanding for the new masters. I was also happy in that this work could be publicly performed. But what it means to study such a work with choristers who are mostly amateur singers – with runaway solos – and an orchestra consisting partly of members of military bands, partly of inexperienced dilettanti, you can form only the haziest notion. Nevertheless the performance was so far successful that a repetition of the same work for Easter was generally requested. This performance is to take place this week in one of the local churches in aid of the poor.

So you see, honoured friend, that I am effectual here in a way in which I could never have been in Prague and, since I have found receptive soil for what is good, I hope to be able to give the direction of art a most pleasurable turn for the better in a very short time. Apart from this I have played a great deal of Wagner, of Schumann and of your works in smaller circles and I found what I was looking for: a receptive public. The inhabitants of Göteborg have, until now, been left so much to themselves that they have no idea what is happening in music. They are mostly very rich merchants who practised art as something rather superfluous and only as much as was necessary to allow them to bandy the word about and in as far as it provided them with light entertainment. But now they really ask for more and it seems that they like both my energy and my obdurate defence of the great masters of the present. I hope to get better and wider results next season. . . .

SMETANA TO DR LUDEVIT PROCHÁZKA IN PRAGUE

Göteborg, 11 March 1860

Honoured Sir,
First of all I would ask you to excuse all my mistakes, both in spelling and grammar of which you will certainly find plenty in my letter, for up to the present day I have not had the good fortune to be able to perfect myself in our mother tongue. Educated from my youth in German, both at school and in society, I took no care, while still a student, to learn anything but what I was forced to, and later divine music monopolized all my forces and my entire time so that, to my shame, I must now confess that I can not express myself adequately or write correctly in Czech. But this reproach falls not only on me, but also on our schools! However, I need hardly repeat that I am Czech, body and soul, and that it is my pride to be the heir to our glory. I am therefore not ashamed to answer you in my mother tongue, albeit imperfectly, and I am glad I am able to show you that my homeland means more to me than anything else. . . .

FROM SMETANA'S DIARY

5 January 1862

It was a Sunday on which my concert was launched in the large precincts of the Zofín Hall. Ugh! how empty and cold it was! Outside the snow was falling fast and it soon covered up the tracks of the few people who came to my concert because they had been given free tickets; shortly after the concert had begun nobody could have traced their tracks in the snow. Yes indeed, a prophet is without honour in his own country. I had thought that if only out of curiosity, people might have wanted to hear a compatriot who, after six years, was once again visiting his home town. Not at all! I had to pay 280 *gulden* deficit.

SMETANA TO HIS FRIEND J. P. VALENTIN IN GÖTEBORG

Prague, 20 April 1865

Attacked by many, by many misjudged, whether purposely or otherwise is of no importance, I see all my endeavours in the field of art put off to some distant and indefinite date when the present deplorable conditions give way to other, better ones. Perhaps this will happen soon. But until today my motto has been: 'Patience and waiting'. From the national point of view the post of conductor at the Czech Theatre is no doubt most important. From here one really has a direct influence on the public in the broadest sense and would be able to influence to the greatest possible extent the refinement of artistic taste as well as, above all, the trend of art. It is therefore understandable that this post would suit me best. But as long as Dr Rieger is the manager it is useless even to think of it, as the present conductor appears to him to be a model for all conductors, in spite of his oft-proved uselessness. . . .

My opera *The Brandenburgers in Bohemia* has been with the theatre management since October. The rehearsals are only now getting under way. It is still impossible to say when it will be performed and the reason for the delay is the tender regard of the present conductor for my person. . . .

SMETANA TO MME FROEJDA BENECKE IN GÖTEBORG

Prague, 3 April 1866

To begin with the same old story, namely my opera [*The Brandenburgers in Bohemia*], this has been put on ten times up to today; each time it drew a full house. It has thus been included in the repertoire and regularly brings me in 10 per cent of the gross takings. Of course, taking into account the size of our provisional theatre, this is not a great deal, even with a packed house. It amounts to around 50 to 60 Austrian *gulden*. Anyhow, that is of no importance to me. Apart from this my opera, which was entered for the prize of 600 *gulden* offered by Count Harrach for the best original Czech opera, has now been awarded this prize by the jury. So you see, dear Lady, that I am beginning to make money out of the products of my brain. Perhaps I may even become rich!

My second opera, *The Bartered Bride*, is already being rehearsed and will be staged during the course of May. I am working on the second act of a third opera, *Dalibor*, and I hope to have completed it by winter. . . .

SMETANA TO HIS WIFE

Prague, 15 September 1866
7 o'clock in the evening

It has happened – I am the conductor! . . . It is little enough, though, that these gentlemen offer me – a salary of 1,200 *gulden* a year and one benefit performance, altogether 1,400 *gulden*. They make excuses for their behaviour on the grounds that they can give no more, that they are having to reduce all salaries and that they could not have given the former conductor a whit more, even if they had wanted to keep him. For the moment then, no more can be done! Later, they say, as soon as it is at all possible, they will see what they can do to make it more. That's their way of promising. Well, we shall see. For the moment I have to be content. My activities have already begun. I have engaged singers, etc. We shall start work as soon as we have the personnel together. . . .

A tragic fate shattered Smetana's career as an organizer and conductor: in 1874 paralysis of the aural nerve made him suddenly deaf. The composer's creative vitality, however, remained unimpaired and he was still able to write some of his most distinguished works, among them the operas 'The Kiss' and 'The Secret' and the great set of symphonic poems called 'Má Vlast' (My Fatherland) during those years of growing despair. But his nervous system was thoroughly shaken and he had to spend the last few months of his life in a lunatic asylum.

SMETANA TO THE CZECH COMPOSER KAREL BENDL

Jabkenice, 24 July 1875

Happy as I was to see that you take such a warm interest in my fate, I have to admit, alas, that I am unable to advise you in any way about the rehearsals which are to take place in Bayreuth in August . . . I am now really sorry that I am not in closer contact with Wagner. But knowing the stories about his overbearing and rude behaviour towards the musical world with the exception of Liszt, I did not care to become acquainted with him, indeed I avoided it on every occasion for I also am sensitive and I cannot stand rudeness. And thus I have never met Wagner personally.

I do know his wife personally, but I presume that she is too proud to put in a word for such an unimportant artist as I doubtless am in her eyes. The only thing which I would suggest in this case is that the gentlemen who wish to travel from Prague to this year's rehearsals in Bayreuth should apply to Wagner direct with the request that he allow them to attend the rehearsals. Of course they would have to give their reasons and flatter him a bit. A diplomatic letter would be needed. Whether Wagner would consent, that is the question, indeed who knows whether he will even answer. But it is always worth trying, there is no harm in that. If he does not consent, then you have saved the journey and money, for he would not admit you on the recommendation of another either. I hear that Jiránek also wants to go there, and it seems, at random. Let him make sure beforehand. You should rather apply to Wagner jointly. Much better if there are more of you!

As regards my illness, my opponents may be satisfied. I shall not soon be in their way again, indeed perhaps never again. My recovery, if indeed it is possible, will require a long time and in as far as I know my condition, I believe that only time will give me back my hearing, at least partially. I also went to see Dr Pospišil, but he began to give me external treatment and that is quite useless. My illness is internal and it has yet to be discovered where the cause lies. That at least is the opinion of all the doctors whom I have consulted. The ear is quite healthy externally. But the inner apparatus – that admirable keyboard of our inner organ – is damaged, out of tune, the hammers have got stuck and no tuner has hitherto succeeded in repairing the damage. In autumn I am going to Leipzig to Dr Hagen who is to give me electric treatment. The last attempt! Then my fate will be sealed!

SMETANA TO HIS FORMER PUPIL CHARLOTTE VALENTIN IN GÖTEBORG

Jabkenice, 29 January 1877

I am deaf, and shall probably remain so for ever. No treatment, no doctors have helped. It is just not possible to bring paralysed nerves to life again. To this unspeakably sad fate come many other worries, and thus it happens that I prefer not to write to you. Such tokens of sympathy as your dear letter are balm to my wounds and I thank you for it most warmly.

You spoke of the ovations accorded me on the occasion of the first performance of my latest opera *Hubička* [*The Kiss*]. They really were ovations the like of which I have never yet experienced. The public rewarded my attempts to introduce our national music into opera in a way that far exceeds my merits. I was called countless times and an unending stream of festively dressed deputations appeared before the public and heaped on me bouquets and wreaths of every description, including a silver one, as well as odes and poems. I was as one stunned, and was so moved that I hardly knew what I was doing. . . .

Unfortunately I was the only one in the packed house who did not hear a single note of the music, my own music into the bargain. . . .

SMETANA TO DR LUDEVIT PROCHÁZKA

Jabkenice, 26 September 1877

Dear friend, believe me that I have to admire myself for bearing up under the terrible blows of a cruel fate. Not only do I suffer from my illness, but I also have to contend with anxiety as to a living. Since May I have been receiving no salary and I have no means of existence. Dr Dašek has stopped my salary until such time as it shall have been approved by the new management. Up to today, however, I have been waiting in vain for this approval and I am thereby plunged into the deepest anxiety.

In such a frame of mind, it is difficult to compose. It has been said that I have rendered certain services to our national art, but they must, it seems, be very small ones since I am rewarded in this way. I swallowed my pride and humbled myself to the extent of sending a written request to the management asking them to leave matters as they stood with the former Young Czech management, that is to say that for the salary of 1,200 *gulden* a year they might have the rights for the performance of my four older operas (without royalties): *The Brandenburgers in Bohemia*, *The Bartered Bride*, *Dalibor* and *The Two Widows*. In addition I paid personal visits to the gentlemen, for instance to Dr Dašek, to Schick, etc., where I was most affably received and . . . put off with fine words. But to this day I have received nothing.

Beethoven received a pension, and the only condition was that he should remain in Austria. For less I have conceded the rights on four major works; this does not, of course, mean that I would dare to compare myself with Beethoven. Forgive me for wasting so many words on this, but I am very bitter about it and I do not know what to do. . . .

SMETANA TO DR LUDEVIT PROCHÁZKA IN PRAGUE

Jabkenice, 10 October 1877

I am longing for my affairs with the Association to be settled; I live in a state of constant anxiety, and think with fear and trembling of my future! I shall be most grateful to you if you can help me in any way to bring matters speedily to a head. The whole matter is most distasteful to those gentlemen, I am a great burden to them and they would gladly be rid of me, and I, believe me, would be only too happy not to have to ask anything from those who give me to understand so clearly that it is only alms that they offer me.

What a sad fate in my old age! And of what have I been guilty, that I am now little more than a beggar? Perhaps of devoting all my forces to my homeland rather than to foreign countries?

I shall say no more about it! The Association put my operas on during the entire period that my salary was stopped, from May until now. But not a *kreutzer* [penny] did they send me, 100 *gulden* in respect of future royalties on *The Kiss* excepted. But that could not keep me for five months with my entire family, and now I am left without a single *heller* [half-penny].

But enough of that, or I might forget myself and in my bitterness go too far!

SMETANA TO HIS FRIEND JAN VLASTIMIL KAREL

Jabkenice, 17 January 1880

I hope that if I have not yet reached the goal I set myself I am at least approaching it. And that goal is to prove that we Czechs are not mere practising musicians as other nations nickname us, saying that our talent lies only in our fingers but not in our brains, but that we are also endowed with creative force, yes, that we have our own and characteristic music. How far I have succeeded in this hitherto, not I but the world will judge. . . .

What a cruel fate is dogging me you doubtless know. It is now the sixth year that I am completely deaf. In autumn, in October 1874 I got up one morning, stone deaf. Since that time, in spite of all the doctors of Prague and foreign countries, for I journeyed to Germany in order to be cured, though vainly, I am as deaf as a post, I hear nothing, neither words, nor notes, neither near nor far. The nerves of my ears are paralysed so that sound cannot penetrate to the brain and I cannot hear a thing. Believe me that I need all my courage and force to keep myself from falling into despair and from putting a violent end to my suffering. Only the sight of my family and the thought that I must go on working for my people and country keeps me alive and inspires me to new work!

SMETANA TO ANNA TRNOBRANSKA

8 May 1883

My disease is drawing a host of others in its wake, troublesome additional complaints which are all due to nervous irritation; this is the main reason why I have not been able for nearly a whole year to read anything that might irritate the fantastic side of my brain. This would cause other morbid conditions, and the doctors have forbidden me to read, write, think, etc. They have not, however, been able to forbid me to listen to what is happening around me, for one mightier than they has done so: 'Fate'. Forgive me for referring to my deafness which has lasted now for nine years, and which has robbed me of everything which makes our life beautiful. I, a musician, have had my hearing destroyed! Why, I have never even heard the little voices of my grandchildren. . . . In this affliction I called to my spirit, and it made it possible for me to imagine my compositions as if I heard them. And I wrote long and difficult works throughout that period, great compositions such as *The Kiss*, an opera, *The Secret*, also an opera, and *The Devil's Wall*; then symphonic works, six large orchestral works under the title *My Fatherland*. And in this way I was able to bear my unbearable fate! If martyrs are still born today, then I am the unhappiest of them, for fate has sentenced me to a silent tomb where the sound of human voices does not penetrate. . . .

FROM REMINISCENCES OF LEOŠ JANÁČEK

My memories of Bedřich Smetana are similar to the picture children make themselves of God: among the clouds. It was during a concert at the Zofín Hall in that for Bedřich Smetana so fateful year, 1875. I was standing right up by the orchestra. At the close of the performance [the first performance of *Vltava*] a tumultuous roar fused into the name *Smetana*! All at once people surging and pressing around me blocked out all light. They were leading the sick composer up the steps. Only his face burned itself into my soul. To this day I remember it faithfully, as though amidst rushing waters and veiled by mist. Surely at that time my eyes devoured only Him and to all others I was deaf and blind. . . .

Antonín Dvořák (*1841–1904*) *had no easy start either: he was hardly acknowledged as a musician in Prague at the time of Smetana's greatest popularity and was still practically unknown in his middle thirties, when Brahms, as an expert adviser to the Austrian Minister of Education on the yearly award of state scholarships to deserving young musicians, became aware of the Czech composer's enormous gift. He recommended him to his publisher Simrock in Berlin, who launched Dvořák's music with immediate international success.*

BRAHMS TO HIS PUBLISHER FRITZ SIMROCK IN BERLIN

Vienna, 12 December 1877

In connection with the State scholarships, I have been receiving a lot of pleasure for several years past from the work of Anton Dvořák, of Prague. This year he has sent in, among other things, some 'Duets for 2 Sopranos with pianoforte', which seem to me to be quite charming and *practical* for publication. . . . Dvořák has written all kinds of things, operas (Czech), symphonies, quartets, piano pieces. He is certainly a very talented fellow. And incidentally, poor! I beg you to consider that! The Duets will show you what I mean, and might 'sell well'. . . .

BRAHMS TO FRITZ SIMROCK

[Vienna] 5 April 1878

I am leaving for Italy in a day or two with Billroth and Goldmark. . . . I would not even have written to say so, except that I am thinking about Dvořák.

I don't know how much further you are prepared to venture with his work. And I know nothing about business, or how much real interest is taken in larger works. Nor am I fond of making recommendations, for after all I have only my own eyes and ears to go by. If you are thinking of anything else at all, you might perhaps ask him to send you two string quartets in Major and Minor and get them played to you. Dvořák has what is most essential for a musician, and it is to be found in these pieces. I myself am a hopeless Philistine, I would even publish my own things for pleasure's sake.

In short, I don't like to do more than recommend Dvořák in a general way. Besides, you have your own ears and your business experience, and that must have its say too. . . .

BRAHMS TO JOSEPH JOACHIM

[*Vienna, May 1879*]

Take a look at Dvořák's Serenade for wind-instruments; I hope you will enjoy it as much as I do . . . it would be difficult to discover a finer, more refreshing impression of really abundant and charming creative talent. Have it played to you; I feel sure the players will enjoy doing it!

DVOŘÁK TO FRITZ SIMROCK IN BERLIN

[*Prague*] *10 October 1883*

My first news is that I have just been on a visit to Vienna, where I spent some delightful days with Dr Brahms, who had just arrived from Wiesbaden. I had never known him so cheerful. We lunched and dined together every day, and talked about all kinds of things. He seemed to enjoy my company, and as for me, I am so enchanted by his kindness as man and artist, that I really love him! What a mind, and what a soul the man has! You know how reserved he is about his compositions, even with his dearest friends and musicians; but he was not so with me. When I asked to be allowed to hear something from his new Symphony [the Third], he was ready at once, and played me the first and last movements. I can say without exaggeration that this work excels his first two Symphonies, perhaps not in the greatness and power of its conception, but certainly in beauty. It has an atmosphere not often found in Brahms. And such magnificent melodies! It is sheer love, and makes the heart leap to hear it. . . .

Dvořák's lovable simplicity and straightforwardness is naïvely expressed in his letters. As a characteristic feature of the time it is of interest to see how a German publisher reacted to a Czech composer's presumption in having his name printed in his own Czech way – Antonín, not Anton – and how conscious the composer was of his success being not merely of personal but of national importance.

DVOŘÁK TO FRITZ SIMROCK

Birmingham, 22 August 1885

Don't laugh at my Czech brothers, and you need not feel sorry for me either. What I asked of you was just a personal wish, and if you cannot grant it I am entitled to regard it as a disobliging reaction which I have not met with from either English or French publishers. You don't seem to realize the conditions in which I live. If I were in Berlin or some such place, it would be quite different. Anyhow, do as you like. . . .

DVOŘÁK TO FRITZ SIMROCK

Vysoka, 10 September 1885

Your last letter, in which you expounded your national political idiosyncracies, amused me considerably. I'm only sorry you should be so ill-informed. That is the talk we hear from all our enemies – or rather, from a few individuals who are employed by newspapers such as the *Kölnische Zeitung*, the *Augsburger*, etc., and are *compelled* to write according to the tendencies and views of the particular politics of the rag they work for. But what do you and I care about politics; let us be glad we can devote ourselves entirely to the service of art! And let us hope that nations which have their own art and stand up for it will never perish, small though they may be. Forgive me, but I only wanted to point out to you that even an artist has a country, and must believe in it firmly and keep a warm corner in his heart for it. . . .

DVOŘÁK TO FRITZ SIMROCK WHO HAD COMPLIED WITH HIS MODEST REQUEST TO ADD CZECH TITLES TO HIS WORKS

[Prague] 7 February 1888

It is producing a great effect here, and is welcomed with open satisfaction. It's almost comic: our Parliament in Vienna has been refusing to print Slav words on the banknotes, and here is Berlin making no bones about recognizing equality! Don't laugh, there is a profound truth involved. So all honour to my friend Simrock!

ANTONÍN DVOŘÁK TO VELEBIN URBÁNEK IN PRAGUE

[London, March 1884]

On Monday there was the first rehearsal with the choir in the Albert Hall, an immense building which can comfortably seat 12,000 people. . . . I must give you an idea of the size of the orchestra and choir. Don't get a shock! 250 sopranos, 160 contraltos, 180 tenors and 250 basses; the orchestra: 24 first violins, 20 second violins, 16 violas, 16 cellos and 16 double-basses. . . . At the concert my appearance was greeted with a storm of applause. The general enthusiasm grew from item to item and at the end the applause was so great that I had to thank the audience over and over again. . . . All this has led me to the conclusion that here in England a happier time, God grant it may be so, has begun for me which, I hope, *will bear Czech art in general good fruit*. The

English are a good, warm-hearted and music-loving nation and it is well known that when once they take a liking to someone, they remain faithful to him. God grant it may be so with me. . . .

DVOŘÁK TO HIS FATHER AT KLADNO, BOHEMIA

London, 21 March 1884

Who could have thought that far across the sea, in this enormous London, I should one day celebrate triumphs such as few foreign artists have known! I shan't make any long story about it, perhaps you have all read in Kladno what the newspapers wrote about my great successes.

Just to give you a slight idea of what this London looks like and how terribly big it is, I shall tell you the following:

If all the Czech inhabitants of the whole of Bohemia were put together, they would not number as many as the inhabitants of London. And if all the inhabitants of the town of Kladno were to visit the enormous hall where I conducted my *Stabat Mater*, there would still be plenty of room – for that is how huge the *Albert Hall* is!

Yesterday I had my second concert in St James's Hall where I again achieved the most splendid success. I cannot tell you how great is the honour and respect the English people here show me. Everywhere they write and talk about me and say that I am the *lion* of this year's musical season in London. Two banquets have already been given here in my honour and, on Monday, a third, and a very great one, is being given by the society of artists, the 'Philharmonia', which invited me to London. In September I shall have to come here again, but still farther beyond London. It is the big industrial town of Worcester, where I shall again conduct my *Stabat Mater*. For next year and '86 I already have offers to come to England and shall have to write new compositions.

From this you can judge how they like me and value me. In some of the papers there was also mention made of you, that I come of poor parents and that my father was a butcher and innkeeper in Nelahozeves and did everything to give his son a proper education. *Honour be to you for that!*

DVOŘÁK TO HIS FRIEND A. GÖBL AT SYCHROV

Birmingham, 21 August 1885

I am here in this immense industrial town where they make excellent knives, scissors, springs, files and I don't know what else, and beside these music too. And how well! It's terrific what the people here manage to do and stand! There will be 8 concerts in all and each will last 4–5 hours. My day is Thursday the 27th at 8 p.m. Please think of me!

I am looking forward to it immensely. The choir and orchestra are first class. 100 sopranos, 100 contraltos, 100 tenors, 100 basses and even more, 40 violins, 16 double basses, 16 cellos and the wind instruments doubled. Just imagine what it will sound like when they start. . . . The Birmingham papers gave me a very warm welcome and the London papers write, too, that my composition is likely to arouse the greatest interest and have the best reception. Maybe it will and maybe it won't. We shall see! And anyhow you will read about it. . . .

FROM THE REMINISCENCES OF DVOŘÁK'S PUPIL JOSEF MICHL

Dvořák: 'I shall never forget how I felt when they made me a Doctor in England: the formalities and the doctors! All the faces so grave and it seemed that none could speak anything but Latin. I listened to my right and to my left and did not know where to turn my ear. And when I discovered that they were talking to me, I could have wished myself anywhere else than there and was ashamed that I did not know Latin. But when I look back on it today, I must smile and think to myself that to compose *Stabat Mater* is, after all, better than to know Latin. . . .'

In 1892, his appointment as director of the National Conservatoire in New York, a post which he held for three years, brought Dvořák to America. As an ardent patriot he liked to spend his holidays at Spillville, Iowa, where he felt thoroughly at home in a Czech community.

DVOŘÁK TO DR EMIL KOZÁNEK AT KROMĚŘÍŽ, MORAVIA

New York, 12 October 1892

Our journey was lovely except for one day when everybody on board was sick except me – and so after only a short period of quarantine, we arrived safely in the promised land. The view from Sandy Hook (harbour town) of New York with the magnificent statue of Liberty (in whose head alone there is room for 60 persons and where banquets, etc., are often held) is most impressive. . . . The city itself is magnificent, lovely buildings and beautiful streets and then, everywhere, the greatest cleanliness. It is expensive here. Our gulden is like a dollar. At the hotel we pay 55 dollars a week for three rooms, of course in the most central part of the city, 'Union Square'. . . . On Sunday the 9th, there was a big Czech concert in my honour. There were 3,000 people present in the hall, and there was no end of cheering and clapping. There were speeches in Czech and English and I, poor creature, had to make a speech of thanks from the platform, holding a silver wreath in my hands. You can guess how I felt! Besides, you will learn about it later from the newspapers. What the Americans write about me is simply terrible – they see in me, they say, the saviour of music and I don't know what else besides. . . .

DVOŘÁK TO MR AND MRS HLÁVKA IN PRAGUE

Boston, 27 November 1892

There are things here which one must admire and others I would rather not see, but what can you do, everywhere there is something – in general, however, it is altogether different here, and if America goes on like this, she will surpass all the others.

Just imagine how the Americans work in the interest of art and for the people. So, for instance, yesterday I came to Boston to conduct my obligatory concert (everything connected with it is being arranged by the highly esteemed President of our Conservatory, the tireless Mrs Jeanette Thurber), at which the *Requiem* will be given with several hundred performers. The concert on December 1st will be given for only *the wealthy and the intelligensia*, but the preceding day my work will also be performed for poor workers who earn 18 dollars a week, the purpose being to give the poor and uneducated people the opportunity to hear the musical works of all times and all nations!! That's something, isn't it? I am looking forward to it like a child. . . .

The orchestra here, which I heard in Brooklyn, is excellent, 100 musicians, mostly German, as is also the conductor. His name is Nikisch and he comes from somewhere in Hungary. The orchestra was founded by a local millionaire, Colonel Higginson, who gave a big speech at my first concert (a thing unheard of here), spoke of my coming to America and the purpose to be served by my staying here. The Americans expect great things of me and the main thing is, so they say, to show them to the promised land and kingdom of a new and independent art, in short, to create a national music. If the small Czech nation can have such musicians, they say, why should not they too, when their country and people are so immense. . . . There is more than enough material here and plenty of talent. I have pupils from as far away as San Francisco. They are mostly poor people, but at our Institute teaching is free of charge, anybody who is really talented pays no fees. I have only 8 pupils, some of them very promising. . . .

The following letters give a charming picture of the way Dvořák liked to spend his free time. Vysoká was a village in Czechoslovakia where he used to holiday and indulge in two of his favourite pastimes, pigeon-fancying and playing 'darda', a popular game of cards.

DVOŘÁK TO DR EMIL KOZÁNEK AT KROMĚŘÍŽ

New York, 12 April 1893

Here, too, some of the critics are against me, but others are all good friends and write fairly and sometimes enthusiastically. I have a good disposition. I can stand a lot and still be quite ready to forgive them. As far as this is concerned, you may be quite at rest. I sit firmly in the saddle and I like it here, except, as I say, for some trifles.

My wish to return to Bohemia will not be realized this year, we have decided otherwise. We shall go straight to Chicago, have a look at the Exhibition, and then set out for *our summer Vysoká* in the State of Iowa, for the village of Spillville, where the teacher and the parish priest and everything is Czech and so I shall be among my own folks and am looking forward to it very much.

The teacher, Mr Kovařík (from Písek and here 26 years) and the priest, Mr Bílý, a very lively fellow, so they say (from Budějovice in Bohemia) will be the people with whom I shall be in closest contact. I shall have pigeons there, and maybe we shall even play *darda*? How grand it will be! The priest has two pairs of ponies and we shall ride to Protivín, a little town near Spillville. Here in America there are *names of towns and villages of all nations under the sun*! . . .

I have not much work at school so that I have enough time for my own work and I am just finishing my E minor Symphony. I take great pleasure in it and it will differ considerably from my others. Well, the influence of America must be felt by anyone who has any 'nose' at all. . . .

DVOŘÁK TO DR KOZÁNEK

Spillville, 15 September 1893

The three months spent here in Spillville will remain a happy memory for the rest of our lives. We enjoyed being here and were very happy though we found the three months of heat rather trying. It was made up for us, however, by being among our own people, our Czech countrymen, and that gave us great joy. If it had not been for that, we should not have come here at all.

Spillville is a purely Czech settlement, founded by a certain Bavarian

German, *Spielmann*, who christened the place Spillville. He died four years ago, and in the morning when I went to church, my way took me past his grave and strange thoughts always fill my mind at the sight of it as of the graves of many Czech countrymen who sleep their last sleep here. These people came to this place about 40 years ago, mostly from the neighbourhood of Písek, Tábor and Budějovice. All the poorest of the poor, and after great hardships and struggle they are very well off here. I liked to go among the people and they, too, were all fond of me. . . .

It is very strange here. Few people and a great deal of empty space. A farmer's nearest neighbour is often 4 miles off, especially in the *prairies* (I call them the Sahara) there are only endless acres of field and meadow and that is all you see. You don't meet a soul (here they only ride on horseback) and you are glad to see in the woods and meadows the huge herds of cattle which, summer and winter, are out at pasture in the broad fields. Men go to the woods and meadows where the cows graze to milk them. And so it is very wild here and sometimes very sad – sad to despair. But habit is everything. . . . Not long ago we went on a trip to the State of Nebraska, to the town of Omaha . . . Omaha is 400 miles from our place, and then we went to visit – guess whom? – Father Rynd whom I met on Czech Day in Chicago – and do you know where? In the State of Minnesota, in the town of St Paul, 400 miles from Nebraska, where there are also many Czechs. . . .

In Russia, the main obstacle to the development of a national school of music was the cultural and economic backwardness of a vast country. When in 1862 Anton Rubinstein, the only Russian musician of European fame and a genuine cosmopolitan, founded the Imperial Conservatoire in St Petersburg, there was hardly any scope yet for professional musicians in the country. Most famous Russian composers of the nineteenth century were amateurs: Glinka (1804–57), the founder of a genuine Russian style, was a landowner, Borodin (1833–87) a chemist, Rimsky-Korsakov (1844–1908) a naval officer, Mussorgsky (1839–81) a civil servant, César Cui (1835–1918) an authority on fortification. The last four mentioned, led by Balakirev (1837–1910), the only professional musician of the group, became influential in the development of Russian music. 'The Five', as they called themselves, or also the 'Mighty Handful', professed the ideals of Berlioz and Liszt and were strongly opposed to German formalism and traditionalism. They were fervent Slavophiles, enthusiastic musicians and devoted friends, although their personal views would often clash. Their overriding common problem was the maintenance of creative activity under the burden of their diverse extra-musical occupations. One finds a great deal of touchiness and aggressiveness in their behaviour, easily explained by the inferiority complex of artists whose control of their material was by no means impeccable. They all had harassed lives, and the tragic ruin of Modest Petrovitch Mussorgsky (*1839–81*) *the eccentric genius who drank himself to death, is poignantly pathetic.*

MILI BALAKIREV TO AVDOTYA ZAKHARINA

31 December 1860

Our entire company lives as before. Mussorgsky now has a happy and healthy appearance. He has written an *allegro* and thinks that he has already accomplished a great deal for art in general and Russian art in particular. Every Wednesday evening now I have an assembly of all the Russian composers; new compositions (when they compose any) are played for us and, in general, good, edifying things by Beethoven, Glinka, Schumann or Schubert, etc. . . .

MUSSORGSKY TO BALAKIREV

Volok, 28 April 1862

In St Petersburg, with only an insignificant distance between them, two schools have been formed, absolute contrasts in character. One is a *Professoria*; the other a free association of those who seek to become kin to art. In one Zaremba and Tupinstein [Rubinstein] in their professorial, anti-musical togas, stuff the heads of their students with various abominations and infect them in advance. The poor pupils see before them not human beings but two fixed pillars to which are nailed some silly scrawls said to contain the laws of music. But Tupinstein is a *tup* [an idiot] – consequently he scrupulously does his duty: to be wickedly dull. But not Zaremba – a bold fellow. He cuts out measures for art. Being raised to the rank of a doctor of music – a cobbler in an academic fool's cap, he is not so childish as to base his opinions and advice on aesthetics and musical logic – oh no! He has learned the rules and uses this as a smallpox anti-toxin to inoculate against free learning anyone who longs to study art. . . .

In the other school, there are you and Gashenka [Lomakin]. But what can be said here: you are a talent, and consequently all bold, free, strong things are yours by nature, and such *people* are needed by the *people*; and because of this – I wish success and prosperous life to your fine enterprise. . . .

CÉSAR CUI TO NIKOLA RIMSKY-KORSAKOV

22 April 1863

Modinka [pet name of Mussorgsky] presented some sort of musical monstrosity to us – supposedly a trio to his *scherzo*, a huge, awkward monstrosity. Here are some church chants of endless length and the usual Modinkian pedalling and so forth – all this is unclear, strange, awkward and by no means a trio. . . .

VLADIMIR STASSOV, CRITIC AND COMPOSER, TO BALAKIREV

St Petersburg, 17 May 1863

What is there for me in Mussorgsky, even though he was with me yesterday at the theatre? Well, yes, his thoughts seem to agree with mine, yet I didn't hear from him a single idea or a single word expressed with real profundity of understanding, with the profundity of a raptured, moved soul. Everything about him is flabby and colourless. To me he seems a perfect idiot. Yesterday I could have flogged him. I believe if he were left without tutelage, if he were suddenly removed from the sphere where you have held him by force, and he were set free to follow his own wishes and his own tastes, he would soon be overrun with weeds like all the rest. There's nothing inside him. . . .

BALAKIREV, ON A VISIT TO PRAGUE, TO GLINKA'S SISTER LUDMILA SHESTAKOVA

Prague, 28 December 1866

I must tell you that evidently [Glinka's] *A Life for the Czar* will not please the local public. Nor will local musicians be pleased, for such heads as Shornik and Smetana can understand nothing sensible that steps out of the German frame. . . . The public attends only operas that are immediately understandable or that suit their vulgar German taste, like *Troubadour* or *William Tell*, and if *A Life for the Czar* is given, it will be only because of the Russophile tendencies of certain local leaders. . . . All the delays with *Ruslan* and *A Life for the Czar* originate with Smetana, who appears to be the worst sort of intriguer, hates Glinka's music and calls it *Tartar*! He belongs to the pro-Polish party and he has dishonourably transferred his hatred of Russia to its art. But I am no fool either, and I will lead the attack myself. . . .

BALAKIREV TO MUSSORGSKY

Prague, 11 January 1867

Here too I am vanquished by a conservatoire: my landlady's nephew is being educated in this worthy institution and, in my absence, saw my collection [of Russian folk songs] on the piano, grew interested in it, became acquainted with me, took the collection home, played it over with his comrades, all of whom shouted in complete rapture: 'This is Slavonic music, while we have German'. Their rapture was so great that they even dared to show this collection or – more exactly – to play several songs to a professor. So that you'll understand how courageous their act was, I'll tell you that here, as throughout Germany, every conservatoire professor is as much a blockhead as our Rubinstein, just as insolent to his awe-struck pupils. In St Petersburg there are protests against the immaculacy of Rubinstein, but not here. So this is what happened: the professor became angry and told them that all this is *ganz falsch* [all wrong] . . . in a succession of chords he had found a hidden fifth, which is strictly forbidden here, and the melodies are in absolute nonconformity with the rules in their melodic course. The students returned with downcast heads and sorrowfully declared that although all this is enchanting, it is *ganz falsch*, and they don't dare not believe the professor, and not one sceptical thought even occurs to them about the immutability of all these calves' laws of harmony and melody. . . .

As you can see, I am spilling about the poison of musical nihilism, as well as organizing a party for the support of *A Life for the Czar*, which the Polish counts (there are plenty here), together with the conductor Smetana and several other gentlemen with musical authority, for example, Mr Procházka, want to chase off the stage as a Tartar opera.

Today I visited classes of schools where the students assemble voluntarily to study Russian (a chair of Russian language is not allowed officially at the university). There are many of them and they are all going to hear *A Life for the Czar* which will probably be given on February 3rd, by the local calendar, conducted by me. . . .

RIMSKY-KORSAKOV TO MUSSORGSKY

St Petersburg, 10 July 1867

In the first place, dearest Modest, you have made me happy by writing to me, and secondly, by your completion of *A Night on the Bare Mountain*. . . . The modulation of G minor and G flat major interrupted by F sharp minor on a trill must be quite beautiful. The glorification of

Satan must certainly be very filthy, and therefore all sorts of harmonic and melodic filth is permissible and fitting, and there should be no reason to send you to the conservatoire. The gentlemen of the conservatoire would of course be horrified by you, but then they themselves aren't able to compose anything decent. . . .

MUSSORGSKY TO RIMSKY-KORSAKOV

Shilovo, 30 July 1868

I want to say that if the expression in sound of human thought and feeling *in simple speech* is truly produced by me in *music*, and this reproduction is musical and artistic, then the thing is in the bag. . . . I have worked briskly – as it happened, but brisk work tells on one: whatever speech I hear, no matter who is speaking (nor what he says) my mind is already working to find the musical statement for such speech. . . .

MUSSORGSKY TO RIMSKY-KORSAKOV

Shilovo, 15 August 1868

Regarding symphonic development: You seem appalled that you are writing in a Korsakov manner rather than in a Schumann manner And I tell you (scorn fear – *vous êtes brave*) that cold *borsht* is a calamity to a German, but we eat it with pleasure – *point de comparaison s'il vous plait, comparaison n'est pas raison.* The German *Milchsuppe* or *Kirschensuppe* is a calamity to us, but it sends a German into ecstasy. Brief, symphonic development, technically understood, is developed by the German, just as his philosophy is. The German, when he thinks, first theorizes at length, and then proves. Our Russian brother proves first, and then amuses himself with theory. . . . . Creation itself bears within itself its own laws of refinement. Their verification is inner criticism; their application is the artist's instinct. If there is neither one nor the other, there is no creative artist; if there is a creative artist, there must be one as well as the other, and the artist is a law unto himself. . . . When he, though contented, revises or, what is worse, adds to it, he *Germanizes, relives* what has already been said. We are not ruminants, but omnivorous animals. This would be a contradiction!—and a contradiction of our nature. . . .

ALEXANDER BORODIN TO HIS WIFE EKATERINA

24–25 October 1871

The alienation of Mili [Balakirev], his obvious turning away from the circle, his sharp remarks about many, especially about Modest, have considerably cooled sympathies towards Mili. If he goes on like this, he may easily isolate himself and this, in his situation, would amount to spiritual death. I, and not I alone, but the others too, feel very sorry for Mili, but what's to be done? . . . There may also be a reason for his estrangement in his strange and unexpected switch to pietism of the most fantastic and most naïve sort. For instance, Mili doesn't miss a single morning mass or a single night mass, breaks a piece from his holy wafer, fervently crosses himself in front of each church, etc. It's quite possible that in these circumstances it is unpleasant for him to meet people who are unsympathetic to all this; he may even be afraid of the tactless and coarse *mitrailleuse* of reproaches from Vladimir Stassov who, whenever he meets him, starts forthwith 'demonstrating' to him that all this is nonsense, that he 'cannot understand' how an intelligent man like Mili, and so on and so on. Moreover, most of the reproaches fall upon his apathy to musical matters, especially during the past year. . . . Modinka is offended by Mili's unjust and high-handed remarks about *Boris* [Mussorgsky's opera], expressed tactlessly and sharply in the presence of people who on no account ought to have heard them. . . .

Cui also is indignant about Mili's apathy and his lack of interest in what happens in our musical circle. Before, Mili was concerned with the slightest novelty, even in embryo. There is no denying that the abyss between him and us grows wider and wider. This is terribly painful and pitiful. Painful chiefly because the victim of all this will be Mili himself. The other members of the circle now live more peacefully than ever before. Modinka and Korsinka particularly, since they began to share a room, have both greatly developed. They are diametrically opposed in musical qualities and methods, one seems to complement the other. Their influence on each other has been extremely helpful. Modest has improved the recitative and declamatory sides of Korsinka who, in turn, has wiped out Modest's tendency towards awkward originality, and has smoothed all his rough harmonic edges, his pretentiousness in orchestration, his lack of logic in the construction of musical form – in a word, he has made Modest's things incomparably more musical. And in all the relations within our circle there is not a shadow of envy, conceit or selfishness; each is made sincerely happy by the smallest success of another. There are the warmest of relations, not even excepting Cui who, for example, ran over to me only for the purpose of hearing the end of my finale. . . .

MUSSORGSKY TO VLADIMIR STASSOV

St Petersburg, 13 July 1872

Maybe I am afraid of technique, because I am poor at it? There are, however, some who will stand up for me as an artist and in this respect also. . . . In truth, until the artist rids himself of his nappies, his leading-strings, so long will the symphonic priests rule, setting up their Talmud 'of the 1st and 2nd editions', as the alpha and omega in the life of art. The little brains sense that their Talmud cannot be used in living art: where there are people, life – there is no place for prejudiced articles and paragraphs. And so they cry: 'Drama, the stage, they cramp us – give us space!' And here they go giving free rein to their brains: 'The world of sounds is unlimited!', yes, but their brains are limited; so what use is this sound of worlds, or rather world of sounds! . . .

It isn't symphonies I object to, but symphonists – incorrigible conservatives. So do not tell me, dear *généralissime*, why our musicians chatter more often about technique than about aims and historical tasks – because, this derives *from that*. . . .

BORODIN TO HIS WIFE

25 October 1873

By the way, here is some news for you: *Boris* [Mussorgsky's opera *Boris Godunov*] is to be given in its entirety. Gedeonov, when he returned from abroad to St Petersburg, as soon as he got out of the railway carriage, said in his first words to Lukashevich: 'Stage *Boris* without fail and as quickly as possible; send the score to Ferrero, I will order it passed'. Now they are already copying the parts. . . . And here is pitiful and sorrowful news: of the author of *Boris*. He has been drinking heavily. Nearly every day he sits in the Maldyaroslavetz restaurant on Morskaya, often drinking himself stiff. This summer the Sorokins saw him completely drunk in Pavlovsk; he caused a disturbance there; the affair reached the police. I have been told that he has already drunk himself to a state of seeing hallucinations and all sorts of trash. . . . This is horribly sad! Such a talented man and sinking so low morally. Now he periodically disappears, then reappears morose, untalkative, which is contrary to his usual habit. After a little while he again comes to himself – sweet, gay, amiable and witty as ever. Devil, what a pity!

BORODIN TO MME IVANOVNA KARMALINA

15 April 1875

Every man is more or less of an egoist and likes to talk of himself. I am a man, and therefore not exempt from this failing; so I shall begin by telling you about myself. Since my last letter I have lived in all manner of ways – rather ill than well. In consequence of the resignation of one of our professors of chemistry, I have been obliged to take over part of his lectures. This work required a lengthy preparation and took up much of my time. Besides, our Academy is on trial and awaits the verdict of its judges. The situation is accidental, but it exercises a very bad influence upon the entire academy, and consequently upon my particular chair. This gives me a great deal to do, and leads to my being taken up with a number of things useful, indispensable, or sometimes even useless. Add to this the troubles of slow promotion and financial embarrassment. All this is not conducive to cheerfulness and leaves me but little time for my favourite occupation. . . . Meanwhile I am like a consumptive who, scarcely able to breathe, still dreams of a goat's milk cure, of a journey to the South, of rambles through meadows carpeted with flowers. I, too, dream of writing an opera.

But what a difference between the consumptive patient and myself! He might carry out his aspirations if health were restored to him, while I can hope for nothing better than to fall ill. In fact, when I am tied to the house with some indisposition, unable to devote myself to my ordinary work, when my head is splitting, my eyes running, and I have to blow my nose every minute, then I give myself up to composing.

I have been thus indisposed twice this winter, and each time I have raised a new stone in my edifice.

This edifice is *Prince Igor*. . . .

BORODIN TO MME IVANOVNA KARMALINA

10 June 1876

As a composer seeking to remain anonymous I am shy of confessing my musical activity. This is intelligible enough. For others it is their chief business, the occupation and aim of life. For me, it is a relaxation, a pastime which distracts me from my principal business, my professorship. I do not follow Cui's example. I love my profession and my science. I love the Academy and my pupils, male and female, because to direct the work of young people one must be always close to them. I have the interests of the Academy at heart. If, on the one hand, I want to finish my work, on the other hand I am afraid of devoting myself to it too assiduously and throwing my scientific work into the shade.

But now, since the performance of the chorus from *Igor*, the public know that I am composing an opera. There is no longer anything to conceal or to be ashamed of. I am in the situation of a girl who has lost her innocence, and by that very fact has acquired a certain sort of liberty; now willy-nilly I must finish the work. . . .

In opera, as in decorative art, details and minutiae are out of place. Bold outlines only are necessary; all should be clear and straightforward and fit for practical performance from the vocal and instrumental standpoint. The voices should occupy the first place, the orchestra the second. . . . It is curious to see how all the members of our set agree in their praise of my work. While controversy rages amongst us on every other subject, all, so far, are pleased with *Igor*. Mussorgsky, the ultra realist, the innovating lyrico-dramatist Cui, our master Balakirev, so severe as regards form and tradition, Vladimir Stassov himself, our valiant champion of everything that bears the stamp of novelty or greatness.

Such is the history of my natural child, *Igor*, whose time has not yet come. . . .

MUSSORGSKY TO VLADIMIR STASSOV

St Petersburg, 19 October 1875

As long as they were held in Balakirev's iron grip, they breathed deep breaths with his powerful lungs (though not quite as his heroic breast did), setting themselves tasks that would have worried even great men. As soon as Balakirev's iron grip was relaxed they felt tired and in need of rest; where to find this rest? – in tradition, of course, 'as our forefathers did, so shall we'. They have put away the glorious banner of battle in some secret hiding-place, hiding it carefully and locking it behind seven locks and seven doors. They have rested and relaxed. Without a banner, without desire, neither seeing nor wishing to see into the distance, they plod away at things already done long before and which no one asks them to do again. And there, from time to time, the croaking frogs [critics], tenderly puffing in their inherited swamp, pass out to them – these artists – their little approvals. And why shouldn't they approve? The 'Mighty Handful' have degenerated into soulless traitors; the 'lash' has become a child's toy whip. I don't believe you'd find people anywhere under the skies more indifferent to the essence of life, more useless to modern creativeness than these artists. . . .

MUSSORGSKY TO VLADIMIR STASSOV

St Petersburg, Night, 29–30 December 1875

The thing is this, my dear, a lad has gone astray, drawn by various desires. And he who has strayed is none other than Count Arseni Kutuzov-Golenishchev – and this is the way it is: he has decided to get married! and this is no joke, he says, it's the *real thing*. So yet another 'takes leave, to go to his native village', never to return. . . . I frankly scolded Arseni and was extremely rude to the aforesaid Arseni. But lying is not for me. He asked me to come to his fiancée (whom I don't know) – but I'm not going; I would have to lie. I don't want him to do what he's doing – and I won't go, that's all. He says that he fell in love with her – all the same, I won't go. It's not necessary. . . .

MUSSORGSKY TO VLADIMIR STASSOV

25 December 1876

My present desire is to make a prognostication, and here it is, this prognostication: *true to life* and not melodic in the classical sense. I'm working with human speech; I have arrived at a sort of melody created by this speech, I have arrived at an embodiment of recitativo into melody (aside from dramatic movements, *bien entendu*, where one may even make interjections possible). I should like to call it intelligently justified melody. And this work pleases me; suddenly, unexpectedly and ineffably, something different from classical melody (so beloved), but at once understandable to everyone and everybody will be sung. If I achieve this – I shall consider it a conquest in art, and it must be achieved. . . .

VLADIMIR STASSOV TO BALAKIREV

3 January 1880

I want without fail . . . to attempt to do something for Mussorgsky. He is sinking; since January 1st he is left without a post and without means of any sort. It would be no wonder if he should drink more! Won't you do something for him – quickly, if possible. Time won't wait! . . .

VLADIMIR STASSOV TO BALAKIREV

February 1881

The doctors now say that these were not paralytic strokes, but the beginning of epilepsy. I was with him [Mussorgsky] today and yesterday, Borodin and Korsakov were there yesterday and the day before, many other friends as well; he looks as if nothing were the matter with him and now recognizes everybody, but he talks the devil knows what gibberish and tells lots of impossible stories. They say that besides the epilepsy and the strokes he is also a bit mad. He is done for, though he may linger on, the doctors say, for a year, or only for a day. . . .

Mussorgsky died some weeks later.

Peter Ilyitch Tchaikovsky *(1840–93) became a civil servant like Mussorgsky, but he soon gave up that uncongenial occupation and entered the Conservatoire at St Petersburg, resolved to take the risk of a most dubious career. Having made his debut as a composer with some success, he found his independence through an extraordinary stroke of luck: a wealthy lady, Mme Nadezhda von Meck, who ardently admired his music, offered him a considerable yearly allowance which enabled him to devote himself without restraint to his creative work.*

PETER ILYITCH TCHAIKOVSKY TO MME VON MECK

Clarens, 25 October 1877

Nadezhda Filaretovna, every note which comes from my pen in future is dedicated to you! To you I owe this reawakening love of work, and I shall never forget for a moment that you have made it possible to carry on my career. Much, much still remains for me to do! Without false modesty, I may tell you that all I have done so far seems to me poor and imperfect compared with what I *can, must* and *shall do* in the future. . . .

TCHAIKOVSKY TO HIS BROTHER ANATOLE

11 August 1869

Balakirev is staying here. We often meet, and I always come to the conclusion that – in spite of his worthiness – his society weighs upon me like a stone. I particularly dislike the narrowness of his views, and the persistence with which he upholds them. . . .

TCHAIKOVSKY TO MME VON MECK

San Remo, 24 December 1877

All the new St Petersburg composers are very talented, but they are all permeated with horrible presumptuousness and a wholly amateurish conviction of superiority to all other musicians in the universe. The sole exception is Rimsky-Korsakov. Like the others, he is self-taught. Recently, however, he has undergone a sharp turn. By nature he is very earnest, very honest, and conscientious. As a mere youth he fell into society that first convinced him that he was a genius and then told him that 'study' isn't necessary, that schools kill inspiration and dry up creative power, etc. At first he believed it. His earliest compositions showed a striking ability and a lack of theoretical training. In his circle they were all in love with themselves and with each other. Each attempted to imitate one or another composition which came from the circle, proclaimed by them to be a masterpiece. As a result the whole group soon sank into a dull mire of uniformity of method, affectation, and lack of distinction. Korsakov is the only one among them who discovered, five years ago, that the doctrines propagated by his circle were without a reasonable basis, and its contempt of the schools, of classical music, its hatred of authority and of models, were just ignorance. I have kept a letter of his written at this period. It both agitated and moved me deeply. He was in despair at the sudden realization of the many years he had wasted, the many years during which he had followed a path that led nowhere. 'What shall I do?', he asked himself. The obvious answer was that one must study, and he began to study with such zeal that academic technique soon became indispensable to him. In one single summer he wrote sixty-four fugues in addition to an incredible number of contrapuntal exercises. Ten of the fugues he sent to me for approval. Though faultless in their way, the fugues showed me that the transition from one type of writing to its opposite had been too violent. From contempt of the schools he went over abruptly to the cult of musical technique. Shortly after that, his symphony and quartet appeared. Though both works are full of tricks, they bear the stamp, as you so justly observe, of dry pedantry. At present he appears to be passing through a crisis, and it is difficult to foresee how this crisis will end. Either he will turn out a great master or he will be completely swallowed up in contrapuntal complexities. Cui is a talented dilettante. His music is graceful and elegant but lacks originality. It is too coquettish, too smooth, and therefore it pleases at first hearing, then one tires of it. The reason for this is to be found in the fact that Cui is a musician only by avocation. Professionally he is a professor of fortification and is very busy lecturing in practically every military school in St Petersburg. He has himself confessed to me that he cannot compose without first picking out little melodies on the keyboard, accompanied by little chords. Once he comes across a pretty little idea, he fusses with it a long time, embellishes and adorns and greases it in every way, and all this takes a lot of time. It took him ten years, for example, to write his opera *Ratcliff*. Nevertheless, I repeat, he undoubtedly has talent; at least he has taste and foresight. Borodin is a fifty-year-old professor of chemistry at the Academy of Medicine. He too has talent, great talent even, but a talent that has perished because of lack of knowledge and a blind fate which led him to the lecture platform of a chemistry class instead of to a living musical activity. He has not so much taste as Cui and his technique is so poor that he cannot compose a single bar without help. Mussorgsky you are quite correct in characterizing as hopeless. His talent is perhaps the most remarkable of all these. But he has a narrow nature, is totally devoid of desire for self-improvement, and is deluded by a blind faith in the absurd theories of his circle and in his own genius. In addition he has some sort of low nature which loves all that is crude, coarse and rough. He is, in short, the direct antithesis of his friend Cui, who, though he swims in the shallows, is at any rate always decorous and graceful, whereas Mussorgsky coquets with his illiteracy and takes pride in his ignorance, rolling along, blindly believing in the infallibility of his genius. But he has a real, and even original, talent which flashes out now and then. The most important personality of the circle is Balakirev. But he has become silent, after having done very little. The great talent of this man has perished because of some fatal circumstances which have turned him to extreme piety after having long taken pride in complete atheism. Today Balakirev practically lives in church. He is continually fasting, preparing himself for the sacrament, and genuflecting to the relics of the saints, and nothing more. His great talent notwithstanding, he has been the cause of much harm. For example, he ruined Korsakov by convincing him that study is harmful. In fact, he is the inventor of all the theories of this strange circle which contains in its midst so many undeveloped, misdirected or prematurely decayed forces.

This then is my frank opinion of this group. What a sad phenomenon! So many talented men from whom, except for Korsakov, we hardly dare expect anything serious. . . . All the same, however, the forces exist. A Mussorgsky, for all his ugliness, speaks a new language. Beautiful it may not be, but it is fresh. So this is why we may expect Russia some day to produce a whole Pleiad of forceful talents who will open new paths for art. Our ugliness is, at any rate, better than the pitiful impotence, masked as serious creative power, of Brahms and other Germans. . . .

Between Tchaikovsky, who soon rose to a prominent position in Russian music, and the 'Mighty Handful' relations were rather strained, as one will have gathered from these letters. One has to take into account, however, the fastidious professional composer's contempt of the amateur, which is felt in his harsh judgement of his colleagues at St Petersburg. All the same he had to pay attention to their public influence, and especially that of Stassov, the acknowledged publicist of the group, a convinced adherent to Liszt's ideals, who gave him his well-meant advice regarding descriptive music. One cannot help smiling at the critic's delightful pedantry regarding Juliet's nurse in the following letter, demonstrating the absurdity of the whole principle.

VLADIMIR STASSOV TO TCHAIKOVSKY

St Petersburg, 21 January 1873

I now hasten to go into further details and rejoice in the prospect of your work [the Symphonic Fantasy *The Tempest*] which should prove a worthy *pendant* to your *Romeo and Juliet.* You ask whether it is necessary to introduce the tempest itself. Most certainly. Undoubtedly, most undoubtedly. . . .

I have carefully weighed every incident, with all their pros and cons, and it would be a pity to upset the whole business. I think the sea should be depicted twice – at the opening and close of the work. In the introduction I picture it to myself as calm, until Prospero works his spell and the storm begins. But I think this storm should be different from all others, in that it breaks out *at once* in all its fury and does not, as generally happens, work itself up to a climax by degrees. I suggest this original treatment, because this particular tempest is brought about by enchantment and not, as in most operas, oratorios and symphonies, by natural agencies. . . .

In your first overture [*Romeo and Juliet*] you have unfortunately omitted all reference to Juliet's nurse, that inspired Shakespearean creation, and also the picture of dawn, on which the love scene is built up. Your overture is beautiful, but it might have been still more so. . . .

TCHAIKOVSKY TO VLADIMIR STASSOV

27 January 1873

I scarcely know how to thank you for your excellent and, at the same time, most attractive programme. Whether I shall be successful I cannot say, but in any case I intend to carry out every detail of your plans. . . . The subject of *The Tempest* is so poetical, its programme demands such perfection and beauty of workmanship, that I am resolved to suppress my impatience and await a more favourable moment for its commencement. . . .

TCHAIKOVSKY TO HIS BROTHER MODESTE AFTER ATTENDING THE FIRST BAYREUTH FESTIVAL

Vienna, 20 August 1876

After the last notes of *Götterdämmerung* I felt as though I had been let out of prison. The *Nibelungen* may actually be a magnificent work, but it is certain that there never was anything so endlessly and wearisomely spun out. . . .

TCHAIKOVSKY TO MME VON MECK

Vienna, 8 December 1877

I have seen Wagner's *Valkyrie*. The performance was excellent. The orchestra surpassed itself. The best singers did all in their powers – and yet it was wearisome. What a Don Quixote Wagner is. He expends his whole force in pursuing the impossible, and all the time, if he would but follow the natural bent of his extraordinary gift, he might evoke a whole world of musical beauties. In my opinion Wagner is a symphonist by nature. He is gifted with genius, which has wrecked itself upon his tendencies; his inspiration is paralysed by theories which he has invented on his own account, and which, *nolens, volens*, he wants to bring into practice. . . . But there is no doubt Wagner is a wonderful symphonist. I shall just prove to you by one example how far the symphonic prevails over the operatic style in his operas. You have probably heard the celebrated *Walkürenritt* [*The Ride of the Valkyries*]? What a great and marvellous picture! How we actually seem to see these fierce heroines flying on their magic steeds amid thunder and lightning! In the concert hall this piece makes an extraordinary impression. On the stage, in view of the cardboard rocks, the canvas clouds, and the warriors who run about awkwardly in the background – in a word, seen in this very inadequate theatrical sky, which makes a poor pretence of realizing the illimitable realm above, the music loses all its powers of expression. Here the stage does not enhance the effect but acts rather like a wet blanket. Finally I cannot understand, and never shall, why the *Nibelungen* should be considered a literary masterpiece . . . Wotan, Brünnhilde, Fricka, and the rest, are so impossible, so little human, that it is very difficult to feel any sympathy with their destinies. . . . For three hours Wotan lectures Brünnhilde upon her disobedience. . . . And with it all, there are many fine and beautiful episodes of a purely symphonic description. . . .

A letter to Mme von Meck expresses a composer's perplexity when his work is misjudged by a trusted expert. The case is striking, because it concerns a work the success of which was not only instantaneous, assured from the very first performance, but which became one of the most popular items of the repertoire, the Pianoforte Concerto in B flat minor.

TCHAIKOVSKY TO MME VON MECK

San Remo, 21 January 1878

In December, 1874, I had written a pianoforte concerto [the Concerto in B flat minor]. As I am not a pianist, it was necessary to consult some virtuoso as to what might be ineffective, impracticable and ungrateful in my technique. I needed a severe, but at the same time friendly, critic to point out in my work these external blemishes only . . . I must mention the fact that some inward voice warned me against the choice of Nicolai Rubinstein [brother of Anton, a distinguished conductor and pianist] as a judge of the technical side of my composition. However, as he was not only the best pianist in Moscow but also a first-rate all-round musician, and knowing that he would be deeply offended if he heard I had taken my concerto to anyone else, I decided to ask him to hear the work and give me his opinion upon the solo part. . . .

I played the first movement. Never a word, never a single remark . . . Rubinstein's silence was eloquent . . . I pulled myself together and played the concerto straight through to the end. Still silence.

'Well?' I asked, and rose from the piano. Then a torrent broke from Rubinstein's lips. Gentle at first, gathering volume as it proceeded, and finally bursting into the fury of a *Jupiter tonans*. My concerto was worthless, absolutely unplayable; the passages so broken, so unskilfully written, that they could not even be improved; the work itself was bad, trivial, common; here and there I had stolen from other people; only one or two pages were worth anything; all the rest had better be destroyed. . . . The chief thing I cannot reproduce: the *tone* in which all this was said. An independent witness of this scene would have concluded I was a talentless maniac, a scribbler with no notion of composing, who had ventured to lay his rubbish before a famous man . . . I left the room without a word. . . . Presently Rubinstein came to me and, seeing how upset I was, called me into another room. There he repeated that my concerto was impossible, pointed out many places where it needed to be completely revised, and said if I would suit the concerto to his requirements, he would bring it out at his concert. 'I shall not alter a single note,' I replied. 'I shall publish the work precisely as it stands.' This intention I actually carried out. . . .

TCHAIKOVSKY TO SERGE TANEIEV

San Remo, 2 January 1878

Very probably you are quite right in saying that my opera is not effective for the stage. I must tell you, however, I do not care a rap for such effectiveness. It has long been an established fact that I have no dramatic vein, and now I do not trouble about it. If it is really not fit for the stage, then it had better not be performed! I composed this opera because I was moved to express in music all that seems to cry out for such expression in *Eugène Onegin*. I did my best, working with indescribable pleasure and enthusiasm and thought very little of the treatment, the effectiveness and all the rest. I spit upon 'effects'! Besides, what are effects? For instance, if *Aida* is effective, I can assure you I would not compose an opera on a similar subject for all the wealth of the world; for I want to handle human beings, not puppets. I would gladly compose an opera which was completely lacking in startling effects, but which offered characters resembling my own, whose feelings and experiences I shared and understood. The feelings of an Egyptian Princess, a Pharaoh, or some mad Nubian, I cannot enter into, or comprehend. . . . Had I a wider acquaintance with the literatures of other countries, I should no doubt have discovered a subject which was both suitable for the stage and in harmony with my taste. Unfortunately I am not able to find such things for myself, nor do I know anyone who could call my attention to such a subject as Bizet's *Carmen*, for example, one of the most perfect operas of our day. You will ask what I actually require? I will tell you. Above all I want no kings, no tumultuous populace, no gods, no pompous marches – in short, none of those things which are the attributes of 'grand opera'. I am looking for an intimate yet thrilling drama, based upon such a conflict of circumstance as I myself have experienced or witnessed, which is capable of touching me to the quick. I have nothing to say against the fantastic element, because it does not restrict me, but rather offers unlimited freedom. I feel I am not expressing myself very clearly. In a word, Aida is so remote, her love for Radames touches me so little – since I cannot picture it in my mind's eye – that my music would lack the vital warmth which is essential to good work. . . .

The opera *Onegin* will never have a success; I feel already assured of that. I shall never find singers capable, even partially, of fulfilling my requirements. The routine which prevails in our theatres, the senseless performances, the system of retaining invalided artists and giving no chance to younger ones: all this stands in the way of my opera being put on the stage. . . . It is the outcome of an invincible inward impulse. I assure you one should only compose opera under such conditions. It is only necessary to think of stage effects to a certain extent. If my enthusiasm for *Eugène Onegin* is evidence of my limitations, my stupidity and ignorance of the requirements of the stage, I am very sorry; but I can at least affirm that the music proceeds in the most literal sense from my inmost being. . . .

TCHAIKOVSKY TO MME VON MECK

Clarens, 19 March 1878

You need not worry, my dear. If fame is destined for me, it will come with slow but sure steps. History convinces us that the success which is long delayed is often more lasting than when it comes easily and at a bound. Many a name which resounded through its own generation is now engulfed in the ocean of oblivion. An artist should not be troubled by the indifference of his contemporaries. He should go on working and say all he has been predestined to say. He should know that posterity alone can deliver a true and just verdict. I will tell you something more. Perhaps I accept my modest share with so little complaint because my faith in the judgement of the future is immovable. I have a foretaste during my lifetime of the fame which will be meted out to me when the history of Russian music comes to be written. For the present I am satisfied with what I have already acquired. I have no right to complain. . . .

TCHAIKOVSKY TO HIS BROTHER MODESTE

Brailov, 27 May 1878

Yesterday I played the whole of *Eugène Onegin* from beginning to end. The composer was the sole listener. I am half ashamed of what I am going to confide to you in secret: the listener was moved to tears, and paid the composer a thousand compliments. If only the audiences of the future will feel towards this music as the composer himself does!

Tchaikovsky's relation with his benefactress was odd indeed. Owing to a curious reluctance on both sides, they never met, although they always maintained a lively correspondence. Tchaikovsky was of a morbid sensitiveness and shyness, which he had to control by a heroic effort when, as he frequently did in his later years, he appeared as conductor of his music.

TCHAIKOVSKY TO HIS BROTHER ANATOLE

Florence, 21 November 1878

On the journey here I was troubled by the thought that Nadezhda Filaretovna would be living so close to me; that we might meet. I even had a momentary suspicion that she might invite me. But a letter from her, which I found upon my writing-table yesterday, set my mind completely at rest. She will be leaving in three weeks, and during that time we shall probably not see each other once. . . .

TCHAIKOVSKY TO HIS BROTHER MODESTE

Simaki [one of Mme von Meck's estates], 9 August 1879

A very, very old house, a shady garden with ancient oaks and lime-trees; it is very secluded, but therein lies its charm. At the end of the garden flows a stream. From the veranda there is a fine view over the village and the forests. The absolute quiet and comfort of the place exactly suit my taste and requirements. I have at my disposal an old manservant called Leon, a cook whom I never see, and a coachman with a phaeton and four horses. I could gladly dispense with the last, since it necessitates my driving occasionally, while in reality I prefer to walk. The proximity of Nadezhda Filaretovna troubles me somewhat, although it is really folly. I know my seclusion will not be disturbed. I am so accustomed to regard her as a kind of remote and invisible fairy that the consciousness of her mortal presence in my neighbourhood is rather disconcerting. . . .

TCHAIKOVSKY TO MME VON MECK

Kamenka, 13 August 1880

Fame! What contradictory sentiments the word awakes in me! On the one hand I desire and strive for it; on the other I detest it. If the chief thought of my life is concentrated upon my creative work, I cannot do otherwise than wish for fame. If I feel a continual impulse to express myself in the language of music, it follows that I need to be heard; and the larger my circle of sympathetic listeners the better. I desire with all my soul that my music should become more widely known, and that the number of those people who derive comfort and support from their love of it should increase. In this sense not only do I love fame, but it becomes the aim of all that is most earnest in my work. But, alas! when I begin to reflect that with an increasing audience will come also an increase of interest in my personality, in the more intimate sense; that there will be inquisitive people among the public who will tear aside the curtain behind which I have striven to conceal my private life; then I am filled with pain and disgust, so that I half wish to keep silence for ever, in order to be left in peace. I am not afraid of the world, for I can say that my conscience is clear, and I have nothing to be ashamed of; but the thought that someone may try to force the inner world of my thoughts and feelings, which all my life I have guarded so carefully from outsiders – this is sad and terrible. There is a tragic element, dear friend, in this conflict between the desire for fame and the fear of its consequences. I am attracted to it like the moth to the candle, and I too, burn my wings. Sometimes I am possessed by a mad desire to disappear for ever, to be buried alive, to ignore all that is going on, and be forgotten by everybody. Then, alas! the creative inspiration returns . . . I fly to the flame and burn my wings once more!

TCHAIKOVSKY TO HIS BROTHER MODESTE

Rome, 26 February 1881

Oh society! What can be more appalling, duller, more intolerable. Yesterday I was dreadfully bored at Countess X's but so heroically did I conceal my feelings that my hostess in bidding me good-bye said: 'I cannot understand why you have not come to me before. I am sure that after tonight you will repent not having made my acquaintance sooner.' This is word for word! She really pities me! May the devil take them all!

TCHAIKOVSKY TO MME VON MECK

Paris, 3 May 1883

I have always written, and always shall write, with feeling and sincerity, never troubling myself as to what the public would think of my work. At the moment of composing, when I am aglow with emotion, it flashes across my mind that all who will hear my music will experience some reflection of what I am feeling myself. Then I think of someone whose interest I value – like yourself, for instance – but I have never deliberately tried to lower myself to the vulgar requirements of the crowd. If opera attracts me from time to time, it signifies that I have as much capacity for this as for any other form. If I have had many failures in this branch of music, it proves only that I am a long way from perfection, and make the same mistakes in my operas as in my symphonic and chamber music, among which there are many unsuccessful compositions. If I live a few years longer, perhaps I may see my *Maid of Orleans* suitably interpreted, or my *Mazeppa* studied and staged as it should be; and then possibly people may cease to say that I am incapable of writing a good opera. . . .

Tchaikovsky's life was cut short in the fullest flower of his creative energy: he was the victim of a cholera epidemic in St Petersburg.

THE WORLD OF YESTERDAY

From Mahler to Schönberg

The most perplexing feature in the musical development of the last two or three generations is an individualism that has hardly permitted any community of aims or tendencies among the outstanding composers. Each stands alone, as it seems, and in most cases set with determination against all others. Occasional alliances look as if they were based mainly on common practical interests, and rather directed against a common adversary than towards identical artistic ideals.

Gustav Mahler (*1860–1911*) *and* Richard Strauss (*1864–1949*), *the most prominent representatives of German music at the turn of the century, could have lived on two different planets: the one passionately subjective and devoted to introspection to the limit of self-torment, the other almost ingenuously extrovert, an unaffected realist. Both, like so many young musicians in Germany, started their careers as operatic conductors; but Strauss, widely acknowledged as a composer right from the beginning, was soon in the fortunate position of being able to restrict his practical activities to a desirable minimum, whereas Mahler, whose work as a composer never brought him any appreciable material reward, had to continue his strenuous activity as a conductor to the end of his life.*

The conductor's career, however, was of dazzling splendour: at thirty-seven he held one of the most prominent positions in European music as director of the Court Opera in Vienna, acclaimed as one of the greatest conductors of his time. With a passionate striving for perfection and an enormous burden of administrative duties on his hands, he found his creative work relegated to a brief summer holiday This was probably the chief cause of a permanently overstrained nervous system and early exhaustion of his vital power.

With his burning idealism and fierce energy, the young beginner was already a terror to his subordinates and most uncomfortable for his superiors. His rise was rapid all the same, as can be seen from his moves from a remote provincial town, Olmütz, to Kassel, Leipzig, Prague, Budapest, Hamburg.

GUSTAV MAHLER TO HIS FRIEND DR FRIEDRICH LÖHR

Olmütz, 20 January 1883

I have to make a tremendous effort to pull myself together and write to you. I am quite paralysed, as though I had fallen from heaven. From the moment I crossed the threshold of the theatre at Olmütz, I have felt like a man awaiting the judgement of God.

If a thoroughbred is harnessed to a cart with oxen, the best he can do is to sweat and haul with them. I can hardly bear to write to you, I feel so defiled.... Up to now, thank heaven, I have had practically nothing but Meyerbeer and Verdi to conduct. I have craftily and perseveringly shouldered Wagner and Mozart out of the repertory – for I could never bear to drag *Lohengrin* or *Don Giovanni*, for instance, down to this. Tomorrow we are giving *Joseph in Egypt* [by Méhul]. An unusually charming work, with a touch of Mozart's grace about it. I really enjoyed studying it. And I must admit that although the orchestra are unimaginably obtuse, they really try hard to please me, and have taken the thing rather more seriously this time. Unfortunately only from a kind of compassion for the 'idealist' – a term of great contempt – for they are quite unable to conceive that an artist may become completely wrapped up in a work of art. Often, when I take fire and try to carry them with me to greater heights, and I see their astonished faces, and the companionable grins they exchange, I get disheartened for a time and I long to rush out of the place for ever. Only the feeling that I am suffering for my Masters and that I may succeed in throwing a spark of their fire into the souls of these poor fellows, braces me even against their mockery; and in better moments I vow to myself that I will hold out for love of the cause....

MAHLER TO FRIEDRICH LÖHR

Kassel, 19 September 1883

This evening I am to conduct [Meyerbeer's] *Robert le Diable* – the classics are the stamping-ground of the Herr Hofkapellmeister [Wilhelm Treiber]; he is the cheeriest beater-out of 4/4 time that I have ever come across. I, of course, am 'the most pigheaded young fellow', stubbornly refusing to receive my initiation into art from his hands....

MAHLER TO FRIEDRICH LÖHR

Kassel, 12 May 1885

My engagement here comes to an end on 1 July. I shall then go to Leipzig for a month. What will happen after that is as much a mystery to me as what we shall be doing 50 years from now. The battle is raging here at present – 'Up with Mahler' – 'Up with Treiber' – party feeling runs high, and I am the one to suffer for it. I'm through with the director, too – since I told him frankly that I didn't see eye to eye with him in matters of art he has ostracized me for insubordination....

MAHLER TO FRIEDRICH LÖHR

Leipzig, [May 1887]

As you probably know, for about the last 3 months my nose has been kept to the grindstone in a way that is without precedent; my colleague has been ill and I have had to do two men's work. I conduct big operas nearly every day and am literally scarcely ever out of the theatre. You can imagine how exhausting this is when one takes art seriously, and what strenuous efforts are needed to acquit oneself worthily of such a tremendous task with practically no preparation. . . .

The composer's progress was punctuated, at intervals of several years, by nine gigantic symphonies, the main work of his life. As regards the conductor's achievements, the ten years during which he was in charge of the Vienna Opera (1897–1907) are still remembered as the Golden Age of that institution.

To his contemporaries, he remained chiefly a great conductor, whom they were even ready to forgive the wayward extravagance of regarding himself as a composer.

MAHLER TO FRIEDRICH LÖHR

Leipzig, March 1888

So – my work [the First Symphony] is finished! I wish I had you beside my piano now, so I could play it over to you!

You are probably the only person who will find out nothing new about me from it; other people are likely to be surprised by many things! It grew so overwhelming – flowing out of me like a mountain torrent! You'll hear it this summer! All the floodgates within me were thrown open at one sweep! Perhaps one day I'll tell you how it happened. . . .

MAHLER TO FRIEDRICH LÖHR

Steinbach am Attersee [Upper Austria], 29 June 1894

This is to announce the auspicious birth of a strong, healthy last movement for the 2nd [his Second Symphony]. Father and child are doing as well as can be expected; the latter is not yet out of danger.

It is to be baptized with the name *Lux lucet in tenebris* [The light shineth in the darkness]. Friends are asked for their silent sympathy; all flowers gratefully refused. Other gifts will, however, be accepted. . . .

MAHLER TO FRIEDRICH LÖHR

Hamburg [*end of 1894*]

Suppose I did come to Vienna. With my attitude to things, what would happen to me there? The first time I tried to impose my interpretation of a Beethoven symphony upon the celebrated Philharmonic Orchestra, trained by the doughty Hans [Richter], the most hateful battle would begin. I have experienced that even here, where my position is unchallenged thanks to the out-and-out championship of Brahms and Bülow!

I should bring a storm round my head whenever I departed from routine and tried to make some contribution of my own. I have only one desire: to work in a small town where there are no 'traditions' and no watchdogs guarding the 'eternal laws of beauty', among simple, unpretentious people, and in that small circle to please myself and the few who can follow me. . . .

MAHLER TO MAX MARSCHALK

Hamburg, 6 December 1896

It's really always the same old story! If a man ever ventures to be *himself*, so much the worse for him! He has to atone for it like a crime. And the deadly sin will not be forgiven until after his death. The world learns nothing from experience, because each case looks different, so that the thing is 'ever new'. . . .

MAHLER TO DR ARTHUR SEIDL

Hamburg, 17 February 1897

Whenever a plan for a great musical structure occurs to me, I always arrive at a point where I have to call in *words* to convey my musical ideas. It must have been the same with Beethoven in his Ninth; only in those days there was no suitable material at hand for him. For when you come down to it, Schiller's poem is not capable of expressing the ineffable things he had in mind. And I remember R. Wagner says the same thing somewhere, quite bluntly. As for me, in the last movement of my Second I ransacked the literature of the whole world, including the Bible, to find the relieving word – and in the end I had to express my thoughts and feelings in words of my own. . . .

With regard to Vienna and the conductors' crisis there, nothing definite can be said as yet. *Between ourselves*, the crisis cannot be solved until the autumn, and the choice now seems to be hovering between Mottl and my humble self.

To be frank, I don't know whether I ought to welcome the idea of the post, for it might turn me aside from my original aims. However, I am completely fatalistic about it, and for the time being I shall think no more of the matter, just waiting to see how things turn out. . . .

MAHLER TO DR ARNOLD BERLINER

Hamburg, 22 April 1897

For the time being, the summons to Vienna has brought me only unprecedented disturbance and the anticipation of battles ahead. Whether it is the right place for me, time alone can show. In any case I must nerve myself for a year's violent hostility on the part of all those who either will not or cannot co-operate (the two things usually go together).

Hans Richter, in particular, is reported to be doing his level best to raise hell against me. However, we shall see! This place has been no bed of roses either, and recently, in particular, I have had to put up with things that were really beneath me.

Another new chapter is beginning. But I am going back to *my own country*, and I shall do all I can to put an end to my wanderings in this life. . . .

MAHLER TO MAX MARSCHALK

[*Vienna, 1897*]

I am in 'the thick of things' as only a theatre director can be. A horrible life that drains one dry! With all my thoughts and feelings turned outwards, I am becoming more and more a stranger to myself. How will it end?

MAHLER TO HIS WIFE ALMA

Dresden, 17 December 1901

I had a very serious talk with [Richard] Strauss in Berlin, and tried to show him that he was in a blind alley. Unfortunately he could not quite see my point. He is a dear fellow, and I find his attitude to me very touching. But I can do nothing for him – for while I see him as a whole, he sees only my pedestal.

MAHLER TO HIS WIFE

Semmering, February 1902

The atmosphere Strauss spreads around him is so arid that one positively begins to doubt one's own personality. If that is the fruit that hangs on a tree, how can one love the tree? You hit the bull's-eye with what you said about him. You agree, don't you, that it is better to eat the bread of poverty together and walk in the light, than to lower oneself to vulgarity like that! A time will come when people will see the chaff sifted from the wheat – and my day will dawn when his sun has set. . . .

MAHLER TO JOSEF REITLER IN PARIS

[*June, 1906*]

For the time being I must rest content with knowing that in a few places there are small circles of art-lovers for whom my work has some meaning, even perhaps some value. The first obstacle to its performance, no matter where, consists in the resources that would have to be employed [Mahler's symphonies demand an outsize orchestra]. Even more of a drawback, however, is the fact that its forms of expression are completely unrelated to what is customary, and at present only a small minority of people recognize that they spring naturally from the composer's character and are not merely arbitrary and freakish.

I frankly doubt whether Paris has any room for my art at present. And frankly it has never occurred to me to go to Paris and try to impose a style that seems so alien even in my own country. I cannot say as yet whether I should advise it even if you, my dear Mr Reitler, are prepared to take on the thankless task of paving the way for me. . . .

MAHLER TO BRUNO WALTER

[*Summer, 1906*]

It cannot be denied that our music involves the purely human (with all that pertains thereto, including the intellectual). As with all art, it is a straightforward question of the actual means of expression, etc., etc. When one is trying to compose music, one mustn't try to paint, write poetry, or present descriptions. But *what* one puts into music, all the same, is the entire (feeling, thinking, breathing, suffering) human being. There can be no particular objection to a 'programme' (even if it is not exactly the highest rung of the ladder) – but it is a *composer* who has to express himself in it, not a writer, philosopher or painter – all of whom are included in the composer.

In short, a man without genius had better keep away, and a man with genius has nothing to fear. It seems to me that all this hair-splitting on the subject is like a man who begets a child and afterwards begins to worry about whether it really is a child, whether it was begotten with the right intentions, and so forth. The point is: he loved – and *he had the vigour*. Basta! And if one does not love and *has no vigour*, then there will be no child! Again, basta! And according to what one is and *the vigour one has*, the child will turn out! Yet again, basta!

My Sixth is finished. I think *I had the vigour*! A thousand times Basta! . . .

MAHLER TO HIS WIFE ALMA AFTER A PERFORMANCE OF STRAUSS'S 'SALOME'

Berlin, [January 1907]

It bears the clear stamp of genius, a powerful work, undoubtedly one of the most significant that has been produced in our time! Under that heap of rubble there is a volcano living and working, a subterranean fire – no mere fireworks. This is probably true of Strauss's whole personality. That is what makes it so difficult to separate the chaff from the grain in him. But I have formed a tremendous respect for the whole phenomenon he constitutes, and now it has gained fresh strength. . . .

MAHLER TO HIS WIFE AFTER A SECOND PERFORMANCE OF THE SAME WORK

Berlin, 14 January 1907

My impression has strengthened still further, and I am firmly imbued with the conviction that this is one of the greatest masterpieces of our time. I cannot explain it in any other way, I can only sense that the voice of the 'Spirit of the Earth' is speaking from the innermost depths of genius – for that spirit builds its dwelling not in accordance with human standards of taste, but in the light of its own incomprehensible needs. Perhaps time will bring me to a still better understanding of this 'material body'. . . .

MAHLER TO HIS WIFE AFTER A PERFORMANCE OF ONE OF HIS SYMPHONIES IN BERLIN

Frankfurt, 15 January 1907

The world is not giving me a very pleasant time just now. I'm like a wild animal with the hounds behind it. But thank God, I am not one of those who fall by the wayside, and the drubbing I have to stand up to from all directions just now (the Berlin critics, too, are almost unanimously 'contemptuous') simply has the effect of a massage. If they throw mud at me, I shall give my suit a good brushing....

MAHLER'S LETTER OF FAREWELL TO THE MEMBERS OF THE COURT OPERA IN VIENNA

Vienna, 7 December 1907

The time has come for our work together to be brought to an end. I am leaving the workshop of which I have grown fond, and this is my farewell to you.

Instead of leaving behind me something complete and self-contained, as I had dreamt of doing, I am leaving something botched and imperfect, as man is always fated to do.

It is not for me to give an opinion on what my efforts have meant to those for whom they were made. But at a moment like this I can say sincerely that I did my best and set myself a high aim. I could not hope to be always successful. The practising artist is more exposed than anyone to resistance from his working materials, to the perfidy of physical objects. But I have always done my utmost, subordinating myself to the matter in hand and my personal inclinations to my duty. I have not spared myself, and so I had the right to demand that others should bring all their strength to the task.

In the thick of the battle, the heat of the moment, we all received wounds and made mistakes. But when we succeeded with a work, completed a task, we forgot all our woes and toil and felt richly rewarded – even with no outward signs of success. We have all made progress, and with us, the institution we were trying to serve.

And now I offer you my warmest thanks – you who have assisted me in my difficult and often thankless task, who have helped me and fought at my side. Please accept my sincerest wishes for your future and for the prosperity of the Court Opera, whose fortunes I shall continue to follow with the keenest sympathy.

Gustav Mahler

MAHLER TO BRUNO WALTER

[*New York, beginning of 1909*]

I have so much to write about myself, that I don't know where to begin. I have been going through such a continuous process of experience (in the last eighteen months) that I can hardly find words for them.

How can I attempt to describe such a tremendous crisis! I see everything in such a new light – I am so constantly on the move; sometimes it would hardly surprise me to discover that I'd suddenly taken on a new body (like Faust in the last scene). My thirst for life is keener than ever, and I find the 'habit of living' even sweeter than before. . . .

I find myself more unimportant with every passing day, yet often fail to understand how one can go jogging along in the old daily rut, amid all the 'sweet habits of life. . . .'.

But how foolish it is to let oneself be sucked into the hurly-burly of life! To be unfaithful, even for an hour, to oneself and the higher powers above! But I am writing just at random – for at the very next opportunity, for instance now when I leave this room, I shall certainly return to being as foolish as everyone else. So what is it that *thinks* in us? And what *acts* in us?

It's a strange thing! When I hear music – even while I am conducting – I hear quite positive answers to all my questions, and feel perfectly clear and confident. Or rather, I feel quite clearly that there are no questions. . . .

MAHLER TO BRUNO WALTER

[*New York, December 1909*]

I can see by now that I'm incorrigible. People like us cannot help being wholehearted about everything we do. And that, I see now, means overworking. I am, once and for all, the eternal beginner. And what little routine I have been able to establish for myself serves, at best, merely to increase the demands I make on myself. . . . My one comfort is that so far I have never really had to strike out a new path, only to keep on along the old one. But of course this in itself leads one so far from all trodden ways that like a settler in a new continent, one is finally obliged to begin laying about one with pick and shovel – which also accounts for the violent resistance I meet with in all my undertakings. . . .

Richard Strauss (*1864–1949*), *the most brilliant and most contradictory of the musicians of his time, offers in his correspondence with Hugo von Hofmannsthal a glimpse into an all-important and very secret corner of the composer's workshop: his relation to his librettist. Hofmannsthal, in his own right a fastidious poet of extreme sensitivity, was by no means a pliable tool in the hands of the composer, such as Mozart's, Bellini's, Verdi's librettists had to be. He played the part of the lofty idealist, Strauss the part of the blunt realist in a relation of the most striking disparity. The musician had the advantage of the widest practical experience of the stage; the librettist, primarily and constitutionally much more a poet than a dramatist and all too often exasperated with what appeared to him sheer vulgarity, would find himself occasionally compelled to yield to his friend's reasoned arguments, as he did, for example, when, for the sake of dramatic effectiveness, he totally reconstructed the second act of 'Der Rosenkavalier' according to the composer's wishes and suggestions. Technical matters regarding the operas would hardly be understood without detailed knowledge. The most thrilling fact, however, in this alliance of two great artists is the gentle but irresistible pull by which the poet led the composer to a style of transparent, spiritualized lightness which was really his, the poet's own vision, and which found its most perfect realization in 'Ariadne auf Naxos'. How the poet was able to sense this latent possibility in the composer's artistic constitution, so much in contrast to the dramatic outbursts of 'Salome' and 'Electra' and still overlaid with Wagnerian sumptuousness in 'Rosenkavalier', appears as a marvel of intuitive instinct.*

RICHARD STRAUSS TO HUGO VON HOFMANNSTHAL

Garmisch (Bavaria), 4 May 1909

Received the first act yesterday: I'm simply delighted. It really is charming beyond all measure: so delicate, maybe a little too delicate for the general mob, but that doesn't matter. The middle part (antechamber) not easy to put into shape, but I'll manage it all right. Anyway, I've got the whole summer before me.

The final scene is magnificent: I've already done a bit of experimenting with it today. I wish I'd got there already. But since, for the sake of symphonic unity, I must compose the music from the beginning to the end I'll just have to be patient.

The curtain is delightful: brief and to the point. You're a splendid fellow. When do I get the rest? . . .

HUGO VON HOFMANNSTHAL TO RICHARD STRAUSS

Rodaun [*near Vienna*], *12 May 1909*

Your apprehension lest the libretto be too 'delicate' does not make me nervous. Even the least sophisticated audience cannot help finding the action simple and intelligible: a pompous, fat, and elderly suitor favoured by the father has his nose put out of joint by a dashing lover – could anything be plainer? The working out of this plot must be, I feel, as I have done it, that is free from anything trivial and conventional. True and lasting success depends upon the effect on the more sensitive no less than on the coarser sections of the public, for the former are needed to give a work of art its prestige which is just as essential as its popular appeal. . . .

RICHARD STRAUSS TO HUGO VON HOFMANNSTHAL

Garmisch, 20 July 1909

Do not, I implore you, let my criticism discourage you. I can only judge from my own experience, but nothing does me so much good, nothing stimulates and fructifies my ambition and creative energy so much as adverse criticism from one to whose judgement I attach some importance. My criticism is intended to spur you on, not to discourage you. I want to draw the best out of you. . . .

In the proposal scene between the Baron and Sophie I feel sure that, during your revision, you'll hit on something even better, more comical and more striking. I know how it is: one feels annoyed when somebody else doesn't like a thing, but it goes on rankling all the same until one's hit on something better. . . .

HUGO VON HOFMANNSTHAL TO RICHARD STRAUSS

Unterach am Attersee, 30 August 1910

Yesterday I read the opera [*Rosenkavalier*] aloud to four or six friends here in one sitting. Both the lyrical and the gay aspects of the whole work made a very considerable impression. A *definite falling off* in interest became apparent in the third act after the Baron's exit, a *longueur* which is wearying. The curtain is almost ready to fall, everything hastens towards the end. Any weariness at this point (and three minutes too much can produce fatal weariness and impatience) would be fatal to the overall success. I then and there made the necessary cuts with some assistance from Felix Salten. . . .

RICHARD STRAUSS TO HUGO VON HOFMANNSTHAL

Garmisch, 7 September 1910

Of course I didn't take your letter lightly, but let me reassure you that (1) I have myself made a few cuts towards the end and (2) neither yourself nor Herr Salten can possibly at this stage judge the musical effect which the conclusion, in particular, will have. That it sounds a bit flat in reading is obvious. But it is at the conclusion that a musician, if he has any ideas at all, can achieve his best and supreme effects—so you may safely leave this for me to judge. I am nearly finished and I believe that the last third has come off brilliantly. . . .

As for the ending, from the Baron's exit onwards, I'll *guarantee* that, provided you undertake to guarantee the rest of the work. . . .

HUGO VON HOFMANNSTHAL TO RICHARD STRAUSS

Rodaun, 6 June 1910

In the final duet between Quinquin and Sophie I was obviously very much tied down by the metre scheme which you prescribed for me, but in the end I found it rather agreeable to be bound in this way to a given tune since I felt in this something Mozartian and a turning away from Wagner's intolerable erotic screaming – boundless in length as well as in degree; a repulsive, barbaric, almost bestial affair this shrieking of two creatures in heat as he practises it. . . .

Strauss had asked the poet for some lines fitting the melody of the duet in question, which he had already sketched.

RICHARD STRAUSS TO HUGO VON HOFMANNSTHAL

Garmisch, 20 June 1912

The rehearsals in Stuttgart [for the first performance of *Ariadne*] have given me very much pleasure. I believe the score is going to signpost a new road for comic opera, for those who are capable. For with this chamber music style the white sheep will quite clearly be divided from the black. . . .

My score is a real masterpiece of a score: you won't find another one like it in a hurry. . . .

HUGO VON HOFMANNSTHAL TO RICHARD STRAUSS

Rodaun, 23 June 1912

Your letter has given me real pleasure. The satisfaction you express with what you have achieved, that calm assurance of the mastery displayed in your work, this has done me good and has, in a sense which you will understand, moved me. It does me good to think that I, who hardly consider myself as standing even at the extreme periphery of your art, should have found – with that instinct which is the common bond between all creative artists, over the heads, so to speak, of the rest of the crowd – the right thing to do in producing this particular work which literally forced upon you a definite style, only to give you back your freedom more fully on a higher plane: and that I should in this way have fulfilled the promise I made to myself in devising this plot, a promise affecting the musician. . . .

HUGO VON HOFMANNSTHAL TO RICHARD STRAUSS

Rodaun, 20 January 1913

It is certainly not chance which made two men like us meet at the same period in history. And I would ask you not to ascribe to a mere freak of creative fancy any single step along the road, which we have to travel together, nor any one step which I have taken and which you have had to take with me. What, between ourselves, I would wish you to appreciate above all as a high merit of mine, and one earned with loving care, is not my libretti as such, but that which is implied in them. After *Salome* and *Elektra* had made it obvious to me that certain things, once done, were not to be repeated – for in art everything can only be done once – I set out in another direction with *Rosenkavalier*, which on the one hand required an unprecedented degree of pithiness and animation in the conversational style, while it re-admitted on the other, through the back door, so to speak, a seemingly remote stylistic method, the method of set numbers. . . . I know where I now am, yet I had rather not demonstrate it in words, but by deeds—that is through a work of art which possesses complete and pure operatic form. I hope this work, when compared with da Ponte's, Goethe's, Wagner's output, will prove itself true and genuine, not excogitated and entirely uncontrived. . . .

RICHARD STRAUSS TO HUGO VON HOFMANNSTHAL

Garmisch, 25 May 1916

As for a new opera, I have the following two things in mind; either an entirely modern, absolutely realistic domestic and character comedy of the kind I have outlined to you before . . . or some amusing piece of love and intrigue . . . a type of play of intrigue for which I've always had a special predilection.

Say a diplomatic love intrigue in the setting of the Vienna Congress with a genuine highly aristocratic woman spy as the principal character – the beautiful wife of an ambassador as a traitor for the sake of love, exploited by a secret agent or some such rather amusing subject, and then add to it the famous session of the Congress when Napoleon's return is announced. – You'll probably say: Trash!

But then we musicians are known for our poor taste in aesthetic matters, and besides, if you were to do a thing like that it wouldn't be trash. . . .

HUGO VON HOFMANNSTHAL TO RICHARD STRAUSS

30 May 1916

I could not help having a good laugh over your letter. The things you propose to me are to my taste truly horrible and might put one off from becoming a librettist for the rest of one's life – I mean put off not just anyone, but me personally. But, you know, it's best not to trouble our heads about it, for the kind of thing you have in mind I could never produce with the best will in the world; even if I did want to do it, I could not bring it off. But – *if it is to be* – I shall hit on something that does appeal to my imagination and holds out the prospect of giving me a certain amount of pleasure in the execution . . . anything conceived in this way is sure to have inherent qualities which will engage your powers in a fresh and unusual manner—that is how it has been every time hitherto, has it not? – and that, after all, is the best we can expect of each other. . . .

You must guide me, I must guide you: perhaps in this way we shall one day reach wholly new and unexplored regions. You have every reason to be grateful to me for bringing you (as now once again with *Die Frau Ohne Schatten*) that element which is sure to bewilder people and to provoke a certain amount of antagonism, for you have already too many followers, you are already all too obviously the hero of the day, all too universally accepted. By all means let them get angry with me and keep harping a while on this 'incomprehensibility', it is a mortgage to be redeemed by the next generation, just like that which appears problematical in *Ariadne*, that which today still provokes people to snort their sullen What then? and What for? . . .

RICHARD STRAUSS TO HUGO VON HOFMANNSTHAL

Garmisch [*September 1916*]

Act III [of *Die Frau Ohne Schatten*] is now finished: but, thanks to our highly beneficial conversation, I have become so uncertain that I no longer know what's successful and what's bad. And that's a good thing, for at my age one gets all too easily into the rut of mere routine and that is the death of true art. Your cri-de-cœur against Wagnerian 'note-spinning' has deeply touched my heart and has thrust open a door to an entirely new landscape where, guided by *Ariadne* and in particular its new *Vorspiel*, I hope to move forward wholly into the realm of un-Wagnerian emotion and human comic opera. I now see my way clearly before me and am grateful to you for opening my eyes. . . . I promise you that I have now definitely stripped off the Wagnerian musical armour.

HUGO VON HOFMANNSTHAL TO RICHARD STRAUSS

Aussee, 16 September [*1916*]

It is good to find a man like you determined not to stand still and get stuck in a rut, but to change and forge ahead, and it is good to know that you and I can occasionally instruct one another in a world where everyone rushes madly on, stupid, stubborn and opinionated, uninstructed and without discipline. . . . A true collaboration between two mature men would be something most rare, ours is as yet only a shadow of what it might be, but we both have good will, seriousness and consistency, and that is more than the God-forsaken 'talent' with which every lout is nowadays equipped. I am of course delighted that you are holding on to me so faithfully, it warms my heart and ties me in turn to you: so does every revelation of a new aspect of your talent like this light and spirited vein which may develop into a 'third manner' and perhaps produce works of lasting value in a yet almost unknown genre. . . .

RICHARD STRAUSS TO HUGO VON HOFMANNSTHAL

[The subject of this letter is the incidental music to Molière's *Le Bourgeois Gentilhomme*, adapted by Hofmannsthal.]

Garmisch, 25 July 1917

Now the main point: but please don't kill me. It seems to me that the piece ought to have a fourth act. The third act with the simple wedding of Lucile and Cleonte is absolutely no ending for a play that is entitled *Der Bürger als Edelmann* and represents a comedy of manners, fitted almost exclusively around that one figure. . . .

To my mind the piece ought to end quite grotesquely, either with a merry eye-opener and cure for Jourdain, like Don Quixote, or as a tragi-comedy with the eye-opening being followed by Jourdain's complete collapse and possibly madness. Do think it over, please! Don't be angry with me! . . .

HUGO VON HOFMANNSTHAL TO RICHARD STRAUSS

Aussee, 2 August 1917

. . . Your proposals, I consider, if you will forgive me, beneath discussion. They demonstrate to me that your taste and mine are miles apart, at least as concerns possibilities of this kind. Pray let me have in due course your decision whether I am free to dispose otherwise of this Molière adaptation, of which I do not intend to alter one iota.

[Continuation]

Aussee, 3 August 1917

Your critical remarks and 'proposals' reveal such absolute incomprehension, indeed such diametrical anti-comprehension of what I have tried to do, and have accomplished with this Molière adaptation by devoting to it for two months every effort of my imagination, my artistic sensitivity, my tact and self-effacement; there was something so devastating in the vista opened up by your finding it possible, after reading this play three times, to put forward proposals of this kind which make nonsense of the whole thing, that it was my first impulse to wire and ask you to leave the whole thing alone and never to speak to me, or write of it, again. But that would have been a sad discord after so many years of amicable and often beautiful joint efforts . . . and so I would not like to make our meeting and discussion of this work impossible, but will endeavour to take the offensive sting out of my absolute and harsh rejection of your ideas and proposals by a calm explanation . . . and so lead you, by the roundabout way of theory, a little closer to the poet's point of view. . . .

Well, I cannot go on filling sheet after sheet with interpretations of my dramatic intentions. All in all I am profoundly saddened by this affair. Taking a lot of trouble I have altered for you, and improved, the structure of an old, somewhat ill-constructed summer-house; out of a couple of windows which were awry I have made a balcony; I have taken out the ugly back-stairs, have given decent proportions to the whole building and have made all the rooms and the main staircase open into a large winter garden which has always been the chief attraction of the whole place. You go over the entire building with me and you don't find one word of approval, you don't even notice any of the improvements I have made in this old refractory structure; the lofty chambers, the fine perspectives, the comfortable rooms. We enter the state room with its fine view out on to the garden, and you throw a brick at the plate glass window, and then, without more ado, you request me to put up a brick wall and so shut out the view over garden and landscape, or at least put a big dung-heap where the fountain now is. My comparison is bitter, but it is in no way exaggerated. The wall is your apalling idea of introducing real madness, the most horrible thing there is in the whole world, as the crowning point of a light and elegant comedy of manners; the dung-heap is the eye-opening' and 'reconciliation' where in fact the various elements face each other as incommensurables and can be reconciled only in the rhythm of the comedy.

I feel as your architect would, exactly. In conclusion I can only ask you – and not for the first time – to make up your mind now, before we meet, whether or not you are willing to decorate with your music *this* my adaptation of the Molière comedy as you now have it, well-rounded, well considered work as it is. These are the only alternatives. . . .

HUGO VON HOFMANNSTHAL TO RICHARD STRAUSS

16 May 1918

From my point of view, too, these days meant a great deal and the *Ariadne* performance, which rounded them off, gave rise to important ideas which I shall try and elucidate to myself and to you at an early occasion. Of all our joint works this is the one I never cease to love best, every time I hear it. Here alone you have gone wholly with me and – what is more mysterious – wholly even with yourself. Here for once you freed yourself entirely from all thought of effect; even what is most tender and most personal did not appear too simple, too humble for you here. You have lent your ear to the most intimate inspiration and have given great beauty; of all these works, this is the one which, believe me, *possesses the strongest guarantee that it will endure*. . . .

RICHARD STRAUSS TO HUGO VON HOFMANNSTHAL

Garmisch, 12 July 1918

Don't be angry that I have 'prodded' you. It was not meant as a reminder – but you cannot blame me for dying to get something from you again soon. I am fifty-four years of age – how long my productive vigour will continue to yield something good, who can tell? And we could both give the world a good many fine things yet. What was it you said at the time? Every few years a delightful little Singspiel, in between a comedy with music (similar to *Bourgeois*), then a satirical operetta, and then – as it goes in the *Magic Flute* – another little Papageno, then another Papagena, until the spring runs dry. . . .

HUGO VON HOFMANNSTHAL TO RICHARD STRAUSS

1 August 1918

. . . In our relationship there is no need for many words and arguments. The passing reference to your fifty-four years does more to prompt me than any amount of persuasion. Rest assured that, whenever I feel in a productive mood, I shall always turn my imagination in the desired direction, in so far as this can be done by an effort of the will. . . .

After the death of Hofmannsthal in 1929 Strauss found a congenial collaborator in another distinguished writer and poet, Stefan Zweig. Their first work in common, however, 'Die Schweigsame Frau' ('The Silent Woman'), coincided with the crisis of the thirties, the advent of Hitler in Germany, which plunged Europe into a cataclysm. Zweig, a Jew, was not acceptable on a German stage. 'The Silent Woman', scheduled for performance in Dresden, caused protracted negotiations between Strauss and the German Minister of Propaganda, but was in the end passed by the Head of State, not without some opposition from the radical wing of the party.

RICHARD STRAUSS TO STEFAN ZWEIG

Garmisch, 20 February 1935

As regards *The Silent Woman*, now that Hitler and Goebbels have given their official permission, there is nothing more to be done, or rather, to postpone. Dresden has already announced the production for June–July, so events must now take their course. But as to the future: if I am so fortunate as to receive another libretto from you, or more than one, it must be agreed that nobody is to know I have received it, or that I am composing music for it. . . .

STEFAN ZWEIG TO RICHARD STRAUSS

Vienna, 23 February 1935

You know my great respect for you, and this in itself entitles me to speak frankly. I sometimes feel – and I honour you for it – that you yourself are not fully aware of your great historical position, that you have too modest an opinion of yourself. Everything you do is destined to have a place in history. Your letters, your decisions, will one day be common property, like those of Wagner and Brahms. So it seems to me hardly possible that anything that happens these days in your life or your art could remain secret; for though I would never let drop a word to reveal that I was working on something for you, this secrecy would one day become public knowledge. A man like Richard Strauss can claim every right in public, he should do nothing in secret; no one must be able to say that you shrank from responsibility. Your magnificent work, which has no equal in the world of art, makes it your duty to refuse all restrictions on your free will and your artistic choice; who else but you has such a right today?

But I fully understand the difficulties a new work would encounter nowadays if I wrote the libretto; it would be regarded as a kind of defiance. And to collaborate in secret seems to me, as I say, unworthy of your rank. However, I will gladly help and advise anyone who works for you, I will sketch out many things for him, and of course without any material return and without ever boasting of it – solely for the pleasure of serving your great art and showing my gratitude for your having made out of *The Silent Woman* a work for the whole world. . . .

Stefan Zweig made his generous offer true: three of Strauss's later operas – 'Der Friedenstag', 'Daphne', and 'Capriccio' – were based on Zweig's suggestions and dramatic sketches. He was wiser than the great composer; a disturbed world does not permit a responsible human being to dodge a question of conscience. There is at least one case on record of a famous musician who had the courage of sticking out his neck when his conscience was troubled. The occasion was the Dreyfus case in Paris which, in the late nineties, caused violent clashes of opinion all over Europe.

EDWARD GRIEG TO MAX ABRAHAM, HEAD OF C. F. PETERS, PUBLISHERS IN LEIPZIG

4 October 1899

On the day when the shocking news of the verdict in the Dreyfus case reached Norway. I received an invitation from Colonne to conduct in Paris. I was staying with Björnson, whose son-in-law, Langen, the publisher, translated my reply into French and asked my permission to have it printed in the *Frankfurter Zeitung*. At first I refused, but later in the conversation I asked 'Do you really think that to publish it would do any good?' and he and several others replied 'Yes, certainly'. So I said 'Well, I don't mind!' The result was that all the leading European newspapers printed the letter in their turn, and now I am getting letters of abuse from France every day, such filthy stuff as you cannot imagine. Mr Henri de Rochefort sent me his noble newspaper *L'Intransigeant* today, addressed as follows: 'To the Composer of Jewish music, Edward Grieg' (!). And as for the contents of the paper, they were really the very limit. I honestly believe that all the basest and vulgarest elements in France have leagued together over this Dreyfus question. . . .

Strauss, with his customary aloofness, tried to temporize, to keep out of trouble and ride the waves. He even accepted the official position of President of the 'Reichsmusikkammer', the obligatory organization of all German musicians recognized as 'Aryans'. At the same time he fully appreciated the value of his librettist and tried to keep him in spite of all difficulties. The result was deep humiliation for the great composer which marked the end of his participation in the public affairs of Hitler's Germany.

In 1933, when Hitler came to power, Bruno Walter was instantly dismissed from his posts as conductor of 'Gewandhaus' concerts in Leipzig and of the Berlin Philharmonic Orchestra. At the same time Toscanini, as a gesture of protest, refused to conduct at Bayreuth. On both occasions Strauss stepped into the breach. In the following letter to Zweig he still cannot see that the ethics of such a course of action are questionable.

RICHARD STRAUSS TO STEFAN ZWEIG

17 June 1935

Your letter of the 15th drives me to despair! This Jewish obstinacy! It's enough to make anyone anti-Semitic! The pride of race, the feeling of solidarity – it gives even *me* a sense of difference! Do you imagine I've ever been influenced in any transaction by the idea that I'm a Teuton (perhaps, *qui le sait*)? Do you imagine that Mozart wrote consciously 'Aryan' music? So far as I am concerned, people fall into two categories, those who have talent and those who have not; and so far as I am concerned the general public exist only from the moment when they form an audience. Whether the audience consists of Chinese, Upper Bavarians, New Zealanders or Berliners, is all the same to me, provided they've paid the full price for their seats. . . . Who told you I had *gone so far politically*? Because I took a concert for Bruno Walter? I did that for the sake of the orchestra – because I stepped into the gap for the other 'non-Aryan', Toscanini? I did that for the sake of Bayreuth. That has nothing to do with politics. It doesn't matter to me how the news-rags interpret it, and you shouldn't bother about that either. That I go through the motions of being President of the *Reichsmusikkammer*? That's in order to do good and safeguard against greater evils. Simply from a sense of artistic duty. . . . So be a good fellow, forget Moses and the other Apostles for a few weeks and just work at your two-act libretto. . . .

THE HEAD OF GOVERNMENT [REICHSSTATTHALTER] IN SAXONY TO ADOLF HITLER WITH A PHOTOCOPY OF STRAUSS'S FOREGOING LETTER

Dresden-A., 1 July 1935

Mein Führer!

The enclosed letter from Herr Dr Strauss to the Jew Stefan Zweig has come into the hands of the Secret State Police in Saxony [the Gestapo], and I beg to send you a photocopy for your information.

With regard to the production of *The Silent Woman* I would like to mention that the first performance was given to a full house, including 500 invited guests, the second performance attracted so few people that the management had to fill it up with free tickets, and the third performance was cancelled, ostensibly because the prima donna was ill.

Heil!

Your devoted
Martin Mutschmann

MEMORANDUM BY RICHARD STRAUSS

10 July 1935

On 6 July I received a visit from Ministerial Counsellor Keudell, sent by the Secretary of State, Herr Funk, to demand that for the sake of my 'impaired health' I should ask to be relieved of my duties as President of the *Reichsmusikkammer*, etc. This I did at once.

Herr von Keudell showed me a copy, underlined in red in many places, of a private letter to my friend and erstwhile collaborator Stefan Zweig; although this letter bore the *full name of the sender* on the outside of the envelope, it had apparently been opened by the State Police of Saxony. I was not aware that, even while President of the *Reichsmusikkammer*, I was under the direct supervision of the State Police, and that my life's work of 80 large compositions, 'recognized throughout the world', did not entitle me to be considered a 'good German' above all criticism. Despite this, Herr Minister Goebbels has taken the unprecedented step of dismissing me without so much as asking for an explanation of the confiscated letter, which must be quite incomprehensible to unauthorized readers who know nothing of what led up to it and see it outside the context of a long correspondence on purely artistic questions. . . . Since Bach's day we have been composing what our talent allowed, and have been Aryans and Germans without giving it a thought. This can hardly be described as high treason, but should be credited to me as loyal service to the fatherland, even when, as in Mozart's case [Da Ponte, Mozart's favourite librettist, was of Jewish origin] and mine, librettos have been provided by non-Aryans.

And now let the sacrifices be reckoned that I have had to accept because I did not hold aloof from the entire National Socialist movement from its inception. These began with my taking over the last subscription concert for Bruno Walter, who had been driven out, which I did for the sake of the Philharmonic Orchestra and after much urging from Kopsch and Rasch. The fee, 1,500 Marks, I presented to the orchestra. This unleashed a storm against me in the Jewish papers in foreign countries, particularly in those of Vienna, which did me more harm and lowered me more in the eyes of all decent people than the German Government could ever have made good to me. I was suspected of being a servile, self-seeking anti-Semite, whereas on the contrary I have always taken every opportunity of making it clear to influential people here (again to my own prejudice) that I regard the Streicher–Goebbels Jew-baiting campaign as a stain on German honour, as a sign of impoverishment, and as an ignoble weapon employed by untalented, lazy mediocrity against superior intelligence and ability. I take this opportunity of declaring openly that I have received so much encouragement from Jews, so much self-sacrificing friendship, generous help and intellectual stimulus as well, that it would be a crime not to make the most grateful admission of the fact. . . .

This loyal declaration came too late.

It would be difficult to find a more drastic demonstration that opportunism does not always pay.

There is a strong unifying force in opposition. It would be no easier to find a positive common denominator for the three great representatives of French music at the turn of the century, Gabriel Fauré *(1845–1924),* Claude Debussy *(1862–1918) and* Maurice Ravel *(1875–1937), than for Mahler and Strauss; what these French musicians had in common was an aversion to German music and all it stood for. It is true that German influence, which had been steadily rising since the time of Beethoven, became more penetrating than ever towards the end of the nineteenth century, when Wagnerism swept Europe and music was regarded almost as an intrinsically German art. As with all movements that develop in a wave, the climax came later than the generating force; the golden age of German music was already a matter of the past when the First World War radically destroyed its international influence.*

Fauré's early development coincided with the high tide of Germanism in music. His opposition to it is characteristically reflected in his letters, but also his perplexity with respect to ways and means of restoring the true character of French music. One can appreciate the antipathy for anything German on the part of a generation that had experienced the war of 1870–1.

GABRIEL FAURÉ TO HIS WIFE MARIE FAURÉ-FREMIET

Bayreuth, 6 August 1896

You think I am going to find the people round me dazzlingly intelligent, because of the atmosphere of intelligence with which Wagner's work surrounds us. But it's just the contrary! I can feel that we are all finding one another even duller than usual. We are incapable of talking about anything except the performances, and each of us is more inept than the other when we try to describe our feelings! We are really stultified by all the splendours, and all our arguments – for we argue a great deal – lead to nothing. That's like the *Tetralogy*, of course; it's packed with philosophy and symbolism that serve merely to demonstrate our poverty, our hopeless emptiness. When it comes to an end it leaves one slightly more convinced of universal misery, of eternal suffering and that's all! You can see how gay and stimulating it is! In fact it is penitence in the noblest meaning of the word, it is almost contrition. . . .

Bayreuth, 8 August 1896

I am full of this *Tetralogy*, it haunts me day and night! I don't think these works are direct examples which could be imitated. But in a general way there is benefit and instruction to be derived from them. The stuff soaks into you like water into sand. . . .

FAURÉ TO HIS WIFE

Cologne, 10 January 1905

They were giving [Bellini's] *Norma*, which I'd never seen. It is full of melodies that enraptured our parents and which require a singing technique now completely lost. And it was being presented in a brand-new theatre, magnificent, lavishly equipped, but designed and decorated with German taste, splendidly heavy and ugly.

The city is enormous, very lively and very clean. There are many beautiful old churches, not to mention the cathedral, the '*Dom*', which stands some thirty yards from my room and is world-famous. But there are so many equestrian Emperors, perched up all over the place! Beside the Rhine – very wide, very handsome – I saw the statue of the unfortunate Frederick. He is gigantic, and is shown making a sweeping gesture as though commanding the whole universe. And when one remembers his reign was plagued by a sore throat, it gives a very true idea of the farcical nature of all things human.

And that's what makes them so formidably powerful, these Germans who are so profoundly different from ourselves. Seeing them still so tough and rough, one wonders what they can have been like in the fourteenth century. But what strength and what orderliness and what substantiality in everything, everywhere, for everything. . . . It's disheartening!

The German Emperor Frederick III died in 1888 of cancer of the throat, after a reign of only three months.

FAURÉ TO HIS WIFE

Frankfurt, 16 January 1905

I'm very tired of all these Germans, despite the trouble they take to be pleasant; and above all, I have had a surfeit of music. They possess very pronounced gifts in that sphere; but they lack our nicety of taste and our sensitivity. And the funny thing is that my music has been criticized for being rather cold, rather too well-bred! We are not of the same race, that is clear beyond doubt. . . .

I have been toiling round all the sights of Frankfurt, and it's cold – eight degrees below zero again today. Another concert this evening. There's at least one every day. And all are listened to with unvarying placidity. Concerts are like meals, they rank among the natural functions. . . .

FAURÉ TO HIS WIFE

Stresa, Lago Maggiore, 31 August 1906

Yesterday, on the boat, an Italian composer called Giordano [composer of *André Chénier*, *Fédora*, etc.] came up to speak to me. During the Italian season last year he was the only composer about whom I could find anything nice to say in *Le Figaro*. Well, it seems there was a lot of opposition to him in his own country, and my article completely altered his situation. That's the sort of thing one would never suspect! They used to call him a lunatic, and one article in the *Figaro* was enough to make him into a great man. Oh, human nature! . . . In short, Giordano, who is a rich man, has a villa near here, and he asked me to come to luncheon one of these days so that all his family can tell me how fond they are of me. . . .

FAURÉ TO HIS WIFE

Lausanne, 20 September 1907

The author of the poem [of the opera *Pénélope*] has given me too much material. He forgets that music makes lines stretch out terribly, and that what takes two minutes to read takes at least three times as long when it's sung. So I am having to cut out couplets or groups of four or eight lines here and there, taking care that the general meaning remains clear. That's not always so easy! Those damned Suitors hold forth interminably!

Lausanne, 23 September 1907

Penelope's speeches are written in a fine style, there's no affectation about them; I like them – but they're too long! It's terrible! When I think of the amount of music I have already written for this first Act, and of how much remains to be done, I'm alarmed at the length it will run to, with practically no action. . . .

FAURÉ TO HIS WIFE

Lugano, 1 October 1907

I've been taking a good look at my work: I think I have made all the actors express themselves in character (both in Act I and in Act II). I made no special effort to do so, I just allowed myself to be guided by the nature of the plot, which is so simple, and the dignity of the characters. . . . And yet the impression produced by the piano is *terribly cold*, the general effect seems to me to be stiff and formal. The only satisfaction I get is when I listen in my own head to what I've composed. I need to ask someone else's opinion. Perhaps if I put the whole thing aside for two or three weeks I may get a clearer view. Wagner's excessive – though always entirely justified – polyphony, Debussy's chiaroscuro, and the contemptibly impassioned writhings of Massenet are the only things by which present-day audiences are moved or gripped. They are indifferent to the limpid, *sincere* music of Saint-Saëns, to whom I feel myself closest. And all this gives me shivers down my spine. On the other hand, if I didn't get into such a funk, if I didn't feel these doubts, I should not be an artist!

FAURÉ TO HIS WIFE

Evian, 25 August 1918

I have had a Festival. In the last month there has been a *Festival Chopin* given here by a pianist, a *Festival Saint-Saëns* arranged by Litvinne, and then mine. After seeing the three successive posters, all different and yet all similar, a little girl of six asked her mother if all these composers really had *Festival* for their first name. . . .

In his old age Fauré was afflicted with distorted aural sensation and progressive deafness.

FAURÉ TO HIS WIFE

Nice, 19 April 1922

It is sheer torture to watch while hearing only a few snatches of singing; and the orchestra can have little or no charm for me. Just imagine, with my poor ears there are moments when I couldn't say *where we have got to in the music*! . . . Neither for myself nor for anyone else have I ever played a single note of *Pénélope* since the first one was written at Lausanne – in 1907 if I am not mistaken. The reason being that my hearing was already defective in those days, and when my fingers played certain notes, it was *other notes* that I *heard*!

Like his music, Debussy's *letters are expressions of a lofty mind and a noble individuality. Fastidiousness, subtlety, wisdom, and critical judgement are combined with a great artist's genuine humility which never permits a word of vanity or self-importance. It seems that this great musician was constitutionally unable to make any comfortable concession to mediocrity, indifference, or routine. No wonder that the atmosphere of the theatre was uncongenial to him; his only opera, 'Pelléas et Mélisande', offered frequent exasperating occasions to a sensitive perfectionist such as he.*

Messager, musical director of the Paris Opéra-Comique, had to abandon 'Pelléas et Mélisande' after its first performance owing to an engagement abroad, leaving the direction of Debussy's opera to the second conductor, Henri-Paul Büsser.

CLAUDE DEBUSSY TO ANDRÉ MESSAGER

Paris, 9 May 1902

Since you went away I have been about as gloomy as a road where no one ever sets foot. . . . But I don't want to bore you with my lamentations, so let us say something about our *Pelléas.*

On Thursday we had a quick run-through, which Büsser needed – between ourselves, the management of the Opéra-Comique might have given time for a full rehearsal – Büsser was nervous and didn't seem to know how to tackle the score. Périer [Pelléas] sang in a voice that seemed to come out of his umbrella! Miss Garden [Mélisande] absolutely refused to look at the aforenamed Büsser, under the pretext that she was accustomed to contemplating another and infinitely more agreeable face. (There's a lot to be said for that opinion.) In brief, a vague and murky impression, one didn't know what might happen.

On Friday a splendid audience, including Monsier de Reszké [a famous tenor]. The public very respectful. Büsser arrived looking like a gentleman who's going to take a cold bath and doesn't like it. (The orchestra was admirable, carrying him along and prompting him over the shading.) He paid no attention to the singers, flinging chords at them with a complete disregard for the latters' harmonic qualities. Anyhow, it all turned out fairly well, and after the fourth Act there were three curtain-calls to reward all these worthy people for their efforts.

In conclusion, a pleasant evening, where only you were lacking – and that completely! What I mean is that you succeeded in awakening Pelléas to musical life with a delicate tenderness that can never be repeated, for there is no doubt whatever that the inner rhythm of any composition is conditioned by the conductor who calls it forth, just as a word is conditioned by the lips that utter it. . . .

DEBUSSY TO HIS PUBLISHER AND FRIEND JACQUES DURAND

25 October 1903

I've received the copy of *Estampes* and take pleasure in thanking you once again for their splendid published appearance; it is perfection . . . the only thing we need now is for these three pieces to be masterworks!

I would have liked to call and thank you personally, but the Opéra-Comique in some ridiculous way takes up all my time [with *Pelléas et Mélisande*]. And this theatrical life disgusts me and wears me out. . . .

DEBUSSY TO J. DURAND

Eastbourne, Friday 19 August 1905

My dear friend, your impatience about the *Images* touches me; but what has happened is this: the first piece, *Reflets dans l'eau*, really doesn't satisfy me, so I have decided to compose another one based on new facts and using the latest discoveries in harmonic chemistry. . . . Excuse me for the slight delay; I trust it will not take me more than a week. I am beginning to see clearly in my imaginative affairs and my thinking mechanism is slowly starting up again.

In short, I'm forgetting the man I am in order to return to being the man I ought to be, the gods willing!

All this metaphysics mixed with mechanics is perhaps neither useful nor very clear, but metaphysics after all is the art of saying very silly things in an obscure way. . . .

The last statement, inimitable in its conciseness and neatness, deserves a place in a manual of philosophy.

DEBUSSY TO J. DURAND

Brussels, 7 January 1906

There's even a chime which ought to be in G and which some imp of perversity has changed to C! . . . It's rather as though someone were ringing the dinner gong in the castle, and it doesn't add much to the sadness of Mélisande's death scene. Up to now, I have seen only half of the tower . . . a fountain made out of unpainted wood . . . underground caverns so realistic that they are impenetrable. The child Yniold is such a child that he doesn't know the music yet, and the *dress rehearsal* is tomorrow. . . . I suppose it would be better to settle down to being one of the illustrious dead with whom they can deal however they like. I assume, moreover, that the orchestra members and the singers are probably already dreaming of me in this role, since it appears that they have never encountered a composer as hard to get along with as I am. . . .

So you will be seeing something that falls short of perfection, dear friend; excuse me beforehand, I've done everything I could for it to be otherwise – even to making myself undeniably unpleasant. May God and the King of the Belgians forgive me. . . .

DEBUSSY TO J. DURAND

Thursday, 1 March 1906

You know, I'm not a bit jealous; the real sea plays with the waves even better than I do, she has more colours and more room to do it in; in any case, I don't hold it against her and hope she'll keep on. . . .

DEBUSSY TO J. DURAND

Tuesday, 20 March 1906

You're very kind, Colonne [conductor in Paris] is very nice . . . you will doubtless think me tiresome if I suggest that *Cortège et Danse* is perhaps too slight to be performed in a season during which *La Mer*, the *Nocturnes* and the *Images* have been played one after another?

I should be quite interested in a historically presented programme of my works, but I am afraid of being accused of scraping the bottom of my desk drawers in my eagerness to keep my name perpetually on the concert posters. . . . I could also be dead – a perfect excuse – which I would rather postpone. . . .

DEBUSSY TO J. DURAND

Le Puys, near Dieppe, 8 August 1906

Here I am again with my old friend the Sea; she is always endless and beautiful. She is really the thing in Nature that best shows you how small you are. Only . . . we don't treat her with sufficient respect. . . . It ought to be forbidden to dip all those bodies deformed by the daily grind into her; but seriously, all those arms and legs churning in ridiculous rhythms, it's enough to make the fish weep. There should only be Sirens in the Sea, and how can you expect those respectable creatures to show themselves in such ill-frequented waters?

The hotel where we're staying is run by a Monsieur X and he is a dangerous man . . . he does his own marketing and brings back the weirdest looking provisions, something awful is sure to happen to any fish or meat that comes his way; in short, he's a professional killer.

Since his hotel is the only one in the place, he laughs at criticism and gets on with his sinister business.

Excuse these housekeeping details, but Carlyle, who knew what he was talking about, being dyspeptic, maintained that the artist has to eat better than anybody else. . . .

DEBUSSY TO J. DURAND

Pourville, near Dieppe, 23 August 1907

Images will be ready, if I can manage to finish *Rondes* to suit me and properly. The music in this piece has a particularly wispy quality and for that reason it's impossible to treat it like a big healthy symphony that walks along on four feet (three, sometimes, but it walks all the same).

Incidentally, I am more and more convinced that music, by its very nature, is something that cannot be poured into a tight, conventional mould. It is all colours, rhythms. . . .

The rest is humbug invented by frigid imbeciles at the expense of the Masters, who almost always wrote nothing but period music!

Only Bach had a vision of the truth. . . .

DEBUSSY TO PAUL-JEAN TOULET

Pourville, 27 August 1907

Of course, this place is ghastly, and although people are no more ridiculous here than elsewhere, they are more in evidence – which doesn't help matters.

Add to this a hotel where 'modern comfort' is represented by a total lack of hot water and tasteless cooking.

The English, who have not become any more pleasant in spite of the *entente cordiale*, nor their wives less stupidly 'angular', add nothing but a slight irritation to an otherwise charming landscape. I would willingly give all nine Beethoven symphonies bound in the skin of R[ichard] S[trauss] to be in Paris. . . .

As one can see, Debussy had no love for German music, past or present, and his fastidiousness was by no means restricted to music.

DEBUSSY TO J. DURAND

March 1908

I find our age so singularly ungracious in its ado about less than nothing. We look down our noses, quite mistakenly, at American bluff, while we produce a kind of artistic bluff which will come home to roost one of these days – most unfortunate for French vanity. . . .

Don't think from the tone of this letter that I've become a pessimist, I hate that kind of mental attitude; it's only that people disgust me now and then and I have to shout it to someone who won't be likely to mistake it for disease. . . .

DEBUSSY TO J. DURAND

London, 13 May 1909

London is bathed in the sulphurous sunlight to be found only here; our hotel is wonderfully situated, but the beds are spartan and I wonder, as I do every time I come here, what the famous English comfort really means.

I have just seen 'Il signor Campanini'. In the first place he has a delicious accent and seems to be a good conductor (we only rehearsed at the piano). There will be four orchestra rehearsals, counting the dress rehearsal! It's not much! and from one country to another, managers are all the same. . . .

Debussy was in London for the performance of 'Pelléas et Mélisande' *at Covent Garden given 22 May.*

DEBUSSY TO J. DURAND

London, 18 May 1909

The first performance of *Pelléas,* which was to have been today, Wednesday, has been postponed until next Friday . . . this news covers lots of unusual or ridiculous happenings! . . .

There is a stage director here called X; he comes from Marseilles, sees ceilings where there is only empty space and imagines wonderful blossoming things on flats as bare as a blind man's stick. You can imagine what heights one might reach with a man of such power! I have rarely had a stronger urge to kill anyone.

I have to act as electrician, stage-hand, God knows where it will end!

Luckily, the orchestra is going well, Campanini has a pretty fair understanding of the piece – a bit too 'showy' – but at least it's warm and alive.

Warnery will be fine, I believe, although I haven't seen her in costume yet.

Marcoux and Bourbon are also good. In short, the performance might be excellent were it not for the same old thing, that is, trying to do a month's work in a week. I've done all I can and my artistic conscience will be clear.

I must add that Higgins and Percy Pitt are charming and ask only to be helpful; but, believe me, it's the fault of the composers who will put up with any kind of makeshift thing so long as they get performed!

All I yearn for now is to get home . . . the theatrical atmosphere makes me ill, no matter how much good will you start out with, some second-rate thing always comes along to trip you up miserably. . . .

DEBUSSY TO J. DURAND

London, 23 May 1909

Here are some further details I've been told about the *Pelléas* première, since as you can well imagine, I did not attend that party!

From the first act on, success was in the air and kept growing until the end. They called for the composer for fifteen minutes. He was peacefully back at his hotel, caring nothing for any sort of glory.

Then Cléofonte Campanini took two bows, after which he telephoned me to tell me that the opera had been an enormous 'soooccess' the like of which has rarely been seen in England. He came around the next morning, confirmed the victory with *commedia dell'arte* gestures and kissed me as though I were a holy medal blessed by the Pope.

Probably at a theatre like Covent Garden – where they think of nothing but effect – all effort is held in reserve for the first performance, since I assure you the dress rehearsal was deplorable. . . .

DEBUSSY TO J. DURAND

London, 27 November 1909

The concert was today and it went off very well: *Fêtes* was encored and I had only myself to thank that the same thing did not happen to the *Prélude à l'après-midi d'un Faune*. . . . However, my knees were buckling . . . a very poor condition in which to conduct anything.

This evening I have to go to a reception given by the English Composers' Society. . . . What face shall I put on? . . . Something resembling a condemned man; it would seem that I can't get out of it because of the *entente cordiale* and other sentimentalities thought up for the purpose of hastening the demise of one's neighbour – most likely. . . .

DEBUSSY TO J. DURAND

Budapest, 4 December 1910

My stay in Vienna was so studded with annoying or ridiculous incidents that I didn't think it worth while reporting it to you. . . .

Well, the concert was a success, especially *Ibéria*. We couldn't play *La Mer* or the *Nocturnes* for lack of time. Of course, I was assured that the orchestra knew *La Mer*, having played it three times. Ah! my friend, if only you had heard it! I even longed for X! The same thing happened with the *Nocturnes*. – Whereupon I decided to stick to the *Petite Suite*, *L'après-midi d'un Faune* and *Ibéria*. And I can assure you that preparing *Ibéria* in two rehearsals represents a pretty considerable effort. Not that I expect this momentous event to be carved on the marble of eternity, but it's worth telling about all the same; my nerves are in shreds. Remember that the only way these people were able to understand me was through an interpreter – namely, a doctor of law – who might very well have been distorting my ideas while he passed them on, one never knows!

For that matter, I used every method I could think of: I sang, I made Italian pantomime gestures, etc. . . . it would have softened a buffalo's heart.

Well, they finally understood and I got in the last word anyhow. I kept taking curtain calls like a ballerina and if the adoring throng didn't unharness the horses from my carriage, it was only because I was in an ordinary taxi-cab.

In fact, if any moral can be drawn from this trip, it is that I am not cut out to play the composer abroad. It takes the heroism of a travelling salesman and a willingness to make the sort of compromise which quite decidedly disgusts me. . . .

DEBUSSY TO ROBERT GODET

6 February 1911

Vienna: raddled old city where one is surfeited with the music of Brahms and Puccini, with officers with women's bosoms and women with officers' chests.

There, an orchestral concert – since that was what I had come for! – Many congratulations in German, which I don't understand, so I am free to take them as I like.

Next, Budapest, where the Danube refuses to be as blue as a famous waltz maintains it is. The Hungarians liars and charming. The best thing they have to offer is a gypsy whose name is spelled Radics but is pronounced Raditch – don't ask me why – who loves music infinitely more than many people who are famous for it.

In a banal, commonplace café, he gives one the feeling of being seated among forest shadows, and from deep down in the soul he draws up that special melancholy we so seldom have occasion to use.

In short, he could wrest secrets from a strong-box.

There, chamber music (1,500 people to listen to the *Children's Corner*, a frightening proportion).

But I brought back some very beautiful embroidery work and some marvellous chocolates from Monsieur Gerbaud's (your compatriot, dear friend), who has a kind of genius. . . .

Gerbaud was the most renowned confectioner in Budapest.

DEBUSSY TO J. DURAND

January 1912

Between ourselves, Mr Russell and the Bostonians seem to me to have discovered the one and only way to perform *Pelléas*!

But I still suspect the Americans to be nothing but transplanted natives of Marseilles. After all, they invented bluff, which is so much like the Mediterranean mentality!

As for me, I am in a fever to find everything I need and in a state of anguish to finish no matter what, at any price! A curious disease, which afflicted Leonardo da Vinci too. Only he had genius as well. That helps a lot. I'm satisfied with having endless patience which – as he said – may sometimes be a substitute for genius. . . .

DEBUSSY TO J. DURAND

12 September 1912

You will find many changes in the last part of *Jeux*. I worked on it up to the last minute. It's an attempt at something rather difficult to bring off, since the music is supposed to help in putting across a rather *risqué* situation! But in ballet, after all, immorality slips through the ballerina's legs and ends in a pirouette. . . .

DEBUSSY TO J. DURAND

June 1914

I'm going to London for a few days to take part in a *soirée* given by Lady Speyer. Caruso would ask as much as I'm getting, just for his accompanist! Still, it's a drop of water in the desert of these ugly summer months.

Let us thank Providence, even if it speaks with an English accent!

The First World War came to Debussy as a shattering experience from which he never recovered, although he was able to resume his creative work in 1915. Disillusioned and physically exhausted, he died of cancer after two operations.

DEBUSSY TO J. DURAND

8 August 1914

You know I have no courage and still less the mentality – never having had occasion to handle a rifle – add to this memories of '70 which prevent me from giving way to any enthusiasm, not to mention my wife's anxiety – her son and son-in-law are both in the army!

All this makes my life extremely tense and filled with worry, in the midst of which I am only a poor atom tossed about by this awful disaster; what I do seems so pitifully small! I am even beginning to envy Satie, who busies himself seriously defending Paris, as a corporal...

DEBUSSY TO J. DURAND

18 August 1914

I've also seen Paul Dukas who, though not at the beck and call of any minister, says he's as ready to get his head knocked in as the next man.

My age and military capacities make me good for nothing more than sentry duty at best. If one more 'head' is absolutely necessary for victory, I'd gladly give my own without arguing about it. . . .

Furthermore, it's almost impossible to work! To tell the truth, I don't care. The side-effects of war are more distressing than people think. . . .

DEBUSSY TO J. DURAND

Pourville, 19 August 1915

The days go by with agonizing rapidity and I no longer have time to take care of the garden . . . for that matter, the last time I did any gardening I was struck in the eye by a dead branch . . . this is probably the way dead branches have of avenging themselves, a fateful warning to get back to music and leave them to die in peace. Which I did straightaway! Dead trees must possess some of the soul of the gods mankind has thrust from its memory: it is better to listen to them than to Madame de Thèbes's prophesies. . . .

Mme de Thèbes was the famous clairvoyant in Paris at that time, who emitted her weekly prophecy of what was to come.

DEBUSSY TO J. DURAND

Pourville, 27 September 1915

We shall be returning to Paris about the 12th of October. Farewell sea, farewell tranquillity! I am definitely ready for life beneath the open sky, among mute trees. Big cities frighten me, one is obliged to shake too many dirty hands. It's not disgust or misanthropy, but the need to concentrate what's left of my powers of thought which 'the city' casually fritters away. Think of the ghastly reporters who try to advertise your plans even before you've been able to realize them! . . .

DEBUSSY TO J. DURAND

Pourville, 9 October 1915

You know my views on the metronome: it might give the correct speed for one measure, like 'les roses, l'espace d'un matin,' but there are 'those' who understand nothing about music and who will use this as a pretext for understanding it even less!

So do whatever you like.

The fatal hour of departure draws nigh!

I shall be writing up to the very last minute, like André Chénier who wrote poetry just before mounting the scaffold! Although macabre, this comparison contains a grain of truth.

The brain is an extremely delicate instrument which is thrown out of gear by the slightest shock and 'atmosphere' is only a trite word. . . .

DEBUSSY TO J. DURAND

8 June 1916

It's still the 'sick man' thanking you for your friendly concern. . . . I confess that daily I lose more of my rather too sorely tried patience; it's enough to make one wonder if this illness is incurable? They would do better to let me know right away 'then! oh! then!' (as that poor creature Golaud says). . . .

My life is really too difficult, and a Claude Debussy who is no longer composing music has no more reason to go on living. I have no hobbies: they taught me nothing except music. . . . This is bearable only if one is productive, but it's rather humiliating to keep knocking on an empty-sounding head! . . .

DEBUSSY TO J. DURAND

5 July 1916

I don't feel well enough to know whether I can do it or not, but I've decided to rise above it, to work and to stop obeying the dictates of an illness which has become a bit too imperious! We shall see. If I am to die soon, I want at least to have made an attempt at doing my duty. . . .

DEBUSSY TO J. DURAND

Le Moulleau, 16 October 1916

No doubt about it, Le Moulleau will have been of no help to me, and I shall return without a single *chef-d'oeuvre* . . . perhaps some useful notes for the future? And then, hotel life never seemed so difficult before . . . the very walls are unfriendly, not to mention this life in a numbered box.

Yesterday I had a visit from X. . . . For a moment he made me sorry I had written a Sonata and doubtful about the soundness of my work! In short, we need never again doubt that there are bad musicians everywhere! Ah well, this experience upset me deeply; it is pregnant with consequences and I am no longer surprised at the lack of understanding which so often greets my poor music. Without overdramatizing, I assure you it frightens me. Why wasn't I taught to polish lenses like Spinoza? I ought never to have relied for my daily bread on what I could earn through music. . . .

It's a miscalculation, I will even go so far as to call it dishonest . . . but it is too late – alas! – to profit from this bitter truth. . . .

DEBUSSY TO ROBERT GODET

3 December 1916

To tell the truth, I go on with this waiting life – waiting-room life, I might say, for I am a poor traveller waiting for a train that will never come again.

They tell me it's the morphine! It's an easy thing to lay the blame on that, for it's far away. No! something is broken in the strange mechanism that used to be my brain.

Who's to blame?

Perhaps this miserable war that loses some of its nobility with every passing day. It was stupid enough to trust the Bulgarians. But it's even more so to trust the Greeks for anything! Those people have been practising lying for too long. And King George looks like a hawker of lead pencils, with no lead in them.

Of course rumours spread like weeds. Everyone appoints a new commander-in-chief every morning. It's like a hunchback changing his tailor in the hope that the new one will be able to conceal his hump. We have no war sense, despite Napoleon.

And then Napoleon was a gambler who didn't know how to stop in time – a real gambler! and after all, what does it matter. . . .

With Maurice Ravel *we find ourselves on a lower plane: he has neither the magnificent, quiet devotion of his older contemporary nor his humility, and his utterance is certainly not free of vanity. Something of this kind may have contributed to his anxiousness to join the army when the Great War started in 1914. At first refused owing to his delicate physique – he was uncommonly small – he succeeded in the end in being accepted as a lorry driver, but was neither temperamentally nor physically fit for the rough conditions of an army in the field; his war service was of short duration.*

Like Debussy, Ravel was a shrewd observer and critical judge of characters and events.

MAURICE RAVEL TO JEAN MARNOLD, MUSIC CRITIC ON THE 'MERCURE'

L'Hermitage, 7 February 1906

I must hasten to tell you that your article quite consoled me for the one in *Le Temps*. Not because of the praise it contained (at least, yes, a little because of that), but because you understood better what I was trying to do. Delicate, subtle, quintessential – mercy on us! I thought I knew myself better.

You have seen something else in my latest compositions, and it's for that that I'm grateful to you. What I'm working at for the moment cannot be called subtle, it's a big waltz, a kind of memorial to the great Strauss, not Richard, the other one, Johann. You know how I delight in those admirable rhythms, and that in my opinion the *joie de vivre* expressed in dance goes much deeper than the puritanism of César Franck. Incidentally, I quite realize what I can expect from the adepts of that neo-Christian movement, but I don't care. . . .

RAVEL TO HIS FRIEND JEAN GODEBSKI

[*Undated, 1911*]

I've tried to do something rather ambitious – to regenerate the Italian *opera buffa*: only the principle of it. This composition does not follow the traditional pattern, like its ancestor, its sole ancestor, Mussorgsky's *Marriage*, which is a faithful interpretation of the play by Gogol.

L'Heure Espagnole is a musical comedy. No changes in Franc-Nohain's text, except for a few cuts. Only the final quintet, in its structure, vocalization and voice effects, bears some resemblance to the standard operatic ensemble. The rest is informal declamation rather than singing. French, like any other language, has its specific accents, its musical inflections. And I don't see why one shouldn't take advantage of those qualities and try a correct prosody.

The spirit of the thing is frankly humorous. I have tried to express irony chiefly by means of the music, by harmony, rhythm and orchestration, and not, as in an operetta, by stringing words together in an arbitrary and farcical style. . . .

I'd been thinking for a long time of composing a humorous work. The modern orchestra seemed to me well suited to emphasize and exaggerate comic effects. When I read Franc-Nohain's *L'Heure Espagnole* it occurred to me that its fantastical, farcical character would just suit my plan. It attracted me for all sorts of reasons, with its mixture of familiar conversation and deliberately absurd lyricism, and the atmosphere of comic and unaccustomed noises that surrounds the characters in the clock-maker's shop. And then there was something to be made out of the picturesque rhythms of Spanish music. . . .

RAVEL TO MME GODEBSKA

St Jean-de-Luz, 8 September 1914

As you foretold, my escapade had a most ridiculous conclusion: they won't have me, because I'm 2 kilos underweight.

Before going to Bayonne I spent a month working from morning to night without even taking time off for a bathe in the sea. I finished my Trio, treating it as a posthumous work. That doesn't mean I lavished genius upon it, but that the manuscript and the notes relating to it are so tidy that no matter who could correct the proofs. . . .

Incidentally, at Bayonne one has no end of difficulty in shaking off a crowd of Red Cross ladies who've given money to clutter up the hospitals, indignant at being asked to wash the feet of the wounded men, pleading ignorance to get themselves out of dressing wounds, and grumbling because no tea-room has been provided for them.

The whole mob – here, at any rate – fusses to and fro, tittering, displaying its arm-bands, and lamenting because the soldiers don't smell good. It's sickening. Personally I think I'm too old for such amusements, and I'm waiting, with other serious people, for these children to go back to their usual occupations – which some of them are beginning to do already. . . .

RAVEL TO JEAN MARNOLD

SENDER: DRIVER RAVEL, MOTORIZED COLUMN,
M.T. SECTION 171, VIA B.C.M. PARIS

[*Undated, March 1916*]

I've been here for a week 'at the front'. It's still a far cry from the real thing, but it's even farther from Paris. Morally, one feels quite close. The planes flying overhead, the motorized columns with their load of men, the signposts, everything is making for . . . over there for the tremendous battle. Chaps are coming back from it all the time. 'It's slowing down, it's hotting up again.'

Every evening the siren at the station and the one at the factory give a Zeppelin warning. When this area is directly threatened, the bugles sound the *stand to arms*.

I'm not too badly off, despite the strict discipline and the discomfort, to put it mildly, of the sleeping arrangements. The food's good, and I take full advantage of it. Almost at once I was assigned to a big Ariès lorry, already half broken down, which was taken away from me two days later. The lieutenant, who knew me by name, suggested I should drive our touring-car, which I modestly refused. They'll give me a light van as soon as they think I can manage it on the road. He's promised to give me some interesting missions. . . .

RAVEL TO JEAN MARNOLD

DRIVER RAVEL
S.P. 4 VIA B.C.M. PARIS

25 May 1916

You know – for you tried to argue me out of it – how, ever since the beginning of the war, I had planned to join the Air Force. You know the outcome of all the attempts I made, and how a friend, with whom I can't be angry, prevented me from being sent into danger. As soon as I joined this unit, three months ago, I wrote to tell Captain Le R. that I was at the front, in other words no longer under Ministry orders, and to remind him that I wanted to become a bomber pilot. I had no answer, and in point of fact my work at once became so interesting that my Icarian dreams were forgotten.

Until the day before yesterday, when I heard that the commander of the squadron had been killed, that the squadron had been disbanded, and that Captain Le R. was in this area, had lost my address, and would be writing to me soon.

This immediately awoke the old craving, I forgot how tired I was and asked to have the examination for my medical certificate. . . .

The Major advised me strongly against flying. I have an enlarged heart. It's not much, nothing serious, they told me. I shouldn't think twice about it if I'd had little heart disturbances all my life, as most men do: but the thing is that at the end of last year, when I had a thorough examination, the doctors found nothing at all. Which means it's accidental, and now I understand that annoying complaint from which my adventurous existence was distracting my attention.

What am I to do now? If I'm examined again by a more thorough doctor I shall be told I'm not fit for driving, and pushed into office work. So even you will understand that I prefer to let things drift. . . .

RAVEL TO HIS PUBLISHER JACQUES DURAND

25 September 1916

Your letter found me in hospital, waiting for an operation. You can guess the results of that dysentery, which lasted a fortnight, due chiefly to the unhealthy life I've been leading for the last 6 months.

However, I don't feel the slightest uneasiness, and am thinking chiefly about my convalescent leave. . . .

RAVEL TO JEAN MARNOLD

Field Hospital No. 20, Ward 7
Châlons-sur-Marne, 7 October 1916

I'm told that Saint-Saëns has informed a delighted public that since the war began he has composed music for the stage, melodies, an elegy, and a piece for the trombone. If he'd been making shell-cases instead it might have been all the better for music. . . .

RAVEL ON TOUR IN THE U.S.A. TO HIS BROTHER ÉDOUARD

Chicago, 20 January 1928

The day before yesterday there was a concert of chamber music. Today it went well. When I came to take a bow, all the brass greeted me with a fanfare.

I'd found spring weather at Chicago, but yesterday, within an hour, it turned freezing cold, with a howling wind, enough to blow your kisser off, and the water and ice tasting of *eau de Javel* [potassium chloride]. This is an extraordinary town, much more so than New York.

Tomorrow evening, second symphony concert. I leave directly it's over for Cleveland, where I shall arrive the following morning. . . .

Cleveland 26 – Hadn't time to finish. The 2nd concert went well. 3,500 people standing. Another fanfare. Then left. . . .

RAVEL TO HIS BROTHER ÉDOUARD

Los Angeles, 7 February 1928

This time it's really summer: 35° C. Glorious sunshine; a big city all in blossom. Flowers that grow in hot-houses in our country; tall palm-trees, in their element. . . . A visit to Hollywood, the film city. Various stars: Douglas Fairbanks, who fortunately speaks French. The journey from San Francisco very pleasant, nearly always on the rear platform; forests of eucalyptus, tall trees one might take for oaks and which are hollies. Varied mountain scenery, rocky or brilliant green. . . . Tomorrow evening, a concert. In the afternoon I shall go and see where they make lions for the cinema. . . .

I was to have lunched with Charlie Chaplin, but I didn't think it would be much fun for either of us. He doesn't know a word of French. . . .

TO HIS BROTHER ÉDOUARD

[Undated, February 1928]

The other day in Chicago I went to dinner with Mrs Rockefeller McCormick, a multi-millionairess. Hurried back to my hotel and had a steak sent up to my room. Dined here with Mrs Cim, who has the finest Lautrecs, Gauguins, Degas, etc., good wine and a splendid cognac. . . .

It is an amusing fact that Arturo Toscanini, the great star conductor who prided himself in the strictest adherence to the most minute detail of the classical scores he performed, was considerably freer in his interpretation when confronted by a work of a living composer. Ravel's 'Boléro' was the occasion of a violent clash of opinion between him and the famous conductor who was not willing to accept any guidance on interpretation.

RAVEL TO MME HÉLÈNE KAHN-CASELLA

Le Belvédère, Montfort l'Amaury, 6 May 1930

A pity you didn't come on the stage; there was a quite amusing dramatic undercurrent. People were in consternation because I'd had the cheek to tell the great virtuoso he had taken the thing twice too fast. That was my only reason for coming . . . but all the same he's a wonderful virtuoso, as wonderful as his orchestra. . . .

RAVEL TO MME GODEBSKA

Le Belvédère, Montfort l'Amaury, 8 May 1930

If I was seen at the Opéra, it was because I knew Toscanini would take *Boléro* at a ridiculous pace, and wanted to tell him so – which caused consternation to everyone, beginning with the great virtuoso himself. . . .

Much more than French music, with its rich undercurrent of national tradition, English music at the turn of the century found itself in the most problematic situation, after two hundred years of provincial seclusion and an almost total disappearance of a national identity expressed in music. Italian, French, and German opera provided the main musical events in London and the rule of German music, firmly established by Haydn, Mendelssohn, Brahms, and Wagner, was unchallengeable when Edward Elgar *(1857–1934) appeared as the first great English composer after Purcell. He had no easy start; it took him twenty years of hard uphill work to be heard, believed, and accepted.*

EDWARD ELGAR TO DR C. W. BUCK

30 March 1888

I had a good success at Birmingham with my Suite, but the critics, save two, are nettled. I am the only local man who has been asked to conduct his own work – and what's a greater offence, *I did it* – and *well* too; for this I must needs suffer. . . .

ELGAR TO FRANK WEBB

Kensington, 29 July 1890

My Overture is finished and I do not think will be liked, but that must take its chance: I find in my limited experience that one's own friends are the people to be most in dread of; I could fill a not unentertaining book with the criticisms passed on my former efforts: when I have written anything slow, they say it ought to have been quick – when loud, it should have been quiet – when fanciful, solemn; in a word, I have always been wrong hitherto – at home. . . .

With a true Edwardian's British insularity, but musically bred on a predominantly German heritage, Elgar shows an unprejudiced feeling for quality and a quizzical sense of humour.

ELGAR TO FRANK SCHUSTER

Bordighera, 8 December 1903

I like the French now but can't get on with the Italian tonguage (good word). Bought some figs today – did not know the name, so asked for 'Frutti, per habilmenti d'Adam et Eva'. I got 'em: but when the Scripture reference or mythology is impossible I don't get on. When left to myself I live on bread and vermouth. . . .

ELGAR TO FRANK SCHUSTER

Kempsey, Worcester, 15 November 1924

I was very sad over Fauré's death – he was such a real *gentleman* – the highest type of Frenchman, and I admired him greatly. His chamber music never had any chance here in the old Joachim days, I fear: I may be wrong but I feel that it was 'held up' to our loss. . . .

Elgar, however, had neither the gift nor the urge for verbal expression. If we want to learn something of the problems of the English composer of the period, we find a fascinating discussion of them in the correspondence of Ralph Vaughan Williams *(1872–1958) and* Gustav Holst *(1874–1934). Both idealists, both fervent believers in a revitalization of English music, they suffered from an oppressive consciousness of a gigantic heritage, insufficiently assimilated, in which the good and the questionable were indiscriminately crossed and combined, owing to a rather casual musical upbringing.*

GUSTAV HOLST TO RALPH VAUGHAN WILLIAMS

Berlin [undated] 1903

Great news – I have written three postcards and two letters in German! The recipients talk of having them framed!! Rather a doubtful compliment, I fear.

I have been trying to think where we (you and I) are and where we come in and what we ought to do.

(Being together so much, I think we work along in much the same way, but I may be wrong.)

To begin with, I think we crawl along too slowly – of course, it is something to get along at all, and I do think our progress is very genuine – but there ought to be more. . . .

Somehow we seem too comfortable – we don't seem to strain every nerve. Anyhow, I know I don't. And composing is a fairly impossible affair as things go even at the best of times. . . .

As for opera, I am bewildered. *Feuersnot* by Rich. Strauss is in reality quite simple and unoriginal *as opera*. Charpentier's *Louise* is idiotic as opera. And I do feel sometimes inclined to chuck *Sita* [an opera on which he was working] in case it is only bad Richard I [Wagner]. Unless one ought to follow the latter until he leads you to fresh things. What I feel is that there is nothing else but Wagner excepting Italian one-act horrors.

As for conducting, (which we ought to learn), it is impossible to attain in England and I fear we must give up all hopes of it. As an orchestral player I really feel sorry, as England is crying out (unconsciously) for real conductors. Henry J. [Wood] is the nearest approach. . . . *And it is not all a question of unlimited rehearsals.* . . .

Of course the matter is made rather worse for me owing to lack of cash, and I feel more and more that my mode of living is very unsatisfactory. . . .

There is also the theory that one should get rich first and then compose. When I was a child, my father told me that Sterndale Bennett worked out that theory during his life very satisfactorily. When I was older, I heard Sterndale Bennett's music. . . .

Getting rich requires a 'teshneek' of its own that some people learn slowly and others never. I don't know which class I belong to and don't care. There is no time to learn that *and* composition. Not that I believe one should cram theory from childhood. But that, once having started (after school, etc., is over) an Englishman may think himself lucky if, after hard work, he writes anything decent before he is fifty. For now I have been abroad, I see what a terrible lot we have to contend against in England.

And I also feel that there is no time for pot-boiling. As tromboning is so damnably uncertain, I must do it, but it is really bad for one, I am sure. I almost feel I can now trace its evil effect in Tchaikovsky, but it is a very insiduous disease. . . .

If money matters were quite satisfactory with me, I still should be as puzzled as to what you and I ought to do – money matters only make things worse.

I think we are 'all right' in a mild sort of way. But then mildness is the very devil. So something must happen, and *we must make it happen*. . . .

HOLST TO VAUGHAN WILLIAMS

Dresden [*1903*]

I hope you bear in mind that all the rot I write is merely a collection of stray thoughts. Well, to begin with, what the hell do you mean by talking about premature decay and getting fat?

I meant 'getting old' in the sense of becoming mature – that is when progress either stops or becomes slower. We must not get old for the next forty years, because we have such a stiff job and (1) you sometimes have said that you feel that 'it is time you did something' after all these years – I forgot your exact words, but I have felt the same myself often, but it is *rot*. We are not old enough and we have not had enough training *of the right sort* (I am coming to that). (2) Sometimes when anything turns out an awful failure, it may teach us more than a thundering success – it does not follow that it *will* but it *may* – which would be of little use, if one was growing old. . . . As I told you once before, Richard II [Strauss] seems to me to be the most 'Beethovenish' composer since Beethoven. Perhaps I am wrong, but anyhow you will agree that, whatever his faults, he is a real life composer.

As far as I can make out, his training seems to have been

(1) Bach, Mozart, Beethoven,
(2) Schumann and Brahms,
(3) Wagner.

Mine has been:

(1) Mendelssohn,
(2) Grieg,
(3) Wagner.

This alone speaks volumes.

Richard II had such a terrific classical training, that Brahms and Wagner never lifted him off his feet. Whereas I (as you say of yourself) don't seem to fit on to their music at all (Mozart and Beethoven). And I believe, as you once said about Richard II himself, that one ought to be able to feel that every composer is the result of those that have gone before him. So we must begin by feeling it about ourselves.

Now if you can prove to me that all this is nonsense, I shall be only too delighted, as it is a serious thing to discover and, if true, it means years and years of *extra* study with the usual lot thrown in. If it is true, there is no one in England to teach us as far as I know. . . .

Then you once said, you were so ashamed of yourself, because your life seemed all holiday. Now if you find that you write better for going away into the country now and then, then it is your *duty* to go and do so. . . . When I thought that composition was merely hard work, I used to worry about it in an irritating sort of way and I believe you do the same sometimes. Whereas, if I am right, we must drop music altogether every now and then so that we never feel stale when we write. . . .

Systematic planning out of the day or anything approaching it is surely out of the question. We must be more thorough when we play each other our things, and we ought to play each one two or three times over at each meeting until the other knows it thoroughly. The only drawback is that, whenever we are together, I have always such a lot to talk about. . . .

HOLST TO VAUGHAN WILLIAMS

Berlin [*1903*]

I really cannot feel concerned about your fears that all your invention has gone. I am sorry, but it is impossible. You got into the same state of mind just before you wrote the Heroic Elegy, so that I look on it as a good sign and quite expect to hear that you have struck oil, when you write again.

I have thought about it a good deal and these are some of my conclusions.

You have never lost your invention, but it has not developed enough. Your best – your most original and beautiful style or 'atmosphere' – is an indescribable sort of feeling, as if one was listening to very lovely lyrical poetry. I may be wrong, but I think this (what I call to myself the *real* RVW) is more original than you think.

But when you are not in this strain, you either write 'second class goods', or you have a devil of a bother to write anything at all. The latter state of mind may seem bad while it lasts, but it is what you want to make yourself do, for however much I like your best style, it must be broadened. And probably it is so each time you get into a hopeless mess. Probably you are right about mental concentration – that is what you want, more than technique. For that reason perhaps lessons would do you good, but it would be a surer way to try and cultivate it 'on your own'. . . .

Another idea of mine is madder and perhaps even harmful, but anyhow you shall have it. Cannot invention be developed like other things? And would it not be developed by your trying to write so many themes every day?

I am sure I am right about us being too comfortable. When you work hard, you merely cover a lot of ground, instead of making sure of your ground as you go on.

Another thing we must guard against, and that is getting old! Especially you – I am more juvenile than ever, I think, but I have my doubts about you. As I said before, we have so much to contend against, and in England there is no one to help, so that progress is sure to be a bit erratic. . . . As for me, I think I have got careless owing to *Worming* [playing the trombone in Stanislaus Wurm's 'White Viennese Band'] and pot-boiling. For I am certain that Worming is very bad for one – it makes me so sick of everything, so that I cannot settle down to work properly. And pot-boiling, as I have done it, is bad, because I got into the way of thinking that anything would do. Whereas we must write now chiefly so that we may write better in the future. So that every detail of everything we do must be as perfect as possible. For the next few years not only ought we to write more carefully than we have ever done before, but more carefully than we need ever write again. My wife has had another idea, which I think I shall adopt. That is that when we return I shall not take any Worming job or go out of London until the Scottish [Orchestra] begins. If I can get a theatre, well and good, if not, I will even accept your offer of lending me money rather than play two or three times a day. . . . Then I should like to try to work systematically from August to November both at writing and studying music. . . .

By the bye, I am certainly going to rewrite the words of *Sita* as you suggest. They are disgraceful and that was largely due to Worming, etc. I used to write them at odd moments, often in the orchestra . . . I used to be proud at writing things at odd times. It was great fun, but it was damned rot and it helped on my present carelessness. . . .

HOLST TO VAUGHAN WILLIAMS

Munich [*1903*]

As to writing at boiling-point: this is the only thing I feel fairly certain about. Writing at boiling-point is *THE* very worst way of composing. Whenever I have done it, it has always turned out badly, and the only good that ever came of it was, when I was able to work the stuff up afresh the next day into something fairly presentable. It *may* be different with you, but anyway I wouldn't worry about it. . . .

VAUGHAN WILLIAMS TO HOLST

The Warren, Meldreth, Cambs. [*1906*]

It was nice to open your parcel and find my initials over your pieces [Holst's *Two Songs Without Words*, dedicated to V.W.] – I don't know what you owe to me – but I know all I owe to you – if I ever do anything worth doing, it will be greatly owing to having such a friend as you 'at my command', as the folk-songs say, always ready to help and advise – and someone whose yea is always yea and nay, nay – which is a quality one really wants in a friend and so seldom gets. . . .

HOLST TO MISS T. R. GRAY

Richmond, Surrey [*Spring, 1907*]

We have at last got a charwoman in, and my brief reign as cook and 'general' has come to a most welcome end.

Oh! The miles of unwashed crockery (N.B.: do you measure unwashed crockery by the mile or the square root?) and unswept floors I left for my successor!

I *must* learn cooking.

The points I most want to learn are

(a) How to cook half a dozen things at once in such a manner, that they don't all boil over or burn at once as you are looking for the tablecloth.

(b) How to persuade potatoes to be just a little quicker.

(c) How to persuade toast not to be so quick!

Holst was poor and he had to work hard for his living. Vaughan Williams was sufficiently well off not to be dependent on earning and he was a generous friend.

VAUGHAN WILLIAMS TO HOLST

Paris [*1908*]

What do you say to £50 at Easter (or when you want it) and £25 more in September?

It might be £50 in September – but I can't be sure yet – so we mustn't count on it. Now is this enough to do you any good? If not, say so and we will try and devise something else – because if we do this job at all, we must do it properly.

It is most important – to my mind – that this should be a real holiday, to make up for all your past years of strain. If you compose during it, all the better – but if you have an idea all the time that you must have something to show for it – then you will spoil your holiday and effectually prevent yourself composing. If – even – you only come back teaching very well, it would mean that it came easier and left you more energy for other work. . . .

The result of this generous offer was a month's holiday in Algeria.

Vaughan Williams shared Holst's devotion to the idea of bringing music to the people and was always interested in humble musical pursuits such as rural choruses and amateur bands. Both realized the tremendous importance of practising music rather than passively submitting to it and Holst, with his restless energy, was indefatigable in stimulating musical activities and irresistible with his enthusiam.

HOLST TO HIS FRIEND W. G. WHITTAKER

Thaxted, Essex [*June 1916*]

It was a feast – an orgy. Four whole days of perpetual singing and playing, either properly arranged in the church, or impromptu in various houses, or still more impromptu in ploughed fields during thunderstorms, or in the train going home.

It has been a revelation to me. And what it has revealed to me, and what I shall never be able to persuade you, is that quantity is more important than quality.

We don't get *enough*. We practise stuff for a concert, at which we do a thing once and get excited over it, and then go off and do something else.

Whereas on this occasion things were different. Take Bach's *Missa brevis*, for instance. The Morleyites had practised it since January. On June 3rd they did it *twice through* at their concert. On June 10th they rehearsed it and other things for three hours in Thaxted church. On Whitsunday we did it during the service in the morning, and again in the evening, and again on Monday morning. And then some enthusiasts went through it again on Tuesday morning.

In the intervals between the services people drifted into church and sang motets or played violin or cello. And others caught bad colds through going long walks in the pouring rain, singing madrigals and folk songs and rounds the whole time.

The effect on us all was indescribable. We weren't merely excited: we were quite normal, only rather more alive than usual.

Most people are overcome by mountain air first. In the same way others are excited by certain music.

The remedy in both cases is, to have more and more and more . . .

I realize now, why the Bible insists on heaven being a place (I should call it a condition), where people sing and *go on singing*.

We kept it up at Thaxted about fourteen hours a day. The reason why we didn't do more is, that we were not capable mentally or physically of realizing heaven any further.

Still, as far as it went, it was heaven. Just as the average amateur's way of using music as a sedative or a stimulant is purgatory, and the professional's way of using music as a topic of conversation or as a means of getting money is hell. . . .

Music, being identical with heaven, isn't a thing of momentary thrills, or even hourly ones. It's a condition of eternity. . . .

On the same event Holst must have written another letter of delight to Vaughan Williams, as can be gathered from the answer of the latter.

VAUGHAN WILLIAMS TO HOLST

Sutton Veney [*June 1916*]

Your letter about Thaxted was splendid – I sometimes feel that the future of musical England rests with you – because every Paulina [pupil of St Paul's Girls' College], and for the matter of that every Morleyite [pupil of Morley College], will infect 10 others, and they in turn will infect 10 others – I will leave you to make the necessary calculation.

Good luck to you – I feel that perhaps after the war England will be a *better* place for music than before – largely because we shan't be able to buy expensive performers, etc., like we did. I wish I could have been there – perhaps next Whitsun: who knows? I read your letter over and over again, it was so inspiring. We don't take music as part of our every-day life half enough – I often wish we could all migrate to some small town where there could really be a musical community – London is impossible from that point of view. . . .

VAUGHAN WILLIAMS TO HOLST

Summer 1918 [On active service]

I wonder whether you will go to Holland – I should feel more inclined for the naval job myself – but still there is the third alternative, I hope, of your stopping at Morley – when all this is over, it will, I believe, be the people who've kept the lamp alight who will count as the heroes.

The war has brought me strange jobs – can you imagine me in charge of 200 horses!! That's my job at present – I was dumped down on to it straight away, and before I had time to find out, which were horses and which were waggons, I found myself in the middle of a retreat – as a matter of fact, we had a very easy time over this – only one horse was killed, so we were lucky. . . .

HOLST TO HIS WIFE ISOBEL

Salonica, 29 December 1918

About going back to the old work, or getting 'something better': I am sceptical about the latter. You see, my old work was very jolly. There was a fearful lot of it, but it was the real thing: real people to teach, and real music to give them, and no 'palaver'. Now the only 'better' thing I can conceive is something to do with committees, education schemes, and co-ordination. In other words, talking about a thing instead of doing it. It may be necessary – I fear it is – but I don't feel it's my job, whereas teaching a kindergarten or the Thaxted choir is. I believe you thought I was going to get away from the teaching atmosphere. I've been in it worse than ever from the day we left! My only consolation is a dear man here, who has been a slum school headmaster for 30 years and who therefore knows that the moment one ceases to think of human beings and dwells mentally amid schemes one is just damned as a teacher.

This is a bit mixed, but all I mean is, that I'm not so keen on a big education job, and I don't see that I should be offered any other sort of 'something better'. . . .

HOLST TO HIS WIFE

Salonica, 15 January 1919

I don't know much about the trains here. There are some, but nobody minds them, and nobody seems to know where, when, or why they go. The trams are a really new thing in overcrowding. A normal one will have six men on the footboard, hanging on to each other. Civilians pay $1\frac{1}{2}$*d*, soldiers $\frac{1}{2}$*d* and fleas, etc., nothing. I go as a soldier. . . .

And I believe my choral music is now being unloaded in the docks. Do you know that all this time I've been trying to make people sing without any music?

HOLST TO HIS WIFE

Salonica, 10 February 1919

I am conducting the remains of the Artillery School Orchestra, founded by Colles of *The Times*. I had a delightful experience with them on Saturday. We were rehearsing in their theatre which has no windows – we had to take out panels in the wall to let in the light, but it also let in a violent snow storm right on to their backs. I gave them as good a time as I could under the conditions (we had one small brazier, which we passed round from one to another), and when it was over, instead of grousing, a man told me it had been his happiest morning in Salonica.

I've never told you anything about this place, although I have often meant to.

It is a ramshackle, untidy, muddled affair. In the burnt-out part, people have collected bricks, etc., and built shanties to live in, often just mere heaps of bricks and boards with a piece of sacking. Some of the churches and mosques are filled with refugees, each family being divided off from the others by walls of sacking hung on cords.

At the back of the city are the ruins of the old walls, where people live in dug-outs, the general effect being weird and squalid. When I first went through that part I thought the plague was on, because so many doors had red crosses, but I found out afterwards that it only meant that the owners were Christian and not Moslem.

As regards people, I have met every race on earth here, except Red Indians and Esquimaux. . . .

HOLST TO VAUGHAN WILLIAMS

Salonica, March 1919

I've learnt what 'classical' means. It means something that sings and dances through sheer joy of existence. And if the *Parthenon* is the only building in the world that does so, then there is only one classical building in the world.

All the old talk of classical v. romantic used to irritate me, but it is only now I realize what twaddle it is. . . .

HOLST TO VAUGHAN WILLIAMS

St Paul's [School, May or June 1926]

I find that I am a hopeless half-hogger and am prepared to sit on the fence as long as possible, partly through laziness and through force of habit, but chiefly through discovering that if I am a fool in music, I am the damnedest of damned fools in everything else. Or to put it in other words, I still believe in the Hindoo doctrine of Kharma, which is one's path in life. If one is lucky (or maybe unlucky – it doesn't matter) to have a clearly appointed path to which one comes naturally, whereas any other one is an unsuccessful effort, one ought to stick to the former. And I am oriental enough to believe in doing so, without worrying about the 'fruits of action', that is, success or otherwise. It applies to certain elementary school teachers I have met, as well as to Bach. Of course, in an emergency one has to throw all this overboard, but I fear I only do so at the last moment. And if I don't – if I try and think things out carefully and calmly – I am always wrong. This has happened so often that I am convinced that Kharma is the only thing for me.

This is all first person singular, but that cannot be helped. I suppose it is really a confession. . . .

Several excursions of Holst's to the U.S.A. became a rich source of experience and stimulation. He was certainly not a conventional teacher.

HOLST TO HIS WIFE

On board R.M.S. 'Scythia'
12 April 1929

If ever I cross the Atlantic again, I want a most exclusive cabin in a very fast boat and my Missus to keep undesirable people away.

But what I really want is to keep off the sea altogether. I'm fed up with the ship (which is a very good one) and the passengers (who are, on the whole, harmless) and above all the *noise* – engines, waves, wind, gramophones, chattering.

I'm expecting great things of Yale – nice men, a quiet room, one or two walks; also my lecture is the least bad I've written, not that that is saying much. . . .

When I get home, I want to live a humdrum monotonous existence with lots of routine work, lots of new 'things' that don't disappoint me too much, and occasional conducting jobs, and three day walks – I want this for the next three or four years!

It doesn't seem an unreasonable desire!

HOLST TO VAUGHAN WILLIAMS

Harvard University, Cambridge, Mass.
5 April 1932

My idea of composition is to spoil as much manuscript paper as possible. But my pupils here would far rather write a thesis on Schönberg's use of the bass clarinet compared with von Webern's; or, better still, talk vaguely about the best method of introducing the second subject in the recapitulation. And some of these boys have really studied hard – if not music, anyhow books on music. Is this University or is it America? I got square with one ultra-modernist wrongnote-merchant by pointing out that I was an old fogey, who was only here for two months more, and that, when I'd gone, he could make up for lost time, but that until then he'd better humour me and even, occasionally, write a tune. And he answered cordially 'sure!'

Giacomo Puccini (*1858–1924*), *the last of a glorious dynasty of Italian composers who ruled opera in Europe for three centuries, had still the chief qualities of his great heritage: dramatic instinct, a true sense of vocality, the gift of shapely melody and an enthusiastic belief in the melodrama as an art form. Successful right from the beginning of his career, he had one disastrous experience of a fiasco in his life, when 'Madame Butterfly' fell flat at its first performance in Milan in 1904. He instantly realized the cause of the disaster, an over-extended second act. By dividing it into two, with minor alterations, he achieved a world success with a work which the publishers were inclined to write off as a dead loss.*

GIACOMO PUCCINI TO HIS FRIEND DON PANICHELLI

[*Milan, 27 February 1904*]

You will be horrified by the vile things the malicious newspapers are saying. But never fear! *Butterfly* is alive, real, and she will soon take flight again. That's what I say, and maintain with unshakable confidence – you'll see – and it will be only a few months from now; I can't tell you where, for the moment. . . .

In his sixties and already afflicted by the insidious disease to which he eventually succumbed, cancer of the throat, Puccini worked with his customary love and devotion at his last opera, 'Turandot'. Near despair sometimes, he felt inclined to attribute his endless difficulties and inhibitions to the exotic subject and its elusive inhumanity. By sheer heroism he succeeded in making it his grandest, most monumental work.

PUCCINI TO HIS LIBRETTIST GIUSEPPE ADAMI

[*1920*]

Gozzi's *Turandot* as a foundation, but from that there should rise a different figure, that's to say (I don't know how to put it) our imagination (and it will be needed!) should produce so much beautiful, tasteful and graceful material that our story will be an absolute *bouquet* of triumphs. Don't overdo it with the Venetian masks – they are to be the *buffoons* and the philosophers who now and then make a joke or express an opinion (carefully chosen, and well-timed); but they must not become importunate and fussy. . . .

PUCCINI TO GIUSEPPE ADAMI

15 May 1920

Turandot! Act I – excellent! I like the *mise en scène* too. The three masks are coming along well. I'm rather afraid the end may not be effective, but I may be mistaken. In short, this first Act is good and well presented. What will the second be like? And shall we need a third? Or will Act II exhaust the subject? Courage – on we go, nimbly and with imagination, and the whole thing will be original and *moving* as well. And that's how I want it and how it *must* turn out. . . .

PUCCINI TO GIUSEPPE ADAMI

Torre del Lago, 30 April 1921

Turandot is going ahead; I think I'm on the right road. I've reached the masks, and shall soon get to the enigmas! I feel I'm doing well. And what about Act II? And Act III? For heaven's sake don't let me get rusty with waiting. . . .

PUCCINI TO GIUSEPPE ADAMI

Viareggio, 30 October 1922

Let us hope that this tune of which you do well to remind me will still come to me in its freshness and touch the soul. And without that, music doesn't exist. I'm working, but there is so much still to be done! and it frightens me to think of my weight of years. But on we go, without fear or hesitation!

PUCCINI TO GIUSEPPE ADAMI

Viareggio, 11 December 1922

The news of *Turandot* is not good. I'm beginning to feel perturbed at my own laziness! Is it that I've had my fill of China in writing Act I and most of Act II? The fact remains that I cannot get going to any purpose. Besides, I'm an old man! That's certain.

If I had had a nice little theme such as I was trying to find for so long, and still am, it would be on the stage by now. But that Chinese world! I'll make up my mind in Milan, perhaps I shall pay back Ricordi and free myself. . . . I can't manage to write the *introduction* to Act II, though I have made many attempts – and I don't feel at home in China. . . .

PUCCINI TO GIUSEPPE ADAMI

Viareggio, 14 April 1923

Work? Slow but good. Turandot's aria is nearly finished, but what a labour! A few changes in the lines will be needed, though. . . . The trio for the masks is going well too. Another horribly difficult piece, and it's of the greatest importance, being a *morceau* with no action and therefore almost academic. In short, I'm plunged in the usual discouragement and the usual brief little pleasures of working. *Turandot* is going forward, with slow steps, but nevertheless. . . .

PUCCINI TO GIUSEPPE ADAMI

Institut Chirurgical, Brussels [November 1924]

Caro Adamino,

Here I am! poor me!
They say I shall be here six weeks.
This was something I didn't bargain for!
And what about *Turandot*? . . .

PUCCINI TO GIUSEPPE ADAMI

[Some days later]

For the time being the treatment isn't too painful. It is only external. But God knows what they will do to me on Monday, to get inside, under the epiglottis! They assure me it won't be painful – and they also say I shall recover. Now I am beginning to hope so. A few days ago I had lost all hope of a cure. And what hours, and what days!

I am ready for anything. . . .

Puccini did not survive this operation; the last scene of Turandot had to be finished from the sketches by his friend Franco Alfano.

The fairy-tale of Leoš Janáček *(1854–1928) and his ascent to fame offers a graphic illustration of the tremendous obstacles a creative artist may have to face when external circumstances are set against him. Living in a situation of extreme provincial narrowness as a humble teacher of music at Brno, the*

Moravian capital, an odd outsider, isolated from the pundits in Prague and still more from the rest of the world, Janáček remained unnoticed, his music gathering dust on the shelves. After years of patient waiting his opera 'Jenufa' was accepted by the theatre in Brno, was given a ramshackle performance in 1904, remained a local event without any wider resonance and was quickly forgotten. Twelve years later a stroke of luck brought this work to the attention of the director of the National Theatre in Prague. Hailed there as an outstanding success, 'Jenufa', in German translation, was performed at the Court Opera in Vienna in February 1918, while the First World War was still being fought, and this performance made the composer famous at the age of sixty-four. It opened his way to a brilliant late period of creative activity and to his being accepted as the greatest exponent of Czech music after Smetana and Dvořák.

LEOŠ JANÁČEK TO MME KAMILA URVÁLEK

Brno, 9 October 1903

Dear Madam,
Yesterday was one of my rare happy days. Perhaps the Almighty has at last decided to turn a smiling face upon me. The management of the National Theatre in Brno sent for the score of my opera, *Jenufa.* When he took it, the clerk certainly carried a great weight on his shoulders; it seemed to me as though he carried many sad years of my life. . . . I will now ask to be pensioned off and so be relieved of my work as Royal and Imperial Music Teacher, and be able to devote my entire time to composing and writing. At last I can see times on the horizon for which I have waited my whole life. Shall I live to enjoy them? Will my spirit be able to bear me up in order to do better work? I think so. . . . Although, who can tell what goes on in his own brain? My brain makes my whole body work so wildly; it can be explained only by guessing and astonishment. It is the will of God and fate. We make our own fate. . . . Here in Brno I am a poor man – as though in a desert – where there is no proper music to be heard. . . .

JANÁČEK TO JOSEF BOHUSLAV FOERSTER

Brno, 24 June 1916

Dear friend,

You cannot imagine what pleasure your letter gave me. I feel as though I were living in a fairy-tale. I compose and compose, as though something were urging me on. I no longer saw any worth in my work, and scarcely believed what I said. I had become convinced that no one would ever notice anything of mine. I was quite down – my pupils had begun to advise me how to compose, and how to orchestrate. I laughed at it all, nothing else remained to me. I now feel that my life is beginning to have some purpose, and I believe in my mission. You have given me strength. Thank you most sincerely.

JANÁČEK TO THE SINGER GABRIELA HORVÁT, OF THE NATIONAL THEATRE IN PRAGUE

Vienna, 12 February 1918

Today was a dress rehearsal at the Vienna Court Opera. The setting was exactly as it will be on the first night. What exquisite colours – 150 costumes – what a wonderfully large stage and everything new and shining! The mill with the beautiful highlands in the background. Sun-flooded – it will certainly make the public perspire. The recruits with the mill-hand on a garlanded horse – yes, I was longing for such a production in Prague, in vain.

Mrs Weidt acts wonderfully – coached by the producer. She is a soprano and therefore has not got your dark, silken voice that fits the part so well – but she acts perfectly. You must see it. At certain moments really it gives you the shivers. And how well imagined – Jenufa is ideal. How these two women compete! There are no words to describe it. The director Gregor told Mrs Weidt that she is singing a part such as she has never known or sung in her life. The rehearsal went off well. Tomorrow there will be another run-through, just to freshen up their memories, and the day after tomorrow is the full dress rehearsal. The Bohemian Quartet is passing through Vienna tomorrow and they asked to be allowed to attend it. The reporters are after me and every day the local press is full of *Jenufa*. . . .

JANÁČEK TO HIS FRIEND, MME KAMILA STÖSSEL

Brno, 5 March 1919

After the Vienna days of old I was once again in Vienna; and today I arrived here from Prague. There is now great jealousy between Prague and Vienna. Where is the best production? Well – it is more heartfelt in Prague. It is home; though poorer, it is nearer to the heart. Believe me, I was so worked up about everything that I am longing for quiet. Now, I have to arrange unpleasant financial problems. All sorts of people are after my money. Will that 'plant of fame' still grow? Look after it well! Fame has gone to my knees, but it hurts there. I have to take hot mud-baths, otherwise I shall start limping. . . .

Janáček visited London for the first time in 1926, during the General Strike. One year before an honorary doctor's degree had been conferred upon him by the University of Brno and he proudly used it in his signature. Otherwise his success never altered his simple way of living nor his sceptical view of things.

JANÁČEK TO MME STÖSSEL

London, 5 May 1926

My dear Mrs Stössel,
Should I continue living as I do now, I would certainly be dead within a month. Nothing but parties, food and sailing around in cars all day long. There is a strike here. The Londoners almost went without milk this morning. Prices are soaring. It is a bad atmosphere for a concert. But I have succeeded well in my mission. I have made many friends and found a patron who will see to it that *Jenufa* is performed within a year. Now it will be better if I return home, otherwise I feel I might never get away from here.

Yours very sincerely,
Leoš Janáček, Ph.D.

JANÁČEK TO MME STÖSSEL

Prague, 13 May 1926

Here I am again in Prague. Soon I shall be in Brno and all will seem to have been nothing but a dream. And yet, what preparations and anxieties it cost me. It is so simple to write something which neither disturbs nor hurts. Unfortunately in the turmoil of life, it seems rather indifferent whether London, or rather that tiny bit of London, heard my works or not. This fact will change nothing in the course of events. Not even in the lives of a single one of its 8,000,000 inhabitants. In short, I am aware of the insignificance of musical work. There is no point in so much discussion of it. Others, on the contrary, take it too seriously; to these I do not belong. And that is that. . . .

Janáček lived to see the rebirth of his country as a national state, in 1919, and he died in time to be spared its downfall twenty years after. Béla Bartók *(1881–1945) was less fortunate; twice in his life he became entangled in the political events of his time, and he died an exile. When, in 1919, after the short-lived communist régime of Béla Kun, a revengeful, reactionary government came to power in Hungary, Bartók, although in no way politically compromised, was treated with suspicion and suspended from his work at the Conservatoire in Budapest. Twenty years later, when with the growing power of Hitler and the beginning of the Second World War central Europe as a whole was thrown into the melting pot, Bartók preferred to emigrate to America, clearly foreseeing the inevitable doom of his country.*

BÉLA BARTÓK TO HIS MOTHER

Rákoskeresztur, June 1919

Dohnányi, myself and Zoltán [Kodály] form, as counsellors assisting Reinitz, the political commissar for music, a musical directorate – though we are assisting not on a political basis but purely as experts in music. This activity leads to a great deal of friction, on the one hand with the musicians' 'Trade Union', on the other, higher up, so that we have contemplated resigning once already. Reinitz left for Vienna three weeks ago and it seems that he is unable to come back yet; not the slightest news from him. Of course, great musical reforms are in preparation, but the political situation is too disturbing, it is impossible to work well or with serious concentration. Reinitz's absence at this moment is very annoying. He was one of the few people capable of nipping unjustified and impossible schemes in the bud. Which is why our friends of the musical trade union speak as if they'd like to hang him. Who knows when the ballet, *The Miraculous Mandarin*, will be put on? . . . However, Galafrès [Mme Dohnányi, a famous actress] would like to produce it. . . .

BÉLA BARTÓK TO HIS MOTHER

Budapest, 23 October 1919

Dohnányi was recently suspended for a year. Thereupon fourteen professors went on strike. After a few days, however, two decided to break the strike, at which the others also returned to work. And now the whole thing is coming to a standstill. The disciplinary investigation of Zoltán and the others is getting nowhere; the whole thing seems to have been a farce. Naturally they are getting their full salary, the only difference is that they are not working for it; in short, they are better off than the professors who are not under disciplinary investigation. In my own case, I am still waiting and waiting. As long as we are stuck here, in a state of siege, it is impossible to budge. But – in so far as it has been possible – I have been inquiring about the possibilities of making a success of things in three other countries. For here it is possible to keep alive, more or less; but it will not be possible to work here, that is to say to work at what I want—folk-music studies – for at least ten years. In short, I want to study folk-music abroad. There is no point in my remaining here; and if it is not possible to live on folk-music abroad, well . . . one can just as well go on teaching in Vienna as in Budapest, for there, there are at least good musical institutions – orchestras, an opera-house and so on . . . everything that they are setting about ruining here by driving away the best, the unique personalities: Tango, Dohnányi, etc. . . .

In a word, I am not having any trouble here, nobody is persecuting me – not because they have absolutely not the least reason to do so (that's a kind of argument they despise here now) but because they wouldn't dare. . . . The three foreign places I had in mind are: Transylvania, Vienna and Germany. An émigré music teacher has taken to Germany all my works on folk-music (on Hungarian, Rumanian and Arabic music) in German translation, and is going to try and say a word on my behalf there. Transylvania is what I would most like myself; for me it would be almost like Hungary, or half Hungary; of all ancient Hungary, it is in fact the land that I like best. I have just learned an interesting thing. Tango has been invited to Rumania by the Rumanian Minister of Culture to work in Transylvania. An official was sent to him with the invitation, and this official made a passing allusion – as if to help Tango to make up his mind – to *my* intention of settling in Transylvania! Tango is off there to reconnoitre the terrain. I am awaiting his return with curiosity. . . .

BÉLA BARTÓK TO HIS MOTHER

Budapest, November 1919

You ask me what I have been up to. Nothing in particular. I am still on leave till the end of December; then I shall ask for a prolongation, which no doubt they will be glad to grant me. Mr Hubay [the newly appointed director] has made his solemn entry into the halls of the National Conservatoire of Music – apparently he himself furnished the 'triumphal march' with which this event was accompanied – and has been spreading himself left and right in interviews with all sorts of newspapers. Thus, for instance, he declared a fortnight ago in the columns of the *Budapesti Hirlap* that he was 'absolutely relying on Dohnányi and Bartók to support him in his great task'; recently, on the other hand, he declared in *Az Ujság* that I could not be expected to interest myself in piano-teaching; a special post would have to be created for me that would enable me to enrich the national musical culture freely, and at my leisure. That is all that I know and nothing more, for of course I haven't met Hubay yet. But you can see from all this that against me personally there hasn't been anything in the least like persecution. You know that for a long time I have been wanting to give up teaching and take another post, for instance in a museum; people like Hubay know this too, and it is possibly of something of this sort that they are thinking. Independently of this, I am making other plans, but naturally I shall not give up the post I have here until I have something absolutely certain and assuredly better elsewhere. When I say 'better' I am not thinking of personal material advantages but of the possibilities of work. The wretched conditions prevailing here certainly make it very questionable whether the state, with the best will in the world, can provide me with the money necessary for buying six hundred phonographic cylinders a year and for the incidental expenses of collecting folk-music. Before the war, that amounted to three crowns a cylinder, 1,800 crowns in all; with the present value or rather non-value of the crown, multiply three by twenty and say 60 crowns a cylinder, or in round figures 36,000 crowns!! That's the greatest bother and the greatest obstacle! For the time being certainly we must wait.

Thank you very much for the sugar; with what a rapt gaze we watched the glittering cubes with their dazzling whiteness pour out of the parcel; it's years since we have seen any. . . .

Still no news about the disciplinary investigation of Zoltán and the others. . . . All work at the ethnographical museum has been suspended for lack of coal! . . .

BÉLA BARTÓK TO MME MÜLLER IN ZÜRICH

Budapest, 13 April 1938

Your friendly letter did me a great deal of good. Yes, those were horrible days for us too. Those days when Austria was attacked. I feel that it is useless to expatiate on this catastrophe – all the more so since you have exactly summed up what we felt ourselves. I should like, however, to add something – the most frightful thing for us at the moment is that we face the threat of seeing Hungary also given over to this régime of bandits and murderers. It is now merely a question of when and how. I cannot imagine how I could live in such a country – or work in such a country, which means the same thing. Strictly speaking, it would be my duty to exile myself, if that is still possible. But even under the most favourable auspices it would cause me an enormous amount of trouble and moral anguish to earn my daily bread in a foreign country (now, at the age of 58, to be forced to take up some hateful task, such as teaching – it is impossible to think of it! In fact, with such a task, I should achieve nothing, for I should not be able to do my really important work). All this adds up to the same old problem, whether to go or to stay. And then there is my mother – can I leave her here for ever during the last years of her life? – no, it is impossible.

What I have been writing now has to do with Hungary where, unfortunately, 'cultured' people, Christians, are almost all submitting themselves to the Nazi régime. Really, I am ashamed to have been born into such a class!

But I am no less worried when I ask myself – after the destruction of Czechoslovakia and Hungary – when will it be the turn of Switzerland, Belgium and so on. . . . In fact, what is the situation with you? . . . However good it is now, it always remains possible for a mere thousand men to ask Germany to occupy the country. . . .

As for my personal situation, at the moment it is rather distressing, for not only has my publisher – Universal Edition – become a Nazi enterprise (the proprietor and the directors have simply been shown the door) but also the A.K.M. (the society which deals with authors' rights – to which both I and Kodály belong) is a Viennese society that has just been nazified. In fact I have just received a scandalous questionnaire about grandparents and other topics, in a word: 'Are you of Germanic race, of similar race, or Non-Aryan?' Naturally, neither Kodály nor I have filled in this questionnaire . . . but really it is a pity that we haven't, because we could have made fun of them, for we should have been able to reply that we are not Aryans – for in fact (as I have learnt from the dictionary) 'Aryan' means 'Indo-European': we Hungarians are Finno-Ugrians, and even perhaps northern Turks, and therefore definitely not Indo-Europeans, therefore not Aryans. Another question is: 'Where and when have you been wounded?' Answer: 'Vienna, the 11th, 12th and 13th of March, 1938!' [The date of the Nazi invasion.]

Unhappily, we cannot permit ourselves these jokes. The only thing to do is to ignore these illegal questionnaires and leave them unanswered. The more the A.K.M. launches into illegal questions, the better it is for us, for the more easily can we get out of their clutches; otherwise we should have to remain their prisoners for the next ten years. . . . We have just heard that two great composers' associations of Western Europe would be glad to accept us as members. We must wait and hope for new violations by the A.K.M. of their constitution; then we can do what is necessary. . . .

BÉLA BARTÓK TO PAUL SACHER IN BÂLE

[*New York 1941*]

Our situation grows worse from day to day. All I can say is that in the whole of my working life, that is to say for the past twenty years, I have never found myself faced with such a terrible situation as that into which I shall perhaps be plunged in the near future. 'Terrible' is perhaps a little too strong, but not very much so. My wife is bearing up against this heroically, and the worse things go with us, the more energetic, confident and serene she becomes. For example, she is trying to find work as a teacher. But how is she to find pupils, or a post? She asks you for some advice on this matter, if possible. You could perhaps send us the prospectus of the agency with which you negotiated last year. What do you think of it all! For myself, I am becoming rather pessimistic; I have lost all my faith in men and nations, in everything. . . .

In a still more tragic way the life of Arnold Schönberg (*1874–1951*) *epitomizes the fate of the central European artist of this century. During a long life of tempestuous ups and downs he maintained a stubborn resistance against anything and everything disagreeing with his own strongly pronounced convictions. With a subjectiveness that hardly allowed a bridge between him and his surroundings, isolated from the world in which he lived and restricted to a small circle of friends and disciples, Schönberg remained a lonely individualist who accepted his inaccessibility and was proud of it. Lacking any practical ability – he was no pianist and an indifferent string player – he had a desperately hard struggle for existence till, at fifty, he found an appointment as teacher of a course in composition in Berlin. Eight years later Schönberg, as a Jew, was dismissed. He found refuge in America like so many of his fellow sufferers.*

The world of paradox in which he lived is well illustrated in his letters. He shows himself a formidable adversary, uncomfortable to everybody, difficult even to his friends. His integrity as a man and artist is as strongly expressed as a gloomy aggressiveness and a burning conviction of the greatness of his work, even as a painter.

SCHÖNBERG TO KARL WIENER, PRESIDENT OF THE ACADEMY OF MUSIC IN VIENNA

Vienna, 19 February 1910

All that might be brought up against me, I think, is that I write a kind of music that does not appeal to those who do not understand anything about it. On the other hand, it must be admitted that it does appeal to those who do understand it. (This is really what the whole thing comes to.) And also that my example leads young people to compose in a similar manner. This objection will not hold water at all. First of all, I do not in fact have this effect on my pupils and do not even wish to have it. In that objectionable sense I influence only those who are inclined that way from the start, whereas those who are constitutionally immune to my art (= untalented) remain so and develop the way they would have developed in any case. Only, they will know a bit more. Secondly, it will not be possible to prevent the young and gifted from emulating my style. For in ten years every talented composer will be writing this way, regardless of whether he has learnt it directly from me or only from my works. Any influence, whether to impede or to encourage such a development, therefore does not depend on whether it is I or someone else who teaches at the Academy. What might hasten it, however, would be continuing to exclude me from everything as has been done in the past. It has been found often enough how dangerous it is to make martyrs. I do not wish to become a martyr. I have no taste for striking attitudes.

Schönberg's application for a professorship was turned down.

SCHÖNBERG TO HIS PUBLISHER EMIL HERTZKA, DIRECTOR OF UNIVERSAL EDITION, VIENNA

Vienna, 7 March 1910

The thing is, I should like to ask you if you could give me some work to do (proof-reading, piano-arrangements, or the like) for Universal Edition since I am compelled to supplement my income somehow. You know I have few pupils this year. My income has shrunk, and my expenses have increased. So I must do something. It doesn't seem likely that being published will bring me in anything for a while.

But there is also something else I wanted to talk to you about. You know that I paint. What you do not know is that my work is highly praised by experts. And I am to have an exhibition next year. What I have in mind is that you might be able to get one or the other well-known patron to buy some of my pictures or have his portrait done by me. I should be prepared to paint a sample portrait for you. I would do your portrait free of charge if you give me your assurance that you will then get me commissions. Only you must not tell people that they *will* like my pictures. You must make them realize that they have to like my pictures, because they have been praised by authorities on painting; and above all that it is much more interesting to have one's portrait done by or to own a painting by a musician of my reputation than to be painted by some mere practitioner of painting whose name will be forgotten in 20 years, whereas even now my name belongs to the history of music. For a life-size portrait I want from 2 to 6 sittings and 200 to 400 kronen. That is really very cheap, considering that in 20 years people will pay ten times as much and in 40 years a hundred times as much for these paintings. I am sure you quite realize this, and I hope you won't make any feeble jokes about a matter as serious as this, but will take it as seriously as it deserves.

As I have said, I am prepared to paint your portrait free of charge by way of a sample if you assure me that I shall get commissions on the strength of it. But there is just one thing; I cannot consider letting the purchase of a portrait depend on whether the sitter likes it or not. The sitter knows who is painting him; he must also realize that he understands nothing about such things, but that the portrait has artistic value, or, to say the least of it, historical value.

SCHÖNBERG TO ALEXANDER VON ZEMLINSKY

[The subject is Schönberg's symphonic poem, *Pelleas und Melisande*.]

Vienna, 20 March 1918

First and foremost; my attitude to cuts is the same as ever. I am against removing tonsils although I know one can somehow manage to go on living even without arms, legs, nose, eyes, tongue, ears, etc. In my view that sort of bare survival isn't always important enough to warrant changing something in the programme of the Creator, who on the great rationing day, allotted us so and so many arms, legs, ears, and other organs. And so I also hold the view that a work doesn't have to live, i.e. be performed, at all costs either, not if it means losing parts of it that may even be ugly or faulty but which it was born with.

The second preliminary question is that of consideration for the listener. I have exactly as little of this as he has for me. All I know is that he exists, and in so far as he isn't 'indispensable' for acoustic reasons (since music doesn't sound well in an empty hall), he's only a nuisance. In any case, a listener who can dispense with my work or with part of it is free to make use of his more fortunate situation and treat me as something he can dispense with entirely.

SCHÖNBERG TO PAUL BEKKER, MUSIC CRITIC IN FRANKFURT

1 August 1924

Intercourse between artists and critics is bound to be somewhat risky for both sides. Now, since I in particular cannot tolerate any criticism whatsoever (for I should not like to think I had written anything that would justify adverse criticism, but cannot, on the other hand, see why I should always be expected to be considerate towards those who understand nothing yet rush in where angels fear to tread, who have not enough insight to suppress lesser or greater qualms about an author of evident merit, and seldom the courage not to intersperse their praise with qualifications, securing their strategic position on several sides), I have up to now as a rule preferred not to become personally acquainted with critics.

However, I too have become somewhat calmer in the course of recent years and have a milder attitude to much of that sort of thing. Today I realize that I cannot be understood, and I am content to make do with respect. That, however, does not mean one can overlook the fact that respect is the very thing that has not been shown me, and this to a quite incredible degree, although at least that stage is now in the main a matter of the past. The most favourable formula was as a rule: 'Whatever one may choose to think of Schönberg', which of course I cannot but regard as great presumption. . . .

Unfortunately the better sort of people become enemies faster than friends because everything is so serious and important to them that they are perpetually in a defensive position. They are driven to this by the great, indeed ruthless honesty with which they treat themselves and which makes them adopt the same attitude to other people as well. This is very wrong, really, for we human beings are far too much in need of tolerance for any thoroughgoing honesty to be helpful to us. If only we could manage to be wise enough to put people on probation instead of condemning them, if we could only give proven friends such extended credit! – I am speaking of my own defects, knowing very well why I have often been more lonely than could well be pleasant.

Perhaps you will gather from all this that I am no longer the bugaboo I used to be. I do not think it means that I stick to my principles less tenaciously than before, but I have come to acquire patience and some knowledge of human nature and am now able to believe that, however sacred I hold my faith, it is no longer so difficult to get on with me as it used to be. So I firmly hope and trust that neither of us will have cause to regret having begun a personal exchange of ideas. . . .

SCHÖNBERG TO RAFFAEL DA COSTA, 'DEUTSCHE ALLGEMEINE ZEITUNG', VIENNA

Berlin, 18 June 1930

For someone as unpopular as I am to answer the question about 'musical life and a shift of the centre of gravity from Vienna to Berlin' means running the risk of making himself still more disliked.

I shall avoid this risk by trying to express unpopular opinions in an unpopular way:

Even before the war people in Vienna were rightly and wrongly proud and ashamed of being less active than Berlin.

Even at that time Berlin showed a lively and intense interest in recognizing and explaining the symptoms of a work of art, something that was missing in Vienna, thanks to centuries of experience in composing.

Even in those days whatever was new was derided after several performances in Berlin, whereas in Vienna it needed only one performance. In extreme cases – in both places – no performance at all.

Even in those days, in both cities, the public had discovered that there is always plenty of time to honour a great man after he is dead. Presumably it had been recognized even in those days that it can then be done more effectively and decoratively and, what is most to the point, more lucratively.

I am looking for a centre of *gravity* and find them all too light.

SCHÖNBERG TO ALMA MAHLER-WERFEL

Hollywood, 23 January 1936

Here we are constantly being offered the earth, which then in the end brings forth sour grapes; at least we are ever and again under the necessity of so regarding them. For a time it looked as though I would be teaching at both universities,[1] which would have brought me in pretty much my Berlin salary. Then I almost agreed to write music for a film, but fortunately asked $50,000 which, likewise fortunately, was much too much, for it would have been the end of me; and the only thing is that if I had somehow survived it we should have been able to live on it – even if modestly – for a number of years, which would have meant at last being able to finish in my lifetime at least those compositions and theoretical works that I have already begun, even if not beginning any more new things. And for that I should gladly have sacrificed my life and even my reputation, although I

[1] The University of South California and the University of California, Los Angeles.

know that others, who have held their own in less strict regard than I mine, would not have failed to seize the chance of despising me for it. . . .

SCHÖNBERG TO OTTO KLEMPERER

Hollywood, 8 November 1934

Dear Mr Klemperer,

Yesterday I was under the necessity of refusing an invitation to a banquet in your honour. You know I have no cause to show you greater respect than you show me. But that is not my motive in the case of this refusal. For you also know that I am thoroughly capable of expressing such things in a much less ambiguous manner. But the fact is: I consider it unspeakable that these people, who have been suppressing my works in this part of the world for the last 25 years, now want to use me as a decoration, to give me a walking-on part to play on this occasion, because I simply happen, entirely at my own pleasure, to be here: and I consider that if these people now have a bad conscience or even indeed want to make good their errors, it is up to them first of all to conciliate me by other means. In any case they will have to recognize that I cannot be fobbed off with bread and butter, however delicious.

Let me repeat it clearly; this refusal is not directed at you, for I esteem your talents sufficiently to adopt much sharper weapons against you. These are jests: please do not misunderstand. With, despite all, very kind regards to you.

SCHÖNBERG TO OTTO KLEMPERER

Los Angeles, 25 September 1940

Dear Klemperer,

You have been misinformed. I did not say that you 'do not like some of my works'.

On the contrary:

I quoted verbatim what you said to me in a discussion that I am sure you have not forgotten:

'Your music has become alien to me'.

That is: not 'some' of my works, but all my works.

There should therefore be no need for any further explanation why I then consider that you should cease to conduct my works. For what can a performance be like if the music has become alien to one?

How it can possibly be insulting to you if I quote your words requires elucidation.

The fact that you have become estranged from my music has not caused me to feel insulted, though it has certainly estranged me. I do not mean to say that I shall take no further interest in you; although I have no notion how the broken (artistic) bridge is ever to function again.

SCHÖNBERG TO HERMANN SCHERCHEN

Los Angeles, 12 November 1945

However gallant it was of you to stay in Europe, I do regret that you didn't come to America. It would be of the greatest importance – at least so far as European art-music is concerned – to have a man like you here, who dares to stand up for modern music. Among the many Europeans here it's only Mitropoulos who has the nerve to do so; since the war all the rest have been kowtowing to the nationalistic endeavours of American composers, and to some extent rightly. But since scarcely one of them (perhaps excepting Reiner) has enough musical education to distinguish between middling, not-so-good, and downright bad, the chaos that prevails here makes the confounding of tongues at Babel seem a veritable (and desirable) Esperanto. – It's a pity, there is plenty of talent, but the teaching is superficial, and the outlook is focused on money-making. . . .

SCHÖNBERG TO OSKAR KOKOSCHKA

Los Angeles, 5 August 1946

You complain of lack of culture in this amusement-arcade world. I wonder what you'd say to the world in which I nearly die of disgust. I don't only mean the 'movies'. Here is an advertisement by way of example: There's a picture of a man who has run over a child, which is lying dead in front of his car. He clutches his head in despair, but not to say anything like: 'My God, what have I done!' For there is a caption saying: 'Sorry, now it is too late to worry – take out your policy at the XX Insurance Company in time.' And these are the people I'm supposed to teach composition to!

Hanns Eisler, one of Schönberg's pupils, was a convinced communist and made no secret of the fact.

SCHÖNBERG TO JOSEF RUFER IN BERLIN

Los Angeles, 18 December 1947

Have you read anything about Eisler and his brother? Do you know anything about the views he had in his Berlin days? I shouldn't damage him any more than he has already damaged himself here. But it's really too stupid of grown-up men, musicians, artists, who honestly ought to have something better to do, to go in for theories about reforming the world, especially when one can see from history where it all leads. I hope that all in all they won't take him too seriously here. Certainly I never took him seriously, I always regarded those tirades as a form of showing off. If I had any say in the matter I'd turn him over my knee like a silly boy and give him 25 of the best and make him promise never to open his mouth again but to stick to scribbling music. That he has a gift for, and the rest he should leave to others. If he wants to appear 'important' let him compose important music.

SCHÖNBERG TO FRANK PELLEG, DEPARTMENT OF MUSIC, MINISTRY OF EDUCATION AND CULTURE, JERUSALEM

Los Angeles, 26 April 1951

I have no words to express how much I should like to make my contribution by taking charge personally, and by teaching at this Academy. I have always had a passion for teaching. I have always felt the urge to discover what can most help beginners and how they can be made thoroughly acquainted with the technical, intellectual, and ethical demands of our art; how to teach them that there is a morality of art, and why one must never cease to foster it and always combat to the utmost any attempt to violate it.

I am unfortunately compelled to resign these hopes. But it seems to me that the half-century by which my experience exceeds that of many of my colleagues entitles me to explain what I would have endeavoured to make of this Academy if I'd had the good fortune and still had the strength to tackle it today.

I would have tried to make this Academy one of world-wide significance, so that it would be a fit kind to serve as a counterblast to this world that is in so many respects giving itself up to amoral, success-ridden materialism; to a materialism in the face of which all the ethical preconditions of our art are steadily disappearing. A universal model must not send forth anyone who is only semi-qualified. It must not produce any instrumentalists whose greatest skill is merely skill, merely the ability to adapt itself completely to the general craving for entertainment.

Those who issue from such an institution must be truly priests of art, approaching art in the same spirit of consecration as the priest approaching God's altar. For just as God chose Israel to be the people whose task it is to maintain the pure, true, Mosaic monotheism despite all persecution, despite all affliction, so too it is the task of Israeli musicians to set the world an example of the old kind that can make our souls function again as they must if mankind is to evolve any higher.

EPILOGUE

It is hardly possible to read the records of great musicians' lives, as they emerge from their own expressions of thought, without being struck by the preponderance of tragedy, of frustration, of self-sacrifice, revealed in such documents: the fate of those who died, as it were, by the wayside, such as Mozart, Chopin, Weber, or had to live in obscurity such as Bach, Schubert, Wolf, or achieved right at the end of lives of untold toil and drudgery a haphazard recognition by a small minority, such as Berlioz or Bruckner. It looks as if the inevitable corollary of greatness were martyrdom. Our world is a jungle for those who have no claws and teeth to defend themselves. Again and again one marvels at the strength of resistance a creative will was able to give to a frail, ailing body, and the meagre encouragement on which such a creative urge could be maintained.

Any conclusion, however, would be misleading without due consideration of an essential redeeming feature: the indescribable bliss the artist finds in his work as the highest fulfilment of his destiny, the satisfaction of the Creator who saw his work 'and saw that it was good'. Creating is the aim and end of the artist's instinct. His struggles and sufferings are but passing clouds; the reality is his work. The Great had to pay the penalty for devoting their lives to the production of a commodity of negligible commercial value: great music. The capacity to disregard everything else was a part of their equipment. They could stand a lot, and the world has treated them accordingly.

The religion of those fortunate few whom Fate permitted to enjoy independence and fame in the end, such as Brahms or Verdi, was stoicism, the disillusioned creed of Ecclesiastes. A magnificent expression of this philosophy may conclude our anthology. It was written to the editor by Ermanno Wolf-Ferrari (*1876–1948*)*, one of the finest, most fastidious artists among musicians of this century, in reply to a letter of spontaneous delight on the occasion of a performance of one of his operas in Vienna.*

ERMANNO WOLF-FERRARI TO HANS GAL

Venice, 6 September 1934

I *share* your pleasure at having found the courage to write to me as you did! It seems as though my music gave you the assurance that you weren't dealing with a conceited man, but with one to whom you could say something kind without having second thoughts. And *that*, too, is brave, in spite of the assurance. Thank you for being so human. It is really the most natural thing, and yet all too rare. And the qualities you find in my music are, properly speaking, simply the most natural. One ought to take it for granted that musical creation must proceed from genuine feeling. It's better not to compose lies, if only because it takes so many notes. And I can't understand how so much music can be written to suit some passing fashion: that can only be deliberate suicide. There is something to be learnt from everything (if it's *good*!), but one can eat veal without turning into a calf: I have never, since I was quite a boy, found any difficulty in disregarding fashion, returning constantly to the study of the great composers, like a perpetual adolescent, and writing in the spirit in which one does a good deed – joyfully, and strictly in accord with that joy. I never worried about success, because I was confident of it. Without haste, of course. Success comes in its own good time, but come it does, in spite of everything. The good – in the moral sense, too – always triumphs, simply because it is good; and the only reason why the bad keeps recurring is so that the good can keep on defeating it. You speak of blockheads; but I say one has to become a saintly blockhead oneself, so as to acquire the patience to cope with all this. As for 'miniature painting', that's another touching foolishness. People are still patting good old 'Papa Haydn' on the back. Every donkey patronizes him. Simply because he has his little joke when he feels like it. And flunkeys who can appreciate nothing but a beating despise him, because he ignores etiquette in dealing with them . . . and so they patronize him. Amen.

The success of *Die Grobiane* [*The School of Fathers*] in Vienna after 28 years gave me *great* pleasure, precisely *because* it came so late. That shows me it was worth while to have a feeling of timelessness. I have always perceived the universal in every detail, and the eternal in every present moment. Musically speaking, I have gone around naked, at the risk of being ugly. Better be ugly than spurious. One must have the courage to be an ass, if that is what one is. I never had any choice.

I'm telling you all this so that you shall not regret having written to me as you did. For you were really writing *to yourself*, not to me: the innermost thought is supra-personal, it is the essence of the I, which knows no You.

Let me hear from you again; it will always give me pleasure. And I hope we shall meet some day.

With the warmest greetings and good wishes.

Yours very sincerely,
Ermanno Wolf-Ferrari

If one considers the expressive and imaginative contents of the letters of several centuries, having gone through a collection such as this, a general 'crescendo' and 'diminuendo' becomes apparent, From more or less crude beginnings in the earlier centuries, letter-writing seems to unfold and develop as an art-form in a curve the apex of which coincides with the middle of the nineteenth century, the decline of which continues in our own time. We do not write proper letters any more; we write for the sake of information and leave everything else to the telephone. This is why this last letter, written by an unfashionable artist, stands out as a lovely anachronism.

It is quite possible that the letter as an art-form has had its day: another reason for us to take a loving interest in those who, without any self-conscious affectation, practised that gentle art.

REFERENCES AND SOURCES

INDEX

REFERENCES AND SOURCES TO TEXT

J. S. BACH

J. S. Bach, Philipp Spitta, Leipzig, 1873–1880

The Bach Reader, H. T. David and A. Mendel, New York, 1945

BÉLA BARTÓK

Béla Bartók, Serge Moreux, transl. G. S. Fraser and Erik de Mauny, London, 1953

LUDWIG VAN BEETHOVEN

Sämtliche Briefe, ed. Alfred Kalischer, Berlin, 1906–1908

VINCENZO BELLINI

Le Lettere di Bellini, ed. F. Pastura, Catania, 1935

HECTOR BERLIOZ

New Letters of Berlioz, 1830–1868, ed. and transl. Jacques Barzun, New York, 1954

Briefe von Hector Berlioz an die Fürstin Carolyne Sayn-Wittgenstein, ed. La Mara, Leipzig, 1903

GEORGES BIZET

Lettres de Georges Bizet, ed. L. Ganderax, Paris, 1908

ALEXANDER BORODIN

Borodin and Liszt, Alfred Habets, transl. Rosa Newmarch, London, 1895

JOHANNES BRAHMS

Johannes Brahms im Briefwechsel mit Joseph Joachim, ed. A. Moser, Berlin, 1908

Clara Schumann–Johannes Brahms, Briefe, 1853–1896, ed. B. Litzmann, Berlin, 1927

Briefwechsel mit Heinrich u. Elisabeth v. Herzogenberg, ed. M. Kalbeck, Berlin, 1907

Billroth und Brahms im Briefwechsel, ed. Otto Gottlieb-Billroth, Vienna, 1935

ANTON BRUCKNER

Gesammelte Briefe, ed. Max Auer, Regensburg, 1924

Bruckner-Brevier, ed. Alfred Orel, Vienna, 1953

FRÉDÉRIC CHOPIN

Correspondence générale, ed. B. E. Sydow, Paris, 1953–60

CLAUDE DEBUSSY

Lettres à son éditeur, ed. Jacques Durand, Paris, 1927

Correspondence de Claude Debussy et P-J. Toulet, Paris, 1929

Lettres à deux amis, Paris, 1942

Lettres à André Messager, Dorbon-Ainé, Paris, 1930

L'Enfance de Pelléas, Paris, 1938

GAETANO DONIZETTI

Vita, musiche, epistolario, ed. G. Zavadini, Bergamo, 1948

ANTONÍN DVOŘÁK

Letters and Reminiscences, ed. Otakar Sourek, transl. Roberta Finleyson Samsour, Prague, 1954

Correspondence with his publisher Fritz Simrock, ed. Wilh. Altmann, Simrock-Jahrbuch, Berlin, 1924

EDWARD ELGAR
Letters of Edward Elgar and other writings, ed. Percy M. Young, London, 1956

GABRIEL FAURÉ
Lettres intimes, ed. Ph.Fauré-Fremiet, Paris, 1951

EDWARD GRIEG
Articler og taler, ed. Gankstad, Oslo, 1957

G. F. HANDEL
A documentary biography, O. E. Deutsch, New York, 1954
The Letters and Writings of G. F. Handel, ed. Erich H. Mueller v. Asow, London, 1935

JOSEPH HAYDN
Joseph Haydn, C. F. Pohl, Leipzig, 1875–1882

GUSTAV HOLST
Gustav Holst, Imogen Holst, London, 1938

LEOŠ JANÁČEK
Letters and Reminiscences, ed. Bohumin Stêdron, transl. G. Thomson, Prague, 1955

JOSEPH JOACHIM
Briefe von und an Joseph Joachim, ed. Andreas Moser, Berlin, 1911–1913

ORLANDO LASSO
Beitrage zur Geschichte der bayrischen Hofkapelle unter Orlando di Lasso, Adolf Sandberger, Leipzig, 1894–5

FRANZ LISZT
Briefe, ed. La Mara, Leipzig, 1893–1905

ALBERT LORTZING
Briefe, ed. G. R. Kruse, Leipzig, 1902

GUSTAV MAHLER
Briefe, 1879–1911, ed. Alma Mahler, Berlin, 1924
Erinnerungen und Briefe, Alma Mahler, Amsterdam, 1940

FELIX MENDELSSOHN-BARTHOLDY
Briefe, ed. Paul Mendelssohn-Bartholdy, Leipzig, 1899
Die Familie Mendelssohn, Seb. Hensel. Berlin, 1898

CLAUDIO MONTEVERDI
Claudio Monteverdi, G. F. Malipiero, Milan, 1930

W. A. MOZART
Briefwechsel und Aufzeichnungen, ed. E. H. Mueller v. Asow, Berlin, 1942
Die Briefe W. A. Mozarts und seiner Familie, ed. L. Schiedermair, Munich, 1914
Mozart's Briefe, ed. W. A. Bauer and O. E. Deutsch, Frankfurt, 1960

MODEST PETROVICH MUSSORGSKY
The Musorgsky-Reader, ed. and transl. Jay Leyda and Sergei Bertensson, New York, 1947

GIACOMO PUCCINI
Epistolario, ed. G. Adami, Milan, 1928

MAURICE RAVEL
Maurice Ravel au miroir de ses letters, ed. Marcel Gerar and René Chalupt, Paris, 1956

GIOACCHINO ROSSINI
Lettere, ed. G. Mazzatinti and G. Manis, Florence, 1902

ARNOLD SCHÖNBERG
Letters, ed. Erwin Stein, transl. E. Wilkins and E. Kaiser, London, 1964

FRANZ SCHUBERT
Briefe und Schriften, ed. O. E. Deutsch, Munich, 1922
Dokumente seines Lebens, ed. O. E. Deutsch, Munich, 1913–14

ROBERT SCHUMANN
Briefe, ed. Karl Storck, Stuttgart, 1906

HEINRICH SCHÜTZ
Gesammelte Briefe und Schriften, ed. Erich H. Mueller v. Asow, Regensburg, 1931

BEDŘICH SMETANA
Letters and Reminiscences, transl. Daphne Rusbridge, Prague, 1953

LOUIS SPOHR AND MORITZ HAUPTMANN
Korrespondenz, ed. Ferdinand David, Leipzig, 1876

RICHARD STRAUSS
The Correspondence between Richard Strauss and Hugo von Hofmannsthal, ed. Franz and Alice Strauss, transl. H. Hammelmann and E. Osers, London 1961
Correspondence with Stefan Zweig, ed. Willi Schuh, Frankfurt a. M., 1957

PETER ILYITCH TCHAIKOVSKY
Life and Letters, Modest Tchaikovsky, ed. and transl. Rosa Newmarch, London, 1906

GIUSEPPE VERDI
Copialettere, ed. G. Cesari and A. Luzio, Leipzig, 1913
Giuseppe Verdi, Arthur Pougin, transl. James E. Matthew, London, 1887

RICHARD WAGNER
Briefwechsel Zwischen Wagner und Liszt, Leipzig, 1887
Richard Wagner an Theodor Uhlig, Wilhelm Fischer und Friedrich Heine, Leipzig, 1888
Richard Wagner an Mathilde Wesendonck, ed W. Golther, Berlin 1904
Richard Wagner an Freunde und Zeitgenossen, ed. E. Kloss, Berlin, 1909
Letters of Richard Wagner. The Burrell Collection, ed. J. N. Burk, Frankfurt, 1953

R. VAUGHAN WILLIAMS and GUSTAV HOLST
Heirs and Rebels, ed. Ursula Vaughan Williams, London 1959

CARL MARIA VON WEBER
Ein Lebensbild, Max Maria von Weber, Leipzig, 1864

HUGO WOLF
Briefe an Hugo Faisst, ed. M. Haberlandt, Leipzig, 1904
Briefe an Oskar Grohe und Frau Grohe, ed. H. Werner, Berlin, 1905

OTHER REFERENCES

Dr Charles Burney, *The Present State of Music in France and Italy*, London, 1771, and *The Present State of Music in Germany, Netherlands and United Provinces*, London 1773

Heinrich Heine, *Ueber die Französische Bühne*, Complete Works, Vol. 11, Hamburg, 1876

La Mara, *Musikerbriefe aus fünf Jahrhunderten*, Leipzig, 1886

Ludwig Nohl, *Musikerbriefe*, Leipzig, 1867

J. G. Prod'homme, *Ecrits de Musiciens* Paris, 1912

Friedrich Reichardt, *Vertraute Briefe, geschrieben auf einer Reise nach Wien*, Amsterdam, 1810

George Sand, *Histoire de ma vie*, Paris 1854–5

Ludwig Spohr, *Selbstbiographie*, Kassel and Göttingen, 1860

Stendhal (Marie Henri Beyle), *La Vie de Rossini*, Paris, 1824

INDEX

Italic figures denote letters written by the person indexed